The Rushing on of the Purposes of God

Studies in Chinese Christianity

G. Wright Doyle and Carol Lee Hamrin,

Series Editors

A Project of the Global China Center

www.globalchinacenter.org

The Rushing on of the Purposes of God

Christian Missions in Shanxi since 1876

ANDREW T. KAISER

◆PICKWICK *Publications* • Eugene, Oregon

THE RUSHING ON OF THE PURPOSES OF GOD
Christian Missions in Shanxi since 1876

Copyright © 2016 Andrew T. Kaiser. All rights reserved. Except for brief quotations in critical publications or reviews, no part of this book may be reproduced in any manner without prior written permission from the publisher. Write: Permissions, Wipf and Stock Publishers, 199 W. 8th Ave., Suite 3, Eugene, OR 97401.

Pickwick Publications
An Imprint of Wipf and Stock Publishers
199 W. 8th Ave., Suite 3
Eugene, OR 97401

www.wipfandstock.com

PAPERBACK ISBN: 978-1-4982-3696-6
HARDCOVER ISBN: 978-1-4982-3698-0
EBOOK ISBN: 978-1-4982-3697-3

Cataloguing-in-Publication data:

Names: Kaiser, Andrew T.

Title: The rushing on of the purposes of god : Christian missions in Shanxi since 1876 / Andrew T. Kaiser.

Description: Eugene, OR : Pickwick Publications, 2016 | Series: Studies in Chinese Christianity | Includes bibliographical references and index.

Identifiers: ISBN 978-1-4982-3696-6 (paperback) | ISBN 978-1-4982-3698-0 (hardcover) | ISBN 978-1-4982-3697-3 (ebook)

Subjects: LSCH: Missions—China—History. | Christianity and culture—China. | China—Church history.

Classification: BV3415.2 .K25 2016 (print) | BV3415.2 .K25 (ebook)

Manufactured in the U.S.A.   12/06/16

Scripture quotations marked (NIV) are taken from the Holy Bible, New International Version®, NIV®. Copyright © 1973, 1978, 1984 by Biblica, Inc.™ Used by permission of Zondervan. All rights reserved worldwide.

Cover image courtesy of Yale Divinity Library

To Heather, Sophia, and Rebekah
My fellow adventurers in Shanxi

Contents

Note on Languages viii

List of Abbreviations ix

Introduction: Why Shanxi? xi

1. The Age of Pioneers (1876–1899) 1
2. The Boxer Turmoil (1900) 61
3. The Golden Age of Mission (1901–1937) 118
4. Shanxi Mission in the Midst of Conflict (1937–1949) 179
5. Legacy (1949–2015) 225

List of Chinese Terms 259

Bibliography 269

Index 281

Note on Languages

For ease of reading, the Chinese terms, place names, and personal names included in this book have been rendered in the standard *hanyu pinyin* romanization. Thus, "Shansi" and "Shensi" from the old missionary letters are referred to in the text by their modern equivalents of Shanxi and Shaanxi, respectively. In the case of quoted materials, older variants have been preserved in order to retain the flavor of the original sources. In a few instances—Chiang Kai-shek, H. H. K'ung, and a few others—alternative romanizations of Chinese proper nouns have been maintained as being more familiar to modern readers. For specialists, a list of selected Chinese characters is included in the back matter.

List of Abbreviations

ABCFM	American Board of Commissioners for Foreign Missions
ABCFMA	Microfilms of the American Board of Commissioners for Foreign Missions Archives, Billy Graham Center, Wheaton College, Wheaton, IL
AG	General Council of the Assemblies of God
BMS	Baptist Missionary Society
BMSA	Baptist Missionary Society Archives, Regents Park College, Oxford
CBM	General Mission Board of the Church of the Brethren
CCC	China Christian Council
CIM	China Inland Mission
CLS	Christian Literature Society for China
CM	*China's Millions*
CR	*The Chinese Recorder and Missionary Journal* or *The Chinese Recorder*
GCPMC	General Conference of Protestant Missionaries in China
HTCOC	*Hudson Taylor and China's Open Century*
LMS	London Missionary Society
MH	*The Missionary Herald*
OSMA	Oberlin Shansi Memorial Association
RMB	*Renmin bi* or Chinese *yuan*, a modern unit of currency

SARA	State Administration for Religious Affairs
SDCK	Society for the Diffusion of Christian and General Knowledge Among the Chinese
SOAS	School of Oriental and African Studies Library, London
SPG	Society for the Propagation of the Gospel
SYM	Independent or Shouyang Mission
TJC	True Jesus Church
TSPM	Three-Self Patriotic Movement
YMCA	Young Men's Christian Association

Introduction

Why Shanxi?

SHANXI MAY SEEM LIKE an unusual location to choose as the subject of a book on the history of Christian mission in China. A remote inland province in north central China, Shanxi rarely makes the headlines today. If you do hear mention of this place it is usually in relation to coal, and either China's energy needs or its pollution woes. For English speakers, even the name is a puzzle: how is it pronounced?[1] And if for some reason a curious reader tries to learn more about Shanxi, a dizzying array of possible spellings resulting from different romanizations and a similar-sounding neighboring province often leaves readers more confused than when they started. Is Shansi the place I am looking for? Or Shan-hsi? How about Shensi? Shaanxi?

Shanxi's name means "west of the mountains," referring to the peaks that physically and culturally separate this inland province from the dynamic and more rapidly developing coastal regions of China. Known for its conservatism, Shanxi is a place where people often seem more comfortable standing still than moving forward. When the national government announced in 2000 a new initiative to promote investment and development in China's western region, inland Shanxi was not included as part of the "west." A pun that circulated widely within the province at the time reflects the kind of self-deprecation mixed with stubborn pride that is indicative of

---

1. It should sound something like "shahn-shee."

Shanxi's relative separation from the outside world: "Shanxi is neither east nor west, Shanxi is nothing."[2]

Shanxi deserves to be more widely known, particularly in relation to its encounter with Christianity. In spite of or perhaps because of Shanxi's isolation, this province has played host to several significant events in the history of Protestant missions in China. One of the first Christian multi-agency, international disaster relief efforts in the world was centered on Shanxi, and those humanitarian actions laid the foundation upon which the first Shanxi church was built. More familiar to most readers, the Boxer turmoil of 1900 was particularly violent in Shanxi, where the vast majority of that year's expatriate deaths occurred. Shortly after the first salvos of World War II lit up the skies of northern China, Shanxi became a center of resistance against the Japanese military, with Chinese and expatriate Christians often entangled in the conflict. In and around these events, a steady parade of missionary giants strode through the province as they sought to build God's Kingdom among the Chinese. Timothy Richard, Hudson Taylor, Pastor Xi, the "Cambridge Seven," Gao Daling, Harry Wyatt, Peter Torjesen, and Gladys Aylward—these individuals and many more, whose names are less familiar or even unknown, have all played their part in the growth of the Shanxi church. And as these Christian men and women endeavored to serve God faithfully in the midst of momentous events, they wrestled with a host of issues that are still discussed within the mission world today.

Enculturation

The narrative of mission history cannot be told without reference to the interplay between culture and Christianity. Effective cross-cultural transmission of the Christian faith requires near constant adjustment, as each instance of dissonance between cultural norms and Christian imperatives is negotiated. In some instances, Christianity speaks prophetically into the culture, challenging and ultimately transforming local practice and understanding. In other instances, Christianity incarnates itself into the local culture, bringing a new and richer sense of fulfillment and completion into local practice and understanding. This process, however, is far from simple: both the senders and receivers of the Christian message are active in the negotiations, each possessing their own authority, producing a host of consequences both intended and otherwise.

These cultural tensions present themselves time and again throughout the history of the Shanxi mission, perhaps most forcefully in the discussion

2. *Shanxi, bu dong bu xi, bu shi dongxi.*

of the causes behind the Boxer violence. Cultural misunderstandings as well as differing cultural values all contributed to the anger and aggression of 1900. The variety of ways missionaries and local Christians in Shanxi responded to local threats illustrates the complexity of this issue. The fact that our modern context is different from that of 1900 Shanxi reminds us that each generation must renegotiate these tensions for themselves.

Evangelism and Humanitarian Aid

Although acts of mercy and the provision of physical aid were key factors in the self-identification and growth of the early church, the Protestant mission community at the end of the nineteenth century was divided over the relative roles of evangelism and humanitarian aid in Christian mission.

This question was inescapable in the case of the Shanxi mission, where opium use and famine were nearly always part of the ministry context. Different agencies and individuals sought to balance the twin impulses to save both souls and bodies in different fashions, and with mixed results. Christians today still struggle to define precisely how physical and spiritual salvation relate to each other, with confusion on this issue leading many contemporary missionaries into personal doubt, or even conflict with their colleagues. This issue is as contentious today as it was when the Shanxi mission pioneers first entered the province nearly one hundred fifty years ago.

Indigenous Principles

Since the Apostle Paul's first journeys around the Mediterranean, Christians have strived to establish faithful churches in previously unchurched places. The methods best suited to achieving this goal, however, have long been the subject of debate.

The agencies that have historically worked in Shanxi were all committed to developing local churches that were self-supporting, self-propagating, and self-governing. Despite this shared ideal, there were different opinions regarding how best to create truly indigenous churches. While this book is primarily concerned with the expatriates who worked in Shanxi, it reveals a gradual but steady movement towards increasing local authority within the church. These issues are presenting themselves in new ways in contemporary China, as an increasingly well-resourced Chinese church begins to explore how it can participate in and contribute to the advance of the global church.

Inasmuch as these issues continue to shape the encounter between Christianity and China in the twenty-first century, the mission past is still alive today.

All survey texts reflect editorial choices regarding which historical details to include in their accounts. In this work, I have chosen to write about Shanxi primarily because this is where my family and I have lived and worked for most of our lives. Initially, this project was intended to help my fellow expatriate Christians in Shanxi understand the historical context of their ministry world, an editorial focus that is still evident in this "curated" selection of individuals and events from Shanxi's past. Many readers will note that Taiyuan receives more attention than other locales, but this is simply because Taiyuan has been the context for my ministry, and thus provides the lens through which I view Shanxi mission.

It is also apparent that I have elected to examine the early years of the Shanxi mission in detail, while presenting the twentieth century in a more sweeping, biographical style. First, those early experiences of famine and violence were formative for the Shanxi mission and thus deserving of special attention. Second, security concerns necessarily limit how much detail and even which events and individuals can be responsibly included in the final chapter—especially since, as this is a historical study, I have elected not to use pseudonyms or otherwise disguise content. Finally, and more personally, I have intentionally allowed my own experience on the field to influence my editorial decisions. I have been impressed many times by the ways certain past personages or events speak directly to the challenges faced by missionaries today on the China field, and these are the things that receive more attention in the narrative. It is my hope that the publication of this book will enable a wider range of readers to benefit from these mission lessons from the past.

Over the years, many individuals have given generously of their time and research to help make this work possible. In particular, I would like to thank my friend Henrietta Harrison for her patience and generous collegiality. Much of what I know about Shanxi can be attributed to her excellent scholarship. Brian Stanley showed me what good historical scholarship informed by faith ought to be, and profoundly influenced my understanding of the nineteenth-century mission project. Carol Hamrin kindly welcomed my manuscript as a fitting companion for Eunice Johnson's *Timothy Richard's Vision* in Global China Center's "Studies in Chinese Christianity," a series with Wipf and Stock's Pickwick Publications imprint.[3] Over the long

---

3. Johnson, *Timothy Richard's Vision*.

course of this project Thomas Askew, Alvyn Austin, Norman Cliff, Katherine Edgerton-Tarpley, and Edvard Torjesen have all helped supply me with relevant materials as well as encouragement and support. I am also grateful to Gordon-Conwell Theological Seminary for inviting my wife and me to serve as Missionaries-in-Residence on two separate occasions, providing valuable library access that made possible a substantial expansion of this work. Thanks as well to my colleagues in Shanxi—too numerous to list here—who have assisted with reading and editing various versions of this text over these many years. Dear friend Amy Park kindly agreed to proofread my manuscript, and her attentions as I approached the end of this process have made my book much better than it otherwise would have been. Finally, this work owes a tremendous debt to the many friends and family members of past Shanxi workers who have shared their family histories with me. I thank them for their generosity, and I thank God for their ancestors' faithfulness. Any errors in fact or judgment are, of course, my responsibility alone.

The title of this book comes from a letter written by Harry Wyatt, an English Baptist medical missionary to Shanxi, during a rail journey shortly after his 1925 arrival in China. As he raced through the Chinese hinterland, Wyatt considered the potentially disruptive nature of his presence. First, he saw himself as a representative of the outside world whose new technologies and ideas were challenging "the serenity of [China's] past centuries." Second, he saw himself as a representative "of a society of Christian people" that had helped establish self-governing and self-supporting churches across China that he believed would weather the coming political and social upheavals. "But there is something deeper here than commercial change or church organization," he wrote:

> Has not God spoken again, and the time now come when these people are being called from the circling sequences of their past ages to a new and progressive spiritual life? Has not the time come when in Christ's name not only are social customs going to change, tumults and wars arise, and many strange things come to pass, but also the humble people are going to put their trust in a Heavenly Father and set their faces towards a better land?
>
> There is something enjoyable about the rush of the train over these brown plains, as the sun sinks lower in the hills. How much more fascinating the rushing on of the purposes of God.[4]

This book is an attempt to trace the history of the rushing on of God's purposes as seen in the Protestant mission's efforts to establish and develop the

---

4. Harry Wyatt, undated letter "Across Shantung on a Train," in Payne, *Harry Wyatt*, 54–55.

church in Shanxi. It is intended as an introduction, a basic key to Protestant missions in Shanxi. By learning from the examples of some of the women and men who contributed to the growth of God's Kingdom in Shanxi during the previous one hundred fifty years, today's cross-cultural workers will be better able to avoid some of the mistakes of the past and to imitate earlier successes. May this work inspire its readers to investigate the past more deeply in order to approach the future more carefully.

[M]issionary history is hardly worth the telling, unless it leads the reader to bring the experience of the past to bear upon the missionary problems of to-day, and enables him to solve the problems of to-day by the insight and the instinct as it were, that reward the patient investigator into the deeds and the purposes of those who have gone before. A knowledge of the history of all the societies is of little service unless the conscience of the reader is enlightened, his love for those for whom Christ died deepened, and his zeal for the furtherance of the great missionary cause strengthened.

—Richard Lovett, *The History of the London Missionary Society, 1795–1895* (London: H. Frowde, 1899), vii–viii.

1

The Age of Pioneers (1876–1899)

FOR MANY CHINESE PEOPLE Shanxi province is the cultural heart of China, the place where "China" was born. Though Shanxi's glorious past might not be obvious to modern visitors, it is a historical reality. This simple fact is now gaining new life as the local tourist trade expands, relying on foreign and national visitors' interest in China's cultural heritage. Shanxi province—China's aboveground archaeological treasure chest—contains over half of the country's existing pre-Qing dynasty structures.[1] Many of these structures are still impressive, pointing back to a far more opulent past when Shanxi's wealth and success earned the province a glorious reputation.

Even as late as the Qing Dynasty (1644–1912), Shanxi enjoyed a degree of relative prosperity due largely to its physical proximity to Russia and Mongolia.

> Shanxi is cut off by mountains from the north China plain to the coast, but forms a corridor linking central China to Mongolia and the Russian steppes. From the fifteenth century to the seventeenth Mongolia was China's main strategic frontier, and the government licensed groups of merchants to provision the frontier armies, allowing them to operate salt and tea trades in return. Shanxi men were well positioned to obtain these licenses and used them to build trading networks that stretched from the tea farms of Fujian on China's southeast coast and the salt fields near Tianjin in the north to the trading posts on the Mongolian frontier where they bought horses and other livestock. Then in the mid-seventeenth century China, along with

---

1. It is commonly said that for underground cultural and historical artifacts one should visit Shaanxi (*dixia kan Shaanxi*), while for aboveground treasures one should visit Shanxi (*dishang kan Shanxi*).

Mongolia, became part of the expanding Qing empire. This put an end to the licensed trade, but the great Shanxi trading houses were well-placed to take advantage of the new opportunities in Mongolia, which they entered in the immediate wake of the Qing armies. They sold tea, silk, and many daily items imported from China to the Mongols, often lending them the money to buy these things, and brought the Mongols' livestock to sell into China. The trade was highly exploitative and extremely profitable. Then in the early eighteenth century the Qing signed a treaty with Russia allowing for trade at the Mongolian border town of Kiakhta, where it rapidly came to be controlled by the Shanxi merchants. Tea and silk were exported to Russia, while sheepskins, woolen cloth, iron, leather, and livestock were imported. When the trade was at its height in the nineteenth century, Russia was China's second largest trading partner after England, and 60 percent of Russian exports flowed to China were passing through Kiakhta.

The profits of this national and international trade flowed into Shanxi, where the great merchant houses were based, and created opportunities and wealth there. One Qing official famously claimed (when proposing a tax increase) that Guangdong and Shanxi were the two richest provinces in the country. This reflected the situation in the 1850s, when much of the [sic] central and eastern China was affected by rebellions, but it does give a sense of how Shanxi was perceived.[2]

When Scottish Presbyterian missionary Alexander Williamson toured North China in the 1860s, he was impressed with the prosperity and number of Shanxi cities, noting in particular the surprising volume of imported goods on display—many from Russia.[3]

Shanxi was also religiously prosperous. Folk religion flourished in the isolated mountain and valley villages, as did various forms of Buddhism. Wutai Shan in north central Shanxi has long been counted one of China's sacred Buddhist mountains. With a large Tibetan Buddhist presence, the holy site still draws huge numbers of pilgrims to this day.

Since its eventual establishment in China near the end of the Ming Dynasty (1368–1644), Catholicism has also maintained a strong and long-lasting presence in Shanxi. The religion of Rome was first brought to Shanxi at the opening of the seventeenth century by Shanxi merchants who, impressed by the Jesuit moral code and respect for learning that they had witnessed

---

2. From Harrison's first chapter in *The Man Awakened from Dreams*, 22–23.
3. Williamson, *Journeys in North China*, 1:151–69, 309–17.

while on business in Beijing, carried the new faith back to their home towns in central Shanxi. Catholicism then began to spread on its own across the province, with the first western missionary—the Franciscan Alfonso Nagnone, a supporter of Ricci and his accommodating attitude toward Chinese culture—not arriving in Shanxi until 1620.[4] Responding to Pope Innocent's prohibition of the Chinese funeral rites, in 1724 the Yongzheng Emperor announced a ban on Christianity ("the religion of the West") throughout the Chinese empire. At that time there were three hundred churches in China and as many as one hundred twenty thousand Catholic believers. The Chinese emperor was offended most by the Pope's pride and arrogance in assuming he could determine what was best for China. As he expressed in the letter he sent back to Rome: "China has her religions. The West has her religions. The Western religions need not visit China—or is it the case that China's religions would be welcome in the West?"[5] Many of the more isolated inland missionaries chose to remain in China, ministering to their congregations until death. Over the next one hundred years the Catholic Church in China came increasingly under the control of local Catholics, resulting in a church that not only survived while officially proscribed, but continued to grow, preserving many of its initial similarities with Chinese religious culture.[6] By 1840, this distinctly Chinese Catholic church counted just under two hundred fifty thousand souls spread across the empire, with twenty or thirty expatriate missionaries serving in country in violation of Chinese law.[7]

During the 1850s the pseudo-Christian Taiping Rebellion raged throughout southern China and in 1853 passed through Shanxi leaving behind a lingering negativism toward Christianity.[8] After the Taipings

---

4. Harrison, *The Missionary's Curse*, 14–18.

5. As recorded in Zhang Wenjian, *Tianguo zhi dao*, 231–35, translation mine. For more on the Chinese Rites Controversy (*liyi zhizheng*) see Minamiki, *The Chinese Rites Controversy*.

6. This is one of the key arguments in Harrison's book. See chapter 1 in Harrison, *The Missionary's Curse*. Williamson claims that one of the two Roman Catholic Chinese who tutored Robert Morrison (the first Protestant missionary to China) was from Shanxi. Williamson, *British Baptists in China*, 10.

7. Zhang Wenjian, *Tianguo zhi dao*, 234.

8. *British Baptists in China*, 23. Though not speaking with specific regard to Shanxi, British Baptist missionary Timothy Richard said that when he arrived in China some six years after the defeat of the Taipings their "baleful effect against the spread of Christianity continued," leaving "a legacy of hatred against Christianity, a hatred which has scarcely melted away." Ibid., 28. For a recent and more nuanced assessment of the Christian nature of the Taiping movement see Kilcourse, "Son of God, Brother of Jesus," 124–44.

captured Nanjing, they sent a Northern Expeditionary Force into Shanxi to take Taiyuan before moving east to Beijing. At Pingyang the Taiping army was welcomed with "spontaneous public support," but the next day at Hongdong, instead of continuing along the Big Road to Taiyuan, they changed their minds and disastrously started eastward through the mountains.[9] The historian Jen Yu-wen attributes the popularity of the Taipings within Shanxi to the desire of the common people for the restoration of Chinese rule in place of the "barbarian" Manchu dynasty and the Taiping Army's high degree of moral discipline.[10] In any event, the Taipings went away and never returned, sparing Shanxi the devastation of the Yangtze cities. Following the conclusion of the Second Opium War (1856–1860), the ratified French-language version of the Sino-French Convention of Peking (1860) included a clause not only guaranteeing the right for foreigners to travel in the interior, but also to buy land and spread Christianity.[11] When foreign priests accordingly returned in numbers to Shanxi after 1860, they found roughly twenty thousand faithful believers residing in villages that had remained Catholic for many generations.[12]

By comparison, Protestant Christianity was a relative newcomer to China, having arrived with Robert Morrison of the London Missionary Society (Lundun Chuandaohui), or LMS, in 1807.[13] It was later still before Protestant mission work began in Shanxi—not until nearly twenty years after the 1860 Convention. By that time, the Protestant mission was already well established in many other parts of China:

---

9. Austin, *China's Millions*, 157–58. The Big Road (*dalu*) refers to the road running from Xi'an through Taiyuan (via Pingyang) and then over the mountains and on to Beijing.

10. Jen Yu Wen and Suddard, *The Taiping Revolutionary Movement*, 179–80.

11. In China the term "foreigner" is used to refer to anyone not ethnically Chinese. An additional clause in the Sino-French Convention stated that in matters of discrepancy the French language version was authoritative. A previous 1846 Imperial Edict had officially restored all former mission property confiscated since the reign of the Kangxi Emperor. Since at that time it was still illegal for foreigners to travel and/or reside inland, this edict was largely irrelevant until after the 1860 Convention. Thompson, "Twilight of the Gods," 54–55, esp. 55 note 6.

12. Latourette, *A History of Christian Missions in China*, 183. Alvyn Austin records a late 1870s figure of 22,780 Roman Catholic converts, led by thirty Western missionaries and eighteen native priests, while another source claims there were twenty-five Roman Catholic missionaries in Shanxi by 1866. Austin, *China's Millions*, 148; Broomhall, *The Jubilee Story of the CIM*, 95. In 1870 there were 250 foreign priests in all of China; by 1885 the total had reached 488. Broomhall, *HTCOC*, 6, *Assault on the Nine*, 370.

13. For more on Morrison, see his wife's compilation of his memoirs Morrison and Morrison, *Memoirs of the Life and Labours of Robert Morrison*. For a recent critical reading of Morrison, see Daily, *Robert Morrison and the Protestant Plan for China*.

missionaries resided at ninety-one centers, had organized three hundred and twelve churches, and Chinese communicants numbered 13,035. In all, twenty-nine societies—twelve American, fifteen British, and two Continental—were on the field, with four hundred and seventy-three missionaries, including seven unconnected.[14]

THE NORTH CHINA FAMINE AND THE BEGINNINGS OF PROTESTANT MISSIONS IN SHANXI

In 1866 Alexander Williamson of the National Bible Society of Scotland (Sugelan Shengjinghui) and Jonathan Lees (LMS)—the first Protestant missionaries to set foot in Shanxi—passed through Shanxi briefly on their way to Xi'an. They were impressed with Shanxi's abundant natural resources, large population, and the beauty of Taiyuan, in particular.[15] They were followed in 1876 by Joshua J. Turner and Francis. H. James, both of the China Inland Mission (Zhongguo Neidihui) or CIM, who had arrived in Shanxi with the goal of establishing the first permanent Protestant residence in the province.[16] After traveling through seven walled cities and a number of smaller villages they were forced by a shortage of funds to return to Hankou.[17]

Timothy Richard was born in Wales in 1845 and arrived in China in 1870 to serve with the English Baptist Missionary Society (Yingguo Jinlihui) or BMS in Chefoo (modern day Yantai), Shandong.[18] Before the end of his first year on the field Richard was left as the only representative of the

14. This is a compilation of statistics from the 1877 General Conference of Protestant Missionaries in China as recorded in the curious 1905 China missions survey textbook Beach, *Dawn on the Hills of T'ang*, 105.

15. Williamson, *Journeys in North China*, 1: 151–69, 247, 309–17. The date of their visit is incorrectly reported as 1869–1870 in Stauffer, *The Christian Occupation of China*, 186.

16. More on Turner below. James left the CIM to join the Shandong BMS work in 1883; in 1892 he left the mission world altogether and went on to a distinguished teaching career that eventually placed him at the Imperial University in Beijing during the Boxer Uprising of 1900. After providing sanctuary within the Legation for some two thousand Chinese Christians, James left the compound on the same day the head of the German legation, Baron von Ketteler, was assassinated. Chinese witnesses say James was then arrested and decapitated by soldiers. Broomhall, *HTCOC*, 7, *It is Not Death to Die!*, 328–30.

17. Broomhall, *The Jubilee Story of the CIM*, 108–9.

18. The port city of Yantai was popularly referred to as Chefoo by the nineteenth-century expatriate community, a misnomer presumably derived from an attempted romanization of the name of nearby Zhifu Island located just off the coast of Shandong.

BMS in China, and by the end of his second year he was already frustrated and disillusioned with the lack of results produced by street preaching in the treaty ports. By 1875 he had moved to the remote inland Shandong city of Qingzhou, where he emphasized the training of local believers to carry out church leadership and evangelism on their own throughout the countryside.[19] The marked degree to which indigenous priorities were expressed in Richard's work with the Qingzhou church inspired Richard's friend John Nevius of the American Presbyterian Mission (Meiguo Zhanglaohui) to write his influential essays on missionary methods.[20] At the same time, Richard became more closely identified with the local people, adopting Chinese dress and developing a method of evangelism that stressed witnessing to "the worthy" individuals in the community—to those whose character and education revealed them to be sincere seekers of truth who Richard felt were predisposed to accept the gospel.[21] These years living in rural Shandong also gave Richard practical experience distributing relief to local villagers during times of disaster (flooding and famine).[22] On the basis of this work, Richard was invited by the LMS's Shanxi Famine Relief Committee (Shanghai) to undertake the twenty-one-day journey over the mountains to inland Shanxi where the famine was said to be severe. He was to espy the state of affairs and then deliver the Committee's alms to the starving people of Shanxi.[23] This disaster provided the initial opening for Protestant mission work in Shanxi—a work in which Timothy Richard's role would prove vital.

First-time visitors to Shanxi are often most impressed by the striking loess formations. Deposited by winds from the Gobi Desert, the dry, porous, light-brownish-yellow loess dirt can be found hundreds of feet deep, covering a landscape made alien by centuries of erosion due to winds and

---

19. John Livingston Nevius, "Mission Work in Central Shantung," *CR* 11, no. 5 (1880) 357–64. For more on Richard's work with the church in Shandong, see Kaiser, "Encountering China," 126–31.

20. Nevius, *The Life of John Livingston Nevius*, 352–53; Nevius, *Methods of Mission Work*; Richard, *Forty-Five Years*, 107. Nevius's 1886 book originally appeared as eight letters each providing advice for new China missionaries with a heavy emphasis on indigenous principles. See *CR* 16, no. 10 (1885) 421–24; *CR* 16, no. 11 (1885) 461–67; *CR* 17, no. 1 (1886) 24–31; *CR* 17, no. 2 (1886) 55–64; *CR* 17, no. 3 (1886) 102–12; *CR* 17, no. 5 (1886) 165–78; *CR* 17, no. 7 (1886) 252–60; and *CR* 17, no. 8 (1886) 297–305. For a detailed analysis of their content, see Chao, "John Livingston Nevius," 259–91.

21. For more on Richard's unique reading of Jesus's Matthew 10:11 instructions regarding "the worthy," see chapter 3 in Kaiser, "Encountering China."

22. The best account of the North China Famine in Shanxi is Edgerton-Tarpley, *Tears from Iron*. For Richard's role in the relief effort, see Bohr, *Famine in China and the Missionary*.

23. Williamson, *British Baptists in China*, 40.

rain. Old roads now travel through canyons where the soft soil has been compacted over time. Cart wheels simply sink into the soil leaving deep ruts that—depending on the weather—vary between impassable sludge and unworkable crevasses. The soil also lends itself to relatively easy excavations—hence the ubiquitous cave homes (*yaodong*) carved into the Shanxi hillsides. When the wind blows, the dust is voluminous and inescapable. Missionaries in the nineteenth and twentieth centuries often complained of the dirt: "Oh! How the wind is whirling and swirling this fine dust into every crack and crevice of our not over tight doors and windows, until a thick coating of dust lies over every thing in the house even to our teeth!"[24] Of course, during years of drought the dust only increased.

In 1875 and 1876 Shanxi had received almost no precipitation, leading to severe drought conditions. As conditions worsened, local people adopted various measures to try and move heaven. For rural residents living at the base of the mountains near Jinci, this involved an elaborate series of processions and prayers.

> For three years the farmers prayed to the Dragon Kings, the deities who lived in pools in the mountains behind the village and were thought to control the rainfall. The [local] men went as a group up into the mountains, where they heaped stones into a cairn, topping them with willow branches and sprinkling water over them. They also joined larger processions from the neighboring village. . . . The men walked in their bare feet, with wreaths of willow branches on their heads, some of them carrying heavy iron implements to express their repentance and the sincerity of their pleas. . . . [T]he families along the main street put little altars outside their doors with candles, bowls of water, and willow branches. As the procession approached they could hear the pleading "*Amitofo, Amitofo, Amitofo,*" as the men called over and over again on the Amitabha Buddha to help them. When the procession passed slowly by, some knelt down, others burned paper money, while yet others dipped willow branches in bowls of water and waved them, scattering the procession with a sign of the rain they so desperately prayed for. The men went on up into the mountains to a temple of the Dragon King that stood beside a small pool. For three days they ate only thin gruel and prayed day and night; when no rain fell they made the gruel still thinner and repeated their prayers.[25]

24. This discussion of loess in Shanxi comes from Brandt, *Massacre in Shansi*, 18–19. The quotation is from Eva Price (ABCFM) of Fenzhou, though the sentiment is universal among early (and current!) missionaries.

25. This account of events in Chiqiao village just north of Jinci is from Harrison, *The Man Awakened from Dreams*, 29.

8   The Rushing on of the Purposes of God

Their prayers did not avail. In 1877, the third year of the Emperor Guangxu's reign (*Guangxu sannian*), a total absence of rainfall resulted in a complete crop failure, and the province fell into a state of disaster. Early that year James and Turner of the CIM finally returned to Shanxi to establish their residence and investigate what became known as the North China Famine.[26] In James's diary of the time he recorded the following scenes from the stricken province:

> People are eating the bark of trees—numbers of trees by the roadside are stripped—and of course this will kill them; much of the country is as bare as a desert. Outside one village we passed to-day there was a group of women who begged us to relieve them, and one called out several times, "Buy my two girls." . . . Never met this before. Cartloads of women and girls have passed us on the way to the capital and other cities to be sold. Saw a dead woman lying close by. . . . *Dogs eat the dead, and the starving eat the dogs.*[27]

Succumbing to famine fever and exhaustion, James and Turner were forced to escape to the coast, leaving the Shanxi capital of Taiyuan two days before Richard's arrival.[28] Arnold Foster of the LMS stationed in Hankou also visited famine-struck Shanxi in 1877. He too left two days before Richard arrived: moved by the suffering he had witnessed, Foster returned directly to London to plead Shanxi's case before the British Minister to China Sir Thomas Wade. The timely arrival of Richard's records of his experiences in Shanxi turned the tide in favor of aid.[29]

When Timothy Richard's arrived in late 1877, there were already two Catholic bishops residing in Taiyuan, an Italian priest running a school for thirteen local boys, and an additional twelve foreign priests spread throughout various counties in Shanxi.[30] According to available records, not one

---

26. The event has many names, but is best known in China as the Dingwu Famine (Dingwu Qihuang), a term based on the two Heavenly Stems that Chinese soothsayers use to mark the years 1877–1878. Edgerton-Tarpley, *Tears from Iron*, 1; Hao Ping, "Shanxi 'Dingwu Qihuang,'" 86.

27. Francis James, "Scenes in the Famine Districts," *CM* (May 1878) 69–70.

28. Evans, *Timothy Richard, a Narrative*, 71. According to Stauffer, they had only managed to last a few months before leaving Shanxi for the second time. *The Christian Occupation of China*, 186.

29. Foster, a close friend of David Hill's, played a significant (and heretofore unrecognized) role in mobilizing missionary relief during the later stages of the North China Famine. See, for example, his lengthy letter discussing relief coordination: Foster to Taylor, 6 October 1877, CIM Papers CIM/JHT/235, SOAS.

30. Xu Shihu, *Li Timotai zhuanlue*, 9.

Protestant believer or missionary was to be found in Taiyuan or anywhere else in the province of Shanxi prior to 1877. According to James's diary from his first journey to Shanxi, Taiyuan in those days had a population of roughly one hundred thousand people.[31] Letters from missionaries printed in the 1878–1879 editions of the CIM publication *China's Millions* give us a general description of what post-famine Taiyuan was like.

> Once a very fine city, but somewhat out of repair. The streets are wide, and many of them well peopled. The wall is said to be thirteen miles in circumference, but much of the ground enclosed is under cultivation. It is not what one would call a busy city, but it is important on account of its official rank and its position in the province. It is situated at the northern end of a plain about ninety miles long by forty broad. This plain contains twelve well to do cities, including the capital.[32]
>
> The houses here are all one-storied, built a foot or more above the ground, the best rooms always facing the south, so as to avoid the keen north winds. . . . The kangs, or heated bedsteads, fill half of each room and are used for putting things upon and sitting upon in the daytime, as well as sleeping on at night. They are heated with coal, which is very cheap here. The floors are brick. . . . We shall miss the fish of other parts of China, but we get abundance of splendid mutton, beef too, and fowls, English as well as sweet potatoes, and cabbages; and there are delicious grapes all through the winter.[33]

The famine, of course, interrupted this supply of plenty. The suffering which Richard witnessed during his winter 1877–1878 investigative excursion into southern Shanxi is difficult to comprehend. The "Famine Administration" section of the *Shanxi Provincial Gazetteer* for the Guangxu reign period observed that "there had never before occurred such extreme distress."[34] Other Qing officials described the famine as causing "distress unseen, and tragedy unheard of" for over two hundred thirty years.[35] Centuries of deforestation and consequent topsoil erosion, the effects of an 1877 locust swarm, looting, cannibalism of the most premeditated kind,

---

31. From an estimate given by a local reported in Francis James, "Scenes in the Famine Districts," *CM* (May 1878) 69.

32. Joshua Turner, "Report of Work in the Province of Shan-Si," *CM* (June 1878) 82.

33. Jennie Taylor, "The Orphanage Work—From Mrs. Hudson Taylor," *CM* (February 1879) 20.

34. Gao Pengcheng and Chi Zihua, "Li Timotai zai 'Dingwu qihuang,'" 135, translation mine.

35. Li Wenhai, *Zhongguo jindai shi da zaihuang*, 81, translation mine.

and a near absolute lack of shelter were found throughout the province but particularly in the areas encompassed by Linfen County and Taiyuan Prefecture where Richard traveled.[36] Each new deprivation compounded the suffering, putting pressure on other already strained resources: by the spring of 1878, local gazettes reported astronomical grain prices that simply "had never occurred before (*henggu weiyou*)."[37] According to David Hill of the Wesleyan Methodist Mission (Daying Xundaohui), in Linfen County alone 1.5 million *mu* of land was laid waste by the famine, leaving no source of revenue for the populace.[38] Neighboring Jiangzhou County was left completely bereft of arable land. As winter approached, the rising cost of coal forced citizens to dismantle portions of their homes for firewood. Between one-half and three-fifths of the houses in Linfen County were taken apart for just this reason, leaving the inhabitants without adequate shelter during the ensuing bitter winter.[39] Richard's own account of the devastation he witnessed is haunting:

> January 30—Passed two men apparently just dead. . . . A few *li* [one *li* equals approximately five hundred meters] farther there was a man of about forty walking in front of us, with unsteady steps like a drunken man. A puff of wind blew him over to rise no more.
>
> . . . Saw fourteen dead on the roadside. One had only a stocking on. His corpse was being dragged by a dog, so light it was. . . .
>
> February 1—Saw six dead bodies in half a day. . . .
>
> Saw men grinding soft stones, somewhat like those from which stone pencils are made, into powder, which were sold for from two to three cash per cutty [a cutty is a measurement weighing just over one pound] to be mixed with any grain, or grass seed, or roots, and made into cakes. I tried some of these cakes, and they tasted like most of them were—clay. Many died of constipation in consequence of eating them.
>
> . . . Farther on I saw two heads in one cage, a warning to those who would attempt violence.
>
> February 2—At the next city was the most awful sight I ever saw. It was early in the morning when I approached the city gate. On one side of it was a pile of naked dead men, heaped on top

---

36. These factors are explored in Bohr, *Famine in China and the Missionary*, 16–23.

37. As reported in Hao Ping and Zhou Ya, "'Dingwu qihuang,'" 85–86.

38. A *mu* is roughly equivalent to one-sixth of an acre.

39. The details on Linfen are from "A Record of the Famine Relief Work in Lin Fen Hien," David Hill, trans., *CR* 11, no. 4 (1880) 260–69; as discussed in Bohr, *Famine in China and the Missionary*, 19 and 22.

of each other as though they were pigs in a slaughter-house. On the other side of the gate was a similar heap of dead women, their clothing having been taken away for food. Carts were there to take the corpses away to two great pits, into one of which they threw the men, and into the other they threw the women.

. . . snow had fallen the night before. On the snow there were the marks of what had been a struggle between two men, and blood was mingled with snow. . . . For many miles in this district the trees were all white, stripped clean for ten or twenty feet high of their bark, which was being used for food. We passed many houses without doors or window-frames, which had been sold as firewood. . . .

February 4— . . . Heard stories at the inn that night of parents exchanging their children as they could not eat their own. . . .

Small wonder that I began to doubt my sense or my sanity, amid such scenes of horror. Was I among the living or among the dead? Terrible as the suffering was, we did not dare to give relief except surreptitiously; for once it was known that we gave relief, we would have been surrounded by such crowds that progress would have been impossible, and our lives would have been endangered, perhaps lost, without any good to the people, while by our safe return and subsequent appeal many of their lives would be saved.[40]

Later, Richard tried to summarize his experience of the famine for those far removed from the suffering: "Think of all the horrors of the destruction of Jerusalem, and those of the most desperate sieges recorded in history. And extend that over hundreds and thousands of towns and villages, and then you will have some conception of it."[41]

It had long been a policy of the Chinese government to operate a series of grain storage centers, supported in various ways and maintained against just such times of famine. Unfortunately, rapid increases in population, a series of expensive wars, and lack of diligence on the part of the officials left only half-full granaries stuffed with rotten grain. Bad roads and official graft further hindered the effectiveness of state relief.[42] According to the British Consul in Tianjin, the limitation of government efforts,

---

40. Richard, *Forty-Five Years*, 130–34.

41. Richard, *Fifteen Years*, 15.

42. For a detailed analysis of government relief efforts, see Edgerton-Tarpley, *Tears from Iron*, 28–39; as well as Bohr, *Famine in China and the Missionary*, 43–82.

was visible in the piles of grain in bags, the broken carts and the foundered mules which strewed the road leading up to the plateau.

[On the one-hundred-thirty-mile mountain trail over the mountains to Shanxi] the most frightful disorder reigned supreme . . . filled with officials and traders all intent on getting their convoys over the pass. Fugitives, beggars and thieves absolutely swarmed . . . Camels, oxen, mules and donkeys . . . were killed by the desperate people for the sake of their flesh (while the grain they were meant to be carrying into Shanxi rotted and fed the rats of Tianjin). Night travel was out of the question. The way was marked by the carcasses or skeletons of men and beasts, and the wolves, dogs and foxes soon put an end to the sufferings of any (sick) wretch who lay down . . . in those terrible defiles. . . . No idea of employing the starving people in making new or improving the old roads ever presented itself to the authorities. . . . Gangs of desperadoes in the hills (terrorised the travelers).[43]

Nevertheless, government relief efforts were the most important source of aid throughout the province.[44] In Taiyuan alone some twenty thousand people received daily pots of gruel from the government; other market towns also received these official food rations, while one hundred copper cash per diems were made available by the government in some of the smaller villages.[45] An imperial official and friend of Richard, Li Hongzhang estimated that out of Shanxi's fifteen million people, only 3.4 million received any degree of government assistance, though this does not take into account gentry-driven aid from Shanxi and the rest of China.[46]

The Committee of the China Famine Relief Fund (initially founded to support Richard's work in Shandong in 1876) expanded with the famine to encompass efforts throughout northern China. When Richard's report returned from Shanxi, the committee began soliciting funds from foreign residents in China and from people all around the world.[47] Since their manpower was limited and transportation difficult and expensive, they chose to have individuals distribute cash in specific, accessible areas.[48]

43. As cited in Broomhall, *HTCOC*, 6, *Assault on the Nine*, 169–70.

44. On the importance of official relief in Shanxi, see Hao Ping, "Guangxu chunian Shanxi zaihuang."

45. Evans, *Timothy Richard, a Narrative*, 72.

46. Bohr, *Famine in China and the Missionary*, 65. For more on gentry responses to the famine, see Edgerton-Tarpley, *Tears from Iron*, 131–55.

47. Janku, "The North-China Famine of 1876–1879," 128–30.

48. Bohr, *Famine in China and the Missionary*, 94–102.

From his earlier work in Shandong, Timothy Richard had learned that it was very important to not surpass or supplant "imperial benevolence" or the work of the local officials, so he sought permission from Shanxi Governor Zeng Guoquan before distributing his funds.[49] The governor was initially suspicious of Richard, fearing that the foreigner had come to stir up trouble among the dissatisfied populace; he may have heard that Richard had already been asked on two occasions to lead uprisings while distributing relief in Shandong.[50] Attempting to "manage" Richard, he first required him to coordinate his relief with the Catholic Bishop of Shanxi (who refused to cooperate) and then required that Richard dispense relief in Taiyuan along with the government efforts.[51] Richard agreed to work under the Taiyuan officials, and began coordinating his door-to-door cash dispersals with the official government grain relief in nearby Yangqu County. Names of Yangqu residents in need had already been collected by local officials, and Richard's job was to hand five hundred cash to each person on the list.[52] In order to tailor the relief to people's actual needs, Richard increasingly relied on trusted Chinese assistants to visit the poor villages ahead of time and record the details of those households where relief was needed. Then Richard himself would visit each home individually and dispense need as he saw fit.[53] Though disappointed at not being given permission to distribute over a wider range of territory, Richard understood the vital necessity of official good will, and thus was content to wait and move slowly. As conditions worsened, Governor Zeng's belief that Richard had come to "steal the hearts of the people" lessened, and Richard was allowed to expand the scope of his work.

In March 1878 the much larger funds from the various societies finally appeared, and Richard and his newly arrived coworkers headed south to Pingyang Prefecture (modern day Linfen is its main city) to distribute the

49. Richard's letter dated 11 December 1877 as reprinted in "China Famine," *MH* 74, no. 4 (1878) 99–100.

50. Bohr, *Famine in China and the Missionary*, 106. Richard had politely refused and then left the district for a while to allow passions to settle. Williamson, *British Baptists in China*, 39.

51. Playing the Protestants and Catholics against each other is a historical Chinese approach to Western foreign relations which Governor Zeng may have learned from his talented brother (Zeng Guofan), who made the practice famous. See Bohr, *Famine in China and the Missionary*, 103.

52. Copper cash (*wen*) was the most common currency denomination in late imperial China. These small coins of limited value were minted with central holes, allowing them to be strung together in strands of one thousand that were roughly equivalent in value to one tael (*liang*), a measure equal to just under forty grams of silver.

53. Bohr, *Famine in China and the Missionary*, 103–6.

aid where the suffering was most acute. One of his new coworkers, David Hill, admitted that although the worst of the suffering seemed to have passed by the time of their arrival, the province was far from fully recovered.[54] As he explained,

> The death-rate in this district is 73 per cent. That is a terrible fact for a single year, isn't it? The food which the people have been compelled to fly to comprises elm bark, roots and stems of wheat and maize, leaves of plum . . . dried earth . . . and alas, in too many cases, human flesh too. Five women were burned alive, hands and feet tied, for killing and eating children they had kidnapped from the streets.[55]

The Pingyang counties of Linfen, Hongdong, and "Wenxi" lost one hundred fifty thousand of their two hundred fifty thousand inhabitants.[56]

Famine relief was not a straightforward task. To disperse aid in an orderly fashion, the missionaries had to use a variety of techniques, ranging from painting people's palms (thus preventing multiple distributions) to using centralized locations (thus limiting travel time for aid workers). Richard was particularly inventive in his approaches to the challenges of distribution. In one instance in Shandong, he imitated Christ's feeding of the five thousand and asked all those seeking funds to be seated on the ground. He found (to the amazement of himself and the local officials) that this made for a quiet, orderly distribution and alleviated the typical press of bodies clamoring for assistance.[57] In an 1878 letter for Hudson Taylor's journal *China's Millions*, Turner recorded some of the distribution techniques employed by the missionaries.

> Our plan is to take the money in cash to the village temple, and then go round to the families on the list, with one of the head men, see the house, make some inquiries, compare their statements with the number of mouths entered on the list, then give them a ticket for money which they take immediately to the temple to be cashed. In some instances we strike off the name altogether. This plan is very laborious, but it brings us into

---

54. Though he ultimately followed Richard's lead, Hill was initially uncomfortable with Richard's deferential approach to local officials—preferring rather to "imitate his Master's methods" and eschew the patronage of the worldly powers. Barber, *David Hill*, 193–95.

55. Ibid., 200.

56. Wenxi may refer to Wenshui. Evans, *Timothy Richard, a Narrative*, 75. Pingyang soon became the first permanent Shanxi station of the CIM in 1879. Beauchamp, *Days of Blessing*, 1–3.

57. Richard, *Fifteen Years*, 13; Richard, *Forty-Five Years*, 102–3.

> contact with the people themselves, and prevents unfairness. . . . We gave money to one village but the next day the headmen brought back the share of twenty people, saying they had (died) since the lists were made, only a few days ago.
>
> Today, one representative of each family from seven villages came by appointment to our temple. They gathered in the open space in front of the door and were admitted, two villages at a time, into the temple yard. Mr. Richard distributed to one, and I to the other. Each person came up to the table when his name was called and received 800 cash (about three shillings) for each needy member of his family. . . . In this way the wants of 1,400 or more persons and their families were supplied.[58]

Sometimes the challenges were more emotional. In a letter from 1878, David Hill recounts one heart-wrenching instance from his experiences dispensing relief.

> . . . A youth came to me complaining that the son of the headman had deprived him of the 2000 cash I had just given him. On inquiring if such were the case, the man said, "Yes, I did, and I had reason for it; that youth killed and ate his own mother," and the looks of the poor lad only too plainly confirmed what the man said.[59]

By the time the famine had subsided, some 145 villages with populations ranging from sixty-three to 1,267 persons had received aid from the multinational, multi-agency group of missionary aid workers led by Richard.[60] David Hill, Albert Whiting of the American Presbyterian Mission, [61] Canon Scott of the Society for the Propagation of the Gospel (Daying Anliganhui or SPG), J. J. Turner (again!), Richard, and the rest of the Protestant missionaries had dispensed over 127,110 silver taels to 100,641 individuals in Taiyuan, Pingyang, and Zezhou Prefectures, while the Catholic missionaries already resident in Shanxi (mostly Italian Franciscans) distributed thirty-five thousand taels among the large Catholic population in Taiyuan.[62]

---

58. As reprinted in Broomhall, *HTCOC*, 6, *Assault on the Nine*, 177–78.

59. Barber, *David Hill*, 201.

60. These aid statistics are from Evans, *Timothy Richard, a Narrative*, 74; compare favorably with the official Shanghai committee reports in the appendices of Bohr, *Famine in China and the Missionary*.

61. According to most sources, Whiting was the only foreign aid worker to die (from disease) during the relief work in Shanxi province. See, for example, MacGillivray, *A Century of Protestant Mission in China*, 78.

62. Bohr, *Famine in China and the Missionary*, 192–93. Bohr's numbers for the Protestant effort in Shanxi, derived from the official famine relief committee reports,

The work in Linfen County was particularly well received: the local magistrate erected a six-foot-tall memorial tablet praising the contributions of the foreign. The tablet closed with the following words: "How profound then and how long-continued must have been the influence of the virtue and beneficence of his sacred Majesty the Emperor, that they [the foreigners] should thus be moved by the call of Heaven."[63] When the rains fell in 1879 and a harvest was finally possible, many people returned to their homes to rebuild their lives. But with the people so weak, and the fields in disarray from years of disuse, little food was planted or harvested. Lower prices for food in general led to massive bouts of dysentery as people gorged themselves on available food—and since poor communication led the West to believe that the famine was "over" there was no aid available. Thus even after the immediate danger had passed, still more people suffered and died.[64] While many lives were saved due to the efforts of the foreign missionaries, the disaster claimed far more lives: by the end of the famine, over five million people had died in Shanxi province alone—amounting to nearly one-third of the province's total population.[65]

It is difficult to measure directly the spiritual fruit that was produced by the missionaries' relief work in Shanxi during the North China Famine. Undoubtedly for some local people, the missionaries and their aid represented hope in the midst of suffering—an alternative means to avert disaster in the "moral meteorology" that shaped popular Chinese notions of natural

---

are still broadly accepted. Thompson, "Twilight of the Gods," 56. Bohr's numbers for Catholic relief (14,416 taels distributed among twenty-eight hundred local families), however, do not include monies raised by Catholics through channels other than the Shanghai Committee. Harrison, *The Missionary's Curse*, 96.

63. See Broomhall, *HTCOC*, 6, *Assault on the Nine*, 186–87; compare with Evans, *Timothy Richard, a Narrative*, 75. Broomhall is quick to mention that Hill, Turner and Richard are listed on the tablet "in that order." Curiously, local observers in Shanxi made no mention of the foreign presence or relief work during the famine. Edgerton-Tarpley, *Tears from Iron*, 131.

64. Broomhall, *HTCOC*, 6, *Assault on the Nine*, 181–82.

65. Cliff, *Flame of Sacred Love*, 84. While Richard estimated the total death count for the famine at between fifteen and twenty million people, Paul Bohr arrives at a figure of something over 9.5 million lives—spread throughout half of China's provinces—lost to famine during the years 1876–1879. Bohr has taken the bottom range of the statistics generated by the Shanghai Relief Committee's report. See discussion in Bohr, *Famine in China and the Missionary*, 113. Regardless, by 1910 Shanxi's total population still numbered only 9,219,287 people. Xu Shihu, *Li Timotai zhuanlue*, 8–9.

All these figures are further confused by the question of population dislocation. As an example, do any of these figures include women sold south during the famine years? An official *yamen* register in Lingqiu County, northern Shanxi, stated that one hundred thousand women and children had already been sold from that one county alone before May 1877. See Broomhall, *HTCOC*, 6, *Assault on the Nine*, 170.

suffering.⁶⁶ Timothy Richard was keenly aware of this, so he actively evangelized alongside his relief work, calling people to prayer and using simple tracts to remind them "that repentance for sin and kind deeds to each other were more acceptable to God than all fasting from meats; that prayer to the true God, and firm resolve to learn all His ways, were better than all their prayers to the other gods combined."⁶⁷ On one occasion in Shandong, Richard was thrilled to lead a thousand men and women in prayer to God for rain.⁶⁸ Some observers at the time, however, doubted the sincerity of Chinese spiritual responses to the missionary efforts. According to one Chinese source, Li Hongzhang met with Richard during the famine years, and while expressing his thanks and appreciation for all the cash being distributed, he also explained that any increase in believers in the areas receiving relief could only be due to people seeking to live financially off of the church.⁶⁹ While no massive influx of believers followed the relief work in Shanxi, it can be argued that the occasion of the famine did lead directly to the firm establishment of Protestant missions in the province.

As a direct result of famine relief work, the first Protestant church in Shanxi was erected in 1878 on Qiaotou Jie in Taiyuan. Out of gratitude for the relief which the missionaries had supplied, some of the local gentry presented the church with a large gold-lettered plaque to be hung over the main entrance inscribed with the words "save the world hall" (*jiushi tang*).⁷⁰ Daily preaching and worship were held here, and in the early years some medical and opium refuge work was carried out as well.

In October 1878 Timothy Richard married Mary Martin (United Presbyterian Mission, Scotland) in Shandong, with the two returning almost immediately and settling into mission life in Taiyuan. Like many missionary wives, Mary Richard was a capable and engaged field worker. In addition to her labors in the various schools and orphanages of Shanxi, Mary Richard was an important scholar of Chinese music, including Chinese hymnody, and was also the author of a multi-volume Chinese-language series of biographies of Christian saints.⁷¹

66. Elvin, "Who Was Responsible for the Weather?" 213–37; Yuan Yingying, "'Dingwu qihuang' zhong chuanjiaoshi zai Shandong," 102.

67. Richard, *Fifteen Years*, 12.

68. Richard, "China," 246.

69. Dong Conglin, *Long yu shangdi*, 198. This same source claims that investigations by the missionaries themselves proved Li's criticism to be largely true.

70. Williamson, *British Baptists in China*, 41–42. The cornerstone plaque on the front of the current church building (completed in 1994) lists 1878 as the initial founding date, while some of the older members of the church (including the younger Mr. Pan) claim to have seen the "Save the World Hall" plaque.

71. Mary Martin Richard, "Chinese Music," *CR* 21, no. 7–8 (1890) 305–14, 339–47; Richard, *Jiaoshi liezhuan*; Richard, *Paper on Chinese Music*.

Immediately following the famine, Richard and Turner had decided to set up a school for boys as well as general orphanages and shelters in the Taiyuan area to care for those left abandoned by the disaster. After her arrival, Mary Richard threw herself into supporting this work. In response to the missionaries' efforts, the governor of Shanxi quickly set up his own shelters, making sure that his projects admitted the most people. David Hill also commenced a similar work down south in Linfen. In early 1878 Richard had written to Hudson Taylor in London, offering to turn the orphanage over to the CIM if Taylor could provide suitable women to run it. In October 1878 Richard's letter received a definite response when Jennie Taylor (Hudson Taylor's second wife), Celia Horne, Anna Crickmay (later Mrs. Turner), Frederick W. Baller, and Francis and Marie James (all of the CIM) arrived to take up work and residence in Taiyuan.[72]

The arrival of Misses Crickmay and Horne in Taiyuan was not only the first instance of women working in Shanxi (Mary Richard did not come to Shanxi until shortly after Jennie Taylor's team had arrived in Taiyuan), but also the first instance of single female Protestant missionaries working in the Chinese interior, establishing a precedent that opened doors for women, married and single, to journey into the farthest reaches of inland China.[73] Jane or "Jennie" Taylor (maiden name Faulding), who accompanied them on their Shanxi adventure, was a courageous woman. Her trip to Taiyuan necessitated her leaving her two small children—three-year-old Earnest and eighteen-month-old Amy—along with Hudson's five children from his previous wife Maria back in England under the care of Hudson's sister Amelia Broomhall (who already had ten children of her own), while Hudson was

---

72. Broomhall lists the following CIM personnel as associated with the early days of Shanxi ministry:

> When the famine died down, David Hill, Turner and James intensified their preaching of the orthodox gospel and distribution of Scripture and soon were joined by (Mrs.) Jennie Taylor, Anna Crickmay, Celia Horne, Elliston, Drake, Pigott, Parrott and for a time James Cameron, George Clarke and their Chinese companions, followed by Robert and Mary Landale, Emily Kingsbury, Agnes Lancaster and Dr. and Mrs. Schofield.

Broomhall, *HTCOC*, 6, *Assault on the Nine*, 290. Unfortunately Broomhall does not include more specific dates. One CIM account records that there were at this time a total of sixty-nine missionary men from various societies serving across Shanxi as part of the general famine relief efforts, though it is unclear how many of these workers were still engaged in Shanxi missions once the crisis had passed. Chang et al., *Christ Alone*, 66.

This same source also claims that Jennie Taylor arrived in May 1878 accompanied by Crickmay and Horne. Ibid., 67. Not surprisingly, Bohr implies that the CIM personnel were sent at the invitation of Richard, while Broomhall is eager to emphasize Turner's formative role. Compare Bohr, *Famine in China and the Missionary*, 110; with Broomhall, *HTCOC*, 6, *Assault on the Nine*, 178–81.

73. Broomhall, *The Jubilee Story of the CIM*, 123–26.

off on his own engaged in other organizational duties—first in England and later in China. In addition to braving separation from her family and breaking the gender barrier to interior missions work, Jennie had earlier been one of the sixteen pioneer missionaries who accompanied Hudson and his first wife Maria and their (at the time) four children back to China in 1866. This group, the first official cohort of CIM recruits to reach China after the founding of the mission in 1865, was later known as the *Lammermuir* Party in honor of the ship that bore them to the other side of the world.[74]

By January 17, 1879 the Shanxi workers were caring for 822 orphans and 334 "Widows and Aged," and the work was still expanding.[75] Jennie Taylor and the other ladies quickly broadened the scope of the already large orphanage and elder care undertakings, establishing among other things an "industrial school" to provide vocational training for young women. Schooling in late Qing China was different in many ways from education in the West, revolving around a strict student-teacher hierarchy with a strong emphasis on memorization and imitation, and with only the most limited educational opportunities for females. One local Chinese scholar writing at the end of the nineteenth century collected some of the local school regulations:

> a school conducted in one of the Jinci town temples, required pupils to sit upright on their bench with their feet together, walk slowly, stand up straight with their hands together, speak quietly, and bow from the waist. . . . [The rules for another] school included walking properly, speaking carefully and playing no games, for "the beginning of study is to keep the body still." Similar rules inculcated a respectful attitude towards books: pupils should wash their hands before sitting down to read, should avoid touching books as far as possible, keeping it a few inches from the edge of the table and using the index finger of the right hand to turn pages.[76]

While books were of course materially valuable, this level of respect reflected their moral significance as well: the Chinese classics contained and embodied the virtues upon which Chinese society was ideally ordered. Timothy Richard records the unusual instance of a local Shanxi scholar who "took up a book of the classics from the table and deliberately placed it on the floor," claiming that he was the only person in the entire province who would dare

---

74. Chang et al., *Christ Alone*, 44, 55–56, 67.
75. Austin, *China's Millions*, 150.
76. Harrison, *The Man Awakened from Dreams*, 27.

commit such an act.[77] Even such tasks as the rote memorization of canonical texts, while certainly essential to advancement through the local, provincial, and eventually national testing regimes, were motivated by a clear moral imperative. As one local scholar from the late Qing dynasty understood the task, "memorizing a book should alter the way a person behaved in everyday life and . . . [one's] reading and actions should be in concord."[78]

In 1879 the small band of missionaries focused their attention on the triennial provincial (*juren*) examinations held that year in Taiyuan.[79] Standing at the entrance to the examination halls, the missionaries handed out twenty thousand tracts titled "The Duty of Thanksgiving for the Cessation of the Famine" along with several other pieces of Christian literature to the degree candidates. Hill and Richard had worked together to select and even write some of the tracts. Richard was a gifted Chinese speaker, but he had not mastered the art of writing in the classical literary style. For this, Richard relied on his recently hired Chinese tutor and secretary Gao Daling, a very gifted scholar from Baibancun in Yangqu who had passed the highest level exams (*jinshi*) at the imperial court. Gao soon converted and became a pillar of the Shanxi Baptist church—although his decision to continue to care for both of his wives after conversion meant he was not eligible to serve as a Baptist elder or pastor. He played a key role in the production of many of both Mary and Timothy Richard's Chinese language publications while they were in Shanxi.[80]

Along with the tracts they received, the 1879 provincial examination candidates were also given a sheet announcing cash prizes to be awarded for winning essays on various moral and religious subjects chosen by the missionaries. Over one hundred essays were received, with three of the prizes being awarded to a traditional Chinese medicine doctor named Xi (Hsi) Zizhi who had submitted four essays, making use of three aliases as well as his own name.[81] Xi met Hill when he went to collect his awards, and he soon agreed to move in with Hill and become his personal tutor. Through reading the Chinese New Testament with Hill, Xi gradually felt the call of Christ. He had a Damascus Road Pauline-type conversion, was delivered

---

77. Richard, *Forty-Five Years*, 165–66.

78. Harrison, *The Man Awakened from Dreams*, 27.

79. Barber, *David Hill*, 213–17. The idea may have originated with David Hill, but he and Richard worked together on it. David Hill, "The Triennial Examinations for the Ku Jen Degree," 463–64.

80. Wei Yisa, *Zhen Yesu jiaohui chuangli*, M10.

81. Williamson, *British Baptists in China*, 42–43. Alvin Austin argues that Xi and his faith were deeply colored by Chinese sectarian religion through Xi's participation in the Golden Elixir sect (Jindanjiao). Austin, *China's Millions*, 163–66, 171–77, 260–67.

of opium by the Holy Spirit, and then baptized by Turner who was by that time working in Pingyang. Xi later changed his name to Xi "Overcomer of Devils" (Xi Shengmo) and became the famous evangelist and anti-opium crusader Pastor Xi of Pingyang County.[82]

During the following years Timothy Richard worked on and presented a series of lectures in Taiyuan on "the law of God in Nature" with such topics as "The astronomical miracle discovered by Copernicus" and "The miracles of chemistry."[83] These lectures, typically involving demonstrations of the latest scientific devices, introduced many members of Shanxi's scholarly elite to the basic concepts of Christianity and modern science.[84] As part of this initiative, Richard secured a set of photographic equipment, training Gao Daling in its use.[85] Alongside these new practical initiatives, Richard also continued his more traditional mission duties: holding regular services, running seven village elementary schools, and instructing the sixty boys of the orphanage in Taiyuan.[86] Nor was the work in vain: as early as 1880 there were already seventeen or eighteen boys and girls in the orphanages who were thought to have become believers.[87]

With the famine relief work behind them, the missionaries initially agreed to work and worship together as one group. There was a sense of cooperation and camaraderie among the group that must have been exciting

82. The main source material on Xi remains Taylor, *One of China's Scholars*. See also Broomhall's discussion of Xi in *HTCOC*, 6, *Assault on the Nine*, 374–75, 401–14, among others.

83. Richard, *Forty-Five Years*, 160–63.

84. Richard was introduced to this method of evangelism by Dr. Calvin Mateer (American Presbyterian Mission) while still in Shandong. Richard's Taiyuan lectures were very well received and a theater was placed at his disposal by the provincial authorities. Williamson, *British Baptists in China*, 34 and 50, respectively. One skeptical modern Chinese source suggests that while some were intrigued by the scientific wonders, few were interested in God. This same author also claims that the missionaries were aware of the shortcomings of their methods. Dong Conglin, *Long yu shangdi*, 198–99.

According to another Chinese source, Richard also has the distinction of being the first person to introduce Marxism to China. In 1898 and 1899, through his affiliation with the CLS, Richard lectured to Chinese audiences on Marxist socialism. In 1899 he also published a Chinese translation of Benjamin Kidd's *Social Evolution* in one of the CLS Chinese language periodicals. Kidd's 1894 book summarized the basic tenets of the then-popular social Darwinism. Ren Fuxing, "'Xinzhou Yesujiao jinlihui shengtu," 112.

85. Gao opened Shanxi's first photography studio on Qiaotou Jie not far from the church. Richard, *Forty-Five Years*, 154, 160.

86. In 1881 (See "Shanxi spirit" below) Richard handed his boys' school over to the CIM in an offer of good will. Williamson, *British Baptists in China*, 50.

87. "Brief Notes: Shan-Si," *CM* (July and August 1881) 99.

even though their numbers were small; in 1880 there were twelve foreign Christian men and women working in Shanxi province. Their common goal: distributing gospel tracts in each of the counties in Shanxi.[88]

THE SHANXI SPIRIT CONTROVERSY: DISPUTE AND CONFLICT ON THE FIELD

In 1881 the "charm of unity and simplicity" that had characterized the cooperation between the various mission societies in Taiyuan came to an end.[89] According to Timothy Richard, Hudson Taylor ordered all CIM personnel in Taiyuan to worship separately from the BMS mission because Richard was in some unspecified way "not orthodox."[90] Shortly after, many of the foreign workers in Shanxi resigned from the CIM. It is difficult to know the exact nature of this dispute, but biographers of Hudson Taylor point to two of Taylor's letters from the time as evidence that there were two factors—one theological and the other personal—behind the schism.

> Hudson Taylor thought [Richard] was "driving a good theory to death" by his reluctance to preach and his preference for moral tracts which spoke about God but not Christ in order gently to prepare the way for the gospel. . . . Taylor didn't see the defections from his mission as necessarily Richard's fault—rather it was the "inevitable result of a strong and attractive character over weaker minds."[91]

The primary reason for the split in the early Shanxi mission community is usually understood to be a theological disagreement over mission methods, rooted in the claim that Richard placed too much emphasis on activities other than evangelism.[92] According to CIM historian A. J. Broom-

---

88. David Hill, "Address at the Fifteenth Anniversary meeting of the China Inland Mission," *CM* (July and August 1881) 89; Richard, *Fifteen Years*, 18. On the number of workers, see Edwards, *Fire and Sword in Shansi*, 47.

89. Barber, *David Hill*, 205.

90. Richard, *Forty-Five Years*, 152–53. This also, according to Richard, resulted in the opening of a separate CIM school in Taiyuan.

91. Steer, *J. Hudson Taylor*, 274–75. In this same passage the biographer describes Richard's thinking as "liberal."

92. The author of the official history of the BMS points out that Richard's concept of salvation as "embracing '*all* sin and misery of the present life'" is actually a rich biblical understanding of the depth and breadth of sin. See Stanley, *History of the BMS*, 196. According to Stanley, Richard's error lay in his application of nineteenth-century evolutionary theory to theology: he believed all other religions could simply be filled in and corrected until they measured up to the full gospel of Christ.

hall, the lack of evangelistic fervor which supposedly resulted from the adoption of Richard's approach to mission was termed "the Shanxi spirit" by Taylor and those critical of Richard within the CIM—a catchall phrase that referred to the "whirlpool of complaints, misunderstandings, derelict spiritual morale and finally resignations from the CIM and BMS."[93] It was seen to be contagious, and those who worked with or at least near Richard were understood to be in danger of infection. In order to focus on winning souls for Christ, Taylor was thus compelled to withdraw his workers from Richard's influence and to put all effort into the preaching of the Word.

A close examination of the relevant archives, however, reveals only a handful of somewhat vague references to the 1881 CIM–BMS split.[94] Even the term "Shanxi spirit" appears to be more an invention of the historian than an actual phrase used at the time. Moreover, the limited evidence that does remain presents the conflict in a somewhat different light. There certainly was, as Richard himself admitted thirty-five years later, some kind of division. But most of the CIM people on the field at the time did not sympathize with Taylor, and in fact continued—if somewhat more sporadically—to fraternize, cooperate, and even worship with the Richards after the split. Eventually, nearly all of the first generation of CIM Shanxi workers either resigned or transferred, many to Richard's BMS. These resignations, however, were driven by dissatisfaction with CIM policies and had little to do with Richard. At the time, many CIM workers in Shanxi and elsewhere were upset by the perceived lack of sufficient financial provision and the strict prohibition of marriage for probationary missionaries.

Modern tendencies to paint Taylor and Richard as diametrically opposed missionaries—one liberal, the other conservative—require significant revision.[95] Taylor and Richard certainly did have their missiological differences. Taylor was at least to some extent driven by premillennial concerns, whereas Richard never discussed millennial matters in any of his writings, personal or public. Richard was convinced that the Kingdom of God had implications for life on this earth as well as for life in the next, an idea which made Taylor somewhat uncomfortable. However, since Richard and Taylor both made the unusual choice to spend their lives in service to God as missionaries in China decades before the rise of the divisive modernist-fundamentalist conflict of the early twentieth century, it would

---

93. This quote comes from Broomhall's account of the controversy in *HTCOC*, 6, *Assault on the Nine*, 288–93.

94. For a more detailed presentation of the information in this paragraph, see chapter 7 in Kaiser, "Encountering China."

95. Pfister, "Rethinking Mission in China," 183–212. See also Walls, "Multiple Conversions of Timothy Richard," 245.

be surprising if they did not share similar outlooks on mission. Both were British Nonconformists (Christians who worshiped outside the established church) with strong Baptist sympathies, both chose to adopt Chinese dress and to engage in medical and other humanitarian work as part of their missionary labors, both were committed to pioneering inland mission work and the development of indigenous churches, and both worked to build the church in Shanxi. Taylor had even applied to join the BMS, before founding his own CIM, owing to the inability of the BMS to guarantee that the next five China workers would be sent to serve under his leadership.[96] These two evangelical missionaries had a great deal in common—even their wives worked together to care for orphans in post-famine Shanxi.

Much is often made of the fact that in his later years Richard, unlike Taylor, focused most of his ministry on reaching Chinese elites, whether through personal contact or through the vast quantities of literature he wrote, published, or translated for this purpose. This, however, had little to do with any supposed "trickle down" theory of evangelism. Richard felt an obligation to evangelize Chinese scholar officials, but he did not expect that many would convert. Rather, he interacted with these elites out of a belief that increased contact with them might soften their hearts toward Christianity. He hoped that this would then encourage Chinese officials to take a more active interest in the living conditions of the Chinese peasants whom Richard had seen suffer so greatly during the recent North China Famine, and to allow greater freedom for Chinese evangelists to take the gospel to the very same common people about whom Taylor was so deeply concerned. Richard chose to take this work upon himself because his recent famine work had positioned him perfectly for this task and no other missionaries seemed willing or able to do so.[97]

Surprisingly, Taylor's first visit to Shanxi did not occur until June 1886, many years after his decision to split the missionary community. During that visit, Taylor delivered a series of addresses to the Shanxi CIM workers who had gathered there. Despite the intervening years, Taylor nevertheless repeated many of the themes that he must have stressed to the troubled team some five years previous, imploring his workers to focus their energies on the oral proclamation of the gospel.

---

96. For some of Taylor's close connections with Richard's BMS, see Richard, *Forty-Five Years*, 28, 32.

97. On the instrumental nature of Richard's focus on Chinese elites, see my "Encountering China," 198–205. Note, as well, that CIM workers were happy to share the gospel with Chinese elites when the opportunity arose.

> Let us feel that everything that is human, everything outside the sufficiency of Christ, is only helpful in the measure to which it enables us to bring Christ forward.
>
> ... If our medical missions bring people nearer to us, and we can present to them the Christ of God, medical missions are a blessing; but to substitute medicine for the preaching of the Gospel would be a profound mistake. If we put schools or education in the place of spiritual power to change the heart, it will be a profound mistake. If we get the idea that people are going to be converted by some educational *process*, instead of by a regenerative *re-creation*, it will be a profound mistake. . . . let all our auxiliaries be auxiliaries—means of bringing Christ and the soul into contact—then we may be truly thankful for them all. . . . Let us exalt this glorious Gospel in our hearts, and believe it is the power of God to salvation. Let everything else sit at its feet, and then all our auxiliaries will indeed be auxiliaries. We shall never be discouraged if we realise that our sufficiency is in Christ.[98]

Undeniably, Timothy Richard was willing to engage in "auxiliary" works: as one typical example, in the early 1880s Richard teamed up with the CIM's own Harold Schofield to survey Taiyuan Prefecture in hopes of alleviating the threat of future flooding.[99] Richard was frequently offered more permanent "secular" jobs by the local and imperial officials—yet he always turned them down. In his memoirs he explained that "however important material advantages were, the missionary was engaged in work of still greater importance and . . . could not permanently leave the higher work for the lower."[100] And as to the "higher" work, Richard's dedication to the spread of the gospel can be shown in the fact that during the two years prior to his arrival in Shanxi, his famine relief work in Shandong province had resulted in a thousand converts and inquirers.[101] Taylor and Richard were both committed to sharing Christ; the difference arose from Richard's willingness to recognize (in comparison with Taylor) more value in mission work that was not direct oral preaching of the gospel.[102] Toward the end of the nineteenth

---

98. Beauchamp, *Days of Blessing*, 90–91.

99. Bohr, *Famine in China and the Missionary*, 166.

100. As quoted in Evans, *Timothy Richard, a Narrative*, 87.

101. Richard was in all respects a Christian of the evangelical persuasion, at least throughout his time in Shanxi. Kaiser, "Encountering China." The astounding figure of "a thousand converts and inquirers" is taken from a brief biographical sketch of Richard found in Forsyth, *Shantung*, 210.

102. In many ways this is the same argument over whether so-called secular labors can be considered "Kingdom-building," which has been present throughout the

century, Richard explained in writing that he was not pushing for secular civilization: he did believe that salvation of individual souls was essential, but he also longed to see

> the application of the healing powers of the Gospel to the social miseries of a great nation; it is a benevolent work, exemplifying the love of Christ, on the grandest scale.... [China] needs most of all character and conscience, purity in family life, integrity in official life, and in order to get these, she needs religious New Birth—she needs Christianity.[103]

While it is possible to demonstrate that there were fewer theological differences between Richard and Taylor than modern readers typically expect, the degree to which differences in personality contributed to the 1881 schism is much more difficult to assess.[104] In the quote cited earlier, Taylor seems to blame Richard's "strong and attractive character" for the division. Taylor and Richard were certainly both men with large, dynamic personalities. With the two of them trying to lead and organize workers on the same field—and with Taylor doing so via correspondence while Richard was present on the ground—it is not surprising that differences arose. Since neither man was fond of compromise and both men resisted being controlled by anyone else, whatever differences that might have arisen would have been very difficult to resolve peaceably. Taylor's preference for top-down leadership and control are well known, as exemplified in the strict and detailed policies of his organization's *Book of Arrangements*.[105] In contrast, Richard strove to avoid limiting anyone's liberty, decrying "co-pastorate[s] of a dozen men on the Mission field" as "impracticable."[106] Accordingly, Richard acquired a reputation as something of a maverick. His own sarcastic comments on the dispute seem to point in this direction (quoted from his autobiography):

---

modern mission age. Richard, like the printer-statesman-missionary Samuel Wells Williams (ABCFM) before him, was one of the earlier missionaries to espouse and promulgate the affirmative position, and as such met with criticism from the more traditional missionaries. See the discussion of subsidiary means in Kaiser, "S. Wells Williams," 70–76.

103. Taken from page four of the *Tenth Annual Report of the Society for the Diffusion of Christian and General Knowledge Among the Chinese* (Shanghai, 1897), written by Timothy Richard.

104. The task of comparison is further clouded by the ascendancy of the CIM and Taylor within the hagiography of post-war evangelicalism. For a modern example of CIM hagiography, see the loyal and glowing portrayal of Hudson Taylor given by the former CIM missionary Herbert Kane in Kane, "J. Hudson Taylor," 197–204.

105. Steer, *J. Hudson Taylor*, 295–96.

106. Correspondence, Timothy Richard to Alfred Baynes, October 19, 1888, BMSA, ch 2.

The matter is now a thing of the past. I see nothing to regret in my attitude at the time, although to this day its consequences follow me. But I am glad to say that in [Taiyuan Prefecture] there is no longer any schism, the Baptist Missionary Society now occupying the whole city.[107]

While a conclusive analysis of the precise ways in which personality differences contributed to the dispute is not possible, it is certainly clear that in this area at least both Taylor and Richard must share the blame.

Immediately following his decision to separate, Taylor called two of CIM administrator Benjamin Broomhall's children to the Taiyuan field to ensure loyalty and orthodoxy in the future. Gertrude Broomhall arrived in Taiyuan in 1885 and spent the next three years traveling throughout Taiyuan Prefecture by donkey to share the gospel with peasant women addicted to opium. In 1894 she married Dixon Hoste (CIM) of the "Cambridge Seven" and joined his work down south in Hongdong.[108] Hudson Broomhall came to Shanxi with his sister, but in 1887 he left Taiyuan for Huolu in Hebei where he met the Pigotts, who shortly after moved to Shouyang, Shanxi.[109] Ultimately, regardless of the exact cause for the split, in God's providence the split in Taiyuan resulted in a division of labor which brought the gospel to more parts of Shanxi more quickly.

According to CIM historian A. J. Broomhall, sometime in 1881 Richard made a trip to Chefoo to try to dissuade Taylor from splitting the local foreign community. Richard even offered to withdraw the BMS from Taiyuan in exchange for unobstructed work in a different city in another province. Richard's overtures were apparently unsuccessful, bringing an inauspicious close to the first of many disputes that would disrupt the Shanxi field during its early years.[110]

One of the larger inter-agency disagreements focused on the nature of conversion. The newer, less developed organizations such as the CIM, Frederick Franson's Scandinavian Alliance Mission,[111] and other Keswick-influenced groups tended to be quicker to baptize new converts, while

107. Richard, *Forty-Five Years*, 153.
108. Cliff, *Flame of Sacred Love*, 85–89.
109. Ibid., 91.

110. There appears to be no mention of this meeting in any of the BMS or CIM archival materials. The only reference to the trip is a brief comment in Richard's autobiography written nearly thirty-five years after the event. Richard, *Forty-Five Years*, 153.

111. Franson's first group of China workers left New York for China on January 17, 1891. These were the first formally trained missionaries of what would later become The Evangelical Alliance Mission (TEAM). Initially, their work focused on neighboring Shaanxi with some activity from European workers in northern Shanxi.

established, more traditional organizations such as the BMS and the American Board of Commissioners for Foreign Missions (Meiguo Gonglihui) or ABCFM were more likely to require evidences of faith and understanding over a certain period of time before welcoming new believers into full fellowship. Given each individual missionary's personal acquaintance with backsliding in his or her own flock, this was no abstract theological debate. On one notorious occasion in 1887, the idiosyncratic Pastor Xi baptized 217 men and women who came to him in Pingyang seeking the ordinance. Another "Baptist missionary operating in South Shansi" baptized two hundred people solely because they came to him and "it was not his place to reject them." One member of the British and Foreign Bible Society working in Shanxi thought it generous to say that one in fifteen of the CIM's converts in Shanxi "were really interested in truth." The ABCFM, by contrast, had a very developed system that distinguished between inquirers and probationers. Unlike the often only vaguely interested inquirers, probationers were required to study doctrine for at least a year and to pass a rigorous examination before being accepted into full communion. Exam questions included: "What is it to be a Christian? What is sin? What is the meaning of baptism? Why did Christ come into the world? What is the work of the holy spirit? Why do you love the Lord?"[112] Regardless of when or under what terms baptism was offered, missionaries were often disappointed with the results of their evangelistic efforts. One Shanxi missionary, upon returning from a brief itineration in the countryside, described the reaction of three individuals to his offer of salvation, reactions which he believed to be quite typical.

> One, a scholar, told [me] that the doctrine of Christ was foolishness, that he himself knew more than Christ did. A second man said that half of the residents of his village were Catholic converts and that he and his family would probably become Christians eventually. The third person, a woman, said she would not be ashamed to become a Christian but that it was unimportant to her.[113]

Looking back on ten years of work in Shanxi, Frank Price of the ABCFM Oberlin Band (see below) outlined eight factors which he saw as the main reasons for the relative lack of evangelistic success: 1) the "mysterious

---

112. The two quotations are taken from Francis Price, "Description of Mission Work in Shansi, 1877–1889," in Brandt, *Massacre in Shansi*, 116–17. Price, as a member of the ABCFM, was almost certainly biased in his assessments, but the disagreement and the issues that contributed to the debate were quite real.

113. Ibid., 57.

providence" in the surprising number of deaths that had occurred; 2) too many missionaries serving "exceedingly short" terms on the field; 3) the very slowness of the work itself made things "trying to those in service"; 4) the "peculiarly difficult" language of Chinese was hard to master; 5) opium enslavement affected so many Shanxi people; 6) "idol worship" was still prevalent in Shanxi; 7) the general "deceitfulness and vileness of the heathen heart"; 8) and, finally, disputes both theological and personal within the mission community.[114]

Returning to Taiyuan in 1886 following his first furlough after fifteen years in China, Timothy Richard found himself embroiled in conflict for the second time, and this time the dispute was explicitly theological and often personal.[115] In his absence, Richard's new BMS Shanxi colleagues—Herbert Dixon, Joshua Turner, and Arthur Sowerby were the main critics—had become dissatisfied with his missionary methods. They accused Richard of teaching "another Gospel" different from that given in the Bible, of advocating ineffective evangelistic techniques, of "leaning Romewards" toward Catholicism, and of being a generally unreasonable person. The dispute, conducted by means of lengthy letters sent back and forth between the Shanxi field and the BMS Committee in England, revealed as much about Richard's new coworkers as it did about himself. Richard's emphasis on concrete demonstrations of the superiority of Christianity over all potential Chinese competitors was too large a departure from the theological training his fellow BMS workers had received back in Britain. The small number of conversions the BMS had seen in its first few years in Shanxi did not match the grand expectations of Richard's less experienced colleagues. And Richard's willingness to use Chinese-language Catholic literature when nothing Protestant was available was unacceptable to Baptist colleagues steeped in mid-century Victorian England's staunch anti-Catholicism. The BMS Committee back in England eventually cleared Richard of all serious charges, requesting only that he place more emphasis on direct evangelism and church work. His accusers were never censured. The lingering ill will led Richard and his family to leave Shanxi, preparing the way for his 1891 decision to serve as director of the Society for the Diffusion of Christian and General

---

114. This list is taken from a typed manuscript of Frank Price's and summarized in ibid., 37. Apart from items one, five, and perhaps six, today's China field would produce a very similar list of challenges.

Charles Price's older brother Frank arrived in China first (in 1884), was quickly invalided home, returned to Shanxi again, and then a few years later left finally with bronchitis. After recovering in the States, he and his family embarked on a long career as missionaries in Micronesia.

115. See chapter 8 in Kaiser, "Encountering China."

Knowledge Among the Chinese (or SDCK), which eventually became the influential Christian Literature Society of China (Guangxuehui) or CLS.[116]

Many of the more esoteric of the theological disputes within the Shanxi mission community centered around particular individuals on the field. Stanley Percival Smith one of the "Cambridge Seven" (see below), initially came under fire from the CIM leadership over his use of Salvation Army-style "drum and cymbal" marching bands: before services, he would send a band crashing through the streets of Lu'an (modern day Changzhi) inviting people to attend.[117] Not long after, Smith attracted further criticism by advocating for annihilationism as an alternative to eternal damnation. After being exposed to the Dowie Sect from America, he eventually came to espouse a sort of "universal restoration" sometimes called "conditional mortality" along with that particular sect's more radical understandings of faith healing.[118] Smith's unique views combined with his stature and influence within the CIM to bring him into frequent conflict with the mission's leaders. In late 1901 Smith wrote to the London Council of the CIM while on home assignment, requesting leave to return to China. On his well-known theological views he commented, "I admit that final restoration is not *clearly revealed* in Scripture, hence I cannot preach it. Any hope I may privately hold concerning it is based on premises which are open to question."[119] Surprisingly, the CIM approved his return to the field! Taylor felt that as long as Smith was hesitant to finally commit himself to his unorthodox views, and did not confuse the people, tolerance was the best policy (Taylor cited Romans 14:1 in his own defense). Once on the field, however, Smith's theological convictions rapidly solidified—convictions that he felt were *not* at odds with the CIM's overall beliefs. Taylor himself finally severed Smith's relationship with the organization in 1902.[120] Smith then left the CIM to work on his own in Zezhou (modern day Jincheng).

---

116. On the SDCK/CLS see Stanley, *History of the BMS*, 189–96; Whitefield, "The Christian Literature Society for China."

117. Broomhall, *HTCOC*, 7, *It is Not Death to Die!*, 58.

118. A congregational minister from Australia, Alexander Dowie founded the conservative Christian sect that bears his name outside of Chicago in 1896. The group emphasized faith healing, operating their own "tabernacle" with healing rooms in Chicago, and denied the traditional Christian belief of eternal suffering in Hell for the unsaved. Harlan, "John Alexander Dowie."

119. Broomhall, *HTCOC*, 7, *It is Not Death to Die!*, 491.

120. For more on Smith, see ibid., 310, 490–97; and Austin, *China's Millions*, 385–87. Personally, Taylor was convinced that "the Holy Scriptures do not hold out any hope for those who die impenitent." Broomhall, *HTCOC*, 7, *It is Not Death to Die!*, 496. However, in later years Taylor softened, noting that had the organization been founded in 1901, the official statements regarding eternal punishment might have been worded

The Age of Pioneers (1876–1899) 31

Taylor's original leniency on this point may seem surprising, but it simply reflects his generosity toward friends and the realities of operating a multi-denominational ministry. As he himself wrote at the time of Smith's dismissal,

> The CIM is not a Church, nor a section of the general Church, but a voluntary union of members of various denominations, agreeing to band themselves together to obey the Saviour's last command in respect to China; holding in common the same fundamental truths, accepting the directorship rule of the Mission, and receiving where needful such ministration as God may make possible from its funds....
>
> If the Directors and Members of our Councils are godly and wise men, walking in the spirit of unity and love, they will not lack divine guidance in important matters, and at critical times; but should another spirit prevail, no rules could save the Mission, nor would it be worth saving. The CIM must be a living body in fellowship with God or it will be no further use and cannot continue.[121]

Taylor's managerial preference for detailed policies and obedience to regulations existed in harmony with a pastoral heart that genuinely longed to see his missionaries faithfully following God's call in their lives.

It is not surprising that in so challenging an environment, with such a promise of potential, where so many bold pioneering personalities were expected to work amicably together, disagreements arose. One critical examiner of Taylor's group's work in Shanxi summarized the contradictions surrounding the early phase of the Shanxi mission:

> Shanxi was the success story of the CIM: the safest province; the largest number of missionaries; the most hospitals, schools and opium refuges; second in the number of converts; and the most experimental methods. Yet it was such a fractious place that some referred to a "Shanxi spirit".... At least fifty Shanxi missionaries resigned from the CIM and left the province; three committed suicide.[122]

---

in a different, less dogmatic fashion. Wigram, *Bible and Mission in Faith Perspective*, 168–70.

121. Broomhall, *HTCOC*, 7, *It is Not Death to Die!*, 496. On the same page it notes that Taylor had read the Bible through in one year over forty times.

122. Austin, *China's Millions*, xxvi.

THE WORDLESS BOOK

The Yellow Emperor of Chinese legend is supposed to have codified the five elements (*wuxing*) and their corresponding color symbols. According to Chinese tradition these materials—metal, wood, fire, water, and soil—are understood to represent the basic composition of the earth. They also play a key role in Chinese traditional medicine, with the colors and their reputed properties being employed by Chinese doctors in their prescriptions.

The five elements would have been well known in Shanxi in particular because of the presence of Wutai Shan, the most important Buddhist pilgrimage site in the province. Located one hundred twenty miles northeast of Taiyuan, "Five Peak Mountain" was (and still is) considered one of Chinese Buddhism's sacred mountains. Dedicated to Manjusri, a bodhisattva associated with transcendent wisdom, the holy site today comprises a vast series of temples and images dating back as early as the Han dynasty. According to one historian,

> Since Manjusri is the Buddha of Grammatical Science, Wutai Shan is laid out with geometric precision as a living *wuxing*. Each of the five peaks is devoted to one of the five celestial colors (one color for each of the elements), and everything—the temples, the images, even the flowers on the hillsides—is red, black, white, green, or yellow.[123]

But these colors would have had very different associations for the early missionaries. In 1866 famed London preacher Charles Spurgeon delivered a message at the Metropolitan Tabernacle entitled "The Wordless Book," in which he told of an unnamed pastor who bound three colored pages together to form a book.[124] The man carried the tome with him, often glancing at the various pages to remind himself of his sin (black), Christ's blood (red), and the forgiveness it brings (white). Spurgeon's simple illustration rapidly spread from the realm of the devotional into the sphere of evangelism. In particular, many groups and individuals began using the book as an effective tool for evangelizing younger or illiterate British children. By 1875 a four-color wordless book was being used by the American evangelist Dwight L. Moody as a refinement of Spurgeon's three-color version. It included an additional gold page to remind readers of "the glories of Heaven." Hudson Taylor was in England during both of these periods, re-

---

123. Ibid., 154–55.

124. Spurgeon's church was a strong supporter of Taylor's nascent CIM from the earliest years onward. Spurgeon's 1866 sermon can be found online as Spurgeon, "The Wordless Book."

cruiting heavily from attendees at Moody's various revival meetings. Given the book's popularity, Taylor and those who signed on to join his fledgling mission certainly would have had early exposure to it. However, it was not until the late 1930s when the newly founded Children's Evangelism Fellowship began printing the books with an additional green page symbolizing "new life in Christ" that the books attained their current five-page form.[125]

When the CIM women first arrived in Taiyuan, they were faced with the immediate challenge of how to feed and clothe one thousand hungry orphans. With winter approaching, they decided to employ local women in sewing wadded clothing for themselves and for distribution to the poor and orphaned. "There was a large pile of [clothes] made, and we very soon got through them; and then another pile was made, and thus, week after week, distribution was made to these poor people in their distress." This soon led to "a new phase of missionary work," when they realized the orphans needed "some kind of industry that might be useful to them in after life." The young girls were taught to braid straw, a common handicraft in Shanxi, to spin cotton, and to embroider articles for sale, such as a "little embroidered comb-case (it is a common thing amongst the Chinese to carry a little comb, with which they comb out their moustache)."[126]

In the midst of teaching stitching and embroidery to the children, one of the missionary women in Taiyuan—probably Jennie Taylor, who would certainly have heard of the book from her husband at the least—came up with the idea of using the "wordless book" within their women's sewing circles, so they could "gossip the Gospel" while they sewed.[127] The Shanxi missionary women organized groups of local women to make gloves with different colors for each of the fingers—explaining as they sewed that gold represented God's heaven, black represented sin, red was for Christ's sacrifice, and white symbolized the new believer's forgiven state. Of course, this was a set of four colors that Shanxi people were already quite familiar with.

Since so many of the CIM recruits had come out in response to Moody and Sankey's preaching tours, they would naturally have been quite familiar with this evangelistic tool and its use in the English urban context.

---

125. This information is found throughout Austin's *China's Millions*. The Child Evangelism Fellowship claims that they added the fifth page "green" in the 1930s, although surely others had thought of this innovation beforehand. In particular, the parallel with China's *wuxing* would likely have suggested just such an addition to the better-informed China missionaries, which raises the question: What color was the fifth finger on the Shanxi missionary women's gloves?

126. Hill, "Address at the Fifteenth Anniversary meeting of the China Inland Mission," 89–93, quotes on 90–91.

127. Austin, *China's Millions*, 167–69.

But employing the same tool in China did not necessarily have the same implications, for in this case they were using an effective tool for reaching illiterate English children to evangelize unchurched Chinese adults. How effective was this technique? What would those Shanxi women have heard? Did the foreign women's simple presentation communicate anything apart from a reaffirmation of traditional Chinese folk understandings of the *wuxing*? Were the missionaries aware of how similar their gospel message sounded to local folk beliefs? Perhaps the missionaries used the similarities to gain a listening audience and then focused on the distinctive aspects of their gospel message. Unfortunately, we have no record of foreign or local opinions on these issues, and so these thoughts are only speculations. But regardless of the scheme's appropriateness, historian Alvyn Austin believes that the women's sewing project in Taiyuan marked the first use of the wordless book in China—and one of the earliest instances of its use in foreign mission.[128]

The first official mention of the book's use in Taiyuan came from Methodist David Hill in his keynote address to the CIM's annual meeting in May 1881. Hill had just returned from Shanxi, immediately upon the completion of his four-year long battle with the Shanxi famine, and thus was one of the first eyewitnesses of Shanxi missions to reach England. Hill had high praise for the CIM men, his colleagues in distributing relief, but he had been particularly impressed by the "adaptiveness" of the women. He then produced a small book given to him by the mission women—a book in the form of "a coloured silk folio, for a lady to use and put her coloured silk thread into." It was made from four different-colored scraps of silk sewn together: black, red, white, and gold. Hill then proceeded to explain its uses to the meeting delegates.

> And what is the lesson that is taught? First of all, the black indicates the blackness of sin—that whoever lives in the habitual commission of sin has his heart blackened by it. The next is the red, pointing them to the blood of our Lord Jesus Christ, which cleanses from all sin. The next is the white, which shows the purity of those who believe in the Lord Jesus Christ for salvation, that their sins are all cleansed away, and that they are washed and made white in His most precious blood. And then the last part is golden, which refers to the golden streets of the heavenly Jerusalem; thus are lessons taught to these poor women.

---

128. Austin was the first modern scholar to bring attention to this fascinating piece of China mission history. Ibid., 167–68.

At the end of his talk, almost in passing, David Hill mentioned another innovation of the CIM women, which was to have far-reaching implications: the first opium refuge. As Miss Crickmay went visiting from house to house, she discovered that many of the women she came across were opium addicts; in fact, after the famine it was estimated that 70 per cent of the adult population of Taiyuan smoked opium, mostly domestic. "At once letters were sent to Pekin [sic], and medicine was purchased; the opium pills were brought down from Pekin, and sold to the people," Hill reported.[129]

R. H. SCHOFIELD AND EARLY MEDICAL MISSIONS IN SHANXI

A distinguished graduate of Oxford University, recipient of numerous awards and distinctions, and an unusually gifted surgeon, Dr. R. Harold Schofield had shocked upper-class Britain with his decision to leave his career behind to serve Christ with the CIM in China. Arriving with his wife in China in 1880, Schofield immediately threw himself into language study and medical work at Chefoo; by October of that same year the doctor and his wife were on a train bound for Taiyuan where he soon established the first medical station in the province.[130] Described by Timothy Richard as "one of the most brilliant medical missionaries who ever came to China," Schofield was considered by the CIM to be their first permanent medical missionary and is generally acknowledged to be the father of medical mission in Shanxi.[131] Despite all this, Schofield was a very humble man. A slip of paper was found in a box along with all of his trophies and certificates with the words written in Schofield's own hand: "God resisteth the proud, but giveth grace unto the humble."[132]

Once in China, Schofield made rapid progress in his language studies. He quickly developed a remarkable Mandarin vocabulary and was said to have kept a personal diary in Chinese. In a letter sent home for publication, Schofield described his work in Taiyuan.

> I would beg the readers of *China's Millions* to pray that God's spirit may work in the hearts of the patients as to produce a sense of sinfulness and need. Thousands have heard the Gospel

---

129. This and the previous quotation are all taken from David Hill, "Address at the Fifteenth Anniversary meeting of the China Inland Mission," 89–93.

130. Edwards, *Fire and Sword in Shansi*, 45–46; Stauffer, *The Christian Occupation of China*, 186.

131. Broomhall, *HTCOC*, 6, *Assault on the Nine*, 316; Williamson, *British Baptists in China*, 52.

132. Broomhall, *The Jubilee Story of the CIM*, 142–45.

for the first time though no actual results are yet apparent; we are certain that sooner or later they will be manifest. At least we can be thankful that the patients characterize the preaching of the Gospel, as "exhorting men to the practice of virtue," often saying, "These are good workers," "It is all good doctrine," etc., but we long to see them really feeling its power.

With the in-patients we have daily morning worship. Many have learnt one or two simple prayers, some few a catechism, and several chapters in the New Testament. Three have expressed a desire to become Christians, and on February 10, 1883, one of them (the young man named K'ao from Ho-nan [Henan] . . .) was baptized, to our great delight. He has been lame for a long time, owing to a chronic disease about both hip joints, and can only walk very slowly with the aid of a stick. At present he remains in the hospital. Being able to read and write well, he is useful in many ways, but especially in putting the Gospel before the other in-patients, and we trust he will soon be used in leading many to Christ.

Schofield went on to explain that after treating 1,851 cases in 1881, hospital visits nearly doubled in 1882 with 3,247 cases, of which 3,110 were outpatients. Among the inpatients that year, there were nineteen medical and eighty-six surgical cases. Out of the total 292 surgical operations, Schofield performed forty-seven with the aid of chloroform. That whole year, only one death occurred in the hospital—from exhaustion after a prolonged spinal disease. Many of the patients came from considerable distances, one traveling five hundred *li*, equivalent to one hundred seventy miles.[133]

In the 1880s and 1890s some of the most commonly treated injuries in Shanxi were wolf bites—an injury that became increasingly common during the lean years of drought and famine.[134] Typhoid was common as well, ultimately infecting thirty-two-year-old Schofield through lice he contracted while caring for a man suffering from a case of virulent diphtheria. As he was dying two months later—a scant three years after his arrival on the field—Schofield told his wife that "these three years in China have been by far the happiest in my life." Schofield's dying prayer was that God would send out from England's highest universities gifted young people for service in mission.[135] A letter sent home just months before his passing records his heart's desire.

133. This and the previous block quotations are from R. H. Schofield, "Medical Mission, Tai-yuen fu, 1882," 134–35.

134. Edwards, *Fire and Sword in Shansi*, 35–36.

135. The quote above, as well as many of the details of Schofield's life and death, are taken from Broomhall, *HTCOC*, 6, *Assault on the Nine*, 315–17.

When I was preparing to come to China three years ago, some of my best friends tried to dissuade me on the plea that there was so much need at home. How I wish that they, and all who use this argument, could just live here for a while, and see and feel the need for themselves! They would then be disposed to ask—not as some did, whether I had a special call to go to China—but rather, whether they themselves had a special call to stay at home. Only a few years ago the interior of China was sealed; now it is widely open, and missionaries can traverse every province, and are settled down, and live in all the provinces but two. Surely this is a loud call to more prayer.

Some of you, I know, are interested in and work for China, others, perhaps, have as yet never seriously considered the subject at all. My object in writing this letter is to implore you all to consider those here who are "sitting in darkness and the shadow of death," as you consider the poor in England at Christmas time. All of you can help by daily, earnest, believing prayer, all can help by giving money, and some, at least, can help by giving themselves to the work.[136]

One of the hospitals in Taiyuan was named for Schofield after his death, while his work was continued by Drs. Millar Wilson (CIM) and Eben Henry Edwards (CIM initially, then SYM, and finally BMS).[137] Dr. Wilson eventually moved on to Pingyang where he established medical work at his own expense, choosing to delay a scheduled Scottish furlough in 1900 so that he could care for the people during the famine of that year: "He could not leave when trial was facing his people." Following the death of Dr. Wilson and his wife at the hands of the Boxers later that summer, and the subsequent destruction of the local mission property, the Wilson Memorial Hospital was founded in his memory in 1908 to treat the sick and infirm in Pingyang.[138] As for Dr. Edwards, he went on to lead a long life of service in Shanxi and Taiyuan, especially through his association with the Schofield Memorial hospital.

Chinese views of medicine and healing differed from contemporary Western understandings in many respects. In ways reminiscent of medieval European beliefs regarding spiritual actions producing physical maladies, Chinese scholars of the time often understood sickness to be heaven's means

---

136. R. H. Schofield, "Letter from Dr. Schofield," 133.

137. Schofield's biography is *Memorials of R. Harold A. Schofield*. The SYM is introduced in the following section. Edwards's first name is given here as Eben based on a conversation with Gary Tiedemann who saw Edwards's actual brith certificate.

138. Chang, et al., *Christ Alone*, 133.

of punishment in cases where virtue was found wanting. Missionary doctors were aware of these tendencies, noting that blind patients often interpreted their condition as a punishment for some kind of crime and were thus more open to Christianity.[139]

Jinci scholar Liu Dapeng provides an interesting example of how sickness and morality were often related in the traditional Chinese medical world. As historian Henrietta Harrison relates,

> In the early spring of 1901, [Liu] became sick with a headache and a pain in his neck and spent much of the New Year holiday resting in bed. His first thought was that his illness must be a divine warning. When the pain continued he put a poultice on his neck and then scraped the sore with the sharp edge of a copper coin. He also tried using vinegar and spirits to wash the sore. At the same time he meditated on the importance of filial piety and brotherly love in preventing illness, "for harmony between family members brings not only the respect of one's neighbors, but also the submission of gods and ghosts. . . . [P]erhaps "Heaven has punished me enough for my sins and will now begin to be merciful, for physical illnesses are all caused by an accumulation of sin which brings down the wrath of heaven.

Over the lengthy period of this particular sickness, Liu had recourse to multiple lancings; moxibustion (the burning of paper within small glass vials to produce vacuum suction on the skin); various poultices consisting of husks, spit, mud, flour, or bear fat; and plenty of powerful laxatives. In addition to insufficient filial piety, fate, tiredness, personal sin, evil winds, and even a curse resulting from the slaughter of hundreds of local Catholics during the recent Boxer Rebellion were all seen as possible causes of physical sickness. These beliefs should not be dismissed as mere ancient superstitions: wind (*feng*) is still commonly blamed for much ill health in Shanxi today.

While these ideas seemed odd to the missionaries, contemporary China Hand and missionary critic Alexander Michie pointed out that they were not that different from Christian notions of faith healing.

> [The missionaries] here meet the Chinese on their own ground of spiritualism, and in cases of sickness or trouble, the missionaries are ready to back the foreign against the native Deity, after the example of Elijah with the prophets of Baal. In other words, they live by prayer, not privately merely, but often openly, and by way of challenging their opponents. When a patient dies for

---

139. These two paragraphs, including the following quotation, are taken from Harrison, *The Man Awakened from Dreams*, 66–67.

> whose recovery special prayer has been made, and the petitioners are self-pledged to a successful issue, they do not look at the material cause of death, but examine the mechanism of their prayer as if it were an experiment in physics that had miscarried.

Because the "poor Inland missionaries" suffered the same ailments as their Chinese neighbors, Michie claimed that missionary influence was therefore limited only to those "within the incandescent sphere of their direct personal attraction."[140]

The kinds of cases and the courses of treatment undertaken by Taiyuan's foreign medical missionaries were described in more detail in a report sent home for publication by Schofield in 1883.

> Malaria and dysentery, which are so frequent in central and southern China, were very rare. Rheumatic fever, so very common in our damp climate at home, appears to be almost, if not entirely, absent in this bright, dry climate. However, rheumatic pains and neuralgia of all sorts are very common, partly, no doubt, owing to the sudden changes of temperature, but chiefly, I think, to the unwholesome habit of sleeping with the absence of flannel under-clothing, renders the body much more susceptible to a sudden chill. Dyspepsia is exceedingly common, due partly to the Chinese habit of bolting food without sufficient mastication, and also to the inevitable overloading of the stomach by those who take only two meals a day.
>
> Eighty-two eye operations were performed in 1882. Twenty-eight patients operated on for cataract. One poor man, aged fifty-five years, with double cataract, for all useful purposes blind, groped and begged his way to the hospital, a distance of fifty miles, taking about a fortnight to accomplish the journey; he recovered good vision in both eyes, and was naturally delighted at being able to walk home in two to three days.
>
> Another patient (a woman, aged forty-seven) was dismissed from her situation being blind, with double cataract. In her despair, she tells us, she twice attempted to commit suicide by jumping into a river and down a well, but was prevented on both occasions. A friend brought her to us. Both eyes were successfully operated on, and she is now able to sew and work, and will probably remain with us as an attendant on the female in-patients.
>
> Small pox is accountable for a large number of deaths annually in China, and also causes a large number of those who

---

140. Michie, *Missionaries in China*, 54–56.

survive to lose one or both eyes. Eleven cases of total blindness, besides many partially blind from smallpox applied to us during the year 1882.

Wolves are very common and often carry off children in the villages. Six cases of wolf-bite were seen; in one little girl, aged eight, the thigh was terribly mangled by three great wounds several inches long, more than half the skin was stripped off and hung down in large folds below the knee. The parents were told that the only chance of life lay in amputation close to or through the hip joint, but of course, would not consent to it, and in about ten days she died.

Out of thirty cases of attempted suicide during the year, in which the friends had applied for help, twenty-seven had taken opium; in the other three cases arsenic, cosmetic powder and oil of almonds were used. In twenty-one cases sulphate of zinc and coffee were sent, with full directions. Most of these recovered; but I was unable to ascertain the exact number of those who did. Rev. A. Sowerby (English Baptist Mission) has attended twelve cases, and Rev. T. Richard one case during the year; of these ten recovered and three ended fatally. This makes the total number of opium-suicide cases treated during the year forty. From the above statement it will be apparent that opium-suicide cases are terribly common in this city, generally they are the outcome of some domestic quarrel—often between daughter-in-law and mother-in-law. Suicide in any form is regarded by the Chinese as the most terrible revenge they can take.[141]

Though the level of medical services provided by missionaries outside of Taiyuan was generally very basic, it was still a common component of mission stations. Practically, the medical care drew people into the orbit of the missionaries. At the same time, the medical needs among the population naturally elicited sympathetic efforts from the missionaries to try and address them. In the case of the ABCFM's mission stations in Taigu, the medical work was even slightly profitable. In 1899 they decided to begin charging small fees (to those who could afford them) for their services. Day patients were charged thirty copper cash, in-patients paid fifty cash for fuel and lights, and in the case of opium poisoning a thousand cash was charged in addition to the cost of cart hire to transport the patient to the dispensary. Sales of medicines—"mostly cod liver oil"—for the year totaled 73,300 cash ($36.65) which, when combined with the income from all the other medical fees, earned the dispensary an annual profit of $147.98 against a total annual

---

141. R. H. Schofield, "Medical Mission, Tai-yuen fu, 1882," 135–36.

budget for the Shanxi ABCFM mission of $14,650. This surplus was then used to support other mission projects.[142]

While a few missionaries were critical of the spiritual value of opium refuges, the facilities quickly became a standard feature of Shanxi mission work, owing to the drug's ubiquitous use throughout society.[143] The earliest record of opium use in Shanxi comes from a Taigu magistrate in 1817, and the drug remained a pastime for the wealthy until its cultivation by Shanxi farmers beginning in the 1850s made the drug available to all. While modern scholars have argued that much of the opium use in nineteenth-century China was merely intermittent and social,[144] missionaries were nevertheless shocked to see the drug used so casually—in many cases given to children as a calmative.[145] Chinese sources from the end of the century all attest to a very high rate of opium usage in Shanxi. Missionaries went further, with many claiming that a large portion of Shanxi's population was addicted to the drug. As a common cash crop, poppies were readily available throughout Shanxi, which was by then one of the biggest opium-growing provinces in China.[146] A popular phrase of the day claimed of Shanxi at the end of the nineteenth century that "eleven out of every ten of its inhabitants are opium smokers."[147] Charles Price (ABCFM) reported a village near Fenzhou (modern day Fenyang) where four hundred ninety out of five hundred or more inhabitants were opium smokers. Because of its popularity, during times of drought the opium crop was typically planted at the first hint of precipitation, while food staples were planted later—if enough rain fell to allow for a second crop.[148]

At least one photo of a local refuge survives, and it is known that George Farthing of the BMS was running an opium refuge for his mission in Taiyuan by 1891.[149] One historian claims that the Schofield Memorial

142. Brandt, *Massacre in Shansi*, 120–22.

143. Norman Cliff informed me in a personal letter (June 29, 2000) accompanying his 2000 book *How the Gospel Came to South East Shanxi* that Stanley Smith and Archibald Glover were driven by their belief in faith healing to shut down the opium clinic in the Changzhi/Lucheng area. See Glover's January 1, 1897 letter to his parents in Glover and Lyall, *Thousand Miles of Miracle*, 246–49. On opium's place in Chinese society, see Zheng Yangwen, "The Social Life of Opium in China," 1–39.

144. See, for example, Newman, "Opium Smoking in Late Imperial China," 765–94.

145. For a detailed discussion of the nature of opium usage in Shanxi, see Harrison, "Narcotics, Nationalism and Class in China," 156–62.

146. Williamson, *British Baptists in China*, 49.

147. Nichols, *Through Hidden Shensi*, 60.

148. Price, *China Journal*, 174 and 79, respectively.

149. The photo (supplied by Edwards) is in MacGillivray, *A Century of Protestant Mission in China*, 79.

Hospital in Taiyuan was one of the first places in China—and perhaps even the world—to begin experimenting with the use of morphine to break opium addictions.[150] By gradually reducing doses of measured morphine administered hypodermically over a three- or four-week period, the opium addict could be released from his or her craving without the mortal risks of sudden abstinence. This form of "treatment was so successful that the gentry presented the hospital with a plaque that proclaimed 'The wonderful needle is like that of old,' as if the hypodermic was a miraculous new kind of acupuncture."[151]

Missionaries were quick to embrace this almost magical technique, and it was soon common to encounter foreigners with virtually no medical training administering morphine and water injections to addicts. Since this was a service initially available only through the missionaries, Chinese began to refer to morphine as "Jesus opium."[152] Pastor Xi's use of morphine (primarily in pill form) for similar purposes also earned him a name for himself, as Chinese people viewed him as part of a long tradition of local Chinese medical practitioners. A fairly fixed cultural entity, these village medical men would use the imagery of the *wuxing* along with traditional Chinese medicine, Chinese *qigong*, and other local folk traditions to peddle their various mystical doses and "golden pills" as efficacious against an almost limitless list of complaints and ailments. In many ways, Pastor Xi's offers of healing and Christian salvation were nothing new, but rather fell very much in line with the practices of these village "doctors." This suggests that there may have been more syncretism involved in the famed evangelist's ministry than is commonly accepted.[153]

Curiously enough, the British government was quick to condemn the morphine trade—even while they continued to condone and profit by the illicit trade in opium. For fear of creating a "panic should it become generally known that a foreign poison was being extensively sold," the British Legation in 1885 encouraged the Zongli Yamen, the Chinese foreign office, to "take steps to prevent the circulation of so dangerous a substance, and promised British cooperation in necessary restrictions." Nevertheless, the trade continued to grow without official restriction through the 1890s.[154]

---

150. Cliff, *How the Gospel Came to South East Shanxi*, 2.

151. Letter from E. H. Edwards, September 27, 1886 as printed in *CM* (February 1887), 28.

152 Austin, *China's Millions*, 246–47.

153. This is one of the more original contributions of Alvyn Austin's book. See, for example, ibid., 14–15.

154. Ibid., 260–64.

MISSIONARY LIFE IN NINETEENTH-CENTURY SHANXI

Throughout the early years of the Shanxi mission, CIM workers continued to expand outside of Taiyuan focusing on the villages and counties to the south. CIM growth in particular was astronomical during the 1880s and 1890s. While in 1881 the CIM total supply of missionaries in China numbered only ninety-six, by 1895 that number would climb to include 621 workers spread all across China with many of them stationed in Shanxi.[155] The arrival of more and more workers from other societies—as well as the ever-increasing number of CIM personnel—seems to have enhanced the dissimilarities that led to the division among the early missionaries in Taiyuan. Non-CIM foreign workers in Shanxi were critical of Hudson Taylor's requirement that his workers live at the same standard of living as the people among whom they were ministering, pointing out that this degree of self-sacrifice was unhealthy and seemed to lead to disease and mental breakdown.[156] Despite these difficulties, Taylor insisted that removing the physical and material differences that separated the missionary from the people he or she lived among was essential to effective Christian mission. Other Shanxi workers were critical of the inflexible attitudes of the "Plymouth Brethren" serving within Taylor's group.[157] Notwithstanding these differences, by 1881 the original goal of that first band of mission workers was nearly complete: every city but two in Shanxi province had been visited.[158]

Just at the moment when the Shanxi missionary community was dividing, their numbers were expanded in 1881 by the arrival of the "Oberlin Band" of graduates in theology from Oberlin College, led by Martin and Emily Stimson. Under the auspices of the ABCFM, they established their

155. The story of God's supply for Hudson Taylor's little mission in China is nothing short of miraculous. Through prayer and hard work, the CIM experienced a series of tremendous years of expansion: 1883 saw twenty new recruits, 1884 had forty-six, and in 1887 a whopping 102 out of a total of 600 volunteers were accepted and sailed for China. And there were still more to come. Figures taken from Steer, *J. Hudson Taylor*, 279, 285, 300, 340–41.

156. Though written mostly in the 1890s, see Eva Price's (ABCFM) comments (including her meeting with Dr. Taylor) in Price, *China Journal*, 60, 107–8, 115. Williamson makes the same case against Taylor in *British Baptists in China*, 335–36.

157. On frustration with the Plymouth Brethren, see the personal letters: Jones to Short, 9 February 1884, BMSA CH/8; and Stimsom to Smith, 13 February 1885, Shansi Mission (ABC 16.3.15), vol. 2, part 2 (Reel 318: 0632), ABCFMA. On the significance of Taylor's Brethren connections, see Wigram, *Bible and Mission in Faith Perspective*, 58–63.

158. Reported in MacGillivray, *A Century of Protestant Mission in China*, 140. For a helpful discussion of the general evangelistic strategies employed during the early days of Shanxi missions, see chapter 10, "After the Fire, the Still Small Voice" in Barber, *David Hill*, 205–19.

first station in Taiyuan before removing to Taigu in an effort to spread out mission work in the province.[159] The ABCFM tended to establish stations in large commercial centers with well-supervised trained Chinese workers and then entrust them with responsibility for developing the surrounding areas, giving the ABCFM a very high ratio of Chinese workers to foreign staff. In 1887 the ABCFM opened their second station—in Fenzhou—and by 1900 the ABCFM had a total of sixteen people working in Shanxi.[160]

The BMS workers in Taiyuan made use of itinerant local evangelists to preach and spread literature throughout the Taiyuan area.[161] In 1882 Timothy Richard visited Xinzhou, a prominent market town northof Taiyuan. Sensing that the area was ripe for evangelism, the BMS opened a permanent preaching station in the area in 1884.[162] Following his visits to Xinzhou, Richard worked in Shandong until 1884 while his wife remained behind in Taiyuan. In 1884 Richard visited Beijing to protest along official channels the anti-Christian rioting that was taking place across China as a result of the Franco-Chinese War of that same year. In 1885 he and his family (including four young daughters) headed to England on their first furlough, leaving Joshua Turner (now with the BMS) to lead the BMS in his absence.

On March 18, 1885, Hudson Taylor's famous "Cambridge Seven" arrived in Shanghai—seen as a direct answer to Schofield's prayers.[163] This collection of seven remarkable men—famous athletes and gifted scholars from Britain's upper-class families—were initially called to service in China through a series of revival/recruiting trips involving D. L. Moody, Ira Sankey, and Taylor.[164] Between 1886 and 1887 Montagu Beauchamp, William Cassels, Dixon Hoste, and Stanley Smith took up posts in Pingyang (Hoste and Smith) and Daning (Beauchamp and Cassels). C. T. Studd was originally posted to Shaanxi but later transferred to Shanxi before ill health led him back to England and eventually Africa. Over the years the Seven made their way through various places in Shanxi such as Lu'an (Smith and Studd) and

159. Robert Landale (CIM) helped the Oberlin folks find a city for their station just before the death of his wife, while the Richards hosted the Stimsons when they first arrived. Brandt, *Massacre in Shansi*, 29; Broomhall, *HTCOC*, 6, *Assault on the Nine*, 316.

160. Stauffer, *The Christian Occupation of China*, 186–88. For a personal account of the ABCFM Fenzhou mission, see Eva Price's letters home published as Price, *China Journal*.

161. MacGillivray, *A Century of Protestant Mission in China*, 79.

162. The date of the BMS's first work in Xinzhou is taken from a Boxer martyr account transcribed in Ren Fuxing, "'Xinzhou Yesujiao jinlihui shengtu,'" 105.

163. Steer, *J. Hudson Taylor*, 288.

164. On their recruitment, see Broomhall, *HTCOC*, 6, *Assault on the Nine*, 321–66. Though a critical examination of the Seven has yet to be written, the classic work on their lives is Pollock, *The Cambridge Seven*.

Hongdong (Hoste and Smith) and then on to other parts of China or Europe. Hoste served the longest in Shanxi, working with Pastor Xi for many years before leaving to become CIM superintendent of Hebei in 1896. The other two of the Seven (A. Polhill-Turner and C. Polhill-Turner) worked in different parts of China—predominantly Sichuan.[165]

In the wake of the famine, educational and medical work continued to be prominent. Although there were no permanent seminaries similar to those developed in some of the coastal provinces, the relatively small size of the Shanxi church and its slow growth meant there was less need for this kind of work. The rural stations of the various missions typically included schools—in the later years women's or girls' schools were increasingly common—although they also hosted periodic short-term Bible training programs.[166] In the urban center of Taiyuan, mission work revolved primarily around hospitals and opium rehabilitation. In 1887 the small scale clinical work commenced by Schofield had been expanded to include ophthalmology, a larger clinic, and fifty beds. At this point it was formally called the Schofield Memorial Hospital—though it was known locally as the "Jesus Church Hospital" (Yesujiao Yiyuan). By this time the Schofield Memorial Hospital was the main medical station in the province, and required a steady stream of committed foreign medical staff throughout this period. Daily consults numbered between thirty and fifty patients.[167]

Many of the young foreign women who spent time in Taiyuan during the 1880s were involved in teaching at mission schools for local children as well as organizing opium rehabilitation programs among the women.[168] Like most women working in the nineteenth-century China mission, Shanxi female missionaries were expected by their agencies to engage in more "settled" work: the rationale was that only women could reach Chinese

165. This information is compiled from various sources: Cliff's *Sacred Flame* is perhaps more helpful with regards to their Shanxi work than most sources, while Broomhall's *Hudson Taylor & China's Open Century* has information on each of the Cambridge Seven scattered throughout the series. None of the Seven was present in Shanxi in the summer of 1900.

166. As an example, the BMS occasionally gathered Chinese teacher-evangelists in Xinzhou for brief training courses. Williamson, *British Baptists in China*, 51.

167. The Schofield Memorial Hospital is at times referred to as the "Taiyuan Men's Hospital," especially in the twentieth century when it is contrasted with the Women's Hospital in Taiyuan (see below). Since the hospital was in fact an expansion of Schofield's own clinic (renamed after his death) the initial date for the founding of Shanxi's first clinical work can be placed as early as 1881. *Shanxi tongzhi* [Shanxi Provincial Gazetteer], vol. 42: 88; Guo Jinfeng, "Jiaohui yiyuan jianzhu," 17–18.

168. The Taiyuan Girls' School, which operated from 1881 to 1900 and was perhaps started by Jennie Taylor, seems to have been staffed by women from many different mission agencies during its existence. Williamson, *British Baptists in China*, 52.

women in their homes through what was sometimes called "gossiping the Gospel."[169] Using simple devices such as the wordless book (see above) and the five-finger mantra ("Thumb: There is one True God . . ."), they were itinerant, but on a more intimate scale. This work was more intensive than that of the men, as they focused on their own courtyards, their neighborhoods, the city, and nearby villages. Miss L. M. Forth described one village trip in Shanxi, where she was taken into a cave that the Christians had transformed into "a little miniature meeting-house . . . Though small, it was beautifully clean; new mats on the tiny *kang*, and a number of small booklets hanging from the wall." After a short prayer meeting, she witnessed a bonfire of idols:

> . . . only pieces of paper – the god of riches, the god of the kitchen, and the god of skill. . . . From there we went into the open air, where we had a very informal meeting for about two hours; the Christians talking to the men, while I sat some distance off, surrounded by a number of women and children, who were charmed by my singing, "Jesus can help little children to be obedient to their mother's words," varied by, "do not swear, or get angry," etc. They made me sing it over and over again, some of the boldest joining in.[170]

From such small beginnings—simply "singing the gospel"—grew the church, for without Christian women and families, it would never have passed from generation to generation. Shandong missionaries Alexander and Isabelle Williamson (National Bible Society of Scotland) both argued that evangelism among women must take strategic precedence over work among men if the gospel were ever to gain a lasting position in China.[171]

While the number of foreign Christian workers serving in Shanxi was increasing rapidly, the kinds of pre-field preparation these new workers had experienced varied greatly in terms of quality and quantity. While the CIM expected formal theological training for all its workers (as Gladys Aylward would famously discover and subvert in the next century), other groups required ordination—a step that some missions would complete for the candidates themselves in a "commissioning" service regardless of how

---

169. Austin, *China's Millions*, 167; Broomhall, *HTCOC*, 6, *Assault on the Nine*, 103. For a fascinating exploration of the changing roles and contributions of women in nineteenth-century China mission, see Hunter, *The Gospel of Gentility*.

170. "Miss Forth," *CM* (January 1893) 11–12. The similarities with Confucian morality are obvious.

171. Williamson, *Old Highways in China*, 6–8; as well as Alexander Williamson's similar comments in Lewis, Barber and Hykes, *Records of the GCPMC: Shanghai, 1890*, 260–61.

much training or preparation for overseas ministry had been undertaken. As a typical example, the ABCFM

> never set up any system or procedure for indoctrinating its China-bound representatives before they left the States. It published no literature or brochures on the subject other than a guide as to what food items and medical supplies, clothing, furniture, and the like to take or send there in advance. It recommended no background material about China or its history; offered no information whatsoever about its people, politics, customs, mores, or culture in general; and provided no explanation of the country's religious heritage. There was no orientation course. . . . The Board relied solely on missionaries in the field . . . to orient new arrivals.[172]

This is not to say that potential candidates were not screened. Most mission agencies were recruiting for very specific sets of qualifications. Mission agencies in Britain sought after "Scottish" qualities: "educational attainment, theological rigour [often defined as membership in the kirk], and practicality."[173] The ABCFM was looking for candidates with

> an unimpaired physical constitution; good intellectual ability, well disciplined by education, and if possible by practical experience; good sense; sound judgment of men and things; versatility, tact, adaptation to men of all classes and circumstances—'sanctified common sense;' a cheerful, hopeful spirit; ability to work pleasantly with others; persistent energy in the carrying out of plans once begun:—all controlled by a *single-hearted, self-sacrificing devotion to Christ and His cause.*

Applicants were also required to answer in writing a series of thirteen specific questions covering a wide range of topics including family background, health, marital plans, the Scriptures, the responsibilities of preachers, and reasons for application. The key difference in attitude between these early pioneers and today's mission applicants is perhaps best seen in one of the last questions: "How do you regard hardship, suffering, and peril incurred in prosecuting the missionary work, and to what extent are you taking them into account and preparing yourself to meet them?"[174]

Once a candidate was accepted into full-time membership in a mission, effective work and service in Shanxi were impossible until he or she

---

172. Brandt, *Massacre in Shansi*, 52.
173. Semple, *Missionary Women*, 10.
174. The previous two quotations are from Brandt, *Massacre in Shansi*, 88–89.

could reach the field and learn the language. To meet the first requirement, prospective missionaries had to somehow get to China from the other side of the world. At the end of the nineteenth century the steamship journey from England to Shanghai took about one and a half months. Though there were many different classes of accommodation, all the passengers struggled with disease and seasickness.[175] Following arrival in China, one still had to travel to Shanxi—a journey that meant a four-day cart trip from Beijing to Baoding, followed by a grueling cart ride across the Taihang Mountains that separate Shanxi from eastern China.[176] The road was a precipitous single-lane dirt track with deep ruts carved into the hard soil. Rain rendered the path impassable, as did accidents of any sort. Oncoming traffic meant backtracking for days to allow other carts to pass. This last leg over the mountains and into Shanxi was arduous, required a massive entourage of guides, colporteurs, and various beasts of burden, and could take many weeks to complete.

Once safely on the ground, the language barrier still remained to be crossed. Many agencies established language schools of their own to prepare their people linguistically.[177] Usually it was only after a period of time in one of these schools that candidates would be sent to their actual stations, where further language study would be pursued as their regular work slowly commenced. Many struggled with mastering the difficult languages of China. From his station in Lu'an, Archibald Glover (CIM) saw these challenges as a manifestation of Satan's power over China:

> Since last mail I have made a slight advance in conducting the evening *li-pai* [*libai*] (or worship service) during Stanley's [Smith] absence in the district. This does not mean much in the way of speaking, but it is a preparation for the next step. One of the strange effects of Chinese upon me is to make me overwhelmingly sleepy as a listener. It is a sore trial to me at the

175. Glover's correspondence gives an interesting account of an 1896 steamship passage. Glover and Lyall, *Thousand Miles of Miracle*, 210–24. Glover seems to have offended or insulted everyone he came into contact with—including, eventually, Stanley Smith, with whom he worked at the Lu'an station of the CIM. He had very strong convictions about what was and was not sinful behavior and he always shared his opinions with others. His austerity most likely came from his belief that, according to his understanding of end-times prophecy, the last days were upon us.

176. Beijing and Baoding were not connected by rail until March 1899. The twice-daily train service reduced the journey to a half-day trip and greatly expedited mail. One missionary in Baoding was stunned to receive a letter from the state of Maine in the United States in just thirty-eight days. Brandt, *Massacre in Shansi*, 169.

177. Some of the mission schools and centers in Wuhu and Anqing, Anhui are described in A.E. Glover's letters in Glover and Lyall, *Thousand Miles of Miracle*, 230–36.

services. The strain of attempting to follow the speaker through a long and quickly spoken address is too much for me, and, ere long, I find myself tumbling over. I believe Satan has more to do with it than might be imagined. In fact the language was made by Satan, doubtless, for it is one of the greatest stumbling blocks to the gospel. Pray for me in this matter.[178]

Nor was Glover alone in his opinion. C. T. Studd and the Polhill-Turner brothers (three of the famous Cambridge Seven) found language study so trying that they decided upon a "more biblical" way of acquiring linguistic proficiency. As they traveled up river to their station in Hanzhong, they put aside their textbooks and devoted themselves to prayer. They persuaded others in Hanzhong to join them until some months later when—with no Pentecostal gifting of tongues in evidence—they realized their error and returned to study.[179] Then as now, only hard work would yield the linguistic proficiency necessary to share Christ with the Chinese. Stanley Smith, William Cassels, and Dixon Hoste (also from the illustrious Cambridge Seven) were sent directly to Pingyang, Shanxi, carrying out their language study on the field with the CIM's rising linguistic star, Frederick William Baller.[180]

Baller had been only twenty years of age when he left his family's carpentry business and sailed for China with the CIM in 1873. After the North China Famine, he served in the CIM as a transport specialist, escorting Jennie Taylor and the single women into Shanxi, another party of men to Shandong, and later a third group to Guizhou. Following the Seven's misguided expectations and great struggles, it was obvious that the CIM had to upgrade its language requirements. At the first China Council meeting, Baller, a scholarly autodidact who insisted that study, not supernatural gifts, was the royal road to learning, was set apart for the "preparation of aids to student probationers."[181]

The curriculum Baller devised for the CIM schools (opened formally in 1886) was published as *Baller's Mandarin Primer* and quickly became the standard language course for most China missions. For CIM workers, the first two years of the course of study (Baller compiled a full six years worth of lessons) were spent in strictly segregated residence at a CIM language school—the men in Anqing with Baller, and the women in Yangzhou under

---

178. From his February 15, 1898 letter written in Lu'an to his parents. Ibid., 265.

179. Broomhall, *HTCOC*, 6, *Assault on the Nine*, 375–76.

180. Austin, *China's Millions*, 223. Baller's famous Mandarin curriculum was developed from his experience training these three men.

181. This and the following three paragraphs are taken primarily from the fuller treatment of Baller and his course for Mandarin language study. Ibid., 228–33.

Marianne Murray. During this time students worked with tutors in order to pass a series of twice-yearly exams—written and oral—in order to be allowed to advance from probationary missionary to "junior missionary," a status that carried certain privileges such as the right to marry. In time even Taylor himself, impressed by this "Course of Study for Probationers," agreed to take Baller's examination. Students who took too long to progress faced the threat of dismissal or transfer to a non-language-intensive posting. In practice not all missionaries managed to achieve Baller's standard of linguistic competency, especially in the coastal treaty ports; in some cases they were advanced after many years on the field solely on the basis of seniority.

According to an 1895 advertisement, "the *Primer* addresses itself to the double task of elucidating the elements of the language and providing some practical means of communication between teacher and scholar," making it "... of the greatest value to beginners."[182] The lessons ranged widely over topics of practical and personal interest for missionaries in China, including home maintenance, Chinese ethics, financial interactions, and evangelistic encounters. English notes on the Chinese texts demonstrate the heavy emphasis Baller's curriculum placed upon mastery of Chinese culture and religion as well as language. Chinese history, geography, and political organization were all covered, along with many selections from China's classic literature in both the vernacular and literary writing styles. Popular Chinese religion was also included, as students were encouraged to track local religious festivals and dates.

The students, according to "Headmaster Baller of Anqing" were not an impressive lot, often proving too eager to emphasize evangelical enthusiasm over practical knowledge.

> A sad procession passes before me of bright promising men who have sacrificed the prospect of great usefulness, yea life itself, and all for the lack of a little common sense ... I knew one young fellow who smiled serenely with an air of ineffable wisdom when urged to use an umbrella ... to shield him from the sun. He said the promise was that the sun should not smite him by day. Need I say that he is now at home with an enfeebled brain? ... [M]any of the strongest die the soonest after coming to this country, while others who could not get their lives insured if they tried, go on year after year and do splendid service for God.[183]

---

182. F. M. Wood, "A Mandarin Primer," *CM* (March 1895) 36.

183. Baller, *Letters from an Old Missionary*, 19–20. Baller originally published his "talks" in several installments of the *Chinese Recorder,* apologizing for "the light vein in which they are written.... The pill is sugar-coated to help it down."

Baller's high standards earned him a reputation at the school for being "by far too authoritarian for mature men to tolerate."[184] Something of his style comes across in his 1907 *Letters from an Old Missionary to his Nephew* which contains his published "talks" to the men at the CIM language school. According to Baller, some of his language students claimed that when they preached in Chinese their

> audience listened with open-mouthed attention. This I can quite believe. I have often listened to preachers in the same attitude myself. You will, however, do well to bear in mind that the open mouth, like the open door, means different things to different people. It may express surprise, admiration, bewilderment, or speechlessness.[185]

Baller's reminder to his missionary students that "words are your tools" found clear expression in his life, even beyond his influential work as a language instructor. In later years Baller shifted his focus to translation work, resulting in a flurry of publications including a Mandarin Bible; Chinese versions of the lives of Hudson Taylor, George Müller, and Pastor Xi; and the authoritative translation of the Kangxi Emperor's *Sacred Edict* into English.[186]

For the new worker living in Shanxi and steadily working toward linguistic competency, there still remained many hardships to be borne. Protestant mission work in Shanxi during these early years enjoyed relative freedom from acts of violence; it was a matter of pride with the missionaries that there had been no instances of anti-foreign or anti-Christian violence at all in the province prior to the summer of 1900.[187] Daily life, however, provided missionaries with more than enough trials. Transportation within the province was grueling, involving lengthy rides in two-wheeled donkey carts (universally decried by all missionaries as phenomenally uncomfortable) over narrow cart paths either riddled with cavernous ruts or mired in mud. Inns were appalling—louse and flea infestation were certain, and robbery likely. Even the food served in the inns was "a trial" to the newly arrived foreign guests:

> *Kua mien*, a kind of macaroni, boiled with cabbage in soup stock; boiled millet served without sugar or salt (rice, grown in

---

184. Broomhall, *HTCOC*, 6, *Assault on the Nine*, 376.

185. Baller, *Letters from an Old Missionary*, 3, 30. These were originally published in several issues of *Chinese Recorder*, 1907.

186. Austin, *China's Millions*, 232.

187. Alexander Saunders claims thirteen years of peaceful and friendly work in Pingyao prior to the summer of 1900. Broomhall, *Martyred Missionaries of the CIM*, 68.

faraway southern China, was a luxury); flapjacks made of sodden buckwheat flour strings, which were boiled in weak soup and served with curds made of fermented beans; or *bo-bos*, steamed dumplings filled with chopped pork and vegetables that were dipped in bitter vinegar before eating.

Most missionaries took comfort in the promise that over time "one can get used to most anything."[188]

For communication with the outside world, the top-notch ABCFM mail system involved two Chinese runners who perpetually traveled back and forth to the relay station at Baoding—a journey of about two weeks' time. From there the mail slowly crept out toward Tianjin and the steamer trade home—three months for a letter was considered a speedy passage. Communication did not improve dramatically until the telegraph line was extended into Shanxi in 1897.[189] Despite the burgeoning of rail in the coastal areas, there were no railways in nineteenth-century Shanxi.[190]

For their residences, missionaries had few options: other than the cave homes common in the more mountainous parts of the province, walled compounds were the principal kind of housing in nineteenth-century Shanxi cities. The enclosing walls benefited the missionaries by helping to stem the otherwise constant flow of strangers and onlookers who flocked to observe and spy on the private lives of the strange foreign people living in their midst, as well as keeping out some of the dirt. The dust, excrement, and refuse that filled the streets of Shanxi's cities and villages meant that disease was an ever-present threat to missionary lives—and the mortality rate among these early pioneers was indeed great. During their first fifteen years in Shanxi, the ABCFM alone lost ten children to disease and the perils of childbirth.[191] The risk of infection was especially acute in the hot, dry summer time; accordingly, most missions encouraged their workers to keep summer homes far from crowded towns (later records proved the wisdom of this policy). The poor nutrition and lack of variety in the typical late nineteenth-century Shanxi diet was also a challenge to Western immune systems perpetually fighting disease. In the end, the loneliness of the Shanxi

---

188. This and the previous quote are from Charles Price (ABCFM) in Brandt, *Massacre in Shansi*, 15.

189. Ibid., 150.

190. 1900 China had a total of 665 miles of track (mostly located in Shandong and connecting Beijing and Tianjin); the United States in 1894 already had some 175,000 miles of track laid. Cohen, *History in Three Keys*, 93 note 102.

191. Brandt, *Massacre in Shansi*, 34–35. In this respect Shanxi was not unique: of the ten children and two wives he cared for, Hudson Taylor saw the death of fully half of his family. Chang et al., *Christ Alone*, 54, 192.

field and the harsh living standards of some of the mission agencies led to a surprising number of mental breakdowns.[192]

Further complicating health matters were the very real financial pressures. While some missionaries, such as the Pigotts and the Edwardses, were of independent means, others at times struggled to support their lives and work on the field. In the early days of the Shanxi field a number of missionaries transferred from the faith-based CIM to denominational mission agencies in pursuit of more secure financial support.[193] Near the end of the nineteenth century, the ABCFM Shanxi mission was doing better than most at generating local income: "native contributions" for maintaining the churches, paying school fees, and supporting the rest of the mission work totaled $634.61—a small portion of the need but a substantial sacrifice from Chinese workers who earned only pennies a day. Half of the mission's total budget went to pay salaries of $1000 per year for married missionary couples, with $500 allowances for children or single female missionaries. Even still, many of the ABCFM missionaries drew against their own meager salaries to help defray mission expenses, often to the extent that they became indebted to the agency.[194]

Regardless of these pressures, there was no denying the relative wealth of the missionaries, and this brought with it a new set of troubles as different agencies and individuals conflicted over which standard of living was most appropriate for expatriates living in Shanxi. Canadian Alexander Saunders—the CIM's first Canadian associate—went to Shanxi in 1886. Perhaps challenged by his small Bible class of blind, orphaned, and unemployed men, Saunders believed that the missionaries in Taiyuan were "living too much above the ordinary people."[195] Stanley Smith felt this distance still more keenly, attributing part of the trouble to excessive reliance on western technologies and possessions:

---

192. The facts alluded to in this paragraph can be found repeated throughout the relevant literature. Eva Price's (ABCFM) personal correspondence from Fenzhou notes several instances of emotional and psychological troubles on the field. See her *China Journal*.

193. Turner and James transferred from the CIM to the BMS over financial matters. Kaiser, "Encountering China," 235–38.

194. Brandt, *Massacre in Shansi*, 120–22.

195 Alexander Saunders, "The Men's Bible-class in T'ai-yuen," *CM* (February 1890) 23; "From Mr. Saunders," *CM* (February 1890) 25. Though rarely discussed, Saunders adapted his missionary methods in ways similar to Timothy Richard, developing a participatory form of Christian worship inspired by the meetings of the local sectarian religious groups. Compare Austin, *China's Millions*, 363–64; and sections 2.3, 4.2, and 4.4 in Kaiser, "Encountering China."

> I am sure the fewer foreign things one has the nearer one is to the lines of the Master. There is a very subtle snare here to speak of western things, and to have them as proofs of the superiority of western intelligence, and as bolsters to the pride of the heart....
>
> I sometimes think the position of a beggar with his one pot, if he have with it contentment, is by no means an undesirable one.... *Possessions*—there is the snare.[196]

Of course, the missionaries were also aware of the unique freedom their material wealth provided, a question of particular import for those on the Shanxi field, such as the Pigott family and the Edwardses, who were independently wealthy. Although her standard of living in America had not been excessive, Eva Jane Price (ABCFM) noticed how greatly her financial and social status differed from that of one of the Chinese nurses of a neighboring mission family. The woman, a Mrs. Chia (Jia), shared the same name in Chinese as Mrs. Price.

> What if my lines were set in such hard places? What if, instead of an earnest Christian, my husband were an opium user with a lot of other bad characteristics? What if, instead of a pleasant home, with all the comforts and advantages that come through Christianity, knowledge, hope, faith, books, pictures, good food, comfortable clothes, beds, cleanliness, I had to live in such a comfortless, poor, mean, barren home as hers? What if, instead of having plenty, with a wide outlook and some aspiration for the future of my dear little girl, I had to go out sewing at seven cents a day, haunted by the fear that my husband, the father of my children, had *sold* my girlie and was using the money for opium? She, this other Mrs. Chia, had that experience once four years ago, when her oldest girl eight years old was sold, and she lives in constant dread that one of the remaining two will soon share a like fate.... She is expecting another baby. What joy of motherhood is hers?[197]

Over and above all of these practical difficulties, missionaries still had to deal with criticism from the larger foreign community in China. One of the loudest voices was that of Alexander Michie, a British opium businessman in Tianjin. In his book *Missionaries in China*, Michie claimed that while foreign merchants were tolerated by Chinese as visitors with understandable motives, missionaries spread throughout the country doing

---

196. "Work in South Shan-si," *CM* (March 1888) 33.
197. Brandt, *Massacre in Shansi*, 70.

"pretty much what they individually like" were stirring up great animosity as they traveled "about the country retailing the figments of their own excited brains as the pure gospel." Many of Michie's readers believed that missionaries—particularly those in remote, inland places like Shanxi—were the main cause of Chinese anti-foreignism. Reflecting a bias held by many in the business and diplomatic communities of the coastal treaty ports, Michie was especially critical of "the most eccentric missionaries . . . , many of them single women, belonging to Mr. Hudson Taylor's China Inland Mission." Nor was there much sympathy for missionary attempts to blend into the local communities. As Michie explained, "To wear the clothes of the poor and eat their food may be nearer to formal condescension than to true sympathy. The thing needful, the entering freely into the spirit of the people, is of exceedingly rare attainment."[198]

Finally, all of these various issues contained within them the potential for further internecine conflict, a stress that invariably took a heavy toll on the workers and their ministries. In 1893, T. W. Pigott, who had been in Taiyuan with the CIM since 1881, resigned with "a few others" to form the Independent or Shouyang Mission (Shouyanghui) or SYM.[199] When the upper class Pigotts returned from their 1898 visit back to England, they brought back with them an English tutor and a French governess and immediately opened a boarding school for missionary children irrespective of organizational affiliation. The Atwaters (ABCFM Fenzhou) were glad to send their two eldest to Shouyang to stay in the Pigotts' home and be educated, since Lizze Atwater had worked as the Pigotts' governess prior to her marriage to Ernest Atwater. This kind of organizational mingling was common, but it made conflicts that much more complicated.[200]

It appears that there were three factors that contributed to the secession from the CIM and the establishment of a new mission. First, different approaches to mission proliferated within the Shanxi mission community,

---

198. Michie, *Missionaries in China*, 52–53 and 38, respectively.

199. Cliff claims that four couples left the CIM to form the SYM, but he implies that this took place earlier—around the time of the initial "Shanxi spirit" controversy. Cliff, *Flame of Sacred Love*, 84. MacGillivray lists the following personnel as eventually joining the SYM: "Mr. Johnson, Mr. McNair, Dr. and Mrs. E. H. Edwards [from CIM], Mr. J. Robinson, Miss Duval, Mr. and Mrs. Stokes [from CIM], Mr. and Mrs. Simpson [from CIM], Dr. and Mrs. A. E. Lovitt and Miss Coombs [from CIM]." MacGillivray, *A Century of Protestant Mission in China*, 88. As for the founding date of the SYM, while MacGillivray gives 1892 for the year when the Pigotts left Taiyuan, Tiedemann lists 1892 as the "China start" date for the new mission; Broomhall says that the SYM was formed in 1893. See "Pigott" biographical entry in *HTCOC*, 7, *It is Not Death to Die!*, 674; and Tiedemann, *Reference Guide to Christian Missionary Societies in China*, 212.

200. Brandt, *Massacre in Shansi*, 110.

often irrespective of organizational boundaries. Second, there seems to have been some disagreement over Pastor Xi and the degree of authority he ought to be granted.[201] Third—and most curious to modern readers—was disagreement on the question of dress. Not everyone agreed with Taylor that dressing like the local people removed unnecessary barriers to effective communication. One western journalist argued that adopting what was called "native dress" had the opposite effect because of the mirth it elicited from Chinese people, and because few foreigners were able to mimic the different posture and body language which went with the clothing.[202] In Shanxi, the workers of the ABCFM, BMS, and most other agencies in the province were free to dress as they saw fit but the CIM workers (and the various CIM-associated Scandinavian missionaries) were all required to adopt Chinese dress and living standards. Not all CIM personnel were convinced of the importance of this point (though Taylor himself was adamant), and it seems "the doctors" in Taiyuan were particularly lax, often wearing Chinese gowns with leather boots and pith helmets. On all three of these points of contention Hudson Taylor was unwilling to compromise, making it clear that observance of the organization's *Principles and Practices* was necessary for membership.[203] In 1896 the CIM completely withdrew from Taiyuan, handing all its work there over to the SYM—including the Taiyuan Girls' School and the Schofield Memorial Hospital; it was at this time that Edwards and most of the rest of the medical staff transferred to the SYM.[204]

At the end of the 1880s there were fifty Protestant missionaries in Shanxi.[205] The BMS, the ABCFM, and the SYM all had stations in and shared responsibility for Taiyuan, along with the provincial representatives for the British and Foreign Bible Society. The BMS expanded over the next twenty years, developing extensive work to the north of Taiyuan in and around Xinzhou, as well as stations in Yangqu, Yuci, Dingxiang, and Shouyang.[206]

201. Austin, *China's Millions*, 279–80.

202. See chapters 44 and 45 in Landor, *China and the Allies*, 1. Note also Landor's praise for Timothy Richard and his reasonableness.

203. For an idea of what the *Principles and Practice* involved, see the account of the 1886 revision in Broomhall, *HTCOC*, 6, *Assault on the Nine*, 420–23.

204. Broomhall is vague here, avoiding names and details surrounding the defection. This paragraph is gleaned from Broomhall, *HTCOC*, 7, *It is Not Death to Die!*, 206–8. The Lucheng field in southeastern Shanxi also experienced a fairly high rate of turnover in its foreign staff, though the exact reasons are unclear. See Cliff's list of Lucheng workers in the appendices of Cliff, *How the Gospel Came to South East Shanxi*, 21–23.

205. Evans, *Timothy Richard, a Narrative*, 84. By 1898, there were just under 2,500 missionaries working in all of China's provinces. Williamson, *British Baptists in China*, 275.

206. MacGillivray, *A Century of Protestant Mission in China*, 79–80.

During these same years the CIM experienced a stunning increase in recruits, and the publicity surrounding the Cambridge Seven helped ensure that many of the new workers came to Shanxi.[207] After their initial posts in Taiyuan and Pingyang,[208] the CIM spread rapidly across the province opening new stations in Quwo (1885), Daning (1885), Xizhou (1885), Datong (1886), Huozhou (1886), Hongdong (1886), Xiaoyi (1887), Pingyao (1888), Yuncheng (1888), Lu'an (1889), and Lucheng (1889).[209]

The result of all this effort was less than what the missionaries and their supporters would have wished. In 1842 there had been six Chinese Protestants in all of China, the only converts since Robert Morrison first arrived in 1807. By 1877 there were 13,035 Chinese Protestant believers in China, and by the year 1890 that number had grown to 37,287. In 1900 the total number of Protestant communicants in China was believed to be around 100,000, or 250,000 including adherents and inquirers.[210] In 1891, a typical year for the CIM, there were 434 missionaries with 148 missionary children (one-third under three years old) scattered among 98 stations in fourteen provinces. In that same year those CIM workers managed 417 baptisms—less than one baptism per missionary. In fact, one half of the stations recorded no baptisms at all, while in most stations the missionaries outnumbered the total "communicants in fellowship."[211] To give an

207. As with the "Cambridge Seven," the CIM often used number goals to drive their recruiting efforts. Gertrude and Hudson Broomhall (who arrived Shanxi in 1885) were part of the "seventy" sent out over the next few years; when Alice Miles reaches China in 1887 she is part of the "hundred." Cliff, *Flame of Sacred Love*, 86, 92. In 1885 the CIM had a total of 163 full members throughout China and the sending countries; by the beginning of 1900 that number had grown to 811. Broomhall, HTCOC, 6, *Assault on the Nine*, 400.

208. These were the two earliest official mission stations in Shanxi, though there is still debate over which society first opened formal work in these locations: Hill (WMS), Richard (BMS), James (CIM the BMS), and Turner (CIM then BMS) were all involved. MacGillivray, *A Century of Protestant Mission in China*, 153; Stauffer, *The Christian Occupation of China*, 186.

209. Based on the CIM publication *Land of Sinim* as recorded in Thompson, "Twilight of the Gods," 56. A more complete (though still only CIM) list can be found in MacGillivray, *A Century of Protestant Mission in China*, 153–54. At times the two lists differ on founding dates, but I have followed Thompson's dates. On Lucheng and Lu'an see Cliff, *How the Gospel Came to South East Shanxi*.

210. The early figures of startling (questionable?) specificity are recorded in Broomhall, *Martyred Missionaries of the CIM*, 258. A Chinese source quoting a 1979 Hong Kong publication gives an 1840 total of "less than 100 believers," though I suspect this total is exaggerated and may include overseas Chinese. Yu Ke, *Dangdai jidujiao*, 291.

211. "Statistics of the China Inland Mission for January, 1892," *CM* (July 1892) 97–98; see also the various provincial reports on 115–21, 127–35, 141–44, and 155–59. The number of missionary children comes from "The Families of the China Inland Mission in December, 1892," *CM* (January 1893) 8.

indication of how the work in Shanxi was progressing, in 1892 the BMS claimed a total of 32 members collected from all three of its stations.[212] By 1900, the Baptist churches in Shanxi had grown to include 256 members.[213] When Dixon Hoste left the CIM station of Pastor Xi in Hongdong in 1896, that district had the largest church membership of any place in Shanxi, with a total of 490 believers.[214] Altogether, in 1898 there were a total of 151 missionaries and spouses in Shanxi with 1,513 Chinese church members "in good standing."[215]

As the nineteenth century drew to a close, the Shanxi mission community hosted two notable but different wedding celebrations. In 1893, Anna Jakobsen (CIM) had attempted to set a new precedent in her mission when she announced her engagement to a local evangelist from her station in Huozhou by the name of Cheng Xiuqi. The CIM leadership, however, convinced her to reconsider, arguing that her cross-racial marriage—the first in the CIM—"would expose all the single girls to unwelcome attention by unsuitable men, if not to danger." Five years later, in early 1898, Anna renewed her declaration and this time persevered despite the strong disapproval of some of her fellow Shanxi missionaries. In her correspondence with the CIM home office, Anna claimed that at least part of her motivation for marrying Cheng Xiuqi was based on her belief that marriage to a local believer would make her more acceptable in some of China's more hostile locations (she particularly mentioned Hunan where she later served). Hudson Taylor's perspective was different: "There was a great danger of her heading a party of [Chinese] and together breaking away from the Mission." Edwards was one of the few supporters of the marriage ("it would be a sin against God to try to stop the marriage"), as was D. H. Clapp (ABCFM), who performed the ceremony in the home of a local Taiyuan "Christian photographer," very likely Richard's former tutor and secretary Gao Daling. Only a handful of foreign missionaries attended the festivities, some with misgivings.[216]

---

212. Six from Taiyuan, sixteen from "Xiao Tianzu," and ten in Xinzhou. Williamson, *British Baptists in China*, 52.

213. Ibid., 53.

214. Cliff, *Flame of Sacred Love*, 102–4.

215. At this time Shanxi's northern border was often considered to extend well up into modern Inner Mongolia. This can make accurate statistics for Shanxi proper very difficult to come by. Edwards's numbers are from his *Fire and Sword in Shansi*, 47.

216. John Gittings, "Lost Souls" *The Guardian* (August 5, 2000). Little is known about the couple's subsequent ministry, although their mission was still operating in Zezhou after Anna's death in 1913. See Tiedemann, *Reference Guide to Christian Missionary Societies in China*, 120–21.

The second significant wedding occurred a few months later, on July 8, 1898, when Ernest Atwater and Elizabeth (Lizzie) Graham (both ABCFM) were united in marriage in the chapel of the old CIM compound in Taiyuan. Over the years many Shanxi missionaries had been married "on the field," but they were typically required by their passport nations to travel to a treaty port for a legally binding ceremony at one of the consul's offices. Held shortly after a change in United States government policy, the Atwaters' was the first legally binding wedding of an American in Shanxi province. There was no controversy in this case, and British and American missionaries joined equally in the festivities. Lizzie was radiant in a cream silk dress trimmed with ribbons, while the men and many of the other ladies wore traditional Chinese robes. A large dinner followed at the residence of one of the Taiyuan missionaries, closing with an impressive wedding cake topped with orange blossoms, leaves, and butterflies made of frosting with the "Am. Eagle and British lion hobnobbing on top."[217]

217. Brandt, *Massacre in Shansi*, 108.

How am I to write all the horrible details of these days? I would rather spare you. The dear ones at Shou Yang, seven in all, including our lovely girls, were taken prisoners and brought to Taiyuen [sic] in irons and there by the governor's orders beheaded. . . .

The pain will soon be over and oh, the sweetness of the welcome above. My little baby will go with me. I think God will give it to me in heaven and my dear mother will be so glad to see us. I cannot imagine the Saviour's welcome. Oh, that will compensate for all the days of suspense. . . . I do not regret coming to China, but I am sorry I have done so little. My married life, two precious years, have been full of happiness. We will die together, my dear husband and I; I used to dread separation. . . .

—Lizzie Atwater (ABCFM Fenzhou)
Letter to "Dear, dear ones," dated August 3, 1900.

2

The Boxer Turmoil (1900)

ORIGINALLY FORMED AS ALTERNATIVE means of defense and protection in the absence of local law, groups such as the Big Sword Society (Dadaohui) and the Spirit Boxers (Shenquan) materialized in various parts of Shandong during the last few years of the nineteenth century. These bands typically revolved around a handful of charismatic leaders who, in their pursuit of local interests and personal gain, at times ran into direct conflict with government forces. Their transformation and development into the phenomenon known in the West as the Boxers is a confusing and wandering tale that arises from the coincidence of a vast number of circumstances.[1]

The rural people who initiated the particular movements which led to what we today know as the Boxers began to band together in the Yellow River basin of Shandong at the very end of the nineteenth century. They were motivated by a need to supply for themselves the security against banditry and rapacious local officials that the overwrought state was failing to provide. For most of the previous one hundred years the Qing rulers had been challenged by a number of ethnic and religiously motivated rebellions, most notably the sectarian White Lotus Rebellion and the later Muslim and Nian Rebellions. The expense and energy devoted to containing these uprisings placed a great strain on the financial, military, and administrative resources of the imperial government, while increasing foreign trade threatened the state monopolies and further drained the imperial treasuries. With the budget for maintaining the imperial household expanding rapidly, the state increased the sale of offices thus lowering the quality of the local officials and creating a class of local tax collectors that were little more than

---

1. For the simplest summary of these circumstances see Fairbank and Goldman, *China: A New History*, 230.

state-licensed extorioners. Public military defeats at the hands of foreigners (France in 1884 and Japan in 1895) only increased popular feelings of discontent. As the end of the nineteenth century approached, the Qing dynasty was in disarray, while the people of China began to look elsewhere for a means to restore China to its past glory and power.

The first of three events which helped bring about the creation of the groups known in the West as the "Boxers" took place on November 1, 1897. Shortly after midnight, two German missionaries of the Society of the Divine Word were brutally murdered outside of a small village in Juye County, Shandong province.[2] The two men, Richard Henle and Franz Xavier Nies, had been visiting local missionary Georg Stenz, who by all accounts was a bitter, grasping missionary with a reputation for interference in local affairs. The Big Sword Society was thought to be behind the attack, though some believed the action to have been motivated by county politics and a desire to create trouble for the local Chinese magistrate. The resolution of what has become known as the Juye Incident resulted in the transfer of many local officials, the erection of two cathedrals at the county's expense in honor of the martyrs, and the demotion of the able Shandong Governor Li Bingheng. On November 14, Germany seized upon the Juye Incident as a pretext for taking the port of Jiaozhou and incorporating it into their sphere of influence, demonstrating to all that the foreigners were now dictating demands to a weakened and impoverished Chinese state.[3] These affronts, combined with a long record of German Catholic interference in local affairs, sparked the kindling of latent anti-foreignism within Shandong.

The formation of a determinedly anti-foreign, anti-Christian group called the "Boxers," however, arose from a second event: a concrete and highly localized conflict between a particular local bandit militia group and a particular group of Christians. In 1869 in Liyuantun, on the border between Hebei and Shandong, the temple dedicated to a deity called the Jade Emperor was ceded to the local Christians. There was local resistance from the beginning, and in the decades that followed, local protective militias formed and then finally moved to show their disapproval of this decision. In 1898 a Shandong-based group called the Plum Flower Boxers (Meihuaquan) staged a martial arts demonstration in Liyuantun under the leadership of Zhao Sanduo—known for his sense of justice and passion for righting wrongs. The show of force worked the locals into a frenzy, and a mob formed and seized the "stolen" temple. Though the local officials at the

---

2. On the Juye Incident see Tiedemann, "Not Every Martyr Is a Saint!" 589–617.

3. Germany's claim to the port of Jiaozhou was soon ratified in treaties with China. Cohen, *History in Three Keys*, 20–22.

time favored the actions of the mob, the power shift in favor of the foreigners that had followed the resolution of the Juye Incident led to the eventual return of the temple property to the Christians. It was in response to this event that Zhao organized a new group of martial artists (referred to in English at the time as "shadow boxers"), composed of members from many different societies ("united") to promote the cause of righteousness and justice over and against the heterodoxy of the foreign-supported Christians (and thus their name: "Boxers United in Righteousness" (Yihequan).[4]

The Boxers as we generally recognize them today, however, derived their final shape from the Shandong Spirit Boxers, rather than the Big Sword Society.[5] Though initially of an almost exclusively religious nature with a large focus on healing (an emphasis which persisted through all its metamorphoses), in late 1898 the Spirit Boxers in Guan County began to call themselves after the Boxers United in Righteousness, who had been so recently active throughout Shandong. The recent arrival of steamships, trains, and the telegraph had meant unemployment for many of the day laborers along the coast. Moreover, the massive inundation of the Shandong flood plain in that same year had combined with the ensuing famine to create a large and desperate refugee population.[6] Having originally drawn heavily from the poorer peasants in Shandong, these new Boxers United in Righteousness suddenly became still more active.

Though the exact reasons are unclear, the combination of the all the factors listed above somehow motivated the Boxers United in Righteousness to begin to engage in expressly anti-foreign and then anti-Christian activities by early 1899. As a natural result of this progression, the third and final event leading to the formation of the Boxers occurred in October 1899, when the Boxers United in Righteousness encountered their first major armed conflict with Qing troops during the Battle of Senluo Temple in Pingyang County on the Hebei border. It was during this battle that the name "Militia United in Righteousness" (Yihetuan) was formally used, and it was here where the "Support/Revive the Qing, exterminate the foreigners" (*fu/xing qing mie yang*) banner was first raised, though such names and slogans had been in sporadic use since the spring of 1899.[7]

---

4. Ibid., 23–24. For a more idiosyncratic understanding of the names of the "Boxers United in Righteousness" see Landor, *China and the Allies*, 1:1–6.

5. The standard work on the origins of the Boxer phenomena in Shandong (with limited reference to Shanxi) is Esherick, *The Origins of the Boxer Uprising*.

6. On August 8 dikes broke at Shouzhang and then Jinan and Dong'e, dislocating millions and "turning much of Northwestern Shandong into a disaster zone." Cohen, *History in Three Keys*, 31.

7. These changes and the historical events (such as the Battle of Senluo Temple)

This final event also raises two other important points which help to illustrate the confusion and contradiction inherent in describing the roots of any phenomenon such as the Boxers. First, not all Shandong militia/bandit groups transformed into anti-Christian groups. As an example, the Spirit Boxers in Zouping County, Jinan experienced the same external and internal challenges, had a significant native and foreign Christian community, and yet never engaged in anti-Christian activities.[8] Secondly, the Shandong Governor Yuxian, who is largely blamed in foreign accounts for most of the Boxer evils, actually criticized the local officials for bungling the Senluo Temple affair. After voicing his doubts (and following the same militia/bandit management technique he had been using all along), Yuxian ordered the major leaders of the boxing clans in Jinan executed and then encouraged the rank-and-file followers to disperse back into the population. He had previously been successful with this policy of decapitation and dispersion in controlling and limiting Boxer activities in southern Shandong; however, by now the Boxers had grown so much in number and popularity that Yuxian's efforts were unable to stem the tide. The Boxers were upset with Yuxian, viewing his criticisms of local officials' failed attempts to control the Boxers as further evidence of his anti-Boxer stance, which had caused them such grief in southern Shandong. At the same time, the foreign community mistakenly thought that Yuxian's criticisms were directed at the local officials' decision to call in the troops to suppress the Boxers, thus misconstruing the criticisms as evidence of Yuxian's supposed pro-Boxer leanings.[9] While for-

---

wherein they found expression are discussed in ibid., 25–33. Broomhall claims that from May 26, 1899 until the battle of Senluo Temple, the Boxers had carried anti-Qing banners: "overthrow the Qing and exterminate the foreigners (*fan Qing mie yang*)." Broomhall, *HTCOC*, 7, *It is Not Death to Die!*, 296. Cohen (with Esherick) sees Boxer adoption of pro-Qing banners as an informed attempt to gain imperial support—support which the Qing were not yet ready to offer.

8. Cohen, *History in Three Keys*, 32.

9. Ibid., 32–33. Missionaries and foreigners at the time universally saw Yuxian (with the support of the Empress Dowager Cixi) as the key figure behind the Boxer violence. This reading is so popular that it permeates all accounts and subjects them to its basic assumptions. See, for example, the recent Catholic account Clark, *Heaven in Conflict*, 112–27. It may be more accurate to view the anti-foreign Yuxian as a staunchly loyal Confucian official; Cohen describes Yuxian as "uncompromisingly anti-foreign." Cohen, *History in Three Keys*, 51. His success at suppressing Boxerism in southern Shandong supports this view, as does the fact that his demotion following the Senluo affair was due to his *failure to suppress the Boxers*. Yuxian was of course welcomed at court because of his loyalty to China and for his suffering the criticisms of the foreign powers. Thus it was his loyalty to the Qing and his bitterness toward the foreigners who constantly criticized him and China that motivated his actions in June and July of 1900 (see below). For a more recent example of the Yuxian-Boxer "conspiracy theory" see Broomhall, *HTCOC*, 7, *It is Not Death to Die!*, 296, 307, and others. For a more sympathetic view of Yuxian, see Thompson, "Reporting the Taiyuan Massacre," 65–92.

eign powers sought the removal of Yuxian from office, the Boxers continued to grow and increase their activity.

Most foreigners believed Yuxian to have been governor of Shandong when, on the last day of 1899, British missionary S. P. Brook (SPG) was murdered outside a small Shandong village by the Boxers—an act that Yuxian supposedly encouraged. Yuxian had in fact already been recalled to Beijing and replaced by the staunchly anti-Boxer official Yuan Shikai.[10] Heedless, the local foreign officials targeted Yuxian, once again demanding action from the Chinese government. The imperial court agreed to formally censure Yuxian and on March 15, 1900, officially demoting him from high-profile coastal Shandong to become governor of the unimportant inland province of Shanxi.

By late May 1900, Boxer activity had escalated and expanded beyond the attack and looting of local Christians to include more destructive behavior impacting local and international trade: in the last week of the month, Boxers tore up the rail and telegraph lines connecting Baoding, Tianijn, and Beijing.[11] Even so, strong orders were being issued by the Imperial State Department (known as the Zongli Yamen) in Beijing calling for fierce repression of the Boxer bandits. However, as increasing unrest throughout May caused the foreign officials in China to call up guards and summon military forces, the pro-Boxer faction at court gained new support for their anti-foreign posturing. On June 10, in response to a unilateral foreign dispatch of soldiers from Tianjin, pro-Boxer Prince Duan Qinwang was appointed head of the Zongli Yamen, signaling a decisive court decision in favor of the Boxers.[12] From this point on, Qing soldiers began to fight alongside Boxer "rebels."

---

10. Cohen, *History in Three Keys*, 35–36. For an example of the foreign belief that Yuxian was governor at the time of Brook's death, see Broomhall, *Martyred Missionaries of the CIM*, 18. Chinese sources list Brook simply as a "British Anglican missionary." Xu Shihu, *Li Timotai zhuanlue*, 56.

11. Brandt, *Massacre in Shansi*, 173. Baoding was the first major city located east of the mountains on the way from Taiyuan to Beijing.

12. Current Chinese historians and party propagandists see the Boxer movement as a response to the foreign invasion of the Eight-Nation Army. While it is true that the June 10 request for Tianjin troops from the various Beijing legations played a role in bringing about Cixi's support for the pro-Boxer faction at court, Boxers had been active and killing Chinese Christians, foreign missionaries, *and* Qing soldiers long before June 10. The Eight-Nation Army did not exist until July 1900. If the foreign war effort was an attempt to protect people from the Boxer violence, then foreign and Chinese Christians who aided the foreign military effort could be said to have been acting in self-defense. On the other hand, if the Boxers can be seen as a response to foreign invasion, then foreign and Chinese Christians who aided the foreign military effort can be seen to have common cause with the militant invaders. The current official

The situation rapidly deteriorated.¹³ On June 11 the Japanese Secretary of Legation was killed by Qing soldiers; on June 13 Beijing was swarmed by Boxer units who immediately set about burning and looting all Christian and foreign-related properties in the city. Tianjin was in a similar state, having been slowly inundated by Boxers since March. On June 17 the German head of legation, Baron Clemens von Ketteler, was shot while passing through the streets of Beijing by Qing soldiers. Foreigners and Chinese Christians took cover in the legations and the various churches as best as they were able. In one act of heroism, missionaries escorted two thousand Chinese Protestants from the Methodist Episcopal mission through the streets of Beijing, giving them a place to live within the protection of the foreign legations.¹⁴ On June 20 imperial soldiers joined by Boxers began firing upon the legations and the cathedral, thus commencing the sieges that would last until August 14 of that summer.¹⁵ For all practical purposes, both Tianjin and Beijing were now under the control of various Boxer factions; fires were rampant, and the suffering and death poured out on local Chinese—both Christian and non-Christian alike—was acute.

On June 21 the Empress Dowager Cixi issued a formal "Edict of War."¹⁶ The Empress Dowager had ruled China from behind (and at times in front of) the scenes for quite some time. Though she was technically only the

---

Chinese interpretation thus describes all the Boxer martyrs as invaders who got what they deserved. This reading of Chinese history persists in many Chinese junior high school history texts, and surfaced again in the various official Chinese responses to the Vatican's 2000 movement to canonize one hundred twenty martyrs from Chinese history. See, for example, the editorial "Fandigang fengsheng shi dui Zhongguo renmin de yanzhong tiaoxin [The Vatican's 'Canonization' Is a Serious Provocation of the Chinese People]" in *Renmin ribao haiwai ban* (October 3, 2000) 1.

13. For the most accurate account of the Boxer sieges in Beijing and Tianjin, see chapter 1 in Cohen, *History in Three Keys*. Since this paper is focusing on Shanxi, the details of the central conflicts in Beijing, Hebei, and Tianjin will be dealt with only in passing.

14. Broomhall, *HTCOC*, 7, *It is Not Death to Die!*, 328–30. One modern Chinese reporter views the labor (wall repair and fortification along with carrying messages) contributed by local Christians during the siege of 1900 as a sign of Chinese oppression at the hands of foreigners. The author fails to take into consideration the lives sacrificed by the foreigners to secure these believers' safety. He also fails to mention the many Chinese Christians who were being killed throughout the city at that same time. Wang Yuhua, "Duli zizhu lai zhi bu yi," *Tian Feng* (May 2000) 4–5.

15. This course of events is summarized from Cohen's more nuanced account in Cohen, *History in Three Keys*, 44–51. For the most detailed account of the siege from a purely Western point of view see Preston, *The Boxer Rebellion*.

16. Strangely, the "edict" was delivered to Chinese officials and not the foreign envoys (although they had previously been officially ordered to evacuate). Cohen, *History in Three Keys*, 51 and 310 note 74.

regent who ruled until the emperor came of age, she controlled real power throughout the court. When she ordered the seizure and imprisonment of the Guangxu Emperor following his failed 1889 Hundred Days Reforms, she secured her reputation as staunchly conservative, anti-foreign, and capable of bold and often violent action. By 1900 the "Old Buddha," as she was called by foreigners in Beijing, was from all practical points of view the ruler of China.[17]

The following day another edict was issued, promising a reward of 50 taels of silver for any foreign man taken alive, 40 taels for foreign women, and 30 taels for any children.[18] The imperial government had suffered too many military defeats of late. It was hoped that focusing civil unrest and hatred on the foreigners would turn the Boxers into a national pro-Qing peasant army (thus staving off the very real possibility of civil war), while at the same time doing away with the foreign influence that had plagued China for the last century.

A staged battle took place over many days in Tianjin, while Beijing itself was turned into a war zone. The Northern Cathedral was crammed with some 3,420 people during the two-and-a-half month siege (mostly women and children), of whom only seventy-two were foreigners. The Catholics there suffered four hundred casualties during the siege, mostly from starvation and disease. The legations held a much broader mix of people: 473 Western civilians, over 400 foreign soldiers, 1,700 Chinese Protestants, and as many as 2,000 Chinese Catholics.[19] Conditions for the Chinese refugees within the legations, though far better than conditions on the streets of Beijing, were nonetheless appalling. Many foreign infants died of starvation during the siege, but the mortality rate due to starvation amongst the Chinese children within the foreign compound was nearly 100 percent. While food was shared equally between foreign and Chinese within the Northern Cathedral, the foreigners within the legations were criminally negligent in supplying food for the Chinese Christians within their walls.[20] Foreign casualties in the legations, on the other hand, were mostly related to combat:

---

17. The most recent biography of Cixi is Chang, *Empress Dowager Cixi*. Cixi's actions in 1900 are probably best understood as being motivated by a powerful drive to preserve the dynasty and her own position of power within that dynasty; in chapter 23 Chang argues that Yuxian encouraged Boxer atrocities, against the will of the more moderate Cixi.

18. Broomhall, *HTCOC*, 7, *It is Not Death to Die!*, 330.

19. These figures are taken from Cohen, *History in Three Keys*, 196–97, especially 197 note 72.

20. This issue is discussed throughout Preston, *The Boxer Rebellion*.

sixty-six foreign soldiers died, while one hundred soldiers and volunteers were wounded.[21]

WHO WERE THE BOXERS?

> There are many Christian converts
> Who have lost their senses,
> They deceive our Emperor,
> Destroy the gods we worship,
> Pull down our temples and altars,
> Permit neither Joss-sticks nor candles,
> Cast away tracts on ethics,
> And ignore reason.
> Don't you realize that
> Their aim is to engulf the country?
>
> ———————————
>
> Their men are all immoral;
> Their women truly vile.
> For the Devils it's mother-son sex
> That serves as the breeding style.
>
> No rain comes from Heaven,
> The earth is parched and dry.
> And all because the churches
> Have bottled up the sky.
>
> When at last all the Foreign Devils
> Are expelled to the very last man,
> The Great Qing, united, together,
> Will bring peace to this our land.[22]

---

21. Cohen, *History in Three Keys*, 54.

22. These two doggerels are samples of the various Boxer songs and verses that circulated at the turn of the century. As translated in Spence, *The Search for Modern China*, 232.

The beliefs of "the Boxers United in Righteousness" emphasized martial arts exercises and spirit possession, drawing heavily from the world of sectarian religious associations such as the famous White Lotus sects.[23] With their selective combining of ideas from each of the "Three Teachings"—the term used by Chinese scholar officials to refer to the widely recognized religions of Buddhism, Confucianism, and Daoism—these secret religious sects were present in many Chinese communities and often deeply integrated in local society.[24] Their use of moral texts, local organizational structures, and confidence in a coming savior has led many scholars and missionaries to compare various sectarian groups favorably with Christianity.[25]

Boxers were readily identified by their opera costumes, typically red silk sashes, turbans, and leggings, though some bands of Boxers were said to favor yellow over red. A small village would typically have only one Boxer group of twenty-five to one hundred males, while larger cities would have many different bands spread throughout the city and organized under different leaders. The nature of those participating in the Boxer movement varied greatly from village to village, as each village's complaints, each village's reserve of charismatic leaders, and each village's supply of disaffected youth was different. As historian Paul Cohen observes, people joined Boxer bands from all walks of life,

> ... including not only peasants but also Daoist priests, Buddhist monks and nuns, demobilized soldiers, members of martial arts organizations, seasonal farm laborers, transport workers hurt by the advent of railway and steamship, urban gang members, and vast numbers of unemployed drifters made destitute by the successive natural disasters that impinged on north China in the last years of the nineteenth century.[26]

23. I am inclined to agree with Cohen and Esherick in seeing the White Lotus (Bailianjiao) influence as incidental rather than essential. As will be seen below I find peasant opera and mythologies to be a much more significant element in Boxer phenomena. On White Lotus influences see Esherick, *The Origins of the Boxer Uprising*, 211–12; as well as the discussion in Cohen, *History in Three Keys*, 38–39. For an argument favoring a stronger connection between sectarianism and the Boxers, see Lu Yao, "Yihetuan yundong fazhan jieduan," 53–65.

24. De Groot, *Sectarianism and Religious Persecution in China*, 155–57. On sectarianism and Christian mission in nineteenth-century China see Kaiser, "Encountering China," 97–112.

25. Bays, "Christianity and the Chinese Sectarian Tradition," 33–55; Tiedemann, "Christianity and Chinese 'Heterodox Sects,'" 339–82. Missionaries at the time also wrote about the similarities. See, for example, Henry D. Porter, "Secret Sects in Shantung," *CR* 17, no. 2 (1886) 65–66; and Nevius, *The Life of John Livingston Nevius*, 300–301.

26. Cohen, *History in Three Keys*, 111.

Within this diversity, there was a definite focus on young boys. This was true to such a degree that in some areas the Boxers were referred to as the "Youth Army" (*tongzijun*) or the "Children's Brigade" (*wawadui*). In July 1900 May Nathan (CIM) wrote a letter home, describing a placard posted in nearby Daning inviting "schoolboys" (*nianshu de haizi*) to form a "Children's Witchcraft Band" (*wawa xiefasi*).[27] This phenomenon was explained by Olivia Ogren (CIM), who was working in Yongning (present day Zhongyang) at the time: "A large proportion of the Boxers were boys, as they were more susceptible to the spirits than mature men. Many children were won from among the poorer people, by the promise of perpetual safety from all calamity if they would give their sons to this righteous crusade."[28] Some contemporary scholars have compared the role of children in the Boxer movement to youth involvement in the Salem Witchcraft Trials, while others suggest that children are in fact more susceptible to trances and spiritual or emotional manipulation.[29]

Alongside the Boxers, groups of young, virginal girls formed, calling themselves Red Lanterns (Hongdengzhao). Less is known about the exact nature of Red Lantern associations, but they were typically pictured using their miraculous powers of flight, healing, and control over the elements to aid their male counterparts in battle. Red Lanterns were believed to possess the power to "rub" dead bodies back to life, and they were routinely credited as responsible for bringing about apocalyptic judgments of darkness, fire, and storm, leading to the death of thousands of foreigners. One Red Lantern told followers on one occasion that she had just returned from a flight to Russia, where she had destroyed an entire city. There are only a few indications of the Red Lanterns ever entering into combat, though it was believed that their magic could make bullets fall out of the air into their baskets. When the Red Lanterns passed through a village, people averted their eyes—especially the young Boxer men. Similar to the austerity and sexual segregation practiced by the Taipings fifty years prior, this kind of sexual purity was seen as empowering and perhaps even the source of the Red Lantern's power.[30]

In response to this particular manifestation of the magical powers claimed by the Boxers, some Shanxi Catholic communities formed their

---

27. Nathan, "From Miss May Nathan's Last Letter," 38. Nathan claimed that the Boxer bands she saw were composed of eleven to fifteen year-old boys.

28. Ogren, "A Great Conflict of Sufferings," 71–72.

29. For a discussion of the role of youth in the Boxer phenomenon see Cohen, *History in Three Keys*, 114–17.

30. For more on the Red Lanterns see Clark, *Heaven in Conflict*, 79–87; Cohen, *History in Three Keys*, 138–45.

own groups of virginal young women, referring to them as "White Lanterns" (Baidengzhao) or "Green-Fisted Lanterns" (Lüshouzhao). Like their Red Lantern counterparts, the Catholic "Lanterns" were young, mostly between the ages of twelve and seventeen. According to one Chinese report from the time, a full-blown battle was supposedly waged outside of Yuci on the sixth day of the sixth lunar month, when a Green-Fisted Lantern took action against her nemesis, the Senior Brother-Disciple of Yuci. Fire, rain, and thunder were all involved in the struggle—as was levitation.[31]

There was no set protocol for establishing a Boxer band, but most often things began with either a new arrival or a local person announcing his status as a Senior Brother-Disciple and his attachment to a particular Chinese deity.[32] Due to the popularity of Chinese folk opera and folk traditions, the figures with the largest following were Guan Di, Guan Yu, Liu Bei, Zhang Fei, Zhao Yun, and Zhuge Liang, all of whom—in the guises of their various courtesy names and titles—were historical characters from *The Romance of the Three Kingdoms*. Also popular were Sun Wukong, Tangseng, Zhu Bajie, and others from *The Journey West*.[33] At the town boxing grounds or near the main temple in town, an altar would be set up to several of these deities. Placards would be posted throughout the area inviting people to attend a martial arts demonstration near the new altar. As a crowd gathered around the leader and his band of Boxers, the members of the group would conduct their ceremonies, enter into a trance, and then begin to perform complicated martial arts drills in unison. A local resident of Taiyuan recalled a Boxer going through his drills during the summer of 1900:

> From the time of the arrival of the Senior Brother-Disciple in Taiyuan, the number of Boxers in the streets of the city grew. They practiced their boxing in small groups on the streets. One time as I was going from Willow Lane [Liu Xiang] to Xixiao Wall [Xixiao Qiang—at that time the name of one of the northern sections of Liu Xiang] I saw a youngster of fifteen or sixteen going through his boxing drills. Facing toward the southeast he performed the *koutou* [sic] and chanted Tangseng, Shanseng, [Zhu] Bajie, [Sun] Wukong, and the like. After this he fell to the

---

31. Qiao Zhiqiang, *Yihetuan zai Shanxi*, 29–30.

32. Apparently, one of the more powerful Senior Brother-Disciples in the Taiyuan area was located in Shentie Town outside of Yuci—and was only twelve years old! See the fascinating account in ibid., 30–31.

33. These figures and the stories and operas they are derived from are still popular today.

ground, scrambled to his feet, and then with greatly increased energy practiced the martial arts.[34]

Impressed by the power and obvious magic of the demonstration, young men and boys from the area would join, the Boxers' numbers and boldness would increase, and the scope of their activities would extend beyond demonstrations to include more violent expressions.

The Boxer ceremonies were most often described as "spirit possession" (*jiangshen futi*) and owed much to the mass possession rituals of the earlier Spirit Boxers of Shandong. Through burning of incense, and the use of charms, prostrations (*ketou*), and chants, a particular deity would be requested to come down and attach itself to the Boxer's body. Having entered into the magic (*shangfa*), the Boxer would have a changed voice, character, behavior, and abilities, in a manner similar to spirit possession in other cultures. A local gazetteer from Anze County in Shanxi described one of these ceremonies:

> The method of the Boxers is as follows: They write an incantation on a piece of paper. After rinsing their mouths [for ritual purification] and chanting the incantation they suddenly fall to the ground. After a short while they get up and begin to dance in a frenzied manner and talk as if in their sleep. Then they either state that Guandi has descended or that Kongming has attached himself to their bodies.[35]

The effect of these mass possessions was startling. In no time at all, a town could become overrun with entranced men and boys practicing their Boxing drills. A Tianjin scholar recorded some of the different kinds of behavior exhibited by the Boxers in his city at the time:

> There are those who move slowly with their eyes closed and those who stare straight ahead and walk forward with erect bearing. There are cases in which a few people hold one person up and cases in which a person supported by two other persons staggers like one who has had too much to drink. In some instances, holding a sword, they dance about wildly, and pedestrians don't have time to get out of the way. In other instances several of them, clutching weapons, walk in single file. Sometimes, mounted on horses, they provide people with protection and guidance. Sometimes they place those who have been wounded or are already dead on their shoulders and take

---

34. As quoted in Cohen, *History in Three Keys*, 97–98.

35. From *Anze xianzhi* in Qiao Zhiqiang, *Yihetuan zai Shanxi*, 140; as translated in Cohen, *History in Three Keys*, 97.

them home. There are even cases in which a bandit [Boxer] will hold a stick embellished on the top with a bloody object which he claims is the heart and liver of a foreigner. Coming or going, they are unaware of what they are doing. Confused, disoriented, they don't seem like normal people.[36]

Similar rituals of boxing drills, charms, prostrations, and chants were performed to attain invulnerability—a legacy from the Big Sword Societies of Shandong. One Boxer leader from Tianjin explained to his followers how this worked: "When you've reached the field of battle, . . . as soon as the gods have entered your bodies you'll go up to heaven, and the devils will have no way to attack you." One author claims that the Boxers demonstrated their invulnerability (complete with a musket shot and the target spitting the bullet out of his mouth) before the Empress Dowager Cixi, who was notably impressed.[37] This was not something new to China, where there was already a tradition of groups whose practice supposedly made them unafraid of firearms (*bu wei qiangpao*). This did not end with the defeat of the Boxers, but invulnerability claims continued into the twentieth century in various peasant uprisings and the supposedly powerful *qigong* masters.[38] Needless to say, this belief in many ways contributed to the slaughter of the Boxers following the arrival of the foreign forces.

The magical powers claimed by the Boxers were not limited to invulnerability; they also claimed to be able to control fire. In varying accounts, Boxers would burn paper and incense, pray, prostrate themselves, and then indicate which buildings should burn and which should not. In some cases, a gesture and the chant "burn, burn, burn" were all that was necessary to incite flames. Although Chinese cities were filled with flammable wooden structures, people were confdient that the Boxers could not only start these fires but control them as well. Some of the Boxer leaders also claimed to be able to instantly heal their warriors during battle. One leader was said to possess a stalk of sorghum which, when pointed at the heads of enemies, resulted in their instant decapitation. Many Boxer leaders were reported to have powers of flight, invisibility, and the ability to be present in two or more locations at one time. The emphasis placed on these miraculous abilities within Boxer culture reflects the self-conceived spiritual nature of

---

36. From the writings of a Tianjin scholar-official as recorded in Cohen, *History in Three Keys*, 99. Confucian elite criticized the "superstition" of the Boxers, empahsizing the heterodox nature of the movement by referring to the Boxers as "bandits" (*quanfei*).

37. Mentioned in Broomhall, *HTCOC*, 7, *It is Not Death to Die!*, 295.

38. On invulnerability see Cohen, *History in Three Keys*, 28, 100–101.

the conflict, a perception shared by both Boxers and Christians.[39] This notion was so strong that from the Boxers' point of view, their losses in battle were due not to superior Western firepower, but rather superior magic. In particular, items associated with female (*yin*) elements (menstrual cloths, female nudity, pregnancies) were considered to be powerful wards against Boxer magic. The Boxer-led siege of the Northern Cathedral in Beijing, for instance, was said to have struggled because of the many women involved and their use of nudity, menstrual cloths, and pubic hair in their defense.[40]

A typical example of how the Boxers spread across Shanxi comes from just south of Taiyuan. A man named Zhang Er, the wealthy owner of the Double Completeness Paper Shop, is widely supposed to have been the instigator of Boxer activity in that county. A previous resident of Xiaodian Village in Yangqu County, Zhang Er was living at the time in Xinzhou near his paper shop in Nanguan Village. Following a mystical fire in the local Guan Di temple in the late fall of 1899, Zhang Er disappeared before returning a month later in total silence, refusing to speak a word to anyone. Upon the later arrival of visitors from Taiyuan, where Boxer bands were already active, he suddenly broke his silence and announced "Time to start!" Zhang Er declared himself the Senior Disciple under the control of Guan Di himself. He immediately began taking students and training them in martial arts. Boxer candidates in Xinzhou were between the ages of eight and twenty, and excluded those with the surname Yang, those born in the Year of the Ram, and anyone whose speech sounded a bit "foreign." All of these involved homophones for the word "foreign" as used in the most common epithet for foreigners in the spoken Chinese of that day: "foreign devil" (*yang guizi*). Zhang Er's Boxer disciples lived and trained at the local Guan Di Temple, and all of their meals were eaten in common, sharing food donated by local people or the Boxers themselves. The group grew in just a few days to include seventy or eighty members, and rapidly expanded out into the surrounding villages until Boxer temples had been established in most every village of the county.[41]

What was it that enabled the Boxer phenomenon to grow and spread across Shanxi so rapidly? Without denying the variety of local contexts within which Boxerism developed, a few general trends can be identified.

39. On the mutual perception of spiritual warfare between Boxers and Christians, see chapters 2 and 3 in Clark, *Heaven in Conflict*.

40. On Boxer magic, see chapter 4 in Cohen, *History in Three Keys*.

41. At the end of the Boxer turmoil, Zhang Er fled to his hometown outside of Taiyuan, where his wife faked his death complete with a mourning hall, a procession of grievers, and a false burial. He was never heard from again. See the account of Zhang Er in Ren Fuxing, "'Xinzhou Yesujiao jinlihui shengtu," 107.

First of all, religion and opera were intimately connected for rural citizens of nineteenth-century north central China.[42] It was only natural that these great *dramatis personae* striding so vividly across the stage would have power in the spirit world. At the same time, the movement's reliance on charismatic local leadership meant that simple imitation of what others did in other locations was often sufficient to attract a following. Thus, the movement could replicate easily, and this rapid spread was seen as further evidence of its truthfulness and divine inspiration. Moreover, once the Boxers in an area reached a critical mass it became impossible to oppose them. Fear contributed to their power and thus their credibility. As Taigu missionary Rowena Bird (ABCFM) explained,

> One of the strongholds the Boxers have got here is through superstition—they teach their tactics first to young boys, and these boys take the lead in every desperate deed, and elder people stand in awe of them and believe that they have supernatural powers. Then the rapid spread of the movement springing up as it has in village after village, hundreds in a day, makes even intelligent people believe it is the revenge of the gods against the religion that disregards their power.[43]

Finally, the mighty claims of Boxer magic were believed by most of the Chinese populace. One Tianjin official estimated that credence was given to Boxer claims by eight out of ten people—including officials.[44] Only fools would choose not to be associated with such power.

RELIGIOUS CONFLICT IN SHANXI

When the Boxers arrived in Shanxi in the spring of 1900, they found a province already boiling over with long-standing dissatisfaction. Although until that point no acts of violence had been committed against Protestant missionaries in Shanxi, there was already a long list of "religious cases" (*jiao'an*) on file with the provincial and imperial governments, describing all the various conflicts that had involved native believers. While some of the cases involved Protestants, most centered on the Catholic community, with its longer history and consequently larger population.

---

42. On opera in Shanxi, see Johnson, *Spectacle and Sacrifice*.

43. Taken from a July 1900 letter from Bird as recorded in Cohen, *History in Three Keys*, 111.

44. Ibid., 110.

A brief list of some of the religious cases recorded during the last half of the nineteenth century will serve to introduce the nature of the majority of the conflicts that occurred between Catholics and their neighbors.[45] The actual number of cases is large, with typical examples including a local drunken quarrel, an unpaid loan, harassment of a Catholic beggar, a soured business relationship, a widow's son's debt and her false complaint, an illegal grain purchase, a dispute over farmland and irrigation, a village school property dispute, marital problems between a husband and his wife and his concubine, hard feelings over a church loan, an overdue loan, and disagreements over the use of commonly owned trees and lands for temple/church repair.[46] Most of these conflicts did not deal directly with matters of faith, but were rather typical village disputes where one of the parties happened to be connected to the local Christian community. More significantly, this list of cases demonstrates the remarkable amount of overlap and interaction between the Catholic and non-Catholic populations in Shanxi at this time, suggesting that the two groups lived together and were at least in some ways still expecting to function as members of a shared community.

Despite or perhaps because of this lingering integration, Chinese Christians did pose a real threat to local community. As part of the official Chinese process for dealing with claims under the protection from religious persecution clause of the unequal 1858 "Treaty of Tientsin," almost any conflict that involved a believer could be treated as a religious case, provided that the believer could convince a missionary to take his or her side. Once a local dispute was registered as an official religious case, it was usually only a matter of time before the foreign ministers, sometimes via their imperial counterparts, became involved in the local adjudication process, giving the local Christians access to a worldly power not available to their understandably bitter non-Christian neighbors. The fact that many of these disputes had little to do with actual matters of faith only made this imbalance of power seem all the more unjust. In some cases, the Catholic party was eventually and justifiably found to be culpable, but this did little to soften local resentment of Christian exceptionalism. These new power dynamics divided local communities in new and disruptive ways.

One concrete example from Shanxi illustrates the interplay between the different forces in these disputes. In 1861 Franciscans in Zezhou, Shanxi

---

45. The following cases were collected from the three chapters written by Litzinger, Sweeten and Thompson in Bays, *Christianity in China*.

46. One Chinese article from 1985 claims that the missionaries in the Xinzhou area had a ferocious attitude, confiscating market stalls and squeezing small shops out of business, but provides no evidence for this accusation. Ren Fuxing, "'Xinzhou Yesujiao jinlihui shengtu," 107.

requested a proclamation from the governor outlining the rights and freedoms of Chinese Christians, providing him with a draft of five articles for publication, each of which concerned money and taxes. The Franciscans claimed that according to the treaties, Chinese Catholics should be exempt from paying any taxes or conscriptions that went toward any activities or projects related to "heterodox" (non-Catholic) practices; accordingly, Chinese Catholics should not be required to contribute toward temple festivals and operas or temple repairs. Moreover, local leaders were also required to punish anyone who attempted to coerce contributions out of Chinese Catholics for such heterodox purposes.[47]

On December 2, 1861, a Catholic missionary in Shanxi filed a formal complaint with the Zongli Yamen in Beijing.[48] Despite the fact that all officials in Shanxi province had received copies of the treaty stipulations, local officials in Yangqu County were supposedly still actively opposing local Catholics. The complaint alleged that village leaders had been visiting the local believers to collect the taxes earmarked for supporting the public opera performances (*gong xi*) that were the focus of the annual temple festivals. Yangqu Catholics who refused to pay were then being beaten and even imprisoned by their village leaders.

After a long series of negotiations between the Franciscans and the French minister on one side, and Chinese officials from the Zongli Yamen and the provincial governor down to the Zezhou magistrates on the other side, the matter was finally resolved, albeit with little input from the villagers themselves. Not surprisingly, the resulting compromise was primarily concerned with the financial aspects of the problem, ignoring the social dimensions. It was declared that Catholic believers could not be required to pay the portion of their taxes that supported local temple festivals, including public opera, but that they still had to pay for public works such as bridge and road repairs, irrigation, security, and shared agricultural labor, as well as the converted corvée labor. The fees supporting the festivals and operas, the French minister declared, were "wasteful" or "useless" expenditures, while the latter projects he deemed "useful" or "public." This determination was accepted, with the government eventually determining that forty percent of the total rural tax burden qualified as "useful," leaving Catholic villagers free to legally withhold the remaining "wasteful" sixty percent of their tax liability. Eventually, this same Catholic arrangement was extended

---

47. Thompson, "Twilight of the Gods," 57.

48. This case, summarized in the following paragraphs, is examined in detail in ibid., 57–60.

to Protestant believers as well. According to the diary of Dr. Harold A. Schofield, the Protestant version reached Shanxi on September 22, 1881:

> a proclamation has just been issued by the Chinese Government in Pekin [Beijing] extending to Protestant native Christians the same privileges which have long been accorded to the native adherents of the Romish priests, viz. complete exemption from all taxes levied for the support of idolatrous rites and ceremonies.[49]

As was often the case, the official settlement failed to address the underlying source of bitterness within the community: Christian free riders. At the local village level, the temple festivals were seen as public benefit services provided for the good of the entire community. Operas were performed for the benefit of local deities with the expectation that happily entertained local gods would then show their gratitude by sending the appropriate rains and generally blessing the community. Since the entire community profited by securing the gods' favor, then it was reasonable to expect the entire community to contribute toward the cost of the opera performances. By refusing to pay, the local Christians were relying on treaty policies based on a secular/sacred distinction that did not yet exist in Chinese rural thinking.[50] Other local disagreements further contributed to this sense of resentment. Lands that were communally contributed and maintained for the support of the local village temple (*cunmiao*), usually a religiously non-partisan temple, were often entangled in disputes, as Catholics leveraged their treaty privileges to recover their contributed lands. And when Christians refused to participate in "pray for rain" processions involving local gods, they were often threatened or punished for not contributing their share to the common good. Significantly, the main cause for bitterness was not so much religious difference as it was the perceived unmerited and unjust exceptionalism of the Catholics within the local community. By refusing to support communal property or bear their share of the financial burdens associated with communal welfare, the Chinese Catholics were posing a fundamental challenge to the meaning of community in rural China.[51]

This is not to suggest that Protestants were completely removed from these conflicts. In one instance, severe drought conditions had driven farmers in Xinzhou to petition their various gods for rain. To demonstrate their piety before the local gods, the community decided not to wear hats

49. Ibid., 56.
50. Austin, *China's Millions*, 159.
51. This is not an exaggeration: as Litzinger has suggested, in much of rural North China "the temple community equals the village community." Litzinger, "Temple Community and Village," 79–82.

to protect their heads from the hot sun while working in the fields. Many local Christians refused on religious grounds to participate in this ban, and accordingly this became a source of local resentment.[52] Even apart from questions of idolatry, the simple step of joining a Protestant church could be perceived locally as removing oneself from the village community. The Protestant church had its own rules and regulations, and its own apparatus for enforcing them, all independent of the local village. The church also demanded that adherents refrain from participating in certain local communal events—and then insisted that they also join in other unique practices that were viewed by their non-Christian neighbors as odd ("you eat whose flesh and drink whose blood?!"). As Fenzhou missionary Charles Price noted, the Chinese word for church (*jiaohui*) made use of a term for an association (*hui*) that was typically applied to China's various heterodox secret societies. The use of this terminology meant that the church "in the mind of the people is only on the same footing [with the secret societies] with the disadvantage of being foreign."[53] On these counts alone, Protestant missions and the churches they established also posed a threat to the local status quo, albeit to a lesser extent (perhaps) than many of the Catholic missions.

While Protestants and Catholics alike were increasingly viewed as forces of destabilization in Shanxi villages as the nineteenth century progressed, it is important to recognize the substantive differences between Protestant and Catholic convictions on intervening in local legal disputes.[54] By 1891 growing awareness of the nature of these local resentments led Dixon Hoste (CIM) and Pastor Xi to curb Xi's previous policy of taking all local legal troubles involving believers to the Provincial officials and claiming treaty protection for the Christians. Significantly, the local church in Hongdong where they served played a key role in driving this decision, having determined that believers suffering for their faith "should trust only in the Lord for protection, and not depend on their treaty rights."[55] One example from early 1900—just months before the Boxer violence hit Shanxi—is typical of Protestant approaches to settling disputes. ABCFM worker George Williams found himself in a difficult situation when a local Taigu Christian

52. Ren Fuxing, "'Xinzhou Yesujiao jinlihui shengtu,'" 107.

53. The terminology did not greatly affect people's perceptions, but rather helped confirm the impressions they received from all the other factors mentioned above. On the question of *hui*, see Brandt, *Massacre in Shansi*, 145.

54. Timothy Richard, "Christian Persecutions in China: Their Nature, Causes, Remedies," *CR* 15, no. 4 (1884) 245–46. While acknowledging the difference in practice, Richard admired the Catholics for confidently asserting before Chinese officials their right to legal protection.

55. Thompson, "Twilight of the Gods," 67.

named Yang came to the mission in a panic looking for protection. Yang had been involved with two other men in the stabbing of a fourth and was being sought by the local magistrate. In the end, Williams decided to surrender Yang to the authorities in order to demonstrate to local officials that "the church is a law-abiding institution." Local Christians were unhappy with Williams's decision: for the Chinese believers who had transferred their primary communal identification from their family or village to the new church, the missionary's failure to protect the church community at all costs was perceived as a betrayal. But Williams's decision was also intended to send a message to church members: missionaries would not protect local Christians if they committed crimes.[56] This stands in stark contrast to the actions of the Catholic missionaries in Shanxi who, even in comparison with their fellow Chinese priests, were typically far more willing to claim their treaty privileges.[57]

Accordingly, when the Boxers first became active in Shanxi, Protestant missionaries were not particularly surprised to see the violence target Catholic communities. From their perspective, the Catholics had become foolishly entangled in webs of local conflict and were now paying the price. As Horace Pitkin (ABCFM Baoding) understood those first acts of violence, "it is paying off old scores, for the [Catholic] priests take up and prosecute law cases for their converts. This creates great enmity and when occasion offers, the return blow is given with great severity."[58] This perspective makes it easier to understand why the Shanxi missionaries were so stunned when the violence broadened to include Protestants as well.

THE POWER AND PREVALENCE OF RUMORS

Missionary letters and diaries at the time were replete with prayers and pleas for detailed reports on what was happening elsewhere. Travel—and thus the transport of hand-carried messages—had been dangerous for foreigner and Chinese alike for quite some time, making news of events in other locations rare and often untrustworthy. Even the most basic national news became unavailable in late May with the end of official postal communications between Shanxi and the coast; from that point onward no one in Shanxi had access to accurate information about what was transpiring elsewhere.[59] Nor was Shanxi unique; by the middle of July the world's leading newspapers

56. Brandt, *Massacre in Shansi*, 149–50.
57. Harrison, *The Missionary's Curse*, 82–86.
58. Brandt, *Massacre in Shansi*, 172.
59. Edwards, *Fire and Sword in Shansi*, 57.

were mistakenly reporting the massacre of every foreigner in Beijing as a fact.[60] Unsurprisingly, this environment proved to be a fecund breeding ground for all manner of rumors.

It is impossible to explain the events in Shanxi during the summer of 1900 without reference to both the prevalence of rumors and the remarkable degree of credence given to them. As Jinci County scholar Liu Dapeng noted in his diary of the times, "For the rampant spread of rumors no time was worse than the juncture of summer and autumn of the twenty-sixth year of Guangxu [July-August 1900]."[61] Liu's daily reflections from that summer portray a terrified populace inclined to violence and ready to believe almost anything. Similarly, Pigott wrote from Shouyang in a June 11 letter to Farthing in Taiyuan that "this place is full of [rumors], the people being fully assured that we shall all very soon be killed . . . I am told that all shopkeepers have received notice in the form of a 'circular' or tract, and that this states that wherever idols have been put away, there all will be killed." In a June 23 letter he listed other rumors he had heard: "The ocean has receded 9 *li* from the shore—no foreign troops can land. A great iron trident has erected itself in the sea. Boxers' food multiplies itself in their hands, so that they may never suffer from want. The foreign legations in Peking are all destroyed."[62] Olivia Ogren reported that after the mid-June arrival of Boxers in Yongning,

> Whispers soon were repeated . . . to the effect that the Boxers wore buttons which kindled fire (celluloid), and that they were stealing girls to recruit [into] the "Red Lantern Society." Absurd stories stating the arrival of foreign soldiers in packing-cases, and that "the Heavenly Soldiers," as the Boxers were called, had flown away into heaven at their approach.[63]

Edwards gives an account of some of the more popular Boxer magic rumors found in 1900 Shanxi. It is important to note that many of the rumors he mentions here had been present in China ever since the earliest contacts with the West.[64]

> The old fable of foreigners and Christians cutting out and scattering the figure of a man in paper, which in a few days came to

---

60. Cohen, *History in Three Keys*, 161. This was supposed to have happened on July 6 and 7. Most of these articles were full of gory details—all false, and all based on rumors.

61. As quoted in *History in Three Keys*, 149.

62. These two quotes taken from Edwards, *Fire and Sword in Shansi*, 73 and 75, respectively.

63. Ogren, "A Great Conflict of Sufferings," 65.

64. See chapter 4 "Westerners as Scapegoats" in Ter Haar, *Telling Stories*.

life and then had the power of doing much harm, was revived, and gained credence. It was further said that men (more especially beggars) were hired by Christians to poison the village wells, and make a mark with some red substance on the doors of the houses—the inhabitants of the house so marked being sure to get ill, and perhaps die. A scurrilous, anti-foreign pamphlet, which was widely circulated through the province [Shanxi], stated that foreign vessels seized at the coast had been found to contain large quantities of human blood, eyes, and the nipples of women's breasts!! If anyone into whose hands the pamphlet fell made one copy and gave it to a friend, he was promised immunity from all evil for himself; if he gave away ten copies, all his family would be safe; but if he distributed one hundred, his whole village would be similarly benefited.[65]

While foreign Christians were the antagonists in most of these tales, Chinese Christians were also implicated. Next to the "foreign devil" missionaries, nineteenth-century Chinese Christians were called "secondary devils" or "secondary hairy ones" (*er maozi*), to show their subordination to the foreigners (sometimes also called "big hairy ones" (*da maozi*)). As an example of how the terms were used, Boxer groups in the Xinzhou region employed this language in their chant "exterminate the foreign devils, sweep away the secondary hairy ones."[66] All Christians, regardless of ethnicity, were considered enemies.

As stated before, the closing years of the nineteenth century had been years of drought for much of northern China—and this was one of the main contributing factors to the growth of the Boxer movement. A Tianjin Boxer's testimony put it rather succinctly: "*Gengzi* [1900] was a drought year and there was nothing to do, so we began to practice Yihe Boxing."[67] This was even more true in Shanxi: as it was in the past and often still is today, water—or rather the lack of it—was at the heart of Shanxi's troubles in the summer of 1900.[68]

As the Boxer groups spread and became increasingly active, water emerged as a key category for Boxer attempts to attack and discredit the

65. Edwards, *Fire and Sword in Shansi*, 54–55.
66. Ren Fuxing, "'Xinzhou Yesujiao jinlihui shengtu,'" 108.
67. Cohen, *History in Three Keys*, 77. The *gengzi* year refers to the year of 1900 as recorded by the lunar calendar system of "earthly stems and heavenly branches." This system of dating is used for fortune telling, and according to this system the year 1900 was destined to bring trouble.
68. Local Chinese gazetteers throughout central and southern Shanxi (including Quwo and Yuci counties) all connected the emergence of the first Boxer groups in mid to late June with the extensive drought conditions they were experiencing. See ibid., 78.

foreign missionaries and their "secondary devil" Christian disciples. One popular 1900 slogan from the Xinzhou region said it simply: If heaven didn't send rain, it was because the foreigners had messed things up.[69] Boxer groups throughout Shanxi began to circulate rumors and post bills around the various towns blaming the local Christians for drought, famine, and crop failure. A. R. Saunders (CIM) of the Pingyao station records one such poster which informed the people that

> ... the present drought was due to the presence of the Protestant and Roman Catholic missionaries, who taught the people to leave idolatry and the worship of ancestors, and that before long the armies of Heaven were to make war against and exterminate the propagators of these religions, and calling on all to aid in carrying this out.[70]

A similar placard was posted in Taigu in mid-summer:

> The gods of happiness and wealth issue these instructions for the information of the members of the Catholic and Protestant religions: You have abandoned the gods and done away with your ancestors, causing the gods to be angry so that the rains do not fall from the sky. Before long heavenly soldiers and heavenly generals will descend to earth and wage a great battle with the adherents of your two religions. It is a matter of great urgency that you quickly join the Boxers and sincerely mend your ways, so that when the time comes [for the great battle], your entire families do not suffer harm.[71]

In an effort to please the gods and bring the needed rain, the number of opera performances also increased, creating more and more interest in Boxerism through its mystic links with the spirits of the larger-than-life characters in the operas.[72]

The missionaries were not insensitive to the precipitation problem. Rowena Bird described their plight in very direct terms in her diary entry for June 25.

> These are most trying times—famine threatens the people with starvation—the dry, hot weather makes all ill, and the Boxers are threatening the destruction of the country by robbing and

---

69. Ren Fuxing, "'Xinzhou Yesujiao jinlihui shengtu," 108.
70. Broomhall, *Martyred Missionaries of the CIM*, 68.
71. Translated in Cohen, *History in Three Keys*, 86.
72. Edwards, *Fire and Sword in Shansi*, 53. Recall that Boxer leaders drew their personae from the opera traditions.

> killing missionaries and Christians.... The country is full of the wildest rumors and threats. The people have nothing to do but talk and they talk of killing the foreigners and Christians and we felt that the end may not be far off for any of us . . . things grow worse and worse and if the rain holds off it is hard to say what violence may not ensue. We know God could send relief thru rain if He thot [sic] best, and we know all our interests are in His hands.[73]

Perhaps the most entertaining of these rumors was recorded by Charles Price (ABCFM) of Fenzhou:

> Various stories were set afloat as to the power of the missionaries to prevent rain, ascribing almost superhuman strength in the way of controlling the elements. Clouds were continuously being driven away by fierce winds, which led to the story—thoroughly believed by all the people—that we went into our upper rooms and drove the clouds back by fanning with all our might. The story was changed as regards the T'ai Yuan Fu [Taiyuan] missionaries, that they were naked when doing the fanning.[74]

Price then went even further, suggesting in one diary entry that the drought conditions actually facilitated the spread of the anti-Christian rumors.

> It was about 1 June that we began to hear vague rumours of unusual unrest and talk against the foreigners and Church. This was caused by the continued drought, which was already being felt in the scarcity of food, and also by the lack of any useful employment for the people, so that they could congregate in the streets and talk over grievances, seeking to find a reason why this suffering should come upon them.[75]

Some of the most persistent water-related rumors in 1900 Shanxi involved accusations surrounding the supposed poisoning of local village wells. It was reported and commonly believed that Christians (Chinese and foreign) were for some reason or other using poison to dry up and contaminate local village wells.

> So great was the terror spread by these reports that numberless persons were killed who had no connection with Christianity whatsoever, for, in consequence of the long-existing drought,

---

73. Quoted in Cohen, *History in Three Keys*, 79–80.
74. Edwards, *Fire and Sword in Shansi*, 269.
75. Ibid. Note that the rumors of unrest appeared before the Boxers arrived.

many people were wandering about picking up a precarious living; and not a few of them were accused of being in the pay of foreigners, and killed at sight. It was extremely dangerous even for respectable foot-travellers to go about singly, especially if they happened to stop at a village well to drink. Immediately they might be seized and their belongings searched, to see if they had anything in the shape of medicine with which they could poison the water. For months many of the village wells were guarded day and night; and even in T'ai Yuan Fu the well-to-do people for three months would not drink any water drawn from the city wells, or employ the usual water carriers, but made their own servants fetch a supply from special wells outside.[76]

One typical Boxer placard included a "divine prescription" for a powerful poison antidote to be swallowed after drinking water from a poison well: mix together half an ounce each of dried black plums, *solanum dulcamara* (also known as bittersweet), and licorice root.[77]

Not all of the people's fears were related to foreign religion. The mining actions of foreign firms were also held accountable for the drought conditions, owing to the vast disturbance in the local *fengshui* which their earth-moving activities created—a pattern of blame that was common throughout Shanxi.[78] In Zezhou representatives from a large mining conglomerate called the Peking Syndicate had recently visited to make observations for a mine.[79] On passing through the city during his flight from the Boxers, A. R. Saunders was threatened and accused of being a member of that firm and was only allowed to proceed after he proved he was a Protestant missionary. Many of the missionaries who survived 1900 and managed to escape from Shanxi reported that their ability to prove that they were neither businessmen (the missionaries wore their hair in queues and dressed in Chinese clothes) nor Catholics (they traveled with their children and wives) secured them passage through the villages.

Opium-induced hallucinations and delusions would almost certainly have exacerbated the fears and stresses common during times of drought and famine. Rumors would have seemed all the more plausible, fears all the

---

76. Ibid., 54–55.

77. The full poster is translated in Landor, *China and the Allies*, 1: 22–24.

78. Broomhall, *Martyred Missionaries of the CIM*, 73. Meaning literally "wind-water," *fengshui* is a traditional Chinese system of geomancy wherein physical space, buildings, geography, and topography are seen as methods for controlling and managing spirits both good and bad.

79. On the Syndicate in pre-Boxer Shanxi, see Thompson, "'If Shanxi's Coal is Lost, Then Shanxi is Lost!,'" 1269–76.

more real when viewed through the haze of narcotics. As discussed above in chapter 2, much of the mission work in the province revolved around rehabilitation centers. Despite these efforts, 1900 Shanxi was still very much in the grip of opium. When Francis Nichols passed through Shanxi in 1902 he reported encountering entire villages lost to the drug. He recorded his impressions on entering one such village:

> Even from a distance the difference between the sad village and the rest is very marked. The walls at the entrance to it are crumbling as though the inhabitants had ceased to take any interest in spirits, good or evil. The roofs of the houses are dilapidated and full of holes. A nearer approach reveals windows from which the paper panes are missing and doors supported by only one hinge. No one is selling vegetables in the road, and the one or two shops which the village possessed are closed. In the shadow of the houses a few men and women are lying or squatting—apparently in a stupor. Their faces are drawn and leathery, their eyes glazed and dull. Their clothes are masses of rags, and, what is most hopeless of all, the men have neglected to braid their queues; their hair is disheveled and matted. Even some of the babies the women carry in their arms have the same parched skins and wan haggard faces. And the cause of this is *opium*.
>
> Such a village, whose wretchedness and degradation I have inadequately described, is known throughout the surrounding country as an "opium village." No matter how cheerful and gay my escort of Shansi police might be, they always became silent, and their faces grave and serious, whenever we passed a place of this kind.[80]

Every year a number of villages in the Shanxi countryside would succumb to the drug and slide into ruin. And while officials, local Chinese doctors, and missionaries alike ran refuges, their scope was still far too small compared to the scale of the problem. Once opium was introduced into a village, the missionaries claimed, it was usually only a matter of time before the entire village became addicted. Southern Shanxi was awash with opium fields; in fact, Chinese production had expanded to the point that by the end of the nineteenth century, Indian opium sales to China had been reduced by half.[81] Efforts by Manchu officials to suppress the cultivation of the drug in Shanxi had only produced riots from the farmers whose livelihoods were

---

80. Nichols, *Through Hidden Shensi*, 57–58.

81. The information within this paragraph is taken from the lengthy discussion of opium contained in chapter 5 "The Blight on the Land" in ibid.

dependent on the poppies. Quite simply, their small plots of land would yield much smaller profits if seeded with simple grain.[82]

And so opium was commonly consumed for recreational purposes and planted for profit throughout the turn of the century, thus supplying another layer of context to the Boxer phenomenon in Shanxi. Regardless of the exact nature of opium use and abuse in Shanxi, rumors shared with the passing of the pipe would surely have taken on increased dread and significance as they swirled around in the smoky air.

Official attitudes toward the Boxers only contributed to the spread of rumors. The ambivalence which the government initially showed toward the Boxers encouraged discussion of the colorful bands and their more exotic claims: "What will the government do?" and other sorts of hand-wringing were only natural. When the government finally decided to side with the Boxers, their decision gave the Boxers and their more fantastical claims a certain legitimacy in the eyes of the people.[83]

VIOLENCE ERUPTS IN SHANXI

Yuxian, the former governor of Shandong, arrived in Taiyuan on April 20, 1900, to take up his new responsibilities as governor of Shanxi. It is claimed that when he traveled to Shanxi he actually brought bands of Boxers with him, and it has even been said that he was personally involved in the founding and organizing of the earliest group of Boxer rebels.[84] Although there is little evidential support for these particular accusations, Yuxian was consistently anti-foreign and consistently loyal to the Qing.[85] Catholic sources claim that immediately after his arrival in Taiyuan, Yuxian began collecting local complaints against the Shanxi foreigners—and even suggest that he "legalized" Boxerism in the province and supplied them with weapons.

---

82. Mentioned in Williamson, *British Baptists in China*, 73.

83. See the discussion in Cohen, *History in Three Keys*, 170–71.

84. Broomhall, *Martyred Missionaries of the CIM*, 18. Broomhall claims Yuxian began recruiting additional Boxers and collecting church membership lists as soon as he arrived in Taiyuan, though he provides no citation. Broomhall, *HTCOC, 7, It is Not Death to Die!*, 313. Western accounts from the time universally hold Yuxian accountable for the Shanxi violence, hailing him as the leader of the Boxers. Modern scholars are less inclined to believe missionary claims of Yuxian-Boxer collusion, though they are also often predisposed to distrust things written by nineteenth-century missionaries.

85. Cohen describes Yuxian as "uncompromisingly anti-foreign." Cohen, *History in Three Keys*, 51.

These actions were supposedly driven by his fear of a Catholic uprising.[86] No doubt, Yuxian was also still bitter over the recent events in Shandong.

It is hard to say exactly when Boxers began to appear in Shanxi, but there seems to be little support for Boxer bands in the province earlier than May. The earliest recorded act of violence took place on May 14 in Hongdong. The local Boxer band announced in the midst of their drilling that they would go immediately to the home of local Christian leader Elder Si and kill him.[87] They then marched on his home, looted the premises, and stabbed Elder Si with a sword. Dr. Millar Wilson (SYM) rushed to treat his wounds, and it was not until many months later that Si succumbed from complications of the wound. Next, on June 6, a "rain procession" in the city of Lu'an turned into an attack on the local mission premises.[88] Although no great damage was done in this instance, from this point on similar acts of protest and attack became increasingly common all across Shanxi. By June 14, Boxers were drilling in Datong and threatening the CIM missionaries stationed there.[89] The general consensus of mission records throughout Shanxi is that the Boxers were not generally active (or even visible) until June.

With the appearance of Boxers around many of the mission stations in the second half of June, tensions in Shanxi rapidly increased. By late June, stories had begun to circulate throughout the province of unrest and uprisings against missionary compounds. These were difficult to corroborate and often slow in arriving. Following her June 21 "Edict of War," the Empress Dowager Cixi took things one step further and on June 24 sent a secret order to officials all across China ordering the death of all foreigners. A sympathetic local official showed a CIM missionary in Henan a copy of the edict by a within which he reported seeing the following phrase: "Foreigners must be killed, even if they withdraw [or escape] they must still [or instantly] be killed."[90] Some of the imperial officials who were aware of the foolishness

---

86. The Catholic complaints against Yuxian are summarized in Clark, *Heaven in Conflict*, 103–6.

87. Broomhall, *HTCOC*, 7, *It is Not Death to Die!*, 321. Following Pastor Xi's death from sickness, Elder Si took up his responsibilities and thus was the leading Christian figure in the communities southwest of Taiyuan.

88. Ibid., 323.

89. Ibid., 327. It is interesting to note that the McKees (CIM in Datong) make no mention of Boxers until this relatively late date. Charles Price (ABCFM) claims that the first Boxers (two of them) did not appear in Fenzhou until June 15. Edwards, *Fire and Sword in Shansi*, 270. Price's observation, in light of Fenzhou's relative proximity to Taiyuan, makes the missionary claims of Boxers traveling with Yuxian and entering the province on April 20 seem less likely.

90. The date of this edict is taken from the diary of a Manchu official named Jingshan who corroborates the general shape and nature of the text as reported by the CIM

of the Empress Dowager's order were able to alter the words "when you meet a foreigner you must slay him," such that many provinces received orders to the effect that they "must protect him."[91] In the south and in places where the foreign presence was substantial, economically powerful, and advantageous, the Empress Dowager's declaration of war was simply ignored. But it was not ignored everywhere: in Shanxi, newly-appointed Governor Yuxian was eager to obey and eager to strike back at the foreigners. Following Cixi's order, things rapidly deteriorated. By the summer of 1900, when things finally turned violent in Shanxi, the Boxers were carrying banners that proclaimed "By imperial command exterminate the Church (*feng zhi mie jiao*)," a substantial development from their earliest Shandong slogans such as "Support the Qing, expel the foreigners (*zhi Qing mie yang*)."[92]

In early June, six CIM women from Pingyao (the Misses Eldred, Gauntlett, Higgs, Johnson, and Rasmussen, all led by the indomitable Eva French) left their station to stay with the Lundgrens (CIM) in nearby peaceful, rustic Jiexiu. On June 26 the Pingyao mission (CIM) was attacked and looted without loss of life.[93] News of this event soon reached Jiexiu, precipitating an attack on the Lundgrens' home that was thwarted through the assistance of a local mandarin who helped smuggle the missionaries safely out of the village.

A Chinese Christian who had been with the missionaries in Jiexiu agreed to carry all this news to Emily Whitchurch and Edith Searell (both CIM) in nearby Xiaoyi. Arriving in Xiaoyi on June 28, he thoughtlessly mentioned the Pingyao riots in the village square. Having heard the news, a mob of villagers rapidly formed and marched on the residence of the two women. A quick summons of the local mandarin defused the crisis, but he then pleaded with the women to leave since he could offer little protection. Early on the morning of June 29 the mob returned, broke down the gate

---

missionary in Henan. See discussion in Broomhall, *HTCOC*, 7, *It is Not Death to Die!*, 330–31. Though incredibly influential, the Jingshan diary has been debunked as a fabrication of the British Beijing resident Edmund Backhouse. Some of the diary's content is indeed accurate, but its more fantastical and uncorroborated portions are most likely not true. See discussion in Preston, *The Boxer Rebellion*, 325–34.

91. Steer, *J. Hudson Taylor*, 354. The Prefect of Fenzhou is said to have actually protested the command to Governor Yuxian himself. Broomhall, *Martyred Missionaries of the CIM*, 19.

92. Broomhall, *Martyred Missionaries of the CIM*, 19; Fairbank and Goldman, *China: A New History*, 230.

93. Following the Xiaoyi murders, the Lundgrens and Miss Eldred quickly removed to Fenyang to stay with their friends the Prices (ABCFM); the other five single ladies left to join the CIM workers in Linfen. Broomhall, *HTCOC*, 7, *It is Not Death to Die!*, 403–4, and 645 note 40.

and door to the women's home, and battered them to death as they knelt in prayer. Their bodies were stripped and defiled, and their premises sacked and looted. Name lists found in their home were then used to hunt down and destroy all Christians in the area. Since the massacre of Christians in Xiaoyi was so complete, it took some time before others in Shanxi knew the details of what had happened. Once word got out, other stations took measures to ensure that baptism and membership lists would not fall into Boxer hands.[94] The violence at Xiaoyi was a shock to the Shanxi Protestant community, and Whitchurch and Searell are often considered the first Shanxi foreign martyrs of the summer of 1900.

On June 24, ten members of the Swedish Holiness Mission were joined by two Christian and Missionary Alliance couples and their children for their annual conference in Shuoping in northern Shanxi. In response to placards posted around town, a mob formed and marched on the foreigners' compound, setting fire to the buildings before forcing local Christians and friendly neighbors into the blaze. The foreigners escaped to the sympathetic local magistrate's official compound (*yamen*), but he confessed that he was powerless to help them. Later on June 29, before they were able to arrange safe passage to Zhangjiakou, the missionaries were escorted to the edge of the town by a group of soldiers who then dragged all sixteen of the foreign men, women, and children out of their carts and stoned them to death. Their bodies were decapitated and burned before their heads were hoisted above the city walls.[95]

In Taiyuan, it was only after Cixi's war declaration that things began to deteriorate rapidly. As discussed above, while Chinese Christians in Shanxi had been suffering attacks since May, Boxer bands generally did not appear in villages with mission stations until the middle of June. And while Boxers were certainly present in Taiyuan (Chinese sources corroborate this), the violence that took place there in June and early July was not an exclusively Boxer phenomenon.

On June 27 the girls' school in Taiyuan under Edith Coombs's (initially CIM, then SYM) direction was dismissing for the summer, as this was the first day of the sixth moon of the lunar calendar. The school was located in one of the far corners of the Schofield Memorial Hospital, and Coombs was still present and superintending the eleven young scholars who, due to various circumstances, were unable to return to their homes on that day.[96]

94. Ibid., 343–44.
95. Ibid., 328, 335–36.
96. It is difficult to reconstruct the exact location of the Taiyuan Girls' School and Schofield Memorial Hospital premises—by 1900 all under SYM authority. Comparing a late-nineteenth-century map of Taiyuan with a similar map from the 1920s, it appears

The day had passed quite typically, with Dr. Lovitt (CIM) seeing around thirty outpatients at the dispensary. A few of the missionaries had read the Imperial Decree which had just been posted in the non-functioning Taiyuan telegraph office, but since it did not bear the official seal they treated it as simply another of the many rumors that circulated so freely that summer.

Later that evening, a crowd collected outside of the front gate of the hospital compound. Efforts by those inside to parley with the crowd were met with stones, and when the crowd reached a certain size they began to set fire to the various buildings of the compound one by one. As midnight approached, the situation became desperate, with few buildings remaining and most of the Chinese helpers gone. The staff decided to force a passage through the mob. Shielding their young charges as best they could, the group of teachers, students, doctors, and patients dashed through the fire set at the entrance to impede their escape. They used their arms to ward off the stones and bricks hurled by the crowd as they raced for the Farthing's (BMS) compound.[97] Coombs, upon exiting the gauntlet, noticed that two girls whose feet were slowly being unbound had been left behind.[98] She raced back into the maelstrom and carried the first child free of the flames. She returned again to the burning compound and as she was dashing out through the fire at the gate with the second child in her arms, she stumbled and fell. Immediately they were assaulted with bricks and stones. The young girl was pulled from beneath Coombs's body and whisked away to safety as Coombs herself was forced back into the fire. Fuel was heaped onto the fire and onto Miss Coombs as she knelt in prayer; though she twice rose from the flames, the crowd would not allow her to escape. The next morning her ashes were recovered and buried by some Chinese friends in the mission garden. Though only Miss Coombs was killed during the raid on the SYM

---

that the hospital and school were located on Dongjia Xiang, a small alley running due south from Xinghualing Xiang, a cross street of Wuyi Lu, one block north of Qiaotou Jie, where the main church was (and still is) located. In the late 1970s Dongjia Xiang was blocked off at its northern and southern ends by a machine shop and a public restroom, respectively, before the whole area was finally demolished in 2008 to make way for high-rise apartments and the new Red Cross Dental Hospital (Hongshizi Kouqiang Yiyuan). For street names, see Williamson, *British Baptists in China*, 64–65, 82–83.

97. Farthing's compound, which he apparently shared with the British and Foreign Bible Society, was located on Qiaotou Jie. The central church and the Taiyuan Boys' School were in the same area. See ibid., 64. One source claims the missionaries fired revolvers during their escape, striking at least one rioter. Miner, *China's Book of Martyrs*, 425.

98. For a firsthand account from one of the pupils that claims Coombs was merely lagging behind the rest of the missionaries as she assisted a lame pupil escape, see Miner, *China's Book of Martyrs*, 423–27.

compound, she was to be the first of many to lose their lives in Taiyuan that summer.[99]

For the next week or so, all of the Protestant missionaries kept indoors, gathered together at the homes of the Farthings, the Whitehouses (BMS), or the Beynons (British and Foreign Bible Society).[100] These premises were all "guarded" by soldiers, as were the now-closed gates and walls of the city proper. Since these homes were in residential areas, they were deemed safe from fire (since their destruction would necessarily imply the torching of all neighboring buildings). This was a tense time as the missionaries became increasingly aware of their tenuous position. Dr. Wilson expressed their mood in a letter to F. C. Dreyer (CIM) of Linfen: "It's all fog, but I think, old chap, that we are on the edge of a volcano, and I fear Taiyuan is the inner edge. I'd rather be where you are."[101] On July 5 a local official made the rounds, recording names of the missionaries and informing them that they must all move to a house where their safety might be better guaranteed.[102] Though rain delayed their departure, they eventually arrived under escort late on June 6 or early on June 7 to find that their band of twenty-six (including children) was to share a residence with the twelve foreigners who comprised the Catholic presence in Taiyuan; they were in fact under house arrest.[103] Having ordered another census of the foreigners just before noon on Monday, July 9, Governor Yuxian pretended to leave Taiyuan on a journey to the north before turning suddenly and leading everyone in the foreign

99. Edwards, *Fire and Sword in Shansi*, 60–67. See especially pages 60 and 67 for lists of who was where on the night of June 27. For the claim that Coombs knelt in prayer, see Williamson, *British Baptists in China*, 64.

100. The paradigmatic account of the July 1900 Taiyuan massacre is found in Edwards, *Fire and Sword in Shansi*, 68–72. Edwards bases his record on eyewitnesses interviewed just one year after the events—though he admits that the exact course of events may never be known. The fact that he finds no evidence to support missionary claims that Yuxian himself swung his sword on that day lends credence to his account. See also the supposedly firsthand accounts of Chinese eyewitnesses in Broomhall, *HTCOC*, 7, *It is Not Death to Die!*, 379–81; Clark, *Heaven in Conflict*, 116–21; and Miner, *China's Book of Martyrs*, 427–29. Broomhall's eyewitnesses, in particular, corroborate many of the details of Edwards's reconstruction.

101. Broomhall, *HTCOC*, 7, *It is Not Death to Die!*, 377.

102. Broomhall claims that the foreigners were held in the "previous headquarters of the Railway Bureau alongside the magistrate's *yamen* in the Boar's Head Lane (Zhu Tou Xiang)." See ibid., 379. This is challenged by a Chinese source, which states that the foreigners were held in a Mining Bureau office on the same street—possibly the same site repurposed. See Xu Shihu, *Li Timotai zhuanlue*, 58. According to an old map of Taiyuan from the 1920s, there was a Zhutou Xiang located south of Fuxi Jie across from Sanqiao Jie, a location that is indeed near the governor's compound.

103. For details of the arrest of the Catholic missionaries, see Clark, *Heaven in Conflict*, 112–16.

compound (including some hapless Chinese workers who were present on business) to his official compound. A group of soldiers was already present, waiting in the courtyard between the compound gate and the main street.[104] The governor lined up the missionaries and began interrogating them, pointedly asking them where they were from. As the foreigners confessed their nationalities, the governor ordered his soldiers to kill them—one by one at first, before impatience led to a swift and final massacre.[105] Later that afternoon seven missionaries recently arrived from Shouyang were first beaten and then killed on the same spot—once again at the governor's command.[106] All told, forty-five foreign men, women, and children were killed that day in front of the governor's compound in Taiyuan.[107]

There is some question as to the authenticity of the execution narratives surrounding the death of the Taiyuan foreign Christians. Roger Thompson has drawn attention to both the lack of substantiation for the massacre in contemporary Chinese and foreign consular records and the many similarities between the "eyewitness" accounts and the traditional martyr narratives

---

104. Some local Christians today believe the missionaries were killed outside the west gate of the governor's compound (a traditional location for executions). An old picture showing the governor's compound in 1902 seems to suggest the more prominent southern entrance as the massacre site. The present entrance to the compound and its location on Fudong Jie match the old photos, save for a large screening wall (*zhaobi*) that originally stood at the end of today's Shipin Jie, creating a small square in front of the gate. See the photos taken from the Central (Bell?) Tower and from the courtyard itself in Edwards, *Fire and Sword in Shansi*, 29 and 72, respectively. Forsyth supplies a suspicious amount of detail on the manner in which the various foreigners in Taiyuan faced death, though his account is generally more laconic than that of Edwards. Forsyth, *The China Martyrs of 1900*, 30–42, and 42 facing.

105. The Empress Dowager's declaration of war on the foreign powers meant that Yuxian was justified in killing the missionaries upon proof (or confession) of their status as foreigners: hence, his line of questioning.

106. Edwards provides a gripping account of the capture, transportation, imprisonment, and execution of the Shouyang group. The seven foreigners were the Pigotts and their son Wellesley, his tutor John Robinson, the governess Mary Duval, and the two Atwater girls (students boarding from the ABCFM team in Fenyang). See Broomhall, *HTCOC*, 7, *It is Not Death to Die!*, 341–42; Edwards, *Fire and Sword in Shansi*, 80–82. Pigott and Robinson supposedly preached to the crowds from the cart as they were carried away in shackles.

107. This total is derived from the generally agreed upon figure of twenty-six Protestants (as held in the former Railway Office), adding the twelve Catholics and the seven from Shouyang. The addition of Ms Coombs would raise the figure to forty-six. See the "martyr roll" in Forsyth, *The China Martyrs of 1900*, 40. According to one local eyewitness, the bodies of the Taiyuan dead (save some of their heads, which were posted as warnings to those who would not recant) were eventually given temporary burial outside the South Gate of the city (near the southwest corner of today's Dananmen). Broomhall, *HTCOC*, 7, *It is Not Death to Die!*, 382.

in older sources such as *Foxe's Book of Martyrs*.[108] Moreover, the memorial sent by Yuxian to the imperial government requesting a bounty for the foreigners he supposedly killed—a document used as evidence in support of Yuxian's role in masterminding the massacre—is also suspect owing to its dissimilarity with Yuxian's other writings, and the existence of other known forgeries attributed to the Chinese scholar who "discovered" the memorial. Rather than a deceitful ploy on Yuxian's part followed by a summary execution, Thompson suggests there was either a more general Taiyuan riot leaving many dead, or a straightforward execution of foreigners and local Christian leaders motivated by Yuxian's need to quell local fears of a coming Christian invasion with the missionaries in the vanguard.[109] While it is certainly true that primary sources relevant to the events of June and July in Taiyuan are sparse, often relying on "eye-witness" accounts with limited verification, the general course of events as portrayed by foreign and local Christians is by no means implausible. On the contrary, the simple fact that this account has stood for so long, giving ample opportunities for contradiction, suggests that while details may be questioned—particularly the more maudlin reports of how the various foreigners faced their deaths—the currently accepted narrative as summarized by Edwards remains the most likely.[110]

It is not known how many Chinese Christians were killed in Taiyuan in 1900.[111] After the foreigners were dispensed with, local Chinese Christians were rounded up for execution as well. One Shanxi missionary who managed to escape reported that once the local Christians were led to the square before the governor's compound, "the (Chinese) Christians had to kneel down and drink their [the foreign missionaries'] blood, and as they

---

108. This paragraph is a coarse summary of Thompson, "Reporting the Taiyuan Massacre," 65–92.

109. On Yuxian's fear of rebellion, see Clark, *Heaven in Conflict*, 115–16. Cohen seems to accept Edwards's accusation of deception on the part of the governor. Cohen, *History in Three Keys*, 51.

110. Clark similarly accepts the basic series of events as reported by Catholic sources in 1900. Clark, "Mandarins and Martyrs of Taiyuan," 98–99.

111. Yuxian's memorial (*zouzhe*) to the Emperor claims that seventeen Chinese "helpers" were killed in front of the *yamen* along with the forty-five foreigners. See Xu Shihu, *Li Timotai zhuanlue*, 58. BMS records claim that nine local Christians died in Taiyuan. Williamson, *British Baptists in China*, 66. One Shanxi Christian reported a rumor that twenty or perhaps even one hundred local Christians were killed in Taiyuan. From an August 22 letter by "C.C.H." as reprinted in Broomhall, *Martyred Missionaries of the CIM*, 267. For the testimony of "C.C.H." (Chang Chih-heng?), see Beauchamp, *Days of Blessing*, 127–28.

knelt, were killed—not one denied Christ."[112] Elder Liu Tingxuan, steward of the Taiyuan church, escaped with his life, leading him to remark in his later years that "God had not counted him worthy to die for Him in 1900."[113]

At roughly the same time (June 26–28), the various mission stations throughout Shanxi were attacked by rioting townspeople. Buildings were torched in many instances, and looting was common. Some missionaries were killed during these initial outbreaks, and these riots set the pattern for the attacks and fear which local Chinese Protestants and Catholics would face for the next few months. With communication so difficult, the missionaries formed into groups by proximity and happenstance and began as best they could to make their way to safety.

On June 29, upon receiving news of the attack on the SYM compound in Taiyuan, the members of the BMS station in Xinzhou fled the city to hide in a local Christian's cave dwelling located in an easily defended mountain pass.[114] After two weeks their location was discovered, but since they were known to possess firearms, their pursuers sent to Xinzhou for military assistance. After a brief struggle the hopelessly outnumbered missionaries surrendered to the soldiers. They were carried back to Xinzhou where they were thrown in the common jail until August 9, when they were told they would be escorted to the coast. Ten guards sent by Governor Yuxian himself led their carts outside the city gates where they were set upon, stripped, beaten, and then cut down with swords.[115] One Chinese source claims that the stain of the martyrs' blood on the walls of the city gate could still be seen when the Communists captured Xinzhou in 1948.[116]

---

112. From an undocumented letter from Matilda Way quoted in Broomhall, *HTCOC, 7, It is Not Death to Die!,* 383–84.

113. On the Sunday following Miss Coombs's death, Elder Liu led a few local Christians in worship at the rear of the Qiaotou Jie church. Williamson, *British Baptists in China*, 66.

114. The BMS missionaries present at the time in Xinzhou were Herbert and Elizabeth Dixon, Adam and Clara McCurrach, Bessie Renaut, and Sidney Ennals—the last two having only arrived in China within the previous year. Thomas and Fanny Underwood (also BMS) were also present on a visit from Taiyuan. Bell and Clements, *Lives From A Black Tin Box*, 175. Written by a Dixon descendant using family letters, this book provides a detailed and fascinating account of the lives of the Dixons, long-serving English Baptist missionaries to Shanxi.

115. Broomhall, *HTCOC, 7, It is Not Death to Die!,* 342, 416. According to Edwards, at least sixteen local believers from the Xinzhou district also perished at that time. Edwards, *Fire and Sword in Shansi*, 180–96. The English text of the Boxer martyr's monument later erected in Xinzhou sets the number of local Christians killed that year at forty. This is taken from the author's own photos of the tablet (for more on the tablet see below).

116. This detail comes from the politicized account of the Xinzhou martyrdoms in

While the rest of Shanxi was being torn apart with violence and persecution, the Christians both Chinese and foreign (ABCFM) in Taigu and Fenzhou enjoyed relative safety. Accordingly, they elected to remain rather than flee. On July 16 they finally heard about the massacre in nearby Taiyuan, by which time the Taigu team was engaged in a heated debate as to whether or not they should use force to defend themselves.[117] Their disagreement came to a sudden end on July 31, when a mob chanting "Kill! Kill!" broke into the Taigu compound, slaying all those they encountered. Some of the foreigners defended themselves with firearms from the flat rooftop, firing on the three hundred Boxers and soldiers below until their ammunition expired. The missionaries were quickly seized and beheaded, their bodies consigned to the burning flames of their homes and their heads delivered in baskets to Yuxian in Taiyuan.[118]

Despite their proximity to Taiyuan and Taigu, the ABCFM missionaries gathered in Fenzhou remained safe for another two weeks. By this time they had enough news of events elsewhere to realize the hopelessness and uniqueness of their own situation. Elizabeth Atwater described their mood in one of her last letters home:

> I have tried to gather courage to write . . . [about the massacre at Taiyuan, when her stepdaughters had been beheaded, and the second massacre at Taigu where her colleagues perished]. We have tried to get away to the hills, but the plans do not work. . . . The people know we are condemned. . . . I long for a sight of your dear faces, but I fear we shall not meet on earth. . . . I was very restless and excited while there seemed a chance of life, but God has taken away that feeling, and now I just pray for grace to meet the terrible end bravely. . . . My little (unborn) baby will go with me. . . . Dear ones, live near to God and cling less closely to earth. There is no other way in which we can receive that Peace from God which passeth understanding . . . My married life, two

---

Ren Fuxing, "'Xinzhou Yesujiao jinlihui shengtu,'" 109. For a more personal account of the flight and murder of the Xinzhou missionaries, see Bell and Clements, *Lives From A Black Tin Box*, 175–94.

117. Clapp, the senior missionary on station, was a pacifist, while the rest favored armed resistance. Brandt, *Massacre in Shansi*, 235–37.

118. Rowena Bird, Howard and Jenny Clapp, Francis Davis, Mary Partridge, and George Williams, along with many Chinese supporters, perished in this attack. Broomhall, *HTCOC*, 7, *It is Not Death to Die!*, 402–3. Brandt reports little or no resistance on the part of the missionaries. Brandt, *Massacre in Shansi*, 249–54. Yuxian used this attack to claim responsibility for a total of fifty-one (forty-five plus six) foreign heads: he then requested a cash reward from the Empress Dowager Cixi in accordance with this total. Broomhall, *HTCOC*, 7, *It is Not Death to Die!*, 381.

precious years, has been so very full of happiness. We will die together. . . . If we escape now it will be a miracle.[119]

Suddenly, on August 13, the local Fenzhou prefect who had been so friendly and sympathetic to the foreigners died and was rapidly replaced by a supporter of Yuxian. This new official confiscated the missionaries' weapons, bound the foreigners in a cart, and told them they were being sent to the coast. Thirty-seven miles out of town, a group of soldiers appeared and joined with their escort in slaughtering the entire group. Thus the last remaining members of the ABCFM in Shanxi perished.[120]

During the summer of 1900 the only way for foreigners to escape death in Shanxi was through flight. In general, fleeing missionaries headed either west for Xi'an in Shaanxi or south through Henan toward Hankou in Hubei. For those who escaped death, the road to freedom was not an easy one. One missionary recounted the experience:

> Most of us were left with only a pair of Chinese trousers on, the upper part of our bodies and heads being entirely unprotected from the awful burning of a July sun. . . . Although we were now almost naked, without either shoes or stockings, the people would not believe that we had no silver secreted about us, and we were beaten most unmercifully in the hope that such treatment would bring some confession as to where the silver was secreted. The people of one village would follow us to the boundary of the next, stoning us . . . and beating us on the back and head . . . from village to village. . . . Mr. E. J. Cooper was dragged to the outside of the village by a rope and left by the roadside as dead [the villagers feared his ghost]. If we sat down anywhere to rest awhile we were stoned and beaten all the more, and the only rest we got was under cover of darkness, when we retired to some lonely spot and slept on the hard ground outside.
>
> The first two days we had nothing to eat and no one who would even give us water to drink. . . . We were stoned into a large market town, and . . . we told the people that we could not go farther till we had something to eat. . . . [A]t last they gave us some bread and water and then escorted us safely out of town. When we had gone about two miles a man, altogether unknown

---

119. As recorded in Broomhall, *HTCOC, 7, It is Not Death to Die!*, 404.

120. All fifteen foreigners attached to the ABCFM in Shanxi died in the summer of 1900 along with (according to Broomhall) "nearly half the Chinese Christians associated with them." See accounts in Brandt, *Massacre in Shansi*, 264–67; and Broomhall, *HTCOC, 7, It is Not Death to Die!*, 403–5.

to us . . . took about three dozen hard-boiled eggs . . . and gave them to us . . . even at this unfriendly time in China. . . .[121]

Many of the deaths suffered by missionaries during that summer resulted from hardships suffered on their journeys to safety. As they fled across the Shanxi countryside, the missionaries faced robbery, nakedness, stoning, starvation, and disease, and in most cases they owed their lives to the whims of the local officials through whose districts they passed. As she and her family journeyed across southern Shanxi, seven-year-old Jessie Saunders remarked, "They treated Jesus like this, didn't they, Mother?"[122] The many hardships endured by the refugee Shanxi missionaries, as well as the faith with which they faced those trials, are both evident in E. J. Cooper's (CIM in Lucheng near modern day Changzhi) August 18, 1900 letter to his mother.

> It is now nearly three months since I wrote you last and as yet I have no letter from home, my last arriving about the end of May. I believe a cable was sent from Shanghai last Tuesday to London. If this was so, you will have learned that dear Maggie has gone to sleep in Jesus. I may as well tell you the worst first. She died at Yangshan, about 100 miles from Hankow, on August 6, after a month's pain and suffering for Christ.
>
> The Lord has honoured us by giving us fellowship in His sufferings. *Three* times stoned, robbed of everything, even clothes, we know what hunger, thirst, nakedness, weariness are as never before, but also the sustaining grace and strength of God and His peace in a new and deeper sense than ever.
>
> We fled from Lucheng on July 6 and reached Hankow (700 miles' overland journey) on August 14. My strength will not allow me to enter into details of the journey. The escape of any of us is a wonderful thing. . . .
>
> Dear Maggie's body was kindly sent down to Hankow by the Yingshan magistrate and was buried here last Tuesday (August 14), another of the party, Miss Huston, who had died still nearer to Hankow from the effect of wounds received in Shanxi, being laid beside her. Dr. Griffith John conducted the service. Dear wee Brainerd, who had come through in a wonderful way, was, within a few days of Hankow, attacked by sun diarrhea, and after his arrival here rapidly sank and peacefully fell asleep yesterday

---

121 From Saunders's letter as reported in Broomhall, *Martyred Missionaries of the CIM*, 70–71. These paragraphs describe the Saunders party's journey from Lu'an to Changzhi.

122. Jessie died on the road during her family's escape journey. Ibid., 21.

at 2 a.m. Dear, wee boy, so changed, oh! so thin. He was buried yesterday evening in the same grave as his dear mother.

Billow after billow has gone over me. Home gone, not one memento of dear Maggie even, penniless, wife and child gone to glory, Edith lying very sick with diarrhea and your son weak and exhausted to a degree, though otherwise well. I have been at the point of death more than once on the road. In one village, after a heavy stoning with brickbats, they put ropes under me and dragged me along the ground that I might not die in the village itself.

And now you know the worst, mother, I want to tell you that the cross of Christ, that exceeding glory of the Father's love, has brought continual comfort to my heart, so that not one murmur has broken the peace of God within.

If God spared not His own Son—all is love—but now we see through a glass darkly, but then face to face. Although wounded and suffering, Maggie said to me, "If the Lord spares us, I should like to go back to Lucheng if possible." Devoted soul denied by her Master of doing the work so near to her heart, she never turned in purpose and desire to win some of the Chinese for Christ. The Lord has accepted her desire and honoured her in her death for Him.

How much it means to me, I hardly realise, and do not know how the Lord will guide. China is in confusion, and probably twelve-month, at least, must pass ere inland work can be resumed.[123]

After all that had happened, Cooper's desire was to return to the work and the people who had cost him so much. Indeed, the cost of the Boxer turmoil was great: all told, 180 missionary men, women, and children were killed across Shanxi that summer, the vast majority (159) of them Protestants.[124] This disparity reflects the simple fact that there were more

123. Ibid., 79–80. Mary Huston and Hattie Rice, both of the CIM, accompanied the Cooper family during their journey. Rice died immediately from the wounds she and Huston received at the hands of Shanxi villagers.

124. The Shanxi figure is from Cliff, *Flame of Sacred Love*, 108. Taking into account the habit at the time of not distinguishing between the two areas, Cohen gives a total of 180 foreign deaths in the *combined* fields of Mongolia/Shanxi with 159 of those being Protestant, while he puts the total number of foreign Protestant Boxer-related foreign missionary deaths at around 178. Cohen, *History in Three Keys*, 52, and 310 note 75. Williamson gives a slightly different total of 171 missionary deaths in Shanxi, with (again) 159 of them being Protestant men, women and children. Williamson, *British Baptists in China*, 69. Of the total Protestant foreign deaths at Boxer hands that year, 79 of them were CIM personnel. Steer, *J. Hudson Taylor*, 356. In 1900 the CIM had 89 missionaries in Shanxi. Broomhall, *HTCOC*, 7, *It is Not Death to Die!*, 318.

Protestant than Catholic *missionaries* in inland China—and many of them were new arrivals in remote locations.[125] The Swedish Holiness Union or Helgelse Förbundet (Ruidian Shengjiehui) and the Scandinavian Alliance Mongolian Mission (Beimei Rui-Nuohui)—both formally associated with the CIM—lost all members but one in the summer of 1900. The Swedish Mongol Mission (Rui-Meng Xuandaohui) was completely destroyed. None of the missionaries attached to the SYM survived, apart from the Edwardses, who were in Britain on furlough at the time.[126] All BMS missionaries in Shanxi were killed.[127] For Chinese believers, Tianjin, Beijing, and all of Hebei were the most violent locations. In Beijing alone it is estimated that fifteen to twenty thousand Chinese Catholics lost their lives during the summer of 1900.[128] In Shanxi around two thousand Chinese Catholics perished, over five hundred of whom were under the age of ten.[129] Protestant losses exceeded four hundred lives—a smaller number but still totaling over a quarter of the Shanxi church population.[130] This difference in the number of Catholic and Protestant deaths was due largely to the fact that there were

---

125. Between 1890 and 1895 alone, some 1,153 *new workers* were added to the various Protestant mission societies working in China. Steer, *J. Hudson Taylor*, 340. Williamson puts the 1898 total for Protestant missionaries in all of China at just under 2,500. Williamson, *British Baptists in China*, 275. Cohen uses Latourette's numbers: the total number of Protestant missionaries in China doubled from 1,296 in 1889 to 2,818 in 1900. Catholic workers grew less dramatically from 639 in 1890 to 886 in 1900. Cohen, *History in Three Keys*, 93 note 100. Broomhall counts sixty Protestant societies with 2,400 members operating in 1900 China. Broomhall, *HTCOC*, 7, *It is Not Death to Die!*, 304.

126. Ibid., 456.

127. Williamson, *British Baptists in China*, 275.

128. The graves of Matteo Ricci and the other Jesuits were desecrated as well. Steer, *J. Hudson Taylor*, 354. Though Catholic statistics are less clear than contemporary Protestant sources, most figures place the total Catholic foreign deaths at around forty, with no sources exceeding forty-eight. Cohen, *History in Three Keys*, 310 note 75.

129. Harrison, *The Missionary's Curse*, 93, 113. On this point Edwards seems a little muddled. While giving a total of 4,500 native Christians (Protestant and Catholic) killed in the Shanxi-Mongolia area, he later claims that the Catholic Church alone suffered some 8,000 casualties across the province. See Edwards, *Fire and Sword in Shansi*, 135, 175. Williamson may be the source for Edwards's numbers: while citing Latourette's figure of 2,000, Williamson prefers to put Roman Catholic deaths at "over 8,000" from a total in the province of "about 15,000" Roman Catholic Christians. Williamson, *British Baptists in China*, 69.

130. Edwards gives a total of 380 Protestant believers dead in Shanxi exclusive of the region "outside the Great Wall," while Miner counts "over 400" local Protestant martyrs. Edwards, *Fire and Sword in Shansi*, 175; Miner, *China's Book of Martyrs*, 422. The total number of Chinese Protestants killed in all of China that summer may be as low as 2,000. Latourette, *A History of Christian Missions in China*, 517.

more Catholic believers in China and they had longer histories of interaction with local people and officials.[131]

Though we have only limited details of how the local Shanxi Christians suffered, the stories that have survived are striking.[132] Many believers took great risks to assist the fleeing missionaries, offering food, carrying bags, fighting off mobs, securing hiding places, or even just publicly befriending them. For those discovered to be aiding foreigners, the destruction of their homes, their possessions, and in some cases their lives was their only reward on earth for their assistance.[133] In many cases, simply being identified as a Christian was sufficient to earn unimaginable suffering, as attested to by the many testimonies recorded in the Protestant post-Boxer literature.[134]

Near Pingyang, crosses were carved into the foreheads of eighteen local Christians who were then made to stand in the sun until their scars became permanent. The local official, in an effort to save their lives, ordered them beaten on the thigh four to five hundred times and then thrown in prison. The women in the group had their hands beaten. Many of this group died.[135] In Taigu the Chinese adherents of the ABCFM mission church suffered greatly, with one prominent believer murdered in the door of the chapel.[136] In Shouyang the losses were particularly severe, with seventy-two local Christians killed during the Boxer turmoil. The Boxers and officials there devised tests to determine whether or not local believers had recanted. Some were brought before mock trials, some were asked to burn incense or kowtow to idols, and some were asked to step outside of a circle drawn in the sand within which was inscribed a cross: in all cases, those who refused met with death.[137] Men were disemboweled, children were killed in their mother's arms, and one woman was buried alive.[138] Sixteen believers attached to the BMS station in Xinzhou were also killed by Boxers.

131. For 1900, compare the figure listed above of one hundred thousand Protestants (from Stauffer's *Christian Occupation*) with Latourette's total of over seven hundred thousand Catholics. Hebei (which at that time was called Zhili) alone had over one hundred thousand Chinese Catholics prior to 1900. Cohen, *History in Three Keys*, 36, 93.

132. The letters of "CCH," a Chinese believer employed by the CIM, have been preserved and give some details of the remarkable faith demonstrated by many of these local martyrs. See the excerpts as translated in Miner, *China's Book of Martyrs*, 263–69.

133. A letter from Eva French includes the names and stories of many of those who helped in her escape. See ibid., 270–72.

134. See especially Edwards, *Fire and Sword in Shansi*, 173–211; and Miner, *China's Book of Martyrs*, 257–82.

135. Edwards, *Fire and Sword in Shansi*, 197; Miner, *China's Book of Martyrs*, 266.

136. Edwards, *Fire and Sword in Shansi*, 175–76.

137. Williamson, *British Baptists in China*, 68–69.

138. Edwards, *Fire and Sword in Shansi*, 152, 176–80.

Four members of the Zhao family in that district boldly sang their favorite hymn—"He Leadeth Me"—as the open cart carried them to their place of execution. One by one they refused to recant and were beheaded.[139]

Adding fuel to the fire, at some point in August an edict was passed by the Shanxi governor ordering all people in the province to practice the Boxer arts.[140] Similarly, on August 15, the provincial government began to provide certificates of protection to Chinese households who renounced Christianity.[141] While this almost certainly saved the lives of many in the province, it also led to recantations and the exodus of many from the church.

On February 16, 1901, Olivia Ogren along with Graham McKie and his two girls reached Hankou, they being the last foreigners to escape Shanxi. With little information, no food or money, and few friends, the story of the Ogren family's capture by and escape from Boxer bands is remarkable for its length and detail. With Ogren's return to safety that February, the torture, privation, murder, and death of the Shanxi missionaries finally came to a close.[142]

Already, those who had survived were looking forward to the future. Their sufferings had only served to increase their longing for God's Kingdom to grow in Shanxi. Matilda May wrote after her escape:

> I rejoice to think of the glorious harvest yet to come. I heard that the Taigu Christians had met for worship, and the Boxers had come and killed all but two . . . My first twelve months in China have been a wonderful experience . . . I am hoping to have a rest, and return to my work in Shanxi.[143]

---

139. Williamson, *British Baptists in China*, 68.

140. A Chinese Christian who supplied information for the CIM at the time claimed the edict was issued on August 7, but other missionary correspondences give other dates (all in August). See Broomhall, *HTCOC*, 7, *It is Not Death to Die!*, 414. Most likely the confusion arises from the different dates on which different localities would have been informed of the order.

141. An example of one such certificate of official renunciation for Yangqu County is reproduced in Edwards, *Fire and Sword in Shansi*, 110 and facing.

142. The full story of the Ogren family in Shanxi is now finally available in English translated from the original Swedish. Ogren, *The Last Refugees from Shansi*. For a shorter version, see Ogren, "A Great Conflict of Sufferings," 65–83.

143. Broomhall, *HTCOC*, 7, *It is Not Death to Die!*, 438.

THE AFTERMATH AND THE INDEMNITY QUESTION

By the fall of 1900 there were hardly any foreigners left in the province, and yet Shanxi's troubles were far from over.

As early as June 17, foreign forces had begun the process of recovering Tianjin and relieving Beijing.[144] On July 14 the "Eight-Nation Army" (Baguolianjun) finally managed to gain full control of all of Tianjin. The Russians and Japanese (supplying by far the largest numbers of soldiers) were particularly rapacious in their looting and destruction following the siege of Tianjin: Russian soldiers razed entire villages, while on one day alone Japanese soldiers delivered over 1.4 million taels of silver in stolen goods to one Japanese port. From Tianjin, however, the path to Beijing looked nearly impossible given the number of Chinese soldiers and Boxers stationed along the way. Further troops were requested and slowly arrived, largely supplied by Japan. Eventually, enough news escaped from the legations to make it clear that further delay would be disastrous, and so the forces set out. On the afternoon of August 14 the allies reached Beijing with British Sikh troops being the first to enter the legation compound.[145]

Once in Beijing, allied cooperation collapsed as the city was cleared of Boxers, Chinese troops, and anything and everything of value. Contemporary accounts are unanimous in decrying the behavior of the foreign troops as being even worse than the destruction and murder suffered by the people of Beijing at the hands of the Boxer and Qing forces. This issue was further confused by the ease with which Boxers could remove their red sashes and turbans and instantly blend back into the population. The commander of the American relief forces remarked to a journalist at the time that "where one real Boxer has been killed since the capture of Peking, fifteen harmless coolies or labourers on the farms, including not a few women and children, have been slain."[146] Over the next few months a series of punitive expeditions were launched from Beijing to suppress Boxer activities throughout various portions of northern China. Again, foreign violence was extreme—especially on the part of the Japanese and Russian armies.

---

144. The most readable account of the relief efforts is found in chapters 6 thru 14 of Preston, *The Boxer Rebellion*.

145. This basic account of the relief of the legations is taken from Broomhall, *HTCOC, 7, It is Not Death to Die!*, 405–15; Cohen, *History in Three Keys*, 53–57. The foreign relief effort was by no means a smooth and well-coordinated campaign, as the various accounts amply testify. Much of this is due to the tensions between the various foreign powers at the turn of the century. See Preston's particularly informative summary of the relations of the various foreign powers in the prologue to Preston, *The Boxer Rebellion*, ix–xxvii.

146. Major General Adna Chaffee quoted in Cohen, *History in Three Keys*, 55.

At four o'clock in the morning of August 15, the Empress Dowager Cixi and the still captive Guangxu Emperor fled Beijing disguised as beggars. On their way to Xi'an, they rested in Taiyuan for several weeks, with Cixi herself staying in the city's Confucian Temple (*wenmiao*). As Cixi and her court approached Taiyuan, labor was conscripted from the surrounding countryside, and small villages were built outside of the city for the majority of the Empress's entourage.[147] Food and other materials were gathered to support the traveling court during its two-week stay in the provincial capital. Despite the privations of the previous year, the people of Shanxi were expected to provide the imperial entourage with one hundred seventy thousand *jin* of grain, one hundred thousand *jin* of coal, over ten thousand *jin* of red meat, hundreds of fowl, and similarly large amounts of other goods as well.[148] Despite her demands, Cixi was not wholly unaware of her position—or the sufferings of the people: sometime during her stay in Taiyuan she issued an edict forbidding the Boxers to drill.[149] On October 1 Cixi and her court finally left Taiyuan for Xi'an. Unfortunately, by this time Shanxi's difficulties had expanded far beyond the Boxers.

As mentioned before, famine was a constant companion to life in Shanxi—especially in the central plain area surrounding Taiyuan—and the turn of the century was no exception. In February 1901 the local scholar Liu Dapeng reported that for every ten people who came to visit him in Jinci County to welcome the new year, eight or nine did not have enough food to eat.[150] Obviously the previous few years had been quite lean, and most of these villages would still have had vivid memories of the massive famine that had struck only twenty years prior.

---

147. One village associated with her visit, Qinglong Guzhen, has recently been restored as a tourist attraction just north of Taiyuan.

148. One *jin* is equal to about half a kilogram. Read Liu Dapeng's account of the visit in Qiao Zhiqiang, *Yihetuan zai Shanxi*, 26–27. When Francis Nichols noted the surprising quality of the roads and guesthouses between Taiyuan and the Shaanxi border he was told that improvements had been made to facilitate the Empress Dowager's flight from Beijing. He reported that the notoriously bad road through Linshi alone required the work of five thousand soldiers for two weeks just to make it passable. See *Through Hidden Shansi*, 88 and 90 respectively.

149. *Fire and Sword in Shansi*, 111.

150. From his diary entry of February 22, 1901. Liu Dapeng, *Tuixiangzhai riji*, 90. The writings of Liu Dapeng are an invaluable source of information for historians of late-Qing and Republican China. A gifted scholar from the Jinci area just outside of Taiyuan and an astute observer, Liu Dapeng kept a daily diary from 1891 to 1941 in addition to writing several other occasional pieces.

The specter of famine was particularly troubling for the Chinese Christians left in Shanxi. A Christian photographer named Chu from Taiyuan described the situation well in a letter written in February 1901.

> At present the Christians are still suffering. With houses burned, their friends killed, their property looted, their grain stolen, and made again to pay the temple taxes, no one inquires into their case. They will soon be either frozen or starved to death. The officials still expect them to pay the taxes. Pray, quickly have a telegram sent to the Governor to say that the Christians need not this year pay the taxes, as they have passed through such heavy troubles. The Christians of Fen Chou Fu, T'ai Yuan Fu, Hsin Chou, and Tai Chou,—altogether fifteen districts,—amounting to more than four thousand people, have had eight-tenths or nine-tenths of their property destroyed. We have also had a very bad year (famine), and if we do not obtain relief by next spring all the Christians will starve. We trust that at an early date our pastors may be able to return to Shansi, by the grace of God, to help His church.[151]

In addition to the famine troubles, many villages were still embroiled in violent local conflicts. At the end of the nineteenth century, the area around Taiyuan and Yuci was peppered with villages that were almost completely Catholic. Beginning in the summer of 1900 and continuing well into 1901, many of these villages were involved in large-scale armed conflicts with their non-Christian neighbors.[152] Motivated by fear, revenge, and hunger, conflicts and rumors of conflicts raged throughout central Shanxi with both Catholic and non-Catholic villages taking turns as the aggressors.[153]

Finally, evangelistic work had been dealt a serious blow, especially in the countryside. Villagers were very much afraid that another outburst of Boxerism was possible; they did not want to be caught on the wrong side. When asked to believe in Christ, cynical villagers often responded with a question of their own: "Do you wish us to believe in a God who couldn't protect his people in 1900?" Recantations and the deaths of many church leaders also posed a significant challenge to the future of the church.[154]

By 1901 the continuing fears of violence and famine which gripped the populace were also exacerbated by the threat of the impending invasion

---

151. As translated in Edwards, *Fire and Sword in Shansi*, 116.

152. Harrison, "Village Politics and National Politics," 1–15.

153. Liu Dapeng gives examples of the kind of fear these conflicts created. See the two translated examples in Cohen, *History in Three Keys*, 158.

154. Williamson, *British Baptists in China*, 81.

of the province by foreign troops. German soldiers stationed in Baoding finally received the order in April to remove the Chinese troops who were guarding the Guguan Pass on the Hebei-Shanxi border. On April 25 the pass was taken with little or no Chinese resistance, and the foreign troops returned to Baoding to await the command to advance into Shanxi. Fearing that the long-awaited invasion had finally come, Chinese troops fled from the border region looting villages, pillaging fields, and stealing women all along the way. This led officials in Taiyuan to believe that foreign troops were in fact pressing the attack and marching toward Taiyuan. Finally convinced of the need to seek resolution, the governor, under the guidance of the head of the foreign affairs bureau in Taiyuan, sent off a telegram imploring Timothy Richard to return to the province and help settle affairs before foreign military occupation was accomplished.[155]

Richard immediately left Shanghai for Beijing, where he and doctors Iranaeus Atwood and Eben Edwards met with the venerable statesman Li Hongzhang to discuss the settlement of the mission troubles. They presented a list of seven proposals which they felt would best resolve the situation and satisfy the demands of all parties. While arguing for leniency toward rank-and-file Boxers, they requested that Boxer leaders be punished and the local people and officials be fined to pay for the support of those orphaned and widowed during the turmoil. Any further trouble from Boxers, however, was to be punished with absolutely no leniency whatsoever. The delegation also asked that monuments be erected in each area where Christians were murdered, stating clearly that the deaths were without cause. Upon the return of missionaries to the province, local officials were to receive them properly with appropriate expressions of apology being rendered by the people, the gentry, and the officials. Finally, a total of five hundred thousand taels of silver collected over a ten-year period was to be extracted from the entire province for the establishment of a Western institution of learning.[156] Chinese statesman Li Hongzhang was sympathetic and supported the missionaries' recommendations.

On June 22 a party of representatives from the various agencies which had been previously working in Shanxi set out from Beijing. Dixon Hoste, Archibald Orr Ewing, C. H. Tjader, and Ernest Taylor represented the CIM;

---

155. The telegram is translated in its entirety in Edwards, *Fire and Sword in Shansi*, 120–22.

156. The list of proposed regulations is translated in full in ibid., 122–24. Edwards values the five hundred thousand tael fine at around £66,000 or approximately £7,000 a year—roughly what Xinzhou, Taigu, and Pingyao each spent annually on their individual opera festivals. Brandt estimated the total Shanxi indemnity to be worth $375,000 in 1900 U. S. dollars. Brandt, *Massacre in Shansi*, 278.

Moir Duncan and Creasy Smith represented the BMS; Atwood represented the ABCFM; Edwards represented the SYM; and Major Pereira of the Grenadier Guards accompanied the group in an unofficial capacity.[157] Having passed through Baoding on their way, the party arrived in Taiyuan—quite by accident—on July 9, 1901, precisely one year after the massacre of the foreign missionaries in that city.

The recommendations earlier presented to Li Hongzhang in Beijing were now accepted and slowly enacted in Taiyuan and the rest of Shanxi. Governor Yuxian was executed. Boxer names were recorded and stored in government offices all across Shanxi, and 107 Boxer "leaders" were executed for their actions.[158] In accordance with missionary wishes, memorials were erected throughout Shanxi—and especially in Taiyuan.[159] The text of one

---

157. Edwards, *Fire and Sword in Shansi*, 126, 131.

158. Ibid., 135. Beach claims that "the archfiend" Yuxian had been executed following "the restoration of order" along with a few other guilty officials. See Beach, *Dawn on the Hills of T'ang*, 142. While Yuxian was certainly executed in 1901, accounts of his death vary widely. Arthur H. Smith claimed in his 1901 account that Yuxian was paraded out of Taiyuan as a hero—with monuments erected in his praise. Edwards claimed that the Empress Dowager welcomed him to Beijing by giving him a scroll personally written by her. Another source has Yuxian banished for life in November until foreign demands for his execution were eventually granted. In another account, Yuxian was having dinner with friends when the order for his execution arrived; he then retired into seclusion before he was beheaded the next day. These accounts are summarized in Brandt, *Massacre in Shansi*, 277–78.

In accord with the traditions of Chinese officialdom, many of those implicated in the Boxer atrocities would likely have committed suicide. Hai Ying, the official in Xinzhou who oversaw the execution of the foreign missionaries there, abandoned his post in the county seat and went into hiding in Ningwu where he later poisoned himself. Ren Fuxing, "'Xinzhou Yesujiao jinlihui shengtu,'" 109.

159. The first monument was erected in the Taiyuan foreigners' cemetery—henceforth known as the Martyr Memorial Cemetery. Next, the Railway Bureau/Mining Bureau (in Zhutou Xiang) where the foreign community was imprisoned was demolished and a pavilion with a garden and memorial tablet erected. Memorial tablets were also placed in a wall near the scene of the massacre at the governor's *yamen*. The SYM compound ruins (school, residences, and hospital in the Xinghualing Xiang and Dongjia Xiang area) were rebuilt, with the Dongjia Xiang gate christened the Coombs Memorial Gate. A large stone was also erected outside the South Gate of the city wall in place of a previous stone praising Governor Yuxian. Finally, a sympathetic official arranged for Pig's Head Alley (Zhutou Xiang) where the foreigners were imprisoned to be renamed "Heaven's Peace Lane" (Tianan Jie). This information is found scattered throughout the literature, especially in Williamson, *British Baptists in China*, 64–67.

One elderly local recalled that it was necessary to remove a large wayside pavilion (*liangting*) before his work unit could build their factory near the western entrance of Xinghualing Xiang in the mid 1970s. This factory was a large beige brick building with yellow accents and cement stars that sat on Xinghualing Xiang between the old Taiyuan Men's Hospital and the newer Red Cross Dental Hospital—since 2008, the site of a large high-rise housing development. The pavilion he mentioned (very likely the Coombs

extant martyr tablet from Xinzhou demonstrates the kind of sentiment that was expressed at the time.[160] The monument was a four-sided stone construction of some size, with texts carved in both Chinese and English. The English text listed the names of the eight foreign missionaries who perished, explaining that the monument was erected in memory of ". . . the Baptist Missionaries who were slain by the sword in the East Gate of Hsin Chou City on August 9th 1900, during the [Boxer rising], and also of the forty Chinese Christians." The main Chinese text is better preserved, and perhaps more instructive.

> The Martyr's Memorial Tablet of the Xinzhou Protestant British Baptist Saints
>
> In the Gengzi Year of the Guangxu Emperor's reign, bandits rose up and on the fifteenth day of the seventh month massacred within the East Gate eight British pastors and teachers. Also, the forty men and women from Xinzhou, Daizhou, Guo County, and Fanshi associated with the church and school who suffered. These Chinese and British honorable devotees were loyal in their deaths. Confucius said, "dying to achieve virtue" and Mencius talked about "laying down one's life for a just cause." Is that not what this represents? This tablet was established so that this will not be forgotten.

The top crosspiece of the tablet was inscribed in Chinese with the text of 1 Peter 2:21, "To this you were called, because Christ suffered for you, leaving you an example, that you should follow in his steps."[161]

Memorial Gate and tablet) was (Yuanlin Ju) to either Yingze Park or the Children's Park (this last location being considered the more likely site). I have been unable to ascertain the exact location, as the City Parks Bureau Director from the 1970s was deaf and senile when I interviewed him in 2003.

160. In October of 2006 Prudence Bell, the granddaughter of Herbert Dixon's eldest son Benjamin, visited Shanxi. During the visit, Bell was generous with materials, providing a wealth of information for this book, including a transcription of the journal Herbert Dixon kept during his few weeks in hiding prior to arrest. During their visit to Xinzhou, Prudence and her husband Stuart were warmly received by local believers who were eager to show the descendants of "their" martyrs various mission properties in addition to the monument. Perhaps most touching, these believers—with tears in their eyes—sought forgiveness from Bell for their forefathers' failure to deliver the Xinzhou foreign martyrs. Bell and Clements, *Lives From A Black Tin Box*, 196–207.

161. The memorial erected to commemorate the deaths of the Dixons and their coworkers in Xinzhou still survives, albeit in disrepair, as a collection of large chunks of masonry strewn about a field. The monument has been disassembled over the years as locals have sought to uncover any valuables buried within or near the spot. Photos in the possession of this author record the various texts still preserved—though many sections are truncated, as reflected in the record of the English text above. The Chinese

On the morning of July 18 the mission representatives and government officials gathered in Taiyuan at a platform located just outside the western gate of the governor's compound and began the funeral procession which eventually led to the "martyr's cemetery" where banners, name placards, and tombstones were on display.[162] Following remarks by the various officials, the funeral ceremony proper was conducted by Dixon Hoste on behalf of the various societies present. Edwards wrote at the time of his impression of the ceremonies.

> It was a beautiful day, and as from the pavilion one looked over the thirty-four new graves to the city and plain beyond and the high mountains to the west, all so peaceful, it was hard, nay almost impossible, to realise what actually happened only a year and ten days before. Outwardly a great difference between now and then, and yet one instinctively felt the difference to be only superficial. It is true that representatives of the gentry were at the cemetery, but neither they nor any of the merchants' guilds gave any tangible token even of respect . . . although six of these guilds combined to erect a memorial tablet extolling the monster Yu Hsien [Yuxian]. The people appeared to be sullen rather than repentant.[163]

Alongside all these formal rituals, practical steps were taken to restore and preserve the peace as well. First, by 1902 a modern provincial police force had been established to escort and protect foreigners traveling legally within Shanxi province.[164] The more pressing issue in 1901, however, was

---

text is recorded in Ren Fuxing, "'Xinzhou Yesujiao jinlihui shengtu,'" 104, translation mine. Note also that this same article incorrectly records the English text as referring to Governor Yuxian, going so far as to attribute the use of an abbreviation and lower case letters as an attempt by the mission community to show their contempt for the Shanxi governor. The English text as engraved makes no mention of the governor—most likely the Chinese author of the article misread the partially obscured English letters for "Boxer rising" as "Gover' yising."

162. Edwards records the path taken to reach the cemetery, and it appears to yield a location similar to the one which Harry Wyatt describes so many years later. Compare Edwards, *Fire and Sword in Shansi*, 137; and Payne, *Harry Wyatt*, 91–93. According to Williamson, Chinese Christian martyrs were also buried there. Williamson, *British Baptists in China*, 66. The martyrs may very well have been buried on land adjoining the original Taiyuan foreigners' cemetery. Eva Price attests to the existence of a cemetery in Taiyuan for foreign workers as early as 1890. Price, *China Journal*, 37. Broomhall claims that a plot of land was given by Governor Zeng Guoquan to bury Whiting's body in Taiyuan following the North China Famine relief efforts that would give a much earlier (ca.1880) date. Broomhall, *The Jubilee Story of the CIM*, 124 note 1.

163. Edwards, *Fire and Sword in Shansi*, 138–39.

164. Nichols, *Through Hidden Shensi*, 45–48. On his trip to Xi'an in 1902 Francis

the question of compensation for lives and property lost during the Boxer turmoil. Though it may seem strange that the foreigners would ask the Chinese government to pay for losses sustained at the hands of a group of local rebels, it must be remembered that at the high point of Boxer turmoil the government, in the person of the Empress Dowager, actually allied with the Boxers and declared war against the foreign powers. Given contemporary international customs it was perfectly acceptable for the Western powers to expect remuneration from the Boxer allies. The Protestant mission societies, though aware of this custom, nevertheless shared a keen desire to distance themselves from the atrocities committed by the soldiers, and by extension the governments, of the foreign nations participating in the suppression of the Boxer turmoil in the summer and fall of 1900. But the question of providing for the surviving local Christians remained, with each of the societies adopting different methods and rationales for settling its affairs.

The LMS, for example, appears to have accepted cash reparations for lives lost—only to later renounce the reparations following further outbreaks of local anger. The ABCFM made no claims for mission property lost, but actively sought land and financial compensation for lives and property lost by the local Christian community.[165] The various American societies felt so strongly about this issue that they petitioned the U. S. Government to include in its official reparations to the Chinese state "indemnities for societies, individuals and Chinese who had suffered 'in person or in property in consequence of their being in the service of foreigners.'" Unfortunately, the mercenary relationship that these funds implied did not help the Chinese church and her struggle for independence. The SYM waived all claims to indemnities on behalf of losses suffered to mission premises or foreign personnel: this understandably impressed the local officials and the people very greatly.[166]

While the CIM is often praised for their desire to have nothing to do with "blood money," they were eager to accept compensation for Chinese believers who lost their lives during the turmoil.[167] Though they were un-

---

Nichols passed through Shanxi, where he was escorted by these new police (proudly displaying their English language "Shansi Police" badges). He was favorably impressed by their efficiency and politeness.

165. All across north China the ABCFM (on behalf of local believers) acquired a total of ninety-six acres of land and had nineteen chapels rebuilt by local Boxer supporters. Broomhall, *HTCOC*, 7, *It is Not Death to Die!*, 464.

166. Edwards includes a full translation of his official settlement with the governor on behalf of the SYM. It is a remarkable document, regrettably too lengthy to reproduce here, providing a detailed tally of losses suffered before renouncing all claims to compensation. See *Fire and Sword in Shansi*, 154–57.

167. For an account of how the exact figures involved were arrived at and distributed, see the CIM account in Broomhall, *HTCOC*, 7, *It is Not Death to Die!*, 476.

willing to have their name associated with Richard's university, they were strongly in favor of its establishment. They maintained their position by separating the mission and its property from the cases of the local Christians. In contrast to the American societies, the CIM treated the sufferings of local believers as matters between the Chinese Christians and their own imperial government. These (unlike the mission's own properties) were not questions for the foreign powers to raise with the Chinese government though, of course, the mission would use its power to help as much as it could.[168] When the CIM presented its rightful demands for the loss of foreign lives and property—and then summarily refused to be compensated for those demands—they were praised by the provincial government. On October 11, 1901, a proclamation was issued in every location where the CIM and its associate missions had worked.

> The Mission [CIM], in rebuilding these churches with its own funds, aims in so doing to fulfill the command of the SAVIOUR OF THE WORLD, that all men should love their neighbours as themselves, and is unwilling to lay any heavy pecuniary burden on the traders or the poor. I, the governor, find . . . that the chief work of the Christian religion is in all places to exhort men to live virtuously. From the time of their entrance into China, Christian missionaries have given medicine gratuitously to the sick and distributed money in times of famine. . . . They regard other men as they do themselves, and make no difference between this country and that. Yet we Chinese . . . have treated them not with generous kindness, but with injustice and contempt, for which we ought to feel ashamed . . . contrasting the way in which we have been treated by the missionaries with our treatment of them, how can anyone who has the least regard for right and reason not feel ashamed of this behaviour.[169]

According to Edwards, the official settlement ultimately granted by the governor for the losses suffered by the Chinese Christians was as follows: the CIM received 73,156 taels for their 156 adherents who were killed, the BMS received 35,776 taels for 112 murdered congregants, the ABCFM was given 25,000 taels for their 79 dead, and the SYM received 5,600 taels in compensation for their loss of 27 adherents. Not only were the demands made by the Protestant societies relatively light, but they also brought with them 26,000 taels of silver to be distributed throughout the province for

---

168. This paragraph is based on the fascinating discussion of indemnities in ibid., 462–70.

169. As translated in ibid., 481.

famine relief. The Protestant negotiators were officially and publicly praised by the governor for their leniency and generosity. He noted in his proclamation that "Everywhere where there had been mischief done by the Boxers [the Protestant missionaries] relieved all according to one rule—not distinguishing between Christians and non-Christians."[170]

While some Protestant mission groups refused indemnification for foreign losses during the summer of 1900, the Catholics in Shanxi were quick to voice their demands once Boxer violence had subsided. The Catholics chose to negotiate their terms through the French government and appropriate ecclesiastical figures as follows: first, either the governor's compound, the Confucian School (called the Lingde Tang), or the military officers' school (*lujun xuetang*) should be handed over to the Church and transformed into a cathedral and a monastery; second, the people of Shentie Town in Yuci County and the people living in Taiyuan's Jinci Town should be expelled and those two areas reserved for the residence of Chinese Catholics (these two towns were thought to be the centers of Boxer activities); finally, an indemnification of ten million silver taels was requested as compensation for the losses suffered by Shanxi Catholics at the hands of the Boxers.[171]

These demands were met with incredulous stares by the Shanxi officials. Shanxi was far too poor to provide these sums, and the officials would rather lose their jobs than grant such requests. Accordingly, the foreign Catholic fathers, local Catholic priests, and local adherents supposedly sent letters to the coast requesting that foreign soldiers enter Shanxi and relieve the suffering of the local believers. Had the foreign powers (in this case the German or French forces) responded favorably to these letters, it is possible that the resulting military presence would have forced the Shanxi government to accede to the Catholic demands. However, political bungling in Beijing by Barnaba Nanetti, one of the few surviving priests from Shanxi, resulted in the loss of foreign diplomatic sympathy for the Catholic Church in the province—and Nanetti's disgraceful recall to Italy.[172] Left with no alternative, the Catholic community took matters into their own hands and forcefully occupied the Confucian School in Taiyuan, while throughout the villages of Shanxi local priests continued to press aggressively for funds from the local populace to support the masses and burial expenses for their dead. Eventually the chief of the Shanxi Provincial Foreign Bureau negotiated a settlement from the Catholics through the French Government. This final agreement provided a greatly reduced indemnity of 2.25 million taels

---

170. Edwards, *Fire and Sword in Shansi*, 157–58.

171. This list of demands is taken from Xu Shihu, *Li Timotai zhuanlue*, 65.

172. Harrison, *The Missionary's Curse*, 118–21.

and made no mention of land; not surprisingly, the Catholics in Taiyuan were still unwilling to return the Confucian School to its rightful owners. The head of the Foreign Bureau finally recovered the school from the Catholics by reminding them that without consular protection, the foreign priests' passports had become invalid; if they did not return the property they would be forcibly removed from the province.[173]

It was also at about this time that the SYM agreed to join with the BMS. As the only surviving member of the SYM, Edwards, after refusing all compensation from the government, personally saw to the rebuilding of the hospital and SYM residences in Taiyuan as well as the church and residences in Shouyang out of his own personal funds.[174] The provincial officials were so moved that they erected a tablet outside the hospital commemorating this generous act, and the governor himself went so far as to contribute seven hundred taels toward the reconstruction of the SYM properties. In September 1902, Edwards formally handed over all properties to the BMS, which he then joined.[175] In the same year, the central church on Qiatou Jie was reopened following its reconstruction funded entirely by local believers, who contributed one tenth of their indemnity for that purpose.[176] The Taiyuan Boys' Boarding School was reopened as the Farthing Memorial School by Arthur Sowerby, while newly arrived Miss M. E. Shekleton reopened the Girls' Boarding School. Both institutions were revived in order to provide for Boxer orphans of local Christian families, although the increasing interest in Western learning during this period led to the eventual acceptance of students from non-Christian families.[177]

Most of the demands of the Protestant societies were quickly met by the Shanxi authorities, but Timothy Richard's proposal to indemnify a Western-style school of higher learning in Shanxi still faced many challenges.[178] Just

173. The story of the Catholic settlement is told with little sympathy in Edwards, *Fire and Sword in Shansi*, 165–72.

174. The names SYM hospital, Schofield Memorial Hospital, Yesujiao Yiyuan, and Taiyuan Men's Hospital all refer to the same building/site. Guo Jinfeng, "Jiaohui yiyuan jianzhu," 24.

175. Williamson, *British Baptists in China*, 80–81.

176. Ibid., 81.

177. The Boys' School may have initially occupied buildings on the Qiaotou Jie property—Williamson lists it as an "adjunct" to the Qiaotou Jie church. Ibid.

178. Eyewitness accounts of the founding of the university are numerous including, Edwards, *Fire and Sword in Shansi*, 160–65; and Richard, *Forty-Five Years*, 299–307. The most recent English-language study of the university is Johnson, *Timothy Richard's Vision*, 89–111. For accounts that emphasize Chinese contributions to the founding of the school, see Li Aisi, "The Founding of Shanxi University"; and Xing Long, *Shanda wangshi*. On the CIM's discreet support for the school see Broomhall, *HTCOC*, 7, *It is Not Death to Die!*, 479.

as Richard began to bring together his "Shanxi University" (Shanxi Daxue) a new Imperial decree ordered local schools to upgrade their status to that of "university." After extended negotiations with Shanxi Governor Cen Chunxuan and the supervisor of the recently upgraded "university" Shen Dunhe, Richard convinced all involved to combine the local Confucian school with his own proposed school, thus creating two departments within one newly established Shanxi "Imperial" University.[179] Richard also had to address local fears that this school would not actually teach anything, but would rather be a blunt tool for proselytizing and indoctrinating Shanxi's brightest young people. Here compromise was needed, and Richard eventually agreed that religion would not be a required course; he was confident that godly teachers and extra-curricular activities would present opportunities for the gospel. He refused, however to disallow Christian teachers and to prohibit religious activities outside the classroom. When pressed on these points by provincial government officials, he reminded them of the religious freedom guaranteed by all of China's treaties with the West—was the governor now authorized to abrogate treaty rights? Richard won his point.[180] Finally, Richard was also criticized by fellow missionaries who thought he was passing up a great opportunity to set up a Christian university in China. Richard was realistic, however, and realized the difficulty of attracting students and winning official support. He also knew that such a school would only sow the seeds for further resentment and bitterness.[181]

Despite these difficulties, Richard's plan was finally adopted. According to the official contract for the founding of the school, after the stipulated ten years the entire school would revert to the ownership and management of the government of Shanxi.[182] In accordance with all the various societies' wishes, the contract made no mention of the word "indemnity." Richard himself was responsible for organizing the school, calling six American and

---

179. The Western Studies Department was referred to as the *xixue zhuanzhai* in all contemporary Chinese literature. The Chinese Studies Department (*zhongxue zhuanzhai*) was formed from the same Confucian School that the Catholics had fought over. The Confucian School itself had taken the name Shanxi University in accordance with the August 1901 official proclamation ordering the elevation of all high-level schools to that of university. This Confucian School (reborn as the Chinese Studies Department) combined with Richard's original idea of a Sino-Western University (now transformed into the Western Studies Department) to become Shanxi Imperial University. For a recent scholarly analysis of these initial negotiations see Li Aisi, "Towards Building Direct Educational Partnership," 188–210.

180. Richard, *Forty-Five Years*, 300–301.

181. Xu Shihu, *Li Timotai zhuanlue*, 77–78.

182. The entire contract (from which most of this paragraph's information is taken) is printed in ibid., 69–76.

European teachers and translators to posts in the Western Studies Department with Moir Duncan to serve as superintendent.[183] His old language helper Gao Daling was asked to serve as a tutor in the new school.[184] Textbooks were to come from a new translation institute in Shanghai also established by Richard with a portion of the Shanxi Boxer funds.[185] Originally, the plan was to offer courses of study in letters, law, engineering, and medicine, but the medical program was never implemented due to insufficient funding. Finally, on June 26, 1902, the Western Studies Department officially opened with an initial enrollment of ninety-eight students.[186]

One of the early buildings from the Western Studies Department of Shanxi University still stands today as a testimony to Christian forgiveness and as proof of the sincere desire of those missionaries to improve the lives of the people of Shanxi province. A former president of Shanxi University from the 1940s voiced his appreciation as follows:

> Given the historical conditions of [1900] Shanxi and her ignorance of Western learning, having Mr. Richard come and personally establish the Western Studies Department in order to bring in Western learning and to train up for the entire province a great number [of students] who accept Western educational techniques, who build railways, who open mines and create

---

183. Following Duncan's death in 1906 Rev. W. E. Soothill (Methodist Missionary Society) served as principal. Williamson, *British Baptists in China*, 80. By 1911 the Western Studies Department had a faculty of thirty-six, of whom fifteen were foreigners. See the list from the commemorative name tablet (*timing bei*) in Xing Long, *Shanda wangshi*, 20–21.

184. Wei Yisa, *Zhen Yesu jiaohui chuangli*, M10. Eventually, Gao rose to the position of bursar for the university. Nyström, *Det nya Kina*, 243.

185. Xing Long, *Shanda wangshi*, 36–42.

186. The initial campus construction was completed in February 1904 with Duncan serving as architect. Both departments moved in simultaneously. For details on the practical arrangements of the campus and the ordering of students' days, see Xu Shihu, *Li Timotai zhuanlue*, 81–83.

Though Shanxi University has long since outgrown its original location and hence moved south to its present site, one old engineering hall (built in 1917) is currently preserved as part of the campus of the Taiyuan Teachers Technical College Middle School (Taiyuan Shifan Xueyuan Fushu Zhongxuexiao) located to the northeast of Wuyi Guangchang. After local scholars successfully protested to prevent the planned demolition of the engineering hall in the late 1980s, two cement-covered tablets were discovered inside its front entryway. The old inscriptions had apparently been covered over (either for protection or in an attempt at their destruction) during one of the various political campaigns following the establishment of the People's Republic of China. The tablets—and the building—have since been restored, preserving the story of the founding of the institution. A helpful reprint of the inscriptions with glosses can be found in Li Weihui, "Shanxi daxue tang," 75–78.

factories—how can this do anything other than create blessings for the people of Shanxi?[187]

On September 7, 1901, the Boxer Protocol was signed, the terms of peace having been dictated by a committee of diplomats representing the various foreign powers. The fruit of a conscious decision on the part of the foreign nations to prop up the Manchu Qing Dynasty, the document called for formal apologies and monuments, enlarged legations, permanent garrisons of foreign troops, and the execution of many (but not all) Boxer "leaders." The total indemnity—the fine exacted to cover all losses of diplomatic life and property during the siege and concomitant battles in Beijing and Tianjin, as well as the cost of the ensuing occupation—amounted to some £67,500,000. It would take China thirty-nine years to clear this debt. Finally, on January 7, 1902, the Empress Dowager Cixi returned to the Forbidden City with the Emperor and the entire court, where she was welcomed and even applauded by a group of foreign officials. The Boxer trouble was over, and China embarked on a rapid set of reforms reminiscent of those attempted by the Guangxu Emperor during the Hundred Days Reform of 1889—but this time with Cixi herself pushing the new policies.[188] For the Qing Dynasty, this was to prove to be too little too late. New ideas were in the air, and change was just around the corner.

---

187. The quotation is from Xu Shihu, taken from his *Li Timotai zhuanlue*, 77, translation mine.

188. See chapters 19 and 20 in Preston, *The Boxer Rebellion*. The indemnity figure is taken from ibid., 310. The United States lobbied to reduce the total fine by one third, but China was surprisingly quick in agreeing to pay the total fee ($335,000,000 at the 1900 rate of exchange or approximately $4,355,000,000 in current U. S. dollars). Note that this figure is completely separate from and independent of any sums awarded to the various mission societies on behalf of their foreign staff or Chinese communicants.

There is perhaps one chance in a hundred that we may escape, but if we must die we are not afraid. If the Lord bids us, we will cheerfully lay down our lives for His sake. All the missionaries are in the same danger; but if we are all killed, and not one escape, there are many more who will be certain to take our place.

—Herbert Dixon (BMS Xinzhou)
Final diary entry dated July 29, 1900.

3

The Golden Age of Mission (1901–1937)

JIMMY GRAHAM AND HIS wife, Sophie, had been serving as missionaries with the American Presbyterian Mission in China for some years. In the aftermath of the Boxer turmoil, Jimmy had used his basic medical training to care for wounded Chinese citizens. Once the dust had settled, Jimmy returned alone to their family's station in Qingjiangpu, Jiangsu, on the Grand Canal, to assess whether or not it was safe for others to return. One night shortly afterwards he had a late night visitor. The man's face was hard, and he was insistent that he needed to speak to a foreigner. Despite the warnings of his staff, Graham welcomed the man into his living room for tea late in the evening. Once assured that they were completely alone, the man introduced himself. He was the head of Shanxi Governor Yuxian's guard. As Graham struggled to control his emotions, the man began to tell his story:

> For several days [Yuxian] kept [the foreign missionaries] [in prison] while his hatred grew. The he called me in and gave me my orders. I am a man trained to obey. I am accustomed to killing. These foreigners—I cared not one way or the other. . . .
>
> We led them out into the prison courtyard and lined them up. Yuxian was there and berated them loudly and angrily. "I do not like you, or your ways, or your foreign teaching." Then he told them they were all to be killed. . . .
>
> Then happened the strangest sight I have ever witnessed. There was no fear. Husbands and wives kissed one another. When the little children, sensing something terrible about to happen, began to cry, their parents put their arms about them and spoke to them of "Yiesu" while pointing up to the heavens and smiling.

> Then they turned to face their executioners, calmly as though this did not concern them. They began singing, and singing they died. When I saw how they faced death I knew this "Yiesu" of whom they spoke was truly God.
> But tell me. Can God forgive my so-great sin?

Graham struggled to contain his rage and desire for revenge. By God's grace he was able to speak calmly to this man of God's forgiveness in Jesus. The man listened attentively, asking only a few basic questions for clarification, and then left quietly on his way to escort Yuxian's wife to the northeast. Graham never saw him again.[1]

On another occasion in the first few years of the twentieth century, noted missionary and revivalist Jonathan Goforth was resting at his home in Henan when a Chinese scholar from Shanxi knocked on his door. The tumultuous events of 1900 were only just concluded, and Goforth's visitor claimed to have been present in the courtyard of the governor's compound in Taiyuan and to have seen firsthand the massacres that took place there at the height of the Boxer summer. The events he witnessed affected him deeply and changed the course of his life forever. Goforth recorded the encounter:

> "I saw fifty-nine men, women, and children killed that afternoon," went on the scholar. "Even in the very moment of death every face seemed to hold a smile of peace. . . . Is it any wonder, therefore, that such marvelous fortitude should have led me to search your Scriptures and to have compelled me to believe that the Bible is in very truth the Word of God?"[2]

The martyrs of 1900 had not suffered in vain.

In the fall of 1908 Goforth himself passed through Taiyuan for a series of "special meetings."[3] This trip came on the tail end of his northern teaching circuit that had helped bring about the famous "Manchurian Revival" of that same year. The first Canadian Presbyterian to serve in China, Goforth arrived in 1888 as one of the pioneer missionaries to northern Henan.

---

1. This encounter and the guard's version of the massacre at Taiyuan are taken from Fortosis and Reid, *Boxers to Bandits*, 36 and following. The discrepancies between this account and other records of the massacre can best be explained by Graham's lack of familiarity with Shanxi or any of its mission workers. It is only natural that he would be less than precise about details, since his record shows his motive for writing was primarily emotional.

2. This testimony is given in Goforth's own words as found in his book *By My Spirit*, 47–48.

3. The details of this trip through Shanxi are recorded by Goforth himself throughout ibid.

Deeply influenced by Charles Finney, the Welsh revivals, and particularly by his firsthand experience with the Korean Revival of 1907, Goforth believed firmly in the application of foreign revivalism to the Chinese church.[4] Typically, Goforth's meetings began with his plain and unimpressive preaching on sin, repentance, confession, and the Holy Spirit. Next would come an open time for confession and contrition of sin. The atmosphere would become charged as people—often church leaders—broke down in repentance and publicly confessed their sins before entire congregations.[5]

In his popular account of his 1908 revival tour, Goforth reported that the Spirit of God had worked "mightily" in the Taiyuan Church during his visit to the city.

> So marked was His presence, indeed, that it was quite a common thing to overhear people in the city telling each other that a "new Jesus" had come. Their reason for saying this was that for years many of the professing Christians had been cheating their neighbours and quarrelling with them. Some, indeed, had gone so far as to revile their parents and beat their wives. It seemed that the other Jesus was too old or had lost His power to keep them in order. But this "new Jesus," it appeared, was doing wonderful things. He was making all those old backsliders get up before the whole church and confess their sins, and afterwards go right back to their heathen neighbours and pay back anything that they owed, and beg forgiveness of all whom they had wronged. But what was the greatest surprise of all was that they should even go so far as to abase themselves before their wives, asking pardon for the way in which they had mistreated them. In this way a Revival served to carry conviction to the great mass of people outside the Church, that the Living God had come amongst His people.[6]

Goforth's revival meetings, intentionally patterned after Goforth's experiences in Manchuria and thus the earlier 1905 revivals in Wales, were an indication that Pentecostalism had arrived in Shanxi. While the miraculous always played a role in the Pastor Xi's indigenized ministry, not since Stanley

---

4. The best single-volume collection of missionary biographies remains Anderson, *Biographical Dictionary of Christian Missions*. For China missions specifically, see "The Ricci 21st Century Roundtable on the History of Christianity in China" located at http://ricci.rt.usfca.edu; and the steadily expanding "Biographical Dictionary of Chinese Christianity" at http://www.bdcconline.net.

5. On revivalism in early twentieth-century China, see Bays, "Christian Revival in China, 1900–1937," 161–79.

6. Goforth, *By My Spirit*, 49.

Smith's 1887 attempt to recreate the Keswick experience and promote the need for a "second baptism" among the Taiyuan missionaries had the miraculous work of the Holy Spirit been featured so prominently in Shanxi missions.[7]

The new growth Shanxi was experiencing was not limited to the spiritual realm. With the resolution of the Boxer troubles of 1900 came a quickening of the pace of modernization within Shanxi. Telegraph offices were opened in Taiyuan, Pingyao, and Houma, with the main Beijing-Europe telegraph line passing through Shanxi before heading north through Mongolia and into Russia where it joined the main Russian east-west trunk. A message from Taiyuan to England required about two days and cost five shillings per word. The missionaries had to wait until 1901, however, for the first postal station in Shanxi with direct links to the coast to open in Taiyuan under the superintendency of the Imperial Maritime Customs office.[8] Shanxi's extensive coal and mineral reserves (first brought to the attention of the outside world by Baron von Richthoffen) were now attracting the kind of foreign investment warranted by their inexpensive pricing: in turn of the century Taiyuan, coal was available at the rate of seven shillings per ton.[9] In 1908, Williamson reported that coal could be delivered to Shouyang residents' doors for a mere half crown per ton.[10]

By the end of 1901, just one year the Boxer events, the surviving missionaries had already begun to return, with Eva French being one of the earliest returnees.[11] The Edwardses also rushed back in order to oversee the

---

7. On the rise of Pentecostalism and its influence on the CIM, in particular, see Austin, *China's Millions*, 448–54. On the 1887 revival meetings in Taiyuan, see Kaiser, "Encountering China," 287–88.

8. The details on communication are from Edwards, *Fire and Sword in Shansi*, 36–37.

9. On the infamous Red Baron and coal see ibid., 33 and 40. Coal has remained inexpensive in Shanxi right up to the present: in the autumn of 2001 a metric ton of coal could be purchased for about 60 RMB (approximately $7.50 at the time). Closures of small-scale mines and other market influences did lead to a brief spike in coal prices during 2003–2004: coal was being sold at that time for over 200 RMB per ton. This produced in Taiyuan a wave of people suffering from "sudden wealth syndrome"—a condition most frequently treated that year in Taiyuan by purchasing the largest BMW available.

10. Middlebrook, *Memoir of H. R. Williamson*, 16. It is incorrect to believe that Shanxi's coal reserves lay dormant until exploited by western mining companies. Coal had been a notable and profitable undertaking in Shanxi as far back as the Ming dynasty. See Harrison, "Village Industries and the Making of Rural-urban Difference," 25–40.

11. After returning to Shanxi, French was joined in Huozhou by her younger sister Francesca and newly arrived teammates Mildred Cable. "The Trio" served for twenty years in Huozhou, travelling extensively throughout China, and authoring many

distribution and reconstruction of all SYM—now BMS—properties. In addition, Edwards also took advantage of the relatively cooperative mood of the local government to set up a museum in Taiyuan. The exhibits were especially popular on weekends and holidays, and they proved a strong draw for the small preaching hall attached to the building.[12] Edwards's repairs to the various Taiyuan properties were finally completed in April 1906, when the Schofield Memorial Hospital opened its doors once again.[13]

The newly rebuilt hospital could accommodate sixty inpatients with two or three missionary doctors and one missionary "nursing-sister." Female patients were initially housed in a nearby courtyard, before poor conditions and the arrival of new workers in 1907 (Dr. Paula Maier and Sister Katherine Lane) led them to expand female medical work using a large Chinese courtyard on Qiaotou Jie. In 1910, the BMS used money from the Arthington Fund to erect a large well-equipped building for female patients on Xinghualing Xiang, just around the corner from the men's hospital.[14] In 1913 the new women's facility was occupied, though work was limited due to the absence of a female missionary doctor. Until the arrival of Dr. Marjory Edwards (Eben's daughter and sister of George Edwards) in 1920, the work was supervised by the male doctors, with Miss E. A. Rossiter (BMS, arrived in 1911) and Miss V. G. Jaques (BMS, arrived in 1916) carrying out the routine work of the facility for many years. They were assisted by a small band of local Christian nurses as well as some Chinese women evangelists. The hospital earned a reputation for exemplary care, especially in midwifery, with a large number of Caesarean sections being performed every year. In 1921 a Chinese nurses' residence and an extra block of buildings for maternity work were erected in memory of BMS doctors John Lewis and George K. Edwards.[15] Unfortunately, the burden of supporting these institu-

---

popular books along the way. In 1923, convinced that the Huozhou station should be handed over completely to local believers, the threesome headed west to carry the gospel to China's Muslims. Benson, *Across China's Gobi*.

12. Williamson, *British Baptists in China*, 203–4. This museum was philosophically an extension of Richard's earlier use of scientific lectures, but on a broader scale. Later, the museum began to model itself after the wildly successful Whitewright Institute in Jinan, Shandong.

13. The opening date is taken from *Shanxi tongzhi*, vol. 42: 88. This source also lists the hospital at this time as having eighty-one beds—contra Williamson's claim of sixty (see below).

14. This is the current location of the Taiyuan City Number One People's Hospital. Williamson, *British Baptists in China*, 82. A few buildings from the days of the Taiyuan Women's Hospital are still standing, though recent plans to expand and relocate the City Number One Hospital do not bode well for these architectural relics.

15. It is claimed by some local Christians that the old two-story building located

tions meant that MBS work was slow to expand into other parts of Shanxi: beyond the main residential centers in Taiyuan and Xinzhou, during these years the BMS was only able to open a "sometimes occupied" station down south in Wenshui and a somewhat more permanent station up north in Tai-chou (Daizhou), known today as Dai County.[16]

In 1909, A. J. Garnier of the BMS began focused work among the students of Taiyuan with the support of Shanxi University's principals and the faculty of the Western Studies Department. Conducted "along YMCA lines," it attracted many university students thus influencing young people from all across Shanxi, while preparing the way for BMS workers some years later to open an official Taiyuan branch of the Young Men's Christian Association (Jidujiao Qingnianhui) or YMCA in 1913.[17] Initially, BMS missionaries were "seconded" (loaned) to the YMCA to work alongside secretaries appointed by the International YMCA. The Board of Managers for the Taiyuan branch had a majority of Chinese representatives, with four members of the Qiaotou Jie church appointed as secretaries. Two large purpose-built buildings were constructed (one for student work and another as a museum/lecture hall similar to the Whitewright Institute in Jinan) using funds from the BMS, but by 1921 the entire sum had been raised locally and was repaid to fund the erection of a new Taiyuan Boys' Middle School in 1921. Activities for the Taiyuan YMCA during these early days were largely religious: Bible studies, Sunday worship, and lectures led by local and foreign evangelists—although they also hosted the usual athletic activities, language classes, cultural events, and literary endeavors. Many church-community cooperative schemes took place under the auspices of the YMCA, and its membership soon grew to over eight hundred students.[18]

These were also exciting days for Richard's Shanxi University, by this time a great success earning the praises of the local officials and people. Graduates were already proving instrumental in developing railways, improving mining techniques, and raising the quality of education all across

---

on the southeast corner of the current Taiyuan City No. 1 People's Hospital was previously used to provide housing for young women nursing students. Could it be one of the Lewis/Edwards memorial buildings? The first class of nurses graduated from the hospital in 1919. See ibid., 106–7.

16. Ibid., 82.

17. Ibid., 80, 82.

18. The Taiyuan YMCA is one of Shanxi's earliest successful self-supporting, self-governing institutions. See ibid., 104–5. Edwards's museum was initially moved into one of the two new YMCA buildings in 1916. The YMCA, however, reacquired the museum rooms in 1921 for expansion purposes at which point the collections were transferred to P. J. Smith's (BMS) small museum attached to the Xinzhou city church. See ibid., 203–4.

the province. Passing through Taiyuan in November 1910, Richard was treated to a banquet by a large representation of the scholars and officials in Taiyuan. He was so moved by their support for the university that he penned a document on the spot officially transferring control and management of the school to the appropriate Shanxi officials—seven months earlier than stipulated in the contract.[19]

In 1901 ABCFM missionary Luella Miner arranged for Taigu resident and former mission school pupil H. H. K'ung (Kong Xiangxi) to study at Oberlin College.[20] K'ung had demonstrated courage and resourcefulness carrying messages for the missionaries and dispensing relief during and after the Boxer Uprising. Once overseas, his distinguished ancestry—K'ung was descended from Confucius—became apparent as he followed up his undergraduate degree from Oberlin with a Masters degree in finance from Yale. He returned to Taigu in 1907 and established the Ming Hsien School—an ersatz Oberlin in China—in memory of the ABCFM Boxer martyrs, locating the new campus on some of the land he had purchased in 1900 to bury the foreign and Chinese Christians.

Around 1910, the ABCFM handed over all of their educational work in Shanxi to the Oberlin Shansi Memorial Association (or OSMA), an organization founded in 1908 in memory of the ABCFM workers from Oberlin who perished in 1900. K'ung—now married to Song Ailing, daughter of the wealthy businessman and Christian minister Charlie Song—served as OSMA representative in Shanxi, where he was also very active in the YMCA. K'ung became an influential supporter of the Nationalist Party, assisting Yan Xishan in the 1911 Xinhai Revolution and then encouraging Yan's efforts to reform Shanxi province; K'ung likely played a key role in shaping Yan's positive attitude toward Christianity and the foreign missionaries.[21] His work at Ming Hsien School in Taigu developed slowly along local lines until 1918 when Oberlin began dispensing graduates to assist with teaching responsibilities, greatly strengthening the school's already solid reputation. Over the next three decades, OSMA expanded Ming Hsien School's mission,

---

19. Xu Shihu, *Li Timotai zhuanlue*, 91–92.

20. This paragraph is based on Carl Jacobson, "H. H. Kung."

21. K'ung served in Chiang Kai-shek's Republican government first as Premier, and then finally as Taiwan's Chancellor of the Exchequer. He was purported to be the richest man in China. Many give the Song sisters credit for the ties their husbands developed. It is commonly said of the three Song sisters that "One loved money (Ailing married K'ung), one loved power (Meiling married Chiang Kai-shek), one loved China (Qingling married Sun Yatsen)." See the popular account of the Song family recorded in Seagrave, *The Soong Dynasty*.

adding an industrial arts section and encouraging students to work in rural reconstruction.[22]

Other organizations also increased their involvement in education during these days, as expanded finances and government support fostered a flurry of institution building within China mission. The educational projects of the Shanxi BMS by this time involved ten different schools, fifteen Chinese teachers and one hundred eighty pupils.[23] In 1910 the CIM opened the Shanxi Bible Institute in Hongdong, the former headquarters of Pastor Xi's work, with support from the Bible Institute of Los Angeles. Initially managed by F. C. Dreyer and his wife, the school grew rapidly, erecting new buildings and enrolling some forty-two students by 1917.[24]

One of the difficulties facing the post-1900 church in Shanxi was how to address the touchy issue of recantation. While the example of those who suffered and died for their faith during the Boxer crisis drew many people to Christ, the same suffering and death had also driven others to abandon the church. In the case of the BMS, the decision was made to require a public confession of recantation from all those who left the church and wished to return. Afterward, a period of discipline was imposed before the person was restored to full fellowship. Unfortunately, there were a few church members who had engaged in the looting of mission property; these individuals were excommunicated.[25] As BMS missionary Arthur Sowerby summarized in 1902,

> It is quite evident already that many of our Christians who suffered death-blows, or imprisonment, have been as brave as any of the great Christian heroes of the days of old. Others have escaped, with no sort of denial of Christ, but these are very few.

---

22. The outbreak of the Korean War in the early 1950s led to the severing of connections between Oberlin and Shanxi province. The Ming Hsien School in Taigu eventually became the Shanxi Agricultural University—a school still in operation and respected today. For more on OSMA, see the helpful summary Ken Grossi and Carl Jacobson, "Oberlin in Asia."

23. *China Mission Yearbook* 1911, 305.

24. The inscription on the dedicatory plaque for the main lecture hall of the school reads: "Shanxi Bible Institute—China Inland Mission—erected by the Bible House of Los Angeles (BIOLA)—Los Angeles, California—To the Glory of God—1914." Chang et al., *Christ Alone*, 134–36. One expatriate Christian working in Shanxi visited Hongdong with James Hudson Taylor IV in the spring of 2003. Some old buildings dating back to the mission days were still standing, but the local Christian community was terribly divided, engaged in battles over the old mission properties. It seemed likely that many of the buildings would soon be torn down. None of Pastor Xi's descendants showed much interest in the gospel, and the church there was struggling.

25. Williamson, *British Baptists in China*, 79 and 76, respectively.

Many have made some form of recantation, apparently by themselves, and others as merely a form. Others have been cowardly, and a few, very few indeed, have shown themselves worthless and wicked.[26]

Between the many deaths and apostasies of 1900, the church's numbers took some time to recover. Understandably, evangelistic work in the countryside was intentionally slow to recommence, for fear of igniting a resurgence of Boxer sympathies. Some of the returning missionaries reported that during their early post-Boxer journeys through the province, their offers of salvation were frequently met with cynicism: "Do you wish us to believe in a God who couldn't protect His people in 1900?" In other cases, missionaries traveling in remote areas encountered open hostility and on occasion they were even stoned.[27] Despite new opportunities for evangelism and the expanding number of foreign and local mission workers that gradually followed in the wake of the Boxer martyrs, the church in Shanxi seemed to lag in growth behind other seemingly less-endowed provinces. By 1911 the members' roll for the BMS's various stations throughout the province listed a meager 364 believers, out of a provincial total of over two thousand Protestant communicants.[28]

SHANXI UNDER THE WARLORDS

On October 10, 1911, fighting began in the southern city of Wuchang. One by one the provinces quickly seceded from the Qing state and established their own legislative assemblies under the leadership of individual provincial strong men. Shortly afterward, on the first day of 1912, the Chinese Republic was established with Nanjing as its new capital and Sun Yatsen as its provisional president. On February 12, 1912, Emperor Puyi abdicated, bringing Chinese imperial rule to a formal close.

The 1911 Xinhai Revolution happened quickly in Taiyuan. The Manchu governor and his guard were killed by revolutionaries, but the other members of the Manchu community were treated reasonably well.[29] While

---

26. Ibid., 79.
27. All the above is taken from ibid., 81.
28. Ibid., 83. The total for Shanxi is an extrapolation from estimates in Stauffer, *The Christian Occupation of China*, 190. For perspective's sake, upon the death of Hudson Taylor in May 1905, the CIM had within China a total of 828 foreign missionaries (not including children), 1,152 Chinese workers, 18,625 baptized communicants, 418 churches, 1,424 mission stations, and 150 schools. Chang et al., *Christ Alone*, 117.
29. This in contrast to Shaanxi where rioting in Xi'an and the northern portions

the commercial quarter of the city was looted and many homes were set afire, the foreign missionaries had been given advance warning by Yan Xishan (who led the rebel military) and a young unnamed radical who was teaching English at Shanxi University (as a youth he had waited table in the home of a missionary before study in England)—both of whom helped arrange for their safety.[30] Taiyuan may have been relatively peaceful, but the disorder across northern China in general was such that many mission societies ordered the evacuation of their foreign associates to the safer coastal cities. Thus for a brief period much of the work in Shanxi was stopped.[31]

Unfortunately, the subsequent 1912 attempt to establish the institutions of modern constitutional democracy rapidly fell victim to Chinese politics as usual. The southern intellectual Sun Yatsen and his faction came into conflict with the northern militarist Yuan Shikai. Sun's party was rapidly crushed, but the ambitious Generalissimo Yuan died in 1916 before he was able to consolidate power and become the next Emperor of a new imperial dynasty. With no strong central authority in evidence, a number of strongmen arose to fill the gap, each establishing his own smaller fiefdom in one or more of China's various regions. In some cases, bandits and organized crime bosses ruled localities for their own personal gain. Shanxi, however, was fortunate in having a more benevolent warlord (*junfa*).

Emerging as Shanxi's "governor" in the wake of the revolution, Yan Xishan was a fascinating combination of old and new China.[32] While a strong advocate of Confucian piety, Yan was also a firm believer in modern militarism. He saw China's future hope rooted in a combination of these two traditions, and he sought to utilize these twin themes in all aspects of

---

of the province brought injury to many in the foreign community (no deaths) and caused foreigners and Manchus alike to seek refuge and adopt siege mentalities. Rescue parties were organized by the British legation for the relief of the beset missionaries, with Christian workers from other cities involved in the relief. See Williamson, *British Baptists in China*, 83–89. Recall also that in imperial Taiyuan one section of the city was walled off for the select residence of local Manchu officials. This area—the Manchu City in the southwest corner of Taiyuan's old walls—would have been easily surrounded and controlled during the 1911 revolution.

30. Middlebrook, *Memoir of H. R. Williamson*, 20–21. Williamson recalls awaking the next morning to find a bullet newly embedded in his mantel!

31. Williamson, *British Baptists in China*, 82–83.

32. It is difficult to form a fair appraisal of just how "benevolent" Governor Yan was. Since he chose to ally with the Nationalist Party during the period of civil war, post-1949 histories are resoundingly critical of him and his policies. This is so pervasive that even elderly people who were alive during his rule can only see him as a "local tyrant" (*tu huangdi*). One elderly gentleman claims it was simply "not possible for people to live" (*min bu liao sheng*) in Warlord Shanxi. From an interview with Mr. Zhang Baoliang as recorded in Stark, "Reexamining Chinese Student Nationalism," 5.

his modernization effort. In Taiyuan, communication poles that carried the essentials of modernization—electricity and communication—were inscribed with Confucian sayings such as "faithfully observe the tenets of filial piety" (*xiaoti zhongxin*) or "observe the rites with honor and integrity" (*liyi lianchi*). One Shanxi University student during those early days recalled all the pupils getting up in the middle of the night and heading over to the Confucian Temple, waiting with empty stomachs until the proper time to offer the regular sacrifices to Confucius. Students were also given free blue-colored exercise clothes and costumes to wear for their mandatory weekly martial arts training sessions. In particular, this same student recalled the fierce discipline and exact order required for the exercises.[33] At the same time, Yan's modernizing tendencies drove him toward the missionaries. While dressing his policy initiatives in the garb of traditional Chinese Confucian virtues, Yan also sought assistance and support from the mission community—support which he generally received, as so many of his efforts aligned with Western mission perceptions of "modern."

In the spring of 1912, the BMS missionaries returned to recommence work in Taiyuan following the Revolution of 1911. Over the next eight years the BMS would see 16 foreign men and women either resign or be transferred out of Shanxi. Sowerby left for Beijing, where he commenced a literary work among the families of high-ranking officials. Turner, who had served in Shanxi so ably since his initial work assisting famine victims, was officially retired in 1920. He, however, chose to continue his residence in Taiyuan where this "ablest of preachers in Chinese" continued to assist and advise the foreign community there until just before his death in 1937. Edwards, known to the people as "the beloved physician," also continued his work in Taiyuan after retirement. A large class of post-war missionary recruits in 1920 further strengthened the field, allowing for some expansion of the work.[34]

Mission work was generally respected by the new provincial government, with Shanxi University now officially enshrined as a full university and referred to publicly as "China's Third University (*guo li di san daxue*)."[35] In 1912 the Men's Hospital in Taiyuan opened again, this time with a new name: Taiyuan Universal Love Hospital (Bo'ai Yiyuan).[36] For its annual operating expenses of three thousand silver dollars, the hospital relied primarily

33. From Shanxi historian Xing Long's article "Wusi qianhou," 89.
34. Williamson, *British Baptists in China*, 103–11.
35. Xing Long, "Wusi qianhou," 88–90.
36. On possible reasons for the name change (affecting both the Men's and Women's Hospitals), see Guo Jinfeng, "Jiaohui yiyuan jianzhu," 24 note 4.

on donations from the Church of England, though from time to time it also received donations, equipment, and medicine from the International Red Cross.37

The 1911 Xinhai Revolution had promised improvements on many levels, but for most of China's citizens—particularly the majority who lived in the rural interior—little changed. A missionary report from Shunde, Shanxi, written just after the revolution recorded the following image of 1911 village life—an image that would have been nearly identical to a snapshot taken a hundred years before, save for the presence of the church and its ministries:

> Shuntehfu [Shunde] has not yet been affected by modern ideas and one may see the typical Chinese life in its many phases. In one home, silks and embroideries were being made ready for the bride. In another were four generations, the younger showing the deference accorded to the aged. Outside the third court, the last wail for an opium suicide was making the bright day gruesome. In most homes one wife was queen of the four mud walls: in several, two wives lived in outward semblance of peace; and in one home often visited, three women owed allegiance to one lord.
>
> One of the visible results of the hospital work is little Jieng Nien, a blind boy who was sent by the doctor three years ago to the Peking School for the Blind. . . . Copies of the Gospels were secured for him, and when one sees the joy that lights his face as his emaciated fingers move over the pages, he cannot but wish that the many hundreds of sightless eyes in China could see in the same way. He reads in the hospital clinics, and to crowds on the street, and sometimes plays the organ for Sunday School. To the Chinese all this is little short of a miracle. Very gratifying is the voluntary contribution made towards his support by some of the Chinese Christians.38

Taiyuan, however, seemed to prosper during the years of Governor Yan's leadership, especially when compared to other parts of China. While these were hard times for the entire country, many observers believed that Shanxi was doing better than most areas, while Taiyuan was positively modern—and most gave the credit to Governor Yan. According to Frederick

---

37. *Shanxi tongzhi*, vol. 42: 88.

38. This report from the American Presbyterian Church (North) includes Shunde as part of their work in Zhili province. As the boundaries are drawn today, however, Shunde is considered part of Shanxi. It is as isolated today by mountains and valleys as it was back then. See *China Mission Yearbook* 1911, 308–9.

Wulsin, an American zoologist/explorer visiting in 1921, Taiyuan was "one of China's most progressive cities" under the leadership of its "model governor."

> With its well-paved streets, its public museum, its college; its electric lights and telephones, its clean and well-disciplined soldiers, it is an example of what the Chinese can do for themselves when the curse of misgovernment is lifted. Here one sees the process of absorbing from the West in full swing—not the westernizing of the Chinese, but the turning of Western ideas to Chinese uses. For that ingenious people always tests, rejects and tests again, but eventually makes over what it adopts into a part of its own strong civilization.[39]

THE WILLIAMSONS IN SHANXI

In 1901, while attending a memorial service in England for the Pigott family of Shouyang who had perished during the Boxer Uprising of the previous year, H. R. Williamson professed his intention to "fill the gap" their untimely deaths had left in the field.[40] The church where the service had been held, the West Street Baptist Church of Rochdale, was also the home church of the Edwards family; thus Williamson had many occasions in the years that followed to strengthen his sense of calling to Shanxi—and Shouyang in particular. Upon completion of his Bachelor of Divinity degree from Bristol Baptist College, H. R. Williamson set off for China. Arriving in Shanghai in November 1908, Williamson and a group of seven other rookies headed off to various fields of service in China. Their steam passage had cost them £37 each.

Williamson was sent immediately to Shouyang, the trip being accomplished by use of a British steamer up the Yangtze River followed by a

---

39. Cabot, *Vanished Kingdoms*, 35. Foreign observers overwhelmingly praised Yan, while Chinese observers at the time were much more circumspect. Today, Yan's identification with the Nationalist regime has led official mainland textbooks and publications to be soundly critical of his contributions to China and Shanxi in particular. Accordingly, all children of a certain age know that Yan had Shanxi's rails set at a different gauge than was common in the rest of China: he did this to prevent invading forces from utilizing his rail network. Since 2008, books and television stories have begun to appear that give testimony to his other more positive contributions in the areas of education, disease prevention, and public works. This means that for the time being his status in China's pantheon of historical figures is still open to debate.

40. This and all the following relies primarily on Middlebrook's 1969 biography *Memoir of H. R. Williamson*.

train ride to Taiyuan along the Belgian-engineered thirteen-hundred-mile Hankow-Peking Railroad. Upon arrival, he quickly set about language study, relying on an elderly toothless opium addict who had served briefly as Timothy Richard's tutor many years ago. The ground Williamson trod was the same earth damped by the feet of the martyred Pigotts, in whose steps he had come to follow. The memorial stone tablet commemorating the sixteen Shouyang martyrs of 1900 was still standing, while one of the local church leaders was a former opium addict, having converted after witnessing firsthand the deaths of the Christians. One can imagine the kinds of thoughts which must have occupied Williamson's mind as he struggled with language study and rural living in those early days—reflections expressed in a pamphlet he wrote in Chinese titled "All for China," which gave an account of the Pigott family's life and death in China. In 1910 Williamson's full probationary period was complete. He immediately raced to Shandong, where his fiancé from his old college days, Emily Stevens, had been serving for a year or so.[41] The two married, and then moved to Taiyuan (apart from a brief stint at the Whitewright Institute in Jinan in 1912), where they threw themselves into ministry. Williamson was given "responsibility . . . for work among students (some 10,000), and also for contacts with the upper official classes to whom Timothy Richard had always directed special attention."[42] They served happily along these lines until their first furlough in 1916.

These were the years of the Great War—a truly world war that reached all the way from Europe to China. Though rarely remarked upon, China joined the allies by recruiting Chinese laborers from the various provinces to assist on the Western Front.[43] Not surprisingly, a number of BMS workers returned to Europe to join the British war effort, many at the cost of their lives. Drs. George Edwards and John Lewis both perished during the war, a severe blow to the medical work in Shanxi. In their absence, two Chinese doctors from the Medical School in Jinan came to Taiyuan to keep the hospital until the war in Europe was over and new foreign doctors arrived (Dr. K. Ford came in 1920; Dr. C. I. Stockley in 1921).[44] The dangers of travel during wartime meant that at the end of the Williamsons' UK furlough, Williamson returned alone to China in 1917, but by late 1918 his wife and

---

41. Williamson technically married before he had secured official permission from the BMS mission offices in London and was consequently censured for his precipitous union. The marriage lasted fifty-six years until death. See ibid., 19.

42. Ibid., 21–22.

43. Williamson, *British Baptists in China*, 100. Seventy thousand Chinese workers were recruited from Shandong alone.

44. Ibid., 106.

two daughters had joined him once again in Taiyuan.⁴⁵ As the war receded into the past, the Williamsons embarked on a lengthy period of fruitful service that saw them involved in an incredible variety of ministries, many of them startling for their progressive nature.

In the winter of 1917–1918, a devastating bout of pneumonic plague broke out in the north of Shanxi, rapidly spreading to threaten all of northern China.⁴⁶ Missionaries from Beijing, Shanxi, and Shaanxi responded to the Chinese officials' cries for help. Edwards and Williamson were sent with official backing to remote northern Shanxi, where their exemplary service was noted by the Governor: Yan personally awarded Williamson the Order of the Beautiful Crop (a decorative riding crop).⁴⁷ The official report of the project, along with Williamson's own diary describe the challenges of

> . . . this onerous task, with its journeys into almost inaccessible places, its difficulties with superstitious and ignorant peasants, its tussles with the apathy and corruptness of officials, and its nearness all too frequently with death in horrible forms.

On one occasion they discovered a young boy free from infection, the sole survivor of his village. Edwards and Williamson brought the boy along with them back to Taiyuan for schooling, where he eventually became an evangelist. The concerted efforts of almost the entire missionary community finally succeeded in stamping out the plague.

Inspired by the effectiveness of the missionary relief efforts during the 1917–1918 epidemic, Governor Yan decided to build upon his reputation as a progressive ruler. Immediately afterward he announced a surprising series of reforms in nearly all areas of life, and he turned publicly toward the local missionary community for advice. As other officials accepted these suggestions, there were great improvements in all spheres of life, including public and private morality.⁴⁸

Williamson credits the missionaries' work during the epidemic of 1917–1918 as being the main influence behind the governor's surprising

---

45. Middlebrook writes in the biography that Emily Williamson traveled first across the Atlantic by steamer (accompanied by her daughters and many disgruntled American soldiers who had been unable to set foot on the continent), and then crossed the American continent by rail, before another steamship carried her and the girls across the Pacific. Yet when H. R. Williamson had traveled the previous year he went by steamer to Bergen and then by train across Siberia and on to Harbin and Beijing. See *Memoir of H. R. Williamson*, 23–25.

46. Williamson, *British Baptists in China*, 103–4.

47. This and the following are all from Middlebrook, *Memoir of H. R. Williamson*, 24–25.

48. Williamson, *British Baptists in China*, 103–4.

eagerness to discuss the positive role foreigners might play in the progress of civil life in China.[49] H. R. Williamson was specifically nominated as the Honorary Adviser to the Governor, not only because of his own distinguished service in the province, but also due to his "quick brain and facility in colloquial Chinese." According to his memoirs, "twice a month on a Friday afternoon" he would meet for an hour with the governor. Out of these meetings came a series of simple texts addressing everything from literacy and hygiene to animal husbandry and democracy. The topics for discussion were decided in advance with the help of a Mr. Wang, a local Chinese man who had studied in England before returning to Shanxi. Then, as various issues were raised, relevant provincial officials would be summoned to attend their conferences. Not only Williamson, but other missionaries as well were frequently invited into the governor's compound, past the site of the 1900 massacre and into the confidence of the highest officials in the province. One wonders what they thought as they passed through that courtyard.[50]

This period of cooperation brought tremendous opportunities to the missionary community. Emily Williamson found that the governor's radical reform of Shanxi's prisons along Japanese lines meant that missionaries were allowed to enter the prisons for preaching and distribution of Scriptures. During her first few visits, Emily Williamson was accompanied by a guard with fixed bayonet for her own protection, but over time the prisoners responded to her visits: one woman who had murdered her husband came to faith and eventually joined the church. Later, Mrs. Williamson was provided with chalk, a blackboard, and even a small organ, which she used to address the female convicts who were allowed liberty from their cells to

---

49. It is hard to know how many of Governor Yan's actions were motivated by altruism and how many by a keen awareness of international politics and economics. Looking toward the Provincial Government compound from the middle of today's Shipin Jie, it is still possible to see a gold and white steeple protruding above the Taiyuan skyline, a red star glued to the top. This church-like building is a topic for debate today, with some suggesting that the governor constructed the edifice to curry favor with the missionaries. Others cite this structure as evidence of Yan Xishan's nascent Christian faith. It seems most likely that this building is the "Meditation Hall" built by Yan Xishan for regular meetings of his moralistic Heart-Washing Society (Xixinshe): "Governor Yen [Yan] is erecting in Taiyuanfu a great structure called a Meditation Hall which is to be used as a place wherein any who wish may at any time enter and meditate in quiet. On Sundays addresses on moral and informing subjects are given upon which attendance from students, soldiers, officials and certain others is compulsory. The building is like a great Gothic cathedral and the finest probably in the province." Editorial in *Fenchow Journal* 1, no. 3 (1919), 18, as recorded in Stark, "Reexamining Chinese Student Nationalism," 14 note 65.

50. See Middlebrook, *Memoir of H. R. Williamson*, 24–30. The quotation is from fellow missionary A. J. Garnier in ibid., 28.

hear her presentations.⁵¹ In addition, the governor had opened a Women's Institute in Taiyuan, where women with their "limited lives and bound feet" could receive training in "English, sewing, cooking, care of children, hygiene and Christian standards of character and conduct." Among the over two hundred women who participated was one of the Governor Yan's wives who was studying English in an attempt to move up a few steps in the wifely pecking order.⁵² Named the "Edwards Memorial Institute" to commemorate the work of E. H. Edwards's wife (known as a "living Buddha" for her generous, loving personality), the Institute was eventually transferred from the BMS to the International Young Women's Christian Association (Jidujiao Nüqinghui), though BMS women—local and foreign—continued their close cooperation with the center.⁵³

In addition to his frequent consultations with Governor Yan, H. R. Williamson was eventually appointed as Shanxi's Provincial Secretary to the new Anti-Narcotics Society of Beijing. Sixteen Chinese Christians were appointed as Inspectors in Shanxi, as it was thought that Christians would be free from the temptations to use official rank for personal profit. When Governor Yan decided to send soldiers out to uproot poppy fields to make way for the planting of wheat and other crops, the peasants rioted. The pitchforks and knives of the peasants resulted in many casualties, which the mission doctors treated gratis throughout the countryside.⁵⁴ Famine was also a constant problem in Shanxi, and one targeted by the "model governor's" new reforms. The missionaries assisted with collecting accurate statistics and distributing grain and water in stricken areas. Williamson and others worked in the mountainous northeast part of Shanxi, where he organized the relief recipients into labor gangs, resulting in the construction of some seventy miles of roadway. For this work he received yet another decoration from the Chinese government.⁵⁵

51. Ibid., 26.

52. The building of "Chinese style architecture" was built "through the visit and generosity of Miss Emily Kemp [sister-in-law of E. H. Edwards] of Rochdale." Ibid., 25. It is hard not to see in the Women's Institute a precursor of some of the community centers and job training programs that many foreigners are seeking to establish in China today.

53. Williamson, *British Baptists in China*, 105–6.

54. Middlebrook, *Memoir of H. R. Williamson*, 26–27.

55. On the road building and famine relief efforts of Williamson see ibid., 27–28. In addition to the awards mentioned here, Williamson received many other commendations from the government, including the Dryandra Leaf for his importation of Australian sheep and his work with the YMCA in the early 1920s, and the Brilliant Star with Cravat from the Chinese Nationalist Ambassador in 1947 for his work in higher education. Ibid., 30 and 63, respectively.

Williamson was responsible for the importation of twelve hundred merino sheep from Australia, a large quantity of cottonseed from America, and even a collection of large American horses. He also secured cinema equipment for the YMCA—all this in addition to his regular mission responsibilities.[56] In 1922 the Williamsons left for a year's furlough before returning again to Taiyuan—this time with four daughters. This transition was particularly difficult as it meant leaving behind Williamson's recently widowed mother, but the entire Williamson clan shared in the burden and committed to serve the family at home while Williamson served Christ in China. Upon his return he purchased a motorcycle and sidecar, much to the alarm of Shanxi's poor mules and muleteers.

China in 1922 was suffused with change, with nationalism gaining increasing force among people of all walks of life. Williamson's diaries recount strikes and protests with slogans such as "Kill all Britishers," "British get out," and even "Kill the *Wei* family [Williamsons]." These were tough times, but throughout Williamson felt that the governor, at least, was still largely friendly toward him and his colleagues.[57] Williamson's biographer, J. B. Middlebrook also hints at brewing trouble in the Taiyuan Church. Apparently an American "sect of some kind" sent workers to Taiyuan to "scoop the pool" and form a "new" church, thus splitting the local Christian community and creating enmity. It is difficult to know exactly what is meant by this, although given the timing and nationality of the trouble it is hard not to think of the various pietistic and Pentecostal offshoots of the Holiness Movement, quite possibly the General Council of the Assemblies of God (Shenzhaohui or Shangdi Jiaohui) or AG who had been active in Taiyuan and Yuci since 1914.[58]

In July 1925, Williamson's fourth daughter, Jessie, died of scarlet fever at the age of three and a half years. She was buried in the Martyr Memorial Cemetery alongside the many other foreign workers who had perished in Shanxi over the last fifty years. The following year, the Williamsons moved to Jinan, where H. R. took up the mantle of leadership for the Whitewright Institute, "the most effective piece of university extension work which can be found in Asia, if not the world."[59] Here he served until 1938 before

---

56. Ibid., 21–22.

57. Ibid., 32.

58. Ibid., 32–33. In Jinyuan just south of Taiyuan, a recently refurbished registered church sits on a property that most likely belonged to the AG. In 2011, the characters "Shenzhaohui" were still visible on the exterior wall of the (derelict) small traditional Chinese worship hall situated on the eastern corner of the property.

59. The quote is from the American Presbyterian missionary Robert E. Speer in ibid., 33.

returning with his family to England to become Secretary of the BMS until his retirement in the 1950s.⁶⁰ His last act before leaving China was to take part in the Taiyuan funeral services for BMS workers Glasby and Wyatt (see "Harry Wyatt" below).

THE CHINESE CHURCH IN THE NEW CENTURY

During these years of relative security, the Shanxi church had been growing. In 1918 the number of Shanxi believers associated with the OSMA and the ABCFM had recovered from a post-Boxer membership total of 125 to nearly 1,500 communicants. The BMS experienced similar expansion, with its twelve missionaries and 76 communicants in 1905 increasing to include thirty-one missionaries and 675 communicants by 1918. The CIM of 1918 had sixty-five missionaries and over 4,400 communicants in Shanxi.⁶¹ Nationwide, 1920 China reported over 350,000 Protestant communicants compared to two million Chinese Catholics.⁶² Across the country there were 7,000 Protestant schools enrolling some 213,000 students, and over 300 mission hospitals of varying sizes in operation.⁶³ By the end of that year, the CIM reported having 1,077 foreign workers and 1,250 Chinese workers serving across China.⁶⁴ In 1917 there were 64 theological and Bible schools in China with 361 professors, teachers, and tutors serving a total of 1,861 pupils.⁶⁵ Perhaps more significantly, the number of Chinese workers serving within the missions had grown from a national figure of 6,961 in 1906 to

---

60. Ibid., 44. Williamson served as Secretary until 1951, and thus oversaw the evacuation and redeployment of the China field during those difficult years. Later on, he also served briefly as Chairman of the BMS Board.

61. Stauffer, *The Christian Occupation of China*, 187. Interestingly enough, the BMS claims to have had fifty-eight "employed Chinese workers," thirty of whom were evangelists (six female) and/or colporteurs. The CIM employed the highest percentage of Chinese women (28 percent female), while the ABCFM had the highest ratio of 6.6 local workers per foreign worker, with lower ratios of 2.5 for the CIM and 1.9 for the BMS. Ibid., 190. Note the helpful chart included in Stauffer's Appendix listing the general state of the Shanxi field circa 1922.

62. From a distillation of Latourette in Lutz, *Chinese Politics and Christian Missions*, 42.

63. Ibid., 43.

64. Reported in *China Mission Yearbook* 1916, 145–46.

65. Interestingly, the theological training carried out in the seminaries of the China Christian Council today serve two to three times the number of students with half the number of schools—not including the massive number of official and unofficial local Bible schools. The 1917 numbers are from *China Mission Yearbook* 1917, 399.

over 28,000 in 1920.⁶⁶ Yet despite all this progress, in 1915 there was still only one Chinese member of the clergy in all of Shanxi.⁶⁷

One church practice not commonly seen today but prevalent in the 1920s was big tent revival meetings. At the invitation of local Christians, teams of Chinese evangelists and missionaries would set up large tents accommodating two hundred fifty to five hundred people on the outskirts of Chinese towns and cities. Focusing on Shanxi's rural districts, the tent missions of the BMS commenced in 1923 with transport and other expenses, preliminary prayer, and follow-up work all being borne chiefly by the local churches. Once the tents were up, the meetings would often go on for weeks at a time. The food stalls and various booths that sprouted up around the tents more than met the Chinese need for "hot and noisy" (*renao*) excitement. On a number of occasions tents were deployed on open ground in Taiyuan city itself, and this practice generally succeeded in attracting great crowds.⁶⁸

F. C. Dreyer of the CIM wrote in a letter to *The Chinese Recorder* advocating yet another ingenious and distinctively modern method of witness: billboards.

> [A] recent journey through several provinces impels me, by your leave, to suggest to your readers the advisability of erecting large Gospel Boards along much frequented highways, at important railway junctions, near busy river ferries, and at prominent points on river and coast where many boats aud [*sic*] steamers pass. The cost of the erection and upkeep of such a board would be comparatively small, yet day by day thousands might by its means be reminded of their duty towards God, of their need of salvation, and of God's offer of Christ. . . . [S]uch boards should be striking and attractive in appearance, having a pointed Gospel message painted in the best possible style, and that they should be kept in good repair by being repainted with a fresh message at intervals.⁶⁹

Protestants were not the only ones engaging in religious proselytism in modern China. The following excerpt comes from a late 1920s Buddhist tract on the efficacy of repeating over and over the name of Amitabha, the

---

66. This statistic is from a list of prayer requests disseminated prior to the 1922 National Christian Conference as listed in *CR* 52, no. 12 (1921) 845.

67. See the "Facts Regarding the Chinese Christian Community" chart in the back of *China Mission Yearbook* 1916. Significantly, this statistic does not include any of the "independent" or non-mission clergy in the province.

68. Williamson, *British Baptists in China*, 204.

69. *CR* 52, no. 8 (1921) 573.

Buddhist God of the Western Paradise. The pamphlet was originally translated for the benefit of Christian missionaries trying to share their faith with those Chinese people who were in the habit of saying "*a mi tuo fa*" in an effort to escape the circle of reincarnation. It is particularly interesting to note how closely the following section follows the outline of a basic Christian apologetic.

> There are some who say, "If at death we repeat the name of Buddha ten times, we are able to escape rebirth. Then I will now diligently do my work, and enjoy myself. When I am about to die, it is only necessary for me to repeat Buddha's name ten times and that is enough. Why should I live on a vegetarian diet or observe the regulations, or morning and evening repeat the name of Buddha, or trouble myself so much?" Uh! You do not know that the span of one's life comprises the time that he breathes. Let the breathing discontinue and at once he is in the after life. Water, fire, sword, soldiers, severe pestilences, poisonous snakes, fierce beasts, any of these can come suddenly, and you will lose your life. How can it be possible for you to see when you are going to die, so that you can slowly repeat the name of Buddha? If at death one is able to be wide awake and quietly repeat the name of Buddha, he will be one who has previously planted Buddha causes. But this is a truly rare thing. The ancients said, "The graves at which there are no descendants to worship are all of young people." If you do not early prepare, will you not be in too big a hurry at that time when your hands are busy and your feet confused?[70]

While Buddhism's remarkable degree of indigenization in China is often remarked on, the Christian religion also adapted quickly to become a Chinese, rather than foreign, religion. By 1903 there were already established groups of self-supporting Chinese churches in the cities of Beijing, Tianjin, Jinan, and Qingdao that operated independently of the Western missionaries or their agencies.[71] Organizations such as the National Association of Chinese Independent Churches and the Federal Council of the Chinese Christian Churches of North China came into existence when local congregations sought mutual cooperation and support after severing rela-

---

70. From "A Simple Talk on Repeating the Name of Buddha *A mi tuo fa*," translated by D. C. Graham in *CR* 59, no. 9 (1928) 577–78.

71. Stauffer, *The Christian Occupation of China*, 380–81. The churches listed here had annual contributions and budgets of between $800 and $3,800 per year (1922 U. S. dollars). For an introduction to the rise of independent Christianity in China, see Bays, "Christianity in China," 307–316.

tions with their original governing mission bodies. These breaks in relationship arose either out of conflicts with individual mission workers or a strong conviction on the part of local and mission personnel that an independent church would be freer to develop in a Chinese way and carry a greater appeal to non-Christian Chinese. By 1920, one congregation in Taiyuan was waiting to join the Federal Council. That same year, a conference was held in Shanghai for the National Association of Chinese Independent Churches: one hundred twenty delegates from 189 churches in sixteen provinces attended representing over ten thousand believers. Of course, there were also many instances of those radically independent religious bodies led by charismatic individuals that are so common today in rural China.[72]

While the 1913 National Conference holds the honor of having been the first conference of its type to include Chinese delegates, the seeds of independence were already being sown during the China Centenary Missionary Conference of 1907.[73] Held in Shanghai, this meeting of the members of the various Protestant societies working in China at that time established a committee on "The Chinese Church" to address the issues involved in the indigenization of the church in China. The resolutions praised increasing independence as an essential hallmark of a healthy Chinese church, while also acknowledging that there was still much work to be done in this area. Typical of the attitudes expressed is the following excerpt from Resolution IV:

> (a) That [the Home Churches which have sent us to China] should sanction the recognition by their missionaries of the right of Chinese Churches planted by them to organize themselves as independent Churches in accordance with their own views of truth and duty, suitable arrangements being made for the due representation of the missionaries on their governing bodies until these Churches shall be in a position to assume the full responsibilities of self-support and self-government.
>
> (b) That [the Home Churches which have sent us to China] should abstain from claiming any permanent right of spiritual or administrative control over these Chinese Churches.[74]

---

72. In the 1920s these types of independent churches could be found in Hubei and Guangdong, as well as most of the coastal provinces. See Stauffer, *The Christian Occupation of China*, 380–81. On the rise of some of the more radically independent forms of Chinese Christianity, see Lian Xi, *Redeemed by Fire*.

73. The claim for 1913 is taken from a photo caption in *CR* 53, no. 3 (1922) 184 and 185 facing.

74. McIntosh, *China Centenary Missionary Conference Records*, 401.

Despite these informed opinions, there still was not a single Chinese Christian present for this major conference on the state of Christianity in China. However, out of this meeting came a newly strengthened conviction that the building of the Church of Christ in China depended essentially on the Chinese themselves. As A. H. Smith remarked just one year later, "The Christian church, to get a footing, must be recognized, respected, approved, or accepted *by the Chinese*."[75] When Beijing pastor Cheng Jingyi attended the 1910 World Missionary Conference in Edinburgh, he not only represented a specifically Chinese church, but he also began a lifetime of advocacy for a unified Chinese church that was not beholden to any foreign denomination or agency.[76]

By 1923 the influential *China Mission Yearbook* was being edited jointly by the CLS and the National Christian Council of China, while throughout the 1920s the portion of contributions to the *Yearbook* from Chinese authors steadily increased.[77] All of these steps toward indigenization reflected a gathering momentum—so much so, that by 1928 one missionary could write that

> . . . Exotic [i.e., foreign] forms of worship are giving way to indigenous modes of expression. These include at times the use of lights (candles), bells and even incense. A carefully prearranged order, which is not announced, suggests a subdued ritualism. Silence also finds its place in this worship. There are also beginnings of a real Chinese hymnology. All this means that some Chinese Christian groups are discarding exotic forms meaningless to them and trying to express their worshipful feelings in indigenous forms that do have meaning. This movement, still

---

75. Deng Zhaoming, "The Church in China."

76. For more on Cheng Jingyi see Ng, "Cheng Jingyi," 14–16; and Wang, "The Church Unity Movement In Early Twentieth-Century China."

77. The number of Chinese-authored articles in the 1926 volume is especially large, though the first number in the volume for 1932 curiously has no Chinese contributors.

It would be fascinating to do a longitudinal study of the influence of the Social Gospel and the modernist schools of biblical interpretation on the China field based on shifts in the content of *CR*. It is certainly the case that in the late teens and early to mid-twenties there seems to be more sympathy than criticism. And yet throughout, we consistently see articles referring to the centrality of Christ and his salvation. What is most obvious to the casual reader is how the evangelism and preaching discussions of the nineteenth century gradually give way to discussions on organization, education, social service, and politics. Of course, following the events in 1922 and all throughout that turbulent decade no issues were more prominent in the pages of the journal than the independence of the Chinese Church (early 1920s) and the relation of missionary money to China's Church (late 1920s).

in its beginnings, has started spontaneously in a number of places.[78]

These same pressures were also being felt in the Taiyuan Christian community. Early on in the twentieth century, local Christians and mission leaders in Taiyuan agreed that in their work they would seek to emulate the "Three-Self Principles" made popular by Roland Allen and John Nevius. Contrary to the common modern perception that the loss of foreign missionaries in 1949 was a sudden blow to the Chinese church, Chinese Christians in Taiyuan had taken control of their ministries from much earlier on.

In 1912, the Taiyuan Chinese Independent Church (Zhonghua Jidujiao Zilihui) was established by Qiao Yisheng in the Dongjihuying neighborhood of Taiyuan; Gao Daling was invited to serve as the congregation's first preacher, despite still having two wives from before his conversion. This new church held strictly to a policy of "Three Don'ts" (*san bu*): don't invite foreign evangelists, don't use money from foreigners, and don't accept foreign control. The independent congregation quickly grew to two hundred people, supposedly with the support of Governor Yan. Before long, however, Gao became disillusioned with the Taiyuan Chinese Independent Church, and set up his own New Jesus Church (Xin Yesu Jiaohui), which, drawing upon Gao's deep connections in the local Christian community, was soon holding nightly meetings of over three hundred people.[79] In 1913 the growing influence of Christianity throughout Shanxi was publicly acknowledged: on a day of prayer in April established by the new national government, Governor Yan along with other high-ranking Shanxi officials attended worship services at the main Protestant (Baptist) church on Qiaotou Jie.[80]

Despite the local popularity of these new independent churches, most of the missionaries eschewed involvement with this movement, supposedly due to "the character of its leaders." Typically, the independent churches appealed to the local (mission) congregations for space to hold services, yet in Taiyuan this was unnecessary. During a 1905 drought, a goddess from a temple to the north of Taiyuan was "successfully" appealed to for rain after all others had failed to supply. The goddess's statues were brought to Taiyuan by order of the acting-governor and ensconced in a new temple erected especially for her honor. This temple was eventually handed over to the Independent Chinese Church and the idols were then buried, causing

---

78. This is from Frank Rawlinson's "New Faces on Old Issues" editorial in *CR* 59, no. 8 (1928) 544.

79. Wei Yisa, *Zhen Yesu jiaohui chuangli*, C18, M10.

80. Williamson, *British Baptists in China*, 108.

an uproar among those who had helped build it some years before.⁸¹ In response to events such as these, the mission community slowly began to urge the local Taiyuan believers to appoint and support their own Chinese pastor, a step finally undertaken in the mid-1920s.⁸²

Stirred by tales of revival, Gao Daling traveled to Beijing in 1919 to witness firsthand the radically independent and charismatic practices and beliefs of "Paul" Wei Enbo's True Jesus Church (Zhen Yesu Jiaohui) or TJC.⁸³ Prior to this visit, Gao had adopted the formal beliefs of the TJC for his Taiyuan New Jesus Church, but now Gao officially embraced the exclusivist TJC and, with the help of Zhang Hanzhong and Li Yuehan, brought the new teaching back to Shanxi. They set up the first Shanxi TJC church in Zhaocheng, Hongdong County, where Pastor Xi Shengmo of the CIM had worked so many years before. Many local CIM followers joined the TJC, drawn by Li Yuehan's excellent medical skills and the TJC's independent status.⁸⁴

In 1921 Gao finally brought the TJC to Taiyuan, converting his old congregation and many others to this pioneering indigenous form of Christianity. The congregation grew rapidly and soon they constructed their own church building. Gao was invited by Chinese church leaders across the province to preach to their congregations, in some cases bringing him into direct conflict with foreign missionaries. Through these travels, Gao proved instrumental in the spread of the independent TJC throughout Shanxi province.

The independence of these churches was a curious kind of freedom. One observer from the 1930s described one such independent church: "They sing hymns and preach sermons just the same as in the American Protestant circles whence they derive their faith. [And yet] They are now entirely unconnected with Western Christianity. Is that all that matters?"⁸⁵ This question was rendered especially poignant by the prevalence of other western influences throughout Republican China. As the same author wrote, "One comes to China with a great respect for her old civilization,

---

81. Reported in a letter from E. H. Edwards as summarized in *The China Mission Handbook*, 1914, 271.

82. Williamson, *British Baptists in China*, 108.

83. On the rise of the TJC see chapters 1 and 2 in Lian Xi, *Redeemed by Fire*.

84. The TJC explicitly claimed that it was the exclusive, one true church. On Gao and the Shanxi TJC, see Hu Shixiang, *Hondong jidujiao shi*, 24–26, 30–32; Lian Xi, "A Messianic Deliverance for Post-Dynastic China," 407–41; Wei Yisa, *Zhen Yesu jiaohui chuangli*, C18.

85. This and the following are from an unknown author's "A Newcomer's Imaginings" in *CR* 63, no. 5 (1932) 291 and 292, respectively.

and it is surprising to find when all is said and done, how almost exclusively western civilization dominates her today—western civilization, that is, with the exception of the West's adopted religion."

As China became increasingly modernized, more and more people began to realize that not all that came from the West was good. One Chinese scholar tried to describe how the combination of Western ideas, traditional superstitions, and political upheavals during the Republican era were combining to sow confusion and immorality throughout Chinese society:

> There is a general breakdown of traditional standards and values. In place of filial attachment there is a more individualistic tendency, and at the same time a social emphasis. Superstitious practices are disappearing, but due to lack of general education they still persist among the illiterate classes, though it should be said that, due to habit perhaps, even people with some education, and especially men of the older type, still have some faith in geomancy and the like. At the same time, clairvoyancy and theosophy are spreading among certain classes of people in certain places, but this I attribute to the unsettled political conditions which make men crave for another world, or some sort of spiritual situation. . . . The most deplorable thing is the breakdown of the old standards of moral worth.[86]

As a response to these tensions, many of the larger city churches in China had already begun by 1922 to take social welfare work—the sorts of things which in Taiyuan were associated with the YMCA—very seriously indeed. While much of this work was educational in nature (e.g., the Jinan Institute attached to Shandong Christian University), other works began to appear as well. The Jiao Dao Gou Church in Beijing ran a school for the deaf and dumb. The "Church of the Triumphant Way" in Nanjing featured an aggressive anti-vice organization called the White Cross Society. The Fuzhou Xiong Yu Dong Church provided winter bathing facilities for local mothers, while the Church of St. Michael and All Angels in Wuchang offered its well and water for communal use as well as its loft for communal sleeping during hot summer months. Grace Episcopal Church in Anqing sponsored the Anking [sic] Colored Cross Stitch Guild, where employment was offered to one hundred thirty women while the proceeds and excess labor were applied to help those less fortunate in the community. Finally, the Nantao Institute in Shanghai operated a Benevolent Loan Society providing small loans

---

86. A letter from Dr. K. S. Liu, Dean of South Eastern University dated October 27, 1923, as quoted in *China Mission Yearbook* 1924, 57–58.

(maximum $5.00) to enable local men to engage in peddling and market sales, the loans to be repaid gradually.[87]

Taiyuan Christians shared in this desire to serve, perhaps none more so than Mrs. Hsu Ling Tsao. Having passed her Chinese Nurses Examination in 1923, Hsu was the first Chinese nurse trained in the Taiyuan Women's Hospital.[88] On June 25, 1924 she opened Taiyuan's first Chinese Christian orphanage, when she agreed to take four children into her care upon the death of their parents.[89] With the support of several local foreign and Chinese Christians, this fledgling orphanage grew rapidly, housing forty-eight children by 1946.

For the first thirteen years of its operation, everything went smoothly: children were given medical treatment at the mission hospital where Hsu had worked as a nurse, and when they came of age the children were educated at the mission school. Two foreign friends of Hsu assisted her with the operation of the orphanage, one of them serving as her treasurer. This was useful since most of the financial support for the orphanage came from foreign gifts. Dr. G. K. Edwards of the BMS (E. H. Edwards's son) agreed to give her a piece of property for her orphanage near the intersection of Shangma Jie and Dongjia Xiang as a perpetual loan—free of charge and with no strings attached.[90]

Hsu was not the only Taiyuan believer to step out into Christian service in his or her community. By the 1920s, local Christian medical professionals

---

87. Stauffer, *The Christian Occupation of China*, 379–80. It is striking to note how similar these works are to the kinds of projects being pursued by foreign and Chinese urban Christians today.

88. Rossiter, "From the Beginning in Shansi," 42. Rossiter, at the time a missionary in Taiyuan, identifies the orphanage director as "Mrs. Hsu (sometimes spoken of as Nurse Djang)." A Chinese version of Hsu's *These Little Ones* (see below) identifies the author as Zhang Lingzao. Perhaps Zhang had a husband named Hsu, leading the foreign missionaries to call her by her "married" name? For the (original?) Chinese text, see Zhang Lingzao, "Shen de weida zuowei."

89. Unless otherwise noted, the information below regarding this private Chinese orphanage is taken from the booklet *These Little Ones*. This brief and highly devotional account was written by the woman who ran the orphanage, Hsu Ling Tsao, and then translated by her daughter (who grew up in the orphanage) in 1946. A letter from Rossiter has been included as part of the preface to the manuscript, suggesting that *These Little Ones* was translated in order to help secure funding for the orphanage. The author's copy is a gift from the Wyatt children.

There are still members of the Taiyuan Christian community who trace their childhood back to Hsu's institution. It is claimed by some in the church that these children were airlifted out to Beijing prior to Taiyuan's "liberation."

90. Hsu Ling Tsao, *These Little Ones*, 23. Until 2008, this property was still standing, having been occupied by the City Civil Affairs Bureau (Taiyuan Shi Minzheng Ju) since at least the time of the Cultural Revolution.

were working in the various hospitals, local Christian teachers were teaching in the schools, and the number of independent churches was growing. The YMCA had Chinese leadership, and local churches were contributing financially to the maintenance of various evangelistic and humanitarian projects throughout Shanxi province.

A fire swept through Xinghualing Xiang and Dongjia Xiang in 1924, severely damaging the Taiyuan Men's Hospital and other BMS mission properties (the orphanage was unharmed). This brought Dr. E. H. Edwards out of retirement in England and back to Taiyuan, where he once again supervised the restoration and enlargement of the hospital, even making a significant financial contribution himself.[91] Shortly afterward (in 1925) R. H. P. Dart was appointed as evangelist and business-manager to the hospital.[92] The same fire also damaged the old CIM properties along Dongjia Xiang. In their place a new Martyr Memorial Church was built to commemorate the Protestant martyrs of 1900.[93] The church was built in the Chinese style with seating for eight hundred. When the Chinese Christian boarding schools on Xinghualing Xiang were in session, worship services packed out the church; otherwise it was usually just over half full.[94]

Just before the fire, in 1923, the BMS had handed over their work southwest of Taiyuan (including nearby Wenshui and Jiaocheng) to the ABCFM. These regions had never been fully developed, due to the demands of the growing institutional work in Taiyuan upon BMS foreign and local staff. Their proximity to the ABCFM's existing work in Fenyang and even

---

91. Williamson, *British Baptists in China*, 107. This final incarnation of the hospital stood on the south side of Xinghualing Xiang just east of Wuyi Lu until 2007 when it was demolished to make way for high-rise apartments. Following the Cultural Revolution, the hospital grounds were occupied by the state-owned Shanxi Medical Electrical Devices Factory (Shanxi Yiyong Dianzi Yiqichang)—an enterprise that was bankrupt by at least the late-1990s.

92. Ibid. Dart is described as "a layman." He contributed to improving both the administrative and evangelistic aspects of the medical work. He was also Dr. Harry Wyatt's first Taiyuan roommate (see below).

93. The Martyr Memorial Church was opened on September 14, 1924, adjacent to the rebuilt Men's Hospital. The names of all the Protestant martyrs from 1900 were inscribed on tablets lining the front porch of the main sanctuary. Located behind today's Red Cross Dental Hospital on Xinghualing Xiang, this building had most recently housed a bankrupt electric transformer factory. In 2004 this structure and its outbuildings were finally demolished, an event that saddened this author but was viewed by the local church as a victory: the church finally received compensation for their loss of the property. Before the old church building was destroyed, this author was able to save a decorative window frame from the main window on the front of the church. This frame now hangs on the wall in Shanxi Evergreen Service's Taiyuan office.

94. Williamson, *British Baptists in China*, 108.

Taigu made this a natural evolution. Likewise, the BMS work in outlying Shouyang was handed over to the care of the Brethren mission in 1919.[95]

Formerly known as the General Missionary and Tract Committee of the German Baptist Brethren Church (Dunkers), the General Mission Board of the Church of the Brethren (You'aihui) or CBM sent its first missionaries to China in 1908. By 1910 the initial team of five missionaries had established their first station at Pingding in Shanxi, where they engaged in evangelistic, educational, and medical work as well as wide-ranging "women's work."[96] A second station was opened at Liaozhou in 1912, and congregations were formally organized at both stations later that year. A primary school was established at Pingding in 1911. With a large staff of expatriate workers in Shanxi and ample funding, the CBM was well positioned to absorb the BMS Shouyang station in 1919.[97] The work expanded rapidly, and by 1924 the mission was operating twenty-seven schools, including four Bible schools and two secondary schools, serving 1,030 students. Medical work had begun in 1914 and reached its height in 1924, with three hospitals—Hiel Hamilton Memorial Hospital in Liaozhou, Brethren Hospital in Pingding, and the Women's Hospital in Shouyang—staffed by sixteen missionary and Chinese workers, with extensive outpatient and public health work. A school for nurses was maintained at Pingding with twelve male and seven female students in 1924.[98]

The early 1920s were a period of growth for the Chinese church—not only in Shanxi, but also throughout the nation. During these years the number of Christians in China increased four or five percent annually, and as the Christian population grew many activities of the church also expanded. In 1921 Christians distributed 578 separate Chinese language periodicals across the country.[99]

---

95. J. C. Harlow and his wife managed the BMS residential station in Shouyang for many years without reinforcements. Ibid.

96. On the early development and expansion of the CBM in Shanxi, see Crumpacker, *Brethren in China*, 9–26; and Horning et al., *Junior Folks at Mission Study—China*, 53–64.

97. Stauffer, *The Christian Occupation of China*, 186.

98. See also Gary Tiedemann's helpful summary of the CBM at the Ricci Roundtable website's "Church of the Brethren Mission." See also "Church of the Brethren Mission" in Tiedemann, *Reference Guide to Christian Missionary Societies in China*, 148–49.

99. From an editorial in *CR* 52, no. 12 (1921) 806–7.

HARLAN AND FRANCES SMITH

In August 1920 Harlan Smith, his wife, Frances, and their infant daughter Pauline stepped off a steamship in Beijing, China.[100] As newly arrived missionaries sent out by the CBM, they had come a long way from their rural home in Ivester, Iowa. Immediately after arrival, they hopped on a train for the two-hundred-fifty-mile journey to Shanxi, where they participated in a full meeting of the mission. When the conference was over they headed straight back to Beijing to begin language study.[101]

The Smiths' first impressions of China and the Chinese people were positive, noting happily "that in temperament and habit [the Chinese] were very similar to we Americans. They could appreciate a joke and they loved to eat noodles, biscuits, pancakes and millet." Such observations were derived from their studies with their language tutors, as well as their experiences practicing the language during frequent excursions

> . . . out into the streets and into the stores [of the local people] trying what words we knew. Even though they wanted to laugh at our strange sounding attempts, they refrained from doing so. They merely said, "Ding How" [*ting hao*], very good.

The Smiths were initially alarmed to note that most Chinese people tended to lump all foreigners together, regardless of motive or disposition, as "foreign devils." However, after one helpful Chinese person suggested that the word so often translated "devil" simply meant "spirit" and thus could be either good or bad, their hearts were put at ease.[102] In order to minimize some of the barriers presented by their foreignness, the Smiths were strong proponents of requiring new missionaries "to give several months to the study of China's past before going into the field." They had also taken to heart the admonition of one elder missionary to remember that Chinese people are generally intellectually superior to most foreigners, as reflected in their ability to memorize vast quantities of written material. These disparate influences encouraged the Smiths to avoid adopting a superior attitude toward the local people.

---

100. The story of the Smiths is taken from Harlan Smith's personal account as preserved by his children. The manuscript, entitled "Compiled in Memory of W. Harlan and Frances J. Smith," was graciously made available to me by Mark A. Strand. Quotations below, unless otherwise noted, are taken from this same source.

101. Brethren missionaries were encouraged to spend the first of their three to four years of language study enrolled at the Peking Language School. Longenecker, "Progressivism and the Mission Field," 63–64.

102. Referring to the phrase *yang guizi*, where the translation "spirit" was proposed for the middle character *gui*.

Shanxi in the 1920s was still somewhat isolated, so when missionaries visited Beijing they invariably seized the opportunity to make extensive purchases of items unavailable on the other side of the mountains. Bedding, clothes boilers, canned butter, and all sorts of goods could be purchased in Beijing, and these items were greatly prized by missionaries in more remote locations like Shanxi. Frances Smith, in one letter home, was impressed by two visiting male missionaries who had bought goods "for the whole mission family . . . everything from ink to clothes."

After completing their initial course of nine months of study in Beijing, the Smiths were dispatched by the CBM to the county seat of Shouyang in Shanxi, where Harlan was delegated to help out with a Red Cross Famine Relief project. His portion of the task involved distributing grain to the day laborers along the eighty-two-mile auto road that was being built.[103] For a period he worked on this project while continuing language study with a tutor they had brought with them from Beijing—though the Beijing tutor was at first reduced to writing characters in order to communicate clearly with the local people. As a final test to mark the end of their formal two years of Mandarin language study, all CBM missionaries were required to speak to a Chinese audience for fifteen minutes. In Harlan Smith's case, the absence of other field workers due to furloughs meant he was forced to take his exam after only eighteen months of study. After a certain amount of anxiety he was "passed" and cleared for full-time mission work. The CBM Shouyang Boys' High School and Grade School required a principal, and Smith was given the job. In addition to his administrative duties he was also expected to teach math and preach in the local chapel—tasks which he worked at steadily until the family's furlough in 1927.

The Smiths' one-year home leave was spent studying evangelism at Bethany Biblical Seminary, after which they returned to Shouyang with a passionate commitment to build an independent Chinese church in their community. Their specific intent was to nurture a local Chinese church that was self-supporting, self-propagating, and self-governing. Though some fellow missionaries felt the Smiths were "ahead of their times," after six years of patient work and prayer the experiment in local autonomy began to bear fruit. One evidence of the church's progress was the local congregation's contribution of $300 annually to provide free tuition for local Christian children to attend the mission school—this in comparison to the $200 contributed annually from churches in America for the same fund.

The Smiths found that the best time to preach the gospel was when the people gathered in the town and neighboring villages for fairs, markets, or

---

103. This was likely the same road Torjesen was involved in building. (See below.)

opera festivals to celebrate traditional holidays. The people came looking to be entertained, and the opportunities for literature distribution were excellent. Since only one out of ten Chinese people at this time were literate, the Smiths only dispensed literature to people who could show proof of reading ability: others were eager to accept the literature, if only to use for wrapping parcels and other such practical employment.[104]

During the summer months, the Smiths along with many other members of the Shanxi mission community would routinely leave the hot, crowded, and supposedly disease-infested cities for various remote natural resorts—the most popular of which was Yudaohe, located in the valley that runs south from Taiyuan at a distance of about eight miles from Fenyang. One fellow Shanxi missionary described the process of vacationing with his family during these summer months.

> It is a lovely place and gives the children a great time. Of course everything is very primitive. We brought most of our furniture and all our clothing, kitchen utensils, etc. See us—sending off at 5 a.m., a cart loaded with over thirty large packages and drawn by four mules because of the muddy cart tracks. Then at 1 p.m. we see off the table boy and the woman, the cook and table boy's respective wives, two goats and a number of packages in rickshaws. We follow by car at 3 p.m. with our four children and all the crevices filled in by inseparable parcels, coats, thermos flasks, etc. The cook had come down the day before to clean out the rooms, build a brick fireplace capable of making bread, etc. We shall have three weeks here before trekking back again. There is enticing mountain climbing and lovely bathing.[105]

The foreigners greatly enjoyed these times of retreat, as they provided families and children with opportunities to frolic on grass (uncommon in crowded Shanxi cities), climb trees (a rare commodity in post-famine Shanxi villages), and swim in sandy pools (the ultimate luxury in drought-ridden Shanxi). These "holidays" were such an established part of Shanxi mission life that the CIM had opened a boarding house in the valley, complete with an English couple to staff it through the busy summer months. In one season, twenty couples passed through the inn, enjoying music and proper English teatime every day, though to the American Smiths it seemed as if the Brits did nothing but eat all day, with their three meals and two teas. A store from Taiyuan that catered to missionary and foreign needs was

---

104. The "one out of ten" literacy rate is Harlan Smith's own figure.

105. This is Dr. Harry Wyatt's own description of his 1935 summer retreat to a temple in a village fifteen miles outside of Taiyuan. Payne, *Harry Wyatt*, 99.

clever enough to move its location every summer out to the valley where the mission community generally stayed, and so keep the foreigners supplied with baking powder, lemons, and other sundries—all at the requisite exorbitant prices.[106]

In 1936 the Smith family returned to the States for a one-year furlough, later extended to three years due to fighting in China. Returning to China in September 1940, they found the Japanese invasion well underway. The ocean liner they sailed on was painted grey and its portholes were blacked out in order to evade detection by the Japanese Navy. Their passenger ship had an anti-aircraft gun mounted on its deck, and each day on board involved "Abandon Ship!" drills for all passengers. It was a very tense time. Once they arrived in Beijing, war was everywhere in evidence: before returning to Shouyang they had to be granted permission from the ruling Japanese government. The train they eventually rode out of Beijing (along a new direct line to Shouyang) took them across rickety bridges hastily reconstructed following bombing raids by Communist guerillas. During the two months they stayed in Shouyang before being evicted by the local Japanese officials, the Smiths heard machine gun fire almost every night and were generally restricted to their mission compound. Much of their time was spent filling out reports for the Japanese authorities. After leaving Shouyang they spent another two months at a missionary school in Tung Chow just outside of Beijing. Finally, the family decided to take the risk and secure passage on a Japanese steamer to America, leaving behind their legacy: Harlan Smith had personally baptized forty or fifty new Christians, the core of a growing and increasingly independent body of Christ in Shouyang, Shanxi.

OSCAR AND ESTHER SCHROEDER

The Schroeders' story begins with the birth of Esther Lenander and her twin brother in 1893.[107] At the time, both children were critically ill. Esther's father prayed that if God would save her life, then he would commit her to the Lord's service for the rest of her days. She was healed, and later, during the series of revivals that swept up and down the West Coast of the United States in the early twentieth century, she dedicated her life to Jesus. In 1909,

---

106. Called "the Taiyuan store" by the Smiths, this business had the foresight to sell "Royal baking powder" for $3.80 and one single lemon for $0.35. It would be fascinating to investigate who owned this surely profitable operation and what else they sold in the store.

107. Thanks to Mark A. Strand for supplying the information given here regarding the Schroeders. Strand's own work in Yuci brought him into contact with the family, and enabled him to interview some of the descendants.

at the age of sixteen, she became convinced that God was directing her life toward missionary service. She obeyed and soon left for China, fulfilling her father's promise to God. Upon arrival, Esther discovered she had a knack for languages, quickly mastering the difficult language of Mandarin Chinese. Some time later she met Oscar Schroeder, a fellow China worker from Norway. They fell in love, and in 1917 the two were married in the northern Chinese city of Shijiazhuang in Hebei province.

Following their marriage, the Schroeders moved to Yuci, Shanxi, where they began their life's work of service under the auspices of the AG.[108] Oscar worked primarily as an itinerant evangelist, soon planting a church in Yuci. In time, he went on to build a sanctuary with seating for around seventy-five people. Like most other Shanxi mission workers at the time, the family spent their summer months outside of the city—Tianlong Shan near Jinci was one of their favorite spots. Throughout their years of service in Shanxi they never felt isolated, thanks to the many Scandinavians who helped them in their work in Yuci, some of whom stayed with them for extended periods of time. In 1921 Esther's six-month-old daughter, Eunice, died in her arms of pneumonia. Following this tragedy, the family took their first and only furlough, spending two years in America and Norway. Two children were born during their home leave.

The Schroeders returned to Yuci with their children and continued building up their young church. Their ministry developed until 1932 when Oscar was kicked by a horse, injuring him severely. According to their children, Oscar and Esther were devastated that God did not heal Oscar immediately in response to their prayers. In 1933, with Oscar's health deteriorating and their financial situation less than sure, Oscar decided to take their oldest son, Gene, with him back to Norway to raise support. He managed to elicit enough funds to send for the rest of the family, and in 1934 Esther and the seven other children closed the mission station and moved to Oslo. At first, the Schroeders viewed their time in Norway as a second furlough, planning to return again to Shouyang after a brief period of convalescence. However, for a variety of reasons they never went back to China.[109] In his later years, Oscar described his philosophy of ministry: "I served God the best I knew how, and left the results to God." Their twenty-five years of

---

108. At that time the Salvation Army was also active in the Yuci area.

109. The war made returning to China almost impossible. Daughter Ruby remembers hiding in a bomb shelter in Norway during the war years. She was just fourteen years old, and with the earth shaking all around her she decided to accept Christ as her savior. When she did, her father said gruffly, "Well I hope it sticks."

faithful service to the people of Yuci laid the foundation for the church that exists there today.[110]

POLITICAL TURMOIL AND THE RISE OF NATIONALISM

By 1918 opium poppies were being cultivated in central and southwestern China once again. While missionaries and some Chinese intellectuals deplored the return of the addictive narcotic, many local and national officials ignored (or in some cases encouraged) the trade to fill coffers with coinage needed to fund war.[111] This was in contrast to Shanxi, where behind Yan Xishan's 1917 ban on opium lay a strong moral conviction regarding the dangers of the drug. As he wrote:

> The ferocity of narcotics is worse than that of floods and savage beasts. They are not only responsible for damaging people and destroying families, but also for the destruction of the country and the extermination of the race. If you overlook a problem as serious as this and do not pay special attention to it then you are not fulfilling your duty as officials to be shepherds of the people.[112]

Opium smoking began to decline during the second decade of the twentieth century, with morphine pills the substitute of choice. But by the late 1920s heroin-based drugs were available, rapidly supplanting other "recreational" narcotics. The rise of these "hard" or powerful drugs eventually contributed to an overall decline in drug usage: the social, financial, and physical costs of addiction were too great. Diarist Liu Dapeng estimated that while 70 to 80 percent of his fellow villagers consumed opium at the end of the nineteenth century, only 30 to 40 percent of them used heroin-based drugs in 1929. Although official bans and permissions affected the levels of drug consumption, usage persisted—especially during the years of the Japanese invasion, when opiates were legalized. At that time it was said of Yuci county town that if one household did not have a heroin user then the next-door neighbor's would. Similarly, in 322 households in three villages in Qi County there were said to be 148 heroin users.[113]

---

110. Two of the Schroeder children returned to Yuci in 2001. Their parents' legacy was evident in the thriving community of local believers worshiping in the new church building paid for by their own tithes and offerings.

111. See the fascinating article in *China Mission Yearbook* 1918, 60–68.

112. From Yan Xishan's *Complete Writings on the Government of Shanxi* as translated in Harrison, "Narcotics, Nationalism and Class in China," 151.

113. These two statistics are from ibid., 154.

Famine struck north China once again in 1920–1921, hitting the same region that had suffered during the North China Famine of 1877–1879. A year of bad crops and a failed spring wheat harvest preceded the poor fall harvest of 1920. In total some fifty-six counties in Shanxi were affected, threatening destitution for over 1.6 million people. By autumn 1920, people in the famine areas were reduced to a diet of food substitutes such as corn cobs, poplar buds, sawdust, elm bark, Sorghum stalks, thistles, leaf dust, and flour made with ground leaves. Houses were torn down for timber, while land was sold at three or four cents on the dollar. In fact, many people classified as "non-destitute" had resources sufficient to survive, but their survival came at the cost of years of indentured servitude to local landlords and loan sharks. The relief program set up to combat the disaster was a cooperative project, with the Chinese government contributing about a third of the total relief package and most of the rest of the funding coming from foreign governments and businesses. Christians played an outsized role in battling the famine, as missionaries comprised 497 out of the total foreign workforce of 584 laborers. Ultimately, these relief efforts helped alleviate some of the worst effects of the disaster, and much was learned about the nature of famine and famine relief in north central China.[114] Both of these issues, opium and famine, became matters of national concern, reflecting the trend toward the politicization of more and more aspects of life.

The growing prevalence of politics throughout Chinese society was largely driven by questions of national identity. In the wake of the 1900 defeat of imperial China by the foreign powers, patriotic Chinese scholars felt free to question everything about their culture and their "race."[115] Chinese intellectuals were looking outside as well as inside to find something new or something different that might save China, and restore her to what they perceived to be her proper place among the nations. This increased awareness of the "other," however, only made the question of what it meant to be Chinese seem more difficult to answer. As traditional sources of central and cultural authority steadily decayed, Chinese elites grappled with the knowledge that

> "Far from being the world, China was now a fragment of the world." . . . To be emancipated from the discredited bonds of Confucianism left one fearfully at sea, in need of a new way to order one's world. A belief in Christianity, or in science,

---

114. See the excellent report of the Famine Relief Committee director Dwight W. Edwards (YMCA Secretary, Beijing) in *China Mission Yearbook* 1923, 242–56.

115. For a sophisticated analysis of the modernizers' response to the Boxer defeat, see Harrison, *China*, 88–130.

including Darwinism, or a dedication to one of the new professions, or to patriotic revolution—all might help one establish one's own self-image. Without intellectual courage, one could hardly survive.[116]

On May 4, 1919, a group of Beijing University students and young intellectuals took to the streets. Filling Tiananmen Square, the protesters were furious over the final form of the Versailles Treaty. Though China had been invited to send representatives to the treaty negotiations in France, their actual demands were ignored. One of the key sources of frustration was the use of Chinese land to appease Japanese militarists, resulting in large portions of northeastern China being ceded to Japanese occupation without regard for China's sovereignty. The angry protesters and the national mood that they represented became known as the May Fourth Movement, recognized today as the first broad public indication that twentieth-century Chinese youth would demand a larger place for their nation on the global stage.

By this time, Shanxi University had earned for itself a national reputation, and as such was soon swept into the national debates. Shortly after May 4, Shanxi University received high level student delegates sent directly from the various Beijing University Student Associations, and over the next few months sent their own delegates to all of the national student conferences. On October 10 Shanxi University entertained two distinguished guests: Beijing University professor Hu Shi and the American educator and philosopher John Dewey. Their lectures on character education and the recent events in Beijing were warmly attended—Dewey was invited to speak twice. More striking, Professor Hu was so impressed with what he saw in Taiyuan that he promised graduates of Shanxi University's college preparatory program that they could enroll directly at Beijing University without any entrance exams, and literature and law students could transfer their enrollments between the schools without any trouble. One scholar of the time described the academic environment as being very much in line with the views of radical reformer Cai Yuanpei. The subjects taught on the Taiyuan campus were wide ranging and debates were constant, often spilling out of the classrooms. Shanxi University was now among the ranks of China's top schools—both in terms of academics and activism.[117]

Ever since China's humiliation at the signing of the Treaty of Shimonoseki in 1895, issues of national sovereignty had occupied priority of place in the hearts and minds of her young, educated urban elite. The events of

---

116. Quoted from Fairbank and Goldman, *China: A New History*, 264.
117. This paragraph is taken from Xing Long, "Wusi qianhou," 90.

The Golden Age of Mission (1901–1937) 155

World War I only further strengthened China's conviction that, while the nation was perhaps still in many ways "behind," the countries of the West were not necessarily the ideal to emulate. Suddenly the old nineteenth-century Social Darwinist nationalism that claimed that the Chinese were not "the fittest" and thus were fated to suffer at the hands of others was being replaced by the easier-to-swallow nationalism of Leninist imperialism. The problem, according to Lenin, was not with China herself, but rather with the imperialist activities of capitalist marauders. According to this philosophy, China's problems no longer came from within, but now the blame could be placed at the feet of foreign capitalists. The students of the 1920s, as heirs of the May Fourth tradition, believed it was their responsibility to speak out for the Chinese nation; as populists, they had faith that the people would support them.[118]

As Marxist and especially Leninist thought spread throughout elite Chinese intellectual salons, the debates over national identity became increasingly confrontational. Editor of the Communist journal *Guide Weekly* (*Xiangdao Zhoubao*) Cai Hesen wrote in 1922 that

> . . . the US, having become the leading capitalist and Christian nation as a result of World War I, was seeking to expand throughout the world. Because England, France and Japan had already established spheres of influence in China, the US was using evangelism, mission education and social service activities to extend its power in China.[119]

More than mere intellectual exercise, as these ideas grew in popularity they became more and more visible in public settings. During a 1922 soccer game between Hunan First Normal College and Yale-in-China, Mao Zedong stood up in the crowd and shouted, "'Beat the slaves of the foreigners.' In the politicized jargon of the time, Mao's chant would have been understood as "defeat those who submitted to the authority of the Yale missionary educators and thereby became denationalized lackeys."[120] Comments such as these were taken seriously by Chinese students.

For the post-May Fourth educated youth, religion—especially foreign religion—was now also suspect. The July 14, 1921 issue of the *Christian Century* reported on the investigations of a group of Chinese students enrolled in American schools into the relation of Christianity to "oriental faiths." The

---

118. This paragraph is distilled from Lutz, *Chinese Politics and Christian Missions*, 57–60.

119. As summarized in ibid., 95–96.

120. This incident is from Stuart Schram's *Mao* as quoted in ibid., 96.

article included a helpful list of the kinds of religious questions being asked by China's young intellectuals:

> Is religion necessary at all? Does China need Christianity? Is not Christianity retarding modern progress? How can the Chinese keep China free from those Western denominational schisms which rose from historical reasons that have little application to China?[121]

The goal for all young Chinese intellectuals and urban elites was simple: China must be forged into a new, strong nation. And while the idealist claims of the Christians and their programs were laudable, it seemed to many young urban Chinese that these same goals could be achieved without the imperialist baggage of foreign missions and religion. In fact, it seemed possible to have the exact same programs without their Christian aspects and achieve the same results. Some went even farther, seeking the elimination of Christianity from China: for these young people, Christianity had proven unwilling or unable to adapt to Chinese culture and now formed a barrier to China's political and social development.[122] In March 1922, a group of nationalistic students gave concrete shape to these criticisms with the formation of the Anti-Christian Students Federation.

The irony of all of this is that in 1922, at the very moment that the anti-Christian movement was becoming institutionalized, many of the accusations of the younger radicals were already being addressed by the larger Christian community. In a move that was far from condescending, the World Student Christian Federation had convened its global conference on the campus of Qinghua University in Beijing. Student representatives attended from all over Asia and the world, including some six hundred Chinese delegates representing over one hundred ninety different schools. The publicity for this event was massive, with articles appearing in all Christian publications in China proclaiming the conference theme as the "Reconstruction of the World according to Christian Plan."[123] 1922 also saw the national meetings of the National Christian Council of China conducted with a strong majority of Chinese delegates.[124] The National Christian Conference of that same year also formed its own committee to address directly China's recent progress toward the Sinification of Christianity. Showing a marked degree of enlightenment, the committee urged "the missionary [to]

---

121. From an editorial in *CR* 52, no. 12 (1921) 804.
122. Lutz, *Chinese Politics and Christian Missions*, 47–49.
123. *CR* 53, no. 3 (1922) 152.
124. Williamson, *British Baptists in China*, 120, 215.

merge himself into the Chinese Christian community; he should not force its development into any Western form but contribute what he may of the spirit of Christianity, leaving that spirit to express itself as it will in purely Chinese fashion." The Commission's report on "The Development of an Indigenous Christianity," listed a number of resolutions and recommendations aimed at advancing a distinctly Chinese church:

> [I]t is our judgment:—
>
> 1. That the ultimate aim and the controlling purpose in the administration and organization of churches and missions should be the development of such an indigenous church that missions can gradually be subordinated and eventually disappear, securing to the Church the full responsibility for the direction of all of its activities, including the use of funds and missionary staff supported by Mission Boards.
>
> 2. That all questions affecting in common the Mission or Missions and the Church be discussed by Chinese and foreigners meeting together.
>
> 3. That it is desirable in certain fields for foreign missionaries to be related to and serve under the direction of constituted ecclesiastical authorities and that they should have the same status as corresponding indigenous workers have.
>
> 4. That in general it is desirable that decisions as to appointment, number, qualification, location and work of missionaries be made by bodies on which there are representatives of the Church or which are themselves the properly constituted courts of the Church.
>
> 5. That the practice now in vogue in many missions and churches of transferring administrative responsibility for evangelistic and primary school work from the missions to committees or organizations representing churches composed exclusively or very largely of Chinese should be encouraged and gradually expanded . . . until it becomes the practice in every mission and church in China.
>
> 6. That representatives of the churches should be associated in the management of educational, medical, and other types of Christian institutional work.[125]

---

125. *CR* 53, no. 3 (1922) 169–70.

This kind of culturally sensitive reflection was already prevalent in the China mission community of 1922, and by the end of the decade would become nearly universal. Indigenous Chinese efforts were also gathering steam: men like Cheng Jingyi of the Church of Christ in China were driving Sinification from within the established churches, while others such as John Sung (Song Shangjie) and later Watchman Nee (Ni Tuosheng) were exploring more radically independent expressions of distinctly Chinese Christianity.[126]

Missionary concern for China's condition, however, was not limited to the state of her church. As one example, missionaries were very much aware of the population pressures constraining all attempts at national development. While decrying abortion as "nothing short of murder," one missionary author argued in 1920 for the inclusion of contraceptive knowledge in missionary "education" work.

> Medical missions and educational missions alike have failed to impart the information so desperately needed if China is to attain that physical health which must be the basis of spiritual well-being; we have kept silent on the one issue which is beyond the shadow of a doubt the answer to the question "What is wrong with China?"[127]

And yet, despite all these attempts by Chinese and expatriate Christians to respond positively to the growing demands of China's increasingly nationalistic youth, emotions among Chinese students continued to run hot through the middle of the 1920s. During these years a number of western secular intellectuals and educators (such as Bertrand Russell and John Dewey) toured China's top universities, giving lectures that typically presented the religious and spiritual claims of the missionaries as outdated, quaint, and foolish. In 1924 a YMCA conference in the United States passed a resolution of interracial goodwill. When this same resolution was presented to mass meetings of students and young people in Shanghai, it was discovered that the Chinese character for hypocrisy had been scrawled across the top of each copy.[128] Growing awareness of China's international status as portrayed through newspapers and print journals further fanned the flames of nascent nationalism, leading more and more Chinese students and intellectuals to

---

126. Wang, "The Church Unity Movement In Early Twentieth-Century China," 163–90; Lian Xi, *Redeemed by Fire*, 131–78.

127. As recorded in Maxwell S. Stewart, "Missions and Population Control in China," *CR* 59, no. 12 (1928) 778–82. Stewart taught at Yanjing University in Beijing.

128. Lutz, *Chinese Politics and Christian Missions*, 87.

view missionaries critically as both imperialists and hypocrites. As one historian described the mood at the time,

> Many Chinese, for their part, saw little need to distinguish between nationalism, anti-imperialism, and anti-Christianism, between the doctrines of Christianity and the actions of evangelists, between resentment of missionaries and the struggle for equality and independence.[129]

The expression of these frustrations over the presence and actions of the foreign mission community took on a more aggressive form as the lingering internal political strife of the previous two decades now burst forth in open warfare. Many regions of China were spiraling toward anarchy as regional warlords, Communists, and Nationalists battled each other for control of various pieces of Chinese territory. As power ebbed and flowed, the battle lines shifted constantly, bringing war, famine, and disease crashing into communities, often suddenly and without warning. The Annual Report of the BMS stated quite simply: "Nineteen hundred and twenty-six was the most perilous and therefore the most anxious year for the mission in China since that year of dread, 1900."[130] Violence was once again a central component in the struggle to develop a new national identity, raising the stakes of all forms of protest and activism.

Anti-Christian and anti-imperialist sentiments combined with internal political war most paradigmatically during the Nanking Incident of March 1927.[131] At the time imperialism was—as always—a convenient bogeyman for internal decay, and the old "eye-gouging" anti-Christian rumors had recently resurfaced in the Catholic regions around Wuchang. As the southern National Revolutionary Army advanced on Nanjing, the transfer of the city into their hands on March 23 was expected to pass peaceably, much like the similar transfer of Hangzhou earlier that year. Accordingly, most of the foreign community ignored their consul's call for withdrawal from Nanjing. Looting of the city began with the arrival of foot soldiers on the morning of March 24, with fixed bayonets and force being used to secure access to foreign properties and goods. As the day wore on and the goods began to disappear, late arrivals expressed their frustration in fits of violence and destruction, in many cases targeting the property and foreign emissaries of the Christian mission presence in China as the clearest visible embodiment of invasive imperialist ambition. Though few were killed and injuries were

129. Ibid., 90.
130. As quoted in Payne, *Harry Wyatt*, 63.
131. The standard account is in Lutz, *Chinese Politics and Christian Missions*, 232–45.

surprisingly low, by mid-afternoon the foreign community had retreated to Nanjing University, the British Consulate, and the Standard Oil Company's quarters on Socony Hill. As a full-out Chinese assault on the Standard Oil properties appeared imminent, British and American ships delivered a suppressing fire of heavy shells to cover the foreign community's flight to the nearby warships, which immediately sailed for Nanjing. This event did nothing to calm already hot tempers, or to assuage Chinese anger over imperialist meddling in China's future. Other similar incidents of violence occurred sporadically in various locations throughout China during these few years, causing damage to property and in some cases bodily injury. Precisely how much damage was sustained by the various foreign missions at the hands of the numerous political and anti-Christian movements during the 1920s is difficult to ascertain but it was not insignificant. As one example, during this decade the Presbyterian Church USA mission in China lost buildings and equipment in seventeen centers spread throughout seven provinces to "warfare and destruction," worth a total value of $279,860.44.[132]

By late 1927 and certainly 1928 the anti-Christian movement was weakening. Partially, this was due to the efforts of local strongmen and authoritarian politicians to suppress the more threatening aspects of the movement.[133] By 1928 the Chinese Nationalist Party (Zhongguo Guomindang) was, at least on paper, in control of a unified China, and strong-arm tactics were tacitly accepted by most local political leaders. In those days, allegations of consorting with Communists or reactionaries could bring arrest in many Chinese cities, so political activism—anti-Christian or otherwise—began to lose some of its luster.

> At a Christian hospital in Taiku, Shansi, a clerk belonging to the Kuomintang unknowingly registered a patient later accused of Communism; fearing that he would be arrested for harboring a Communist, he left his position and fled for home.

---

132. The figure is given in 1928 U. S. dollars as recorded in "The Present Situation," *CR* 59, no. 12 (1928) 801.

133. Lutz cites one example from Chongqing where the military governor who seemed to dislike leftists and nationalists alike organized a giant anti-imperialist, anti-Chiang Kai-shek rally in the spring of 1927. Thousands gathered, and as the leftist speakers approached the podium, the governor's agents opened fire, killing a number of prominent Communists. Over two hundred people were shot or trampled to death in the riot that ensued. In many cases, similar strong-arm tactics succeeded in quelling student violence and even forcing a return to "normalcy" on various campuses. Clearly, political activism had become a risky endeavor by the latter half of the 1920s. Lutz, *Chinese Politics and Christian Missions*, 258–59.

The hospital cashier was imprisoned for eighteen days during investigations.¹³⁴

Significantly, the heavy-handed approach to governance employed by the Nationalists and their warlord accomplices often resulted in decreased influence and authority of foreign missionaries throughout society, thus meeting many of the goals of the original anti-Christian activists and removing the urgency of their cause.

At the same time, disillusionment had set in as idealistic dreams of political activism clashed with actual experience, revealing a far grittier reality than many students had expected. In particular, factionalism and strife within the various rebel cliques were pervasive, diverting precious resources from the original goal of national salvation. Moreover, it became clear that the revolution sought by so many was largely to be the possession of the educated and privileged. Political manifestos from this period assumed that China's future would be determined by a new emerging set of young educated men and women. This realization cooled the ardor of the many would-revolutionaries who had no claim to the elite status so prized by student unions and political leaders, whether Confucian or Communist.¹³⁵

Finally, it was clear by the end of the 1920s that many of the imperialist complaints against Christianity as a foreign rather than Chinese institution were no longer valid. With the evacuation of missionaries from the interior following the Nanking Incident, Chinese naturally stepped into vacated roles serving as principals, acting as presidents, and heading the committees of the various mission organizations. Educational institutions now had Chinese majorities on their boards and had voted to make religious activities voluntary; many of the Christian schools were actively pursuing government registration. By 1930 or 1931, all of the Protestant colleges in Shanghai save St. John's had either registered with the Nationalist government or were in the process of registering. The Church of Christ in China (non-denominational) held its first assembly in October 1927, adopting a working constitution that minimized "Western traditions and sectarian theology." In 1926, Pope Pius XI consecrated six Chinese bishops, the first Chinese believers to achieve the rank since the seventeenth century. And when a Maryknoll Father sought compensation for anti-Christian looting through the United States State Department, he was denied and "informed that Vatican policy now discouraged such diplomatic intervention."¹³⁶

---

134. This incident is taken from "Midnight Watch," an April 1929 report on the Taigu mission by C. and A. Hausske, as recounted in ibid., 260.

135. Ibid., 283.

136. This paragraph is summarized from ibid., 263.

162   The Rushing on of the Purposes of God

This is not to say that the church was fully Sinicized; that process would continue for at least another fifty years. Nevertheless, missionaries were absent from college campuses and in many cases were withdrawing their authority from ecclesial and mission bodies. Historian Jessie Lutz explains:

> Sinification was actually to take longer and to be less complete than indicated in 1927 but for the moment the missionaries, who had been labeled instruments of cultural aggression, were absent from most campuses and churches. Chinese Christians, many of whom shared the goals of the moderates, would bear the brunt of any continued campaigning. If occasional outbursts over special issues were still possible, radicals would find it difficult to inspire more than short-term involvement by the majority.[137]

Through the events of the 1920s, the Chinese church had been forced into a heightened degree of self-reliance. With mission property confiscated, foreign missionaries withdrawn to safe ports, and the lives of local Christians threatened, the church had no choice but to care for its own as best as it was able.

CHALLENGES TO TRADITIONAL MISSIONS IN REPUBLICAN ERA SHANXI

In 1925, the total manpower committed to the Protestant evangelization of China peaked with 8,158 foreign workers assigned to the field.[138] It was estimated that in 1925, Americans gave as much as $10,000,000 to support missionary work being accomplished in China through three or four thousand American citizens stationed in country.[139] Despite this impressive figure, many missions suffered financially due to the global economic recession that followed World War I. In some cases missionaries were forced to leave the field due to lack of financial support. Other missionaries—perhaps the majority—chose to retrench financially, a practice that helped to further the indigenization of mission work in China.

The Smiths of Shouyang are a typical example of how the global recession impacted missionaries working in China. In a letter written home in

---

137. Ibid.

138. Williamson, *British Baptists in China*, 274–75.

139. The figures are from Julean Arnold, "The Missionaries' Opportunity," *CR* 56, no. 10 (1925) 639.

1933, Frances Smith commented on their family finances as she balked at paying high prices for imported foodstuffs:

> I guess we'll have to live more like the Chinese. If we could have Pauline [their daughter] at home we'd get along fine, but the school expenses are so far beyond her allowance. But then everybody in the world seems to be having the same financial problems these days. If we keep well we'll be thankful.[140]

In one remarkable exception to this pattern, Dixon Hoste (CIM General Director at the time) reported in 1923 that CIM contributions had exactly *doubled* during the war years—a striking blessing. While acknowledging that exchange rates overseas still affected many missionaries adversely, he attributed his own mission's good fortune to prayer and God's divine providence.[141]

Despite the financial constraints affecting most missionaries, there were other compensating developments that were making life easier for Shanxi missionaries. Perhaps most notable, travel between Beijing and Taiyuan had improved dramatically. In the 1920s Janet and Frederick Wulsin made several expeditions across northern and western China. As professional "explorers" this upper class American couple traveled through China's vast hinterland collecting photos, stories and biological specimens for Harvard, the Smithsonian Institution, and anyone else interested. Their diaries and letters testify that by 1921, express trains left Beijing regularly for Hankou, where passengers bound for Shanxi would then disembark before boarding another northbound train to Taiyuan. The entire trip could now be made in just three days.[142] This journey was also a much more comfortable affair, as the increased availability of consumer goods meant that expatriates traveling in China now did so with a host of previously unimagined luxuries. In addition to the requisite silk pajamas for warding off flea infestations, the Wulsins included the following items as part of their outfit:

> toilet articles, a mirror; toilet paper, a flash light, 2 notebooks, 1 sweater, 2 films, 1 package of tobacco and 2 slabs chocolate, . . . a bottle of malted milk, a bottle of Epsom salts in a sock, a can of insect powder, a book of the essays of Rabelais, and a collection of O. Henry short stories.[143]

---

140. Taken from a July 2, 1933 letter written from "Yutao Ho" as recorded in the manuscript "Compiled in Memory of W. Harlan and Frances J. Smith," 7.

141. See his report in *China Mission Yearbook* 1923, 102–3.

142. Cabot, *Vanished Kingdoms*, 34.

143. Ibid., 33.

Once within Shanxi the Wulsins had no choice but to submit to traditional modes of transport: mule litters and two-wheeled wooden carts.

The litter was built on a frame of poles shaped like a hospital stretcher, with one mule in front and another behind, while the mule driver ran alongside. The top was made of bowed wooden slats covered with matting and Chinese oilcloth to keep out the rain, open at the front but closed at the rear and sides. Once [the passenger] had crawled in from the front and installed herself on the cushions, four men would first lift the back poles of the litter onto one mule, then hoist the two other poles onto the front mule.

... [T]he time came to ford [the] first river in the mule litter. The water rose above the mule's shoulders. "I felt a bit timid at the thought, as I perched on my dja-wher, but an army of Chinese Adams, clad like our first ancestors (only minus the fig leaf) led my mules over safely, while my muleteer, with his baggy trousers tied around his neck, and his shoes tucked into one of the mule's pack saddles, waded over."

Mules and carts were the mainstay of travel in Western China. The Wulsin expedition used mules for bad mountain roads, and carts for better ones; they had two types of carts, both without springs and almost impossible to destroy, even if they toppled from a high bank or bumped over a boulder. The stylish Peking cart, a small-bodied two-wheeled carriage with a hooded top and a baggage rack behind, was used as a taxicab in the towns and for the weddings and funerals of important people in the countryside. The larger two-wheeled wooden carts, without hoods, were used for carrying baggage and freight. One mule would be positioned between the shafts, while two or three others, mules, donkeys, or occasionally oxen, pulled through ropes which ran from their collars to the bed of the cart or axle....

However, even the hardiest of Chinese carts could not travel everywhere. Many mountain trails were only three feet wide, with steep rocks rising on one side and a sheer drop on the other. To travel roads like this, the expedition hired additional mules in nearby villages and then loaded its supplies onto mule trains. Each mule would be loaded with up to two hundred pounds of baggage, with a driver for every three or four animals.

These mule drivers generally worked for local innkeepers. Travelers hired the transportation by specifying the destination, the number of days it would take to get there, the marches and halting places along the road, the weight of the baggage, and the number of animals and carts required. After much negotiation, a price was agreed upon and the sum paid in advance, with the innkeeper held liable for the contract's execution.[144]

While some degree of discomfort was practically unavoidable, developments in international finance had made travel and expatriate life in general at least more convenient. By this time the national Bank of China allowed travelers to open checking accounts, which made it possible to draw money from post offices at the larger cities. Foreigners conducted financial transactions in Mexican silver dollars, the standard used for all foreign exchange in China at the time. In 1921 the rate of exchange was twenty-three Mexican cents to the U. S. dollar.[145]

A fascinating survey of 1,577 of the total 2,200 foreigners listed in the 1920 *Directory of Protestant Missionaries in China* revealed that missionaries in China during this period had an average of 2.66 children in their families, with these children having spent an average of 67 percent of their lives in China. The infant mortality rate for the first six months after birth was lower than among professional families in England, but the second six months saw the rate of death rise to two or three times the English average. This was due to infectious diseases—particularly of the intestines. While sickness rates were highest in central and southern China (malaria, parasites, and other debilitating diseases), the death rates were highest in northern China—sometimes nearly three times as high—where the most common diseases often resulted in death. Dysentery (19 percent of all deaths), respiratory infections (13 percent), diarrhea (12 percent), childbirth complications (10 percent), and diphtheria (6 percent) were the leading killers among all China missionaries. "Nervous Breakdown" was listed as the fourth most common disease among foreign adults—preceded by malaria (number one), dysentery, and typhoid.[146]

A mere twenty years after the tremendous upheaval of 1900, Christian missions in Shanxi were booming. In total, 244 foreign workers along with 566 local workers were employed in the forward movement of the gospel in 1920 Shanxi.[147] These workers came from a wide range of missionary societies, including the American Board of Commissioners for Foreign Missions, the American Presbyterian Mission (North), the Apostolic Faith Missionaries (Shitu Xinxinhui), the General Council of the Assemblies

---

144. Ibid., 38–39.

145. Ibid., 33, 35.

146. As summarized in Stauffer, *The Christian Occupation of China*, 441–42.

147. Organizations and statistics compiled here are taken directly from the tables and charts in *Christian Occupation*, though it is unclear whether or not Stauffer has included statistics for the Brethren mission in his reports.

of God,[148] the Baptist Missionary Society, the China Inland Mission, the Church of the Brethren Mission, the CIM-associated Norwegian Mission in China or Norske Mission i Kina (Nuoweihui), the Salvation Army (Jiushijun), the CIM-associated Swedish Holiness Union, the CIM-associated Swedish Mission in China or Svenska Missionen i Kina (Rui-Huahui), the independent Tsechow Mission (Shenzhaohui),[149] and the Young Men's Christian Association of China.

Catholic work in Shanxi during these years was divided between two Franciscan Vicariates: one centered in Taiyuan caring for northern Shanxi and a second operating out of Lu'an in the south.[150] In 1920 the Roman Church reported a national total of 1.97 million Chinese Catholics, of whom 94,122 were found in Shanxi.[151] They were ministered to in Shanxi from over nine hundred evangelistic centers serviced by sixty foreign and thirty-five Chinese priests and nuns.[152]

During this time of global upheaval, the mission community was also experiencing change as it led, dragged, or in some cases followed China into the modern world. World war and Chinese nationalism, as well as a growing appreciation for the strengths of China's own cultural traditions, were leading many foreign missionaries to question some of the assumptions that had driven the grand nineteenth-century mission project.[153] As this earlier mission consensus began to crumble, four trends emerged that dramatically altered the China mission world.

First, the Great War and the global depression that followed on its heels had produced a significant shift in mission power. As America rose to surpass Great Britain on the world political stage, the two countries' relative contributions to global missions also changed accordingly. Increasingly, it

---

148. According to the "Assemblies of God Mission" entry at the Ricci Roundtable website, "in 1948 there were 88 missionaries, 148 Assemblies, and 6 Bible schools, with 7,500 members in China."

149. Tsechow, "Dzezhou," or Zezhou is modern day Jincheng. Norman Cliff states that in 1902 Stanley Smith moved south from Lucheng to Zezhou where he worked steadily until his death in 1931. The eventual solution to the theological disagreements between the CIM and Smith, the "Tsechou Fu" or Tsechow Mission was Smith's own project, established after he left the CIM. Cliff, *How the Gospel Came to South East Shanxi*, 10; Tiedemann, *Reference Guide to Christian Missionary Societies in China*, 224. The Tsehchow Mission was known in Chinese as the *shenzhao hui*, a name that is also at times given for the AG. Compare ibid., 122 and 224.

150. Stauffer, *The Christian Occupation of China*, 459.

151. Ibid., 461. The figure of 94,122 *includes* 19,237 believers from the Ordos Region and another 9,845 from Central Mongolia.

152. Ibid., 188.

153. Lian Xi, *The Conversion of Missionaries*, 10–16.

was money and missionaries from North America—particularly in terms of smaller, independent missions—that would influence the future of the gospel in China. According to the 1928 editors of *The Chinese Recorder*,

> During the last twenty-five years or so the western subsidization of Christian effort in China has been [China missions'] most marked characteristic. The curve of subsidization has risen rapidly, if not more so, than that of any other aspect of Christian work in China. This has correlated with the rapid shift of economic power in the West which has made the United States the chief economic power in the world and the leading contributor to Christian work in China.[154]

Even the quintessential non-traditional British sending agency was affected, with the CIM getting more and more of its missionaries and finances from outside of the United Kingdom. While Europeans would continue to participate in China mission, North Americans would set the course for expatriate contributions to the development of the Chinese church during the first half of the twentieth century.

Second, Christian missions in China were now increasingly defined by institution building. The "curve of subsidization" mentioned above refers primarily to the increase in financial outlays required to maintain the massive growth in institutional work (schools and hospitals) that was becoming more and more representative of mission work during this period.[155] Though the process had begun in the closing decades of the nineteenth century, the evils of war in Europe, as well as increasing awareness of the good within the people and cultures of China, drove many early twentieth-century China missionaries to question the heretofore-assumed superiority of Western Christianity. The resulting doubt led many missionaries to retreat from the exclusively religious claims of their faith and to emphasize the "unquestionable" good of social reforms. And for expatriate Christians, these humanitarian efforts were primarily expressed through the institutions of China mission. The violent anti-foreignism of the mid-1920s briefly challenged this trend toward institutionalization, as "the occupation of Christian property, the temporary stoppage of much economic help, and the threats to life" led many missionaries to return to earlier emphases on spiritual matters.[156] However, this was a temporary phenomenon. While missionaries from independent and Pentecostal backgrounds tended to

---

154. *CR* 59, no. 11 (1922) 705.

155. For a look at the earliest phases of this trend, see Hyatt, "Protestant Missions in China, 1877–1890."

156. *CR* 59, no. 11 (1922) 708.

continue the evangelistic pursuits of previous generations of China workers, the integration of the humanitarian priorities associated with the so-called Social Gospel into the institutional center of mainline Protestant mission in China progressed with only limited interruptions, profoundly shaping the legacy of China missions.[157]

The scale and impact of the mission institutions during these years were impressive. According to an article by J. Leighton Stuart, China in 1930 had forty-five national, provincial, and private colleges, plus an additional twenty-three technical or professional schools of college level, thirteen Christian colleges and universities, and two theological and three medical college level schools associated with the churches. Of the total students in China at the time, 9 percent of collegiate scholars and 24 percent of the students enrolled in professional training programs matriculated at Christian schools.[158] As early as 1912, the influence of Christian schools and missionary interest in national politics were readily apparent: some 65 percent of officials within the republican government identified themselves as Christian.[159]

Growing popular interest in China's status as a nation lent further support to the new emphasis on humanitarian concerns expressed through institutions, as the politicization of Chinese society placed pressure on all faiths to be of service to some other "larger" ends. At the beginning of 1932, the editors of *The Chinese Recorder* listed increasing economic burdens, Communism, and the reality of war and militarism as the three great challenges facing China. According to these influential missionaries, the proper role of the Chinese church was to offer an alternative to war and Communism in order to present China with a legitimate chance of attaining the "abundant life"—a phrase here understood almost exclusively with respect to this world.[160]

This same drive toward the "institutionalization of good works" naturally resulted in an increased reliance on "professional" missionaries,

---

157. On the importation of Social Gospel theology by the mainline China mission community, see Lian Xi, *The Conversion of Missionaries*, 153–57. Note that nineteenth-century evangelicalism understood both evangelism and humanitarian aid to be legitimate expressions of Christian love. The radical dichotomy between conversion and social welfare that we today associate with the Social Gospel is a twentieth-century phenomenon—and one that was not even embraced by all those associated with the Social Gospel movement. Bebbington, "Evangelicalism," 247–48; Fishburn, *The Fatherhood of God*, chapter 1.

158. J. Leighton Stuart, "Higher Education in the Nation's Life," *CR* 63, no. 10 (1932) 292.

159. Stauffer, *The Christian Occupation of China*, 33.

160. From an editorial in *CR* 63, no. 1 (1932) 1–6.

understood to be Christian workers whose primary work identity was something other than pastor or evangelist. The resulting change in the makeup of the missionary population reflected a third and deeper transformation in China mission: beneath the impulse toward social reform and the institutions that promoted it, there was a shift in the theological assumptions underlying and driving Christian mission.

While some foreign workers in China continued to be motivated by traditional evangelistic concerns, the increasing popularity within Western Christianity of theologies that substituted an inclusive Social Gospel for the more traditional message of salvation from sin found exclusively through Jesus was combining with recent political upheavals in China and throughout the world to lend a tremendous sense of uncertainty to every aspect of mission life and work in China. Along with these doubts, growing appreciation within many missionary circles for Chinese culture was making it increasingly difficult for expatriates to maintain faith in the superiority of the Christian beliefs of their home countries.[161] These new theological currents were threatening to denude China mission of its explicitly spiritual content. As Chinese theologian T. C. Chao (Zhao Zicheng) remarked presciently in 1928, "the battlefield in China is not the realm of the non-Christian religions, but in the realm of secularism."[162]

At its most basic level, this theological shift was simply the expression within the China mission community of the fundamentalist-modernist debates that raged across North America during the early part of the twentieth century. It was claimed by some in 1921 that three thousand out of the seven thousand-plus missionaries in China were "modernists." While this claim is unverified, it is true that over 50 percent of the missionary force in China in 1921 had been on the field for fewer than ten years, suggesting that they almost certainly would have had opportunity to be exposed to modernist ideas.[163] The influence of these ideas within the institutions of mission was apparent, as revealed in YMCA secretary Xu Baoqian's claim that "Christianity and the New Culture Movement (Xin Wenhua Yundong) supplemented each other because both stood for science and democracy and both encouraged youth to dedicate themselves to social service." Still more striking, Xu went on to state that "essential Christianity was not

---

161. Lian Xi, *The Conversion of Missionaries*, 8–16.

162. *CR* 59, no. 7 (1928) 406.

163. From an editorial in *CR* 52, no. 12 (1921) 806–7. For more on the largely North American fundamentalist-modernist conflict and its effect on global mission, see Patterson, "The Loss of a Protestant Missionary Consensus," 73–91.

necessarily identical with the Christian church or the Christian nations, but was the spirit of actualized Christianity."[164]

This erosion of confidence in the exclusive nature of Christianity's truth claims was also affecting the home bases of overseas mission. No longer viewed by many of the traditional sending congregations as an unequivocal good, the worldwide missionary enterprise was now crumbling at its foundations. As one author described the new global context for mission,

> The machine age which helped produce the present policy of foreign missions is now breaking up that same policy with its modern means of travel and international press. The tourist groups and the press are carrying conflicting reports to the home constituency. Search-lights [sic] are being turned upon foreign missions strong enough to organize the Laymen's Fact Finding Commission. The young people at home are uncertain as to the content and method of the foreign mission program they are asked to support. The art of superficial propaganda at home is breaking down. Facts are wanted.[165]

This skepticism was more than incidental, reflecting a general hesitancy to promote back home the specifically spiritual goals and methods of mission and also yielding further impetus toward institutionalization in mission. "It was evident in 1922, generally speaking, that support, or part of it, was easier to secure for schools, hospitals and enterprises like the YMCA, than for purely church work."[166]

As missionaries and their sending agencies abandoned the evangelistic imperatives that had formed the center of the missionary enterprise during the previous centuries, their shift in theological priorities began to affect the many Chinese churches still associated with mission. One foreign observer referenced the changing understanding of Christmas evinced by some local believers in the early 1930s as an indication of the continuing erosion of Christianity's distinctly spiritual content.

> Last year someone in this town who had been educated overseas sent the writer a Christmas card—he was not a Christian, and the act was simply one of charming friendliness and most pleasant. But it was significant; he regarded Christmas as simply a

---

164. Xu Baoqian as summarized in Lutz, *Chinese Politics and Christian Missions*, 46.

165. B. M. Flory, "New Foundations for Chinese Church," *CR* 63, no. 2 (1932) 80. Flory had served with the CBM in China since 1917. At the time of this article's publication he resided in Shouyang.

166. From the third installment of "Western Money and the Chinese Church," *CR* (June 1928 to July 1929).

time of holiday and merrymaking—a sad, bitter comment on the Christianity of the western world. . . . [Christmas] is not simply and solely a time for amusement. . . . In one church the writer knows the order of events last Christmas was this. A communion service was held, but not in the main church, and at an unusually early hour, to make room for the more important events to follow. At the usual church hour, and in the usual place, a morning service was held, which changed by almost imperceptible degrees into a bunfight, with strangers admitted, and a program of songs. This festivity was a quite admirable example of Christmas joy. Yet it seemed to one person present that it might have been better . . . to avoid giving the impression that the religious part was something to be got over first.[167]

Fourth, developments in Chinese politics were combining with a growing sensitivity toward and appreciation for Chinese culture to compel expatriate missionaries to embrace a more distinctly Chinese church. By the 1920s there was already some awareness that mission Christianity was often just Western Christianity, and some missionaries were vocal in demanding change.

In the August 1921 edition of *The Chinese Recorder*, a newly arrived missionary named Rachel Brooks wrote of her impressions of China, the Chinese church, and the missionary effort. With her fresh perspective, Brooks's thoughts represented the view of the new generation of Western Christians that began to appear on the field in the 1920s. After expressing her admiration for the spiritual openness and freedom she found characteristic of China—she juxtaposed China's vibrant colors and easy smiles with the strict puritan nature of her own tradition—Brooks went on to describe her desire to draw closer to Chinese believers:

> I have rejoiced . . . in the devoted service of the missionaries but there is a lack of initiative among Christians, and among the missionaries I feel remote and isolated from the Chinese life, as withdrawn from reality, as a nun. The strong idealistic currents in modern China, such as those of the Renaissance, are outside of the Christian community.
>
> . . . To sum it all up, the words I have heard most frequently among missionaries are the words "protect" and "careful." We must protect our movement from the Chinese Renaissance and be careful over the differences of theological opinion among missionaries. But this use of "protect" and "careful" is not the speech of freedom, it is the speech of fear. Consequently I am

---

167. "A Newcomer's Imaginings," *CR* 63, no. 5 (1932) 299.

> making two resolutions for my own policy. First, that Christian truth needs to be explained so that it can be understood, but it does not need to be protected. It can stand exposure to all the winds that sweep the world. Second, I will live for a time if possible, with Chinese, to try and get their point of view, understand their attitudes towards the unseen, and begin my work at the point at which the Chinese themselves are. [168]

Other missionaries, however, questioned whether Western missionaries were truly capable of setting aside their own preferences and embracing a different culture. Noting the "house pride" of evangelical British missionaries, one missionary wrote to the editors of the *Chinese Recorder* to decry how a love of middle-class comforts often erected a barrier between the missionary and the Chinese. Calling for a "straight fight with that school of thought represented by the Bible Union people," this author was critical of what he saw as the "magical views of Christianity" taught by older missionaries. The "fundamental weakness of the evangelical churches," he wrote, was "that they are mainly middle-class, that is lovers of solid comfort."[169] For this particular contributor, strong identification with the evangelical imperatives of mission made cultural accommodation almost impossible: only by abandoning the exclusive claims of salvation from sin through Jesus could Christian mission hope to become Chinese in any meaningful way.

This fourth shift in mission involved not only missionaries becoming increasingly in tune with Chinese cultural proclivities, but also Chinese believers becoming progressively prominent within Chinese Christianity. In some cases, this was expressed in a radical repudiation of Western Christianity and the establishment of independent Chinese churches like the True Jesus Church. In other cases, the missionaries themselves pushed for the transfer of authority to local believers within the missions and their dependent churches —an often-daunting task. As mission leader Donald MacGillivray noted, the organizational prerogative to develop indigenous ministries

> . . . is a huge one and the tendency is to enlarge it, with the corollary of ever more new secretaries. As if the evangelization of China and the unavoidable problems of the Chinese Church were not themselves a sufficiently staggering program, nevertheless we must infinitely increase our burden in order to Christianize society, politics, and international relations!

168. *CR* 52, no. 8 (1921) 554–55. By "Renaissance" it is presumed that Brooks is referring to the New Learning and the liberalism and knowledge that accompanied this movement.

169. These quotes are from H. Marsden's letter to the editor as printed in *CR* 59, no. 12 (1928) 796–97.

> We often hear mutterings about the intolerable burden of western creeds and rites imposed on the Chinese Church. Some of us would gladly repent in dust and ashes, if repentance would do any good. But does the Chinese Church realize that the western passion for organization is busy shackling her with a portentous chain of committees, for the most part of western origin and little suited to her particular genius?[170]

Statements of this sort became increasingly common within the mission community. On one hand, they reflect a longing among evangelical missionaries for the simpler, early days of preaching "Christ and Him Crucified." At the same time, these comments reveal a mission community in the midst of a growing debate over what in their message was universal and what was culturally conditioned. Some persisted in their confidence that Christianity was capable of finding faithful expression within any culture. But for a growing number of missionaries, the cultural arrogance of Western Christianity was inescapable. The words of author and China missionary daughter Pearl S. Buck rang true for an increasing number of missionaries: when faced with China's own rich cultural heritage, the modern Western missionary simply "has no message to give."[171]

At an address delivered to the 1928 Sixth Annual Meeting of the National Christian Conference held in Shanghai, missionary H. T. Hodgkin mentioned four areas in particular where he hoped to see the Chinese church improve over the next few years. Here again, doubts about foreign mission presence and a concomitant desire for increased local Christian leadership are strongly evident.

> First, I hope to see the Christians of China more deeply and truly unified as one body in facing their splendid opportunity. . . .
>
> I hope, in the second place, to see a Church that is becoming an increasing power in the life of the nation. . . .
>
> Third, I hope to find the Church in China becoming increasingly a field for the exercise of the finest gifts and energies of the best Chinese. . . .
>
> Fourth, I hope to see a more deeply spiritual Church. . . .
>
> How then may these ideals be realized? May I refer just to three directions which have been especially upon my mind?

---

170. Quoted from a letter of D. MacGillivray included in *CR* 59, no. 8 (1928) 521–22.

171. Pearl S. Buck, "Is There a Place for the Foreign Missionary?" *CR* 58, no. 2 (1927) 104.

(a) There is a need of clear, constructive thinking in relation to the issues facing us. . . .

(b) There is a call for fearless creative action [and living]. . . .

(c) Above all, we need dynamic prayer.

Am I going home because I think there is no more place for missionaries in China? Certainly not! What then can the missionary do? I think we may turn back to our three points [points (a), (b) and (c) above], and we may humbly say that if the missionary can humbly and patiently help along each of these three lines, his presence will be a great gift to the Church of China.[172]

Not surprisingly, many missionaries responded to the chaos presented by a mission community in the grips of these four trends (North American preeminence in mission, focus on institution building, increased emphasis on the Social Gospel, and the growing mandate for indigenous leadership) by resigning and leaving the mission field. According to one missionary observer, the primary reason for young workers leaving the field seemed to be "the inability of the missionary to find his place in the program of the mission," this likely reflecting difficulties in resolving the tension between the evangelistic and humanitarian impulses in mission.[173] Next, some missionaries left over questions related to mission method: some feared that the older generation of workers would require the new workers to follow a certain method of direct and aggressive evangelism. While missionaries had always squabbled over which methods of mission were "the best," the spread of theological doubt within the expatriate Christian community made early twentieth-century debates over the whys and hows of preaching Christ in China especially demoralizing. As one veteran missionary stated the issue,

I have no objection whatsoever to giving the Gospel to the Chinese; in fact I have, I hope, a flaming enthusiasm for it. But I am beginning to wonder . . . whether or not the Chinese would lean more toward the Gospel if we did not preach it to them so much. When there are few accessions to the Church, instead of merely

---

172. From Hodgkin's October address "My Hopes for the Chinese Church" as printed in *CR* 59, no. 12 (1928) 745–52. By "fearless creative action" in point (c), the author has in mind a believer who is "more fearless in his following of Christ" going wherever and doing whatever the gospel of Jesus demands.

173. Richard H. Ritter, "Why Should We Quit," *CR* 59, no. 12 (1928) 766–69. Ritter, a member of the Presbyterian Mission (North) in China on staff at Yanjing University in Beijing since 1923, was responding to T. T. Brumbaugh's July 19, 1928 *Christian Century* article "Why Young Missionaries Quit."

> putting more pressure on to the evangelization program, let us put more pressure on to the educational, medical, and above all social service programs. Then perhaps people would trust us more, love us more, accept us more readily as friends, and—if our lives are anywhere near Christian themselves—would probably become gradually, more Christian in their own attitudes and impulses. In the end, through fellowship with us and naturally ensuing conversations about what Christianity really is, we have every reason to hope that they would attain that supremely lovesome and precious fellowship—the saving fellowship with Christ.[174]

Third, this same observer noted that some young missionaries quit the field over the question of increasing institutionalization in mission. For many missionaries, the church in China as an institution now seemed awkward and foreign. At the same time, the indigenous independent forms of Christianity often seemed to struggle for lack of an organizational/institutional framework. Awareness of this contradiction led some to wonder whether the withdrawal of the foreign presence might create a church in China that was both stronger and more independent.

Finally, many of the departures simply reflected the general disillusionment that had grown to characterize so much of the China mission enterprise. Though much effort and great amounts of resources had been expended, the record of Christian missions in China was not one of unmitigated success. Newly arrived foreign workers saw little reason to hope for growth as they surveyed a China mission still struggling to recover from the popular disaffection with Christianity that lingered after the Chinese nationalistic critiques of the 1920s. As one observer wrote, in one town ". . . the ground seems strewn with people, many of them educated, who have been connected with the Church but are now utterly aloof. One goes to a country district, and is told that the greatest obstacle is the old (lapsed) church members, of whom there are so many."[175]

> In one man's view of up-country work, Christianity has every appearance of being a dying cause. We must tell the truth, and the truth in this case is not soothing syrup—it is no good purring while the Church in China burns (or more accurately burns out). One would think that here at least the Church would not suffer from the disadvantages of tradition and convention—the first Christian work was begun here barely more than thirty

---

174. Richard H. Ritter, "Why Should We Quit," *CR* 59, no. 12 (1928) 766–69.
175. "A Newcomer's Imaginings," *CR* 63, no. 5 (1932) 292.

years ago—yet we seem to have the ill effects of tradition without the strength it can give.[176]

Christians used to be moved by the thought of so many thousands dying without hearing the Gospel. Now we are a stage further on: most people with a burning desire could now listen to the Christian Message, even though presented very inadequately. And the situation that now faces us is that nine hundred and ninety in each of those many thousands simply do not care two pins for it all. . . . The time now demands not so much preaching as persuasion, and this is vastly more difficult.[177]

At the end of his discussion of why missionary workers left the field, Richard H. Ritter offered several suggestions for reducing the number of early withdrawals. Most of his ideas had to do with allowing young missionaries room to experiment, all the while counseling them that disillusionment was not a problem endemic to the China field in particular. He also insisted that the sending boards needed to

> . . . recognize as a fundamental principle that the choice of missionaries is to be limited to those who will fill specific positions for which they are trained and which are open at the time; emphatically to warn the candidates of drab days and blank discouragements ahead; to have [candidates] meet as many missionaries on furlough as possible; and to test their qualities of spirituality and fitness for the specific task by some short-term job in the homeland first.[178]

The number of missionaries serving in China had dropped off dramatically by 1932.[179] To fill this gap, many felt that a new kind of missionary was needed. Who would or should supply the shortfall? What should the new missionaries look like? Fundamentally, all concerned with China mission recognized that there was a new context for expatriate service in China: "missionaries who come, for instance, expecting as heretofore to fill places of dominant and prominent leadership cannot fit into a Christian Movement rapidly passing under Chinese leadership." Apart from this basic shift, many proposed requirements remained little changed from a century

---

176. Ibid.

177. Ibid., 295.

178. Richard H. Ritter, "Why Should we Quit," *CR* 59, no. 12 (1928) 770.

179. This claim and the information on missionary qualifications and testing that follows comes from Rawlinson's editorial in *CR* 63, no. 2 (1932) 65–69. In his description of the ideal candidate, Rawlinson tended to emphasize professional excellence over theological qualifications—a significant departure from earlier mission practice.

ago: good health was considered essential, as well as a bright intellect and special academic and professional training. Undergirding all these traits were the essential "inner resources—poise, vision, ideals and above all a vivid consciousness of God as made known in Jesus" that had always been looked for in potential missionary candidates. Alongside these familiar recruiting priorities, however, a number of new emphases emerged. Adaptability, resourcefulness, and creativeness were now explicitly valued, while those who imitated and reproduced others' work were considered handicapped for modern China mission. It was also understood that in 1930s China the missionary would build upon whatever he found in place culturally and religiously, rather than destroying everything local to impart his or her own program. This necessarily implied a degree of receptivity to the local culture. Unfortunately, it was often difficult to ascertain the suitability of a given candidate for service in China. To that end, modern Christian missions now employed "tests of personality" as part of the pre-field assessment process. These tests were to examine five areas: missionaries must (1) be able to engage in a cooperative search for solutions to China's problems; (2) know how to engage in cooperative service; (3) know how to share personal ideas without leading in working them out; (4) be satisfied to exercise all their labors in subordinate administrative positions; (5) have the ability to make and work through friendships. Finally, it was suggested that these tests should also include examination of the candidates' actual work records. Such examinations were to be administered outside of narrow denominational affiliations, with Chinese nationals sitting on the central selection committees.

Over the next few decades the church and all of China were to be subjected to still greater pressures. Was the church adequately prepared? How would the mission community respond to yet another wave of challenges? More fundamentally, what kind of nation would China become, and what role would the church play in that transformation?

The spreading of Christianity is not something akin to throwing a copper to a beggar. It is like the rescue of a drowning man by slipping off one's clothes, and plunging into the dark waters—without reserve or hesitation. There is no cheap way of missionary service. A starving Chinese can witness for the Lord by sharing his crust; a comfortable English church member can only do the same work by a financial sacrifice which costs as much. We get no further by talking about God or writing books about Him. We must see the face of the Master in every [Chinese] face; our lives must be proofs of a God of love.

This means for us, in our generation, an appreciation of the present tragedy, and the glorious possibilities of the Chinese. . . . If our spiritual experience is to ring true, it means sharing our education, our medical facilities and often our food. At the mention of cheapness the whole effort collapses as a pack of cards.

The Christian witness cost Christ everything. What must it cost us?

—Dr. Harry Wyatt (BMS Taiyuan)

Written from Taiyuan in the early 1930s
as recorded in Payne, *Harry Wyatt*, 104–5.

4

Shanxi Mission in the Midst of Conflict (1937–1949)

When Sun Yatsen died in 1925, he left behind a far-from-unified Republican Government. Warlordism and the accompanying concentration of power at the local levels had fostered years of anarchy within China. One of Sun's last acts was to consent to an uneasy alliance between his Nationalist Party, the Soviet Union's Comintern, and China's up-and-coming national Communist Party. In June 1926 a force composed of soldiers mostly from Guangzhou's Nationalist Whampoa Military Academy began to march north toward Beijing. Under the leadership of recent Whampoa graduate Chiang Kai-shek (Jiang Jieshi), this "Northern Expeditionary Force" was tasked with bringing national unification to China's disparate local warlords, while representatives of the two parties (Communist and Nationalist) traveled ahead of the advancing armies to secure the good will of the people in the countryside.

Fighting, broken alliances, and the cold-hearted manipulation of protestors and various factions lasted until 1928. With the Japanese assassination of the main warlord in northeast China, Chiang Kai-shek's Nationalist Party finally consolidated its hold on China. Zhang Xueliang—the erstwhile warlord of Beijing—pledged loyalty to the Nationalist flag, even as the pro-Nationalist Shanxi warlord Yan Xishan struggled to extend his independent control over the Yellow River Basin. While the regionalism brought about by the stifling grip of local warlords would never again command China's future, this newfound national unity did not extend geographically to all of China, nor did it yet represent any kind of consensus about how or even by whom China should be governed. In particular, the Nationalist picture of a unified China left no room for the far-from-defeated Communist Party.

Communism as enshrined in China today is something quite different from what Marx and even Lenin envisioned at the turn of the century. The Chinese Communist Party (Zhongguo gongchangdang) or CCP founded in Shanghai by Li Dazhao, Chen Duxiu, and others in 1921, was initially under the authority and direction of the Soviet Comintern. From its early efforts to mobilize students and urban workers, the fledgling CCP grew in influence, gradually achieving sufficient status to enable it to ally with and eventually contest the more entrenched republican Nationalist Party. As the years passed and various attempts were made to realize European socialist ideals within China, it became increasingly clear that China's unique context demanded that its future ruling party be more Chinese and less Communist than the Soviet Union originally intended. The aggressive actions of Japan in the late 1930s further heightened this sense of nationalism. Ultimately, a more explicitly Chinese version of Communism emerged that wedded Leninist theories of imperialism and Marxist ideas of economic redistribution with an idealistic emphasis on rural peasants—an emphasis that was quite foreign to Stalin's Soviet Communism.[1]

By the 1930s, Governor Yan Xishan was driving many positive changes in Shanxi—often with the assistance of the foreign mission community. Education along "modern lines" was finally spreading throughout the province, carrying with it various new ideas and technologies that brought practical improvements to many aspects of life. The provincial army was also modernizing, as Governor Yan oversaw the construction of new armories throughout the province and a general expansion of Shanxi's military forces. While many residents struggled to provide for their families in the midst of political and social chaos, Shanxi's traditional prominence in Chinese national and international trading networks meant that many villagers still believed that financial opportunities awaited those willing to leave home in pursuit of work.

> One Taigu village surveyed in 1935, after years of economic troubles, still had 36 men working in the county town, 14 in other villages in the county, 24 in other counties in Shanxi, and 28 in other provinces, primarily in the northeast and Manchuria. This was 17 percent of the total male population of the village, but over 30 percent of men in their late teens to their late twenties.[2]

---

1. The coarse summary here leaves unmentioned many factors that shaped China's development during these tumultuous years. For a more complete treatment of Republican China see, among others, Harrison, *China*.

2. Harrison, *The Man Awakened from Dreams*, 23.

At first, 1930s Shanxi missionaries continued their work as best as they could, seizing whatever ministries arose from the comings and goings of Nationalist and Communist forces throughout the province. The CIM reported in January of 1932, "Movements of many troops have hindered traveling and itinerant work in Shansi. Some of the soldiers have been converted. The Luanfu Hospital had been reopened with two doctors, and nurses, after having been closed for some time. People generally are very friendly and open for Christian work."[3]

This pattern lasted until the beginning of formal hostilities in 1937 and the invasion of Shanxi from the north by the Japanese Imperial Army. Many cities were sacked, including the BMS stations of Taizhou and Guo County (modern day Guoyangzhen). The siege of Guo County was particularly gruesome. The local inhabitants resisted, and when the Japanese finally entered the city many citizens were roped together and forced to kneel outside the city walls for twelve, twenty-four, even thirty-six hours before being machine-gunned to death. The bodies were quickly interred in large heaps, resulting in some being buried alive. Chinese casualties were estimated at about four thousand dead, including two local BMS evangelists, a schoolteacher, and two deacons.[4] Williamson tells of a Pastor Ch'in Liang of Guo County who, upon being seized and bound, protested and demanded that the Japanese kill him right there in the church of which he was a pastor. The Japanese consented, sparing Ch'in some of the indignities borne by those who died outside the city gates. In Xinzhou one of the local deacons was shot, while two other Christians were imprisoned and beaten. Once set free, they called all the local believers to the church on the city's hill to thank God that they had been counted worthy to suffer.[5]

Governor Yan Xishan's priority throughout these tumultuous years was to maintain his position of authority in Shanxi. Initially, he tended to side with the Nationalists, perceiving Communism as a threat to his aristocratic style of rule. However, the Nationalist focus on suppressing Communism—a "disease of the heart," in Chiang Kai-shek's famous words—meant relatively fewer resources were devoted to defeating the Japanese invaders. As the mountains of Shanxi became one of the key areas of guerilla resistance to the Japanese, the local people increasingly favored the explicitly anti-Japanese Communists. Rural Shanxi sympathy for the Chinese Communists was further strengthened by physical proximity to Communist leader Mao Zedong's base in Yan'an, and the relative easy access this provided to

3. "The Present Situation," *CR* 63, no. 1 (1932) 62–63.
4. Price, "From Taiyuan to Shanghai," 45.
5. Williamson, "Our Church in Post-War China," 202.

Communist supplies. Not surprisingly, Yan switched sides. Ever the pragmatist, Yan would partner with anyone who might help him retain control of Shanxi: Communist guerillas from Shaanxi, Nationalist forces from the coast, and after 1945 even former Japanese soldiers.

THE JAPANESE OCCUPATION OF TAIYUAN

In October of 1937 Japanese forces laid siege to Taiyuan, commencing a lengthy period of air and artillery bombardment. During the early phase of the siege, Marcel Beney and his wife (Salvation Army) joined with the BMS missionaries in Taiyuan to listen to worship services from England over short wave radio. This kept the expatriates in touch with the outside world for the first week or so until the city lost all electrical power. Coal and food were already scarce, and the fighting was growing in intensity. For safety, the missionaries set about constructing a narrow forty-foot-long air-raid shelter eighteen feet below the ground of their compound.[6] On November 8 the city fell to Japanese forces following several months of battle in the surrounding countryside. Immediately, the population of the city plummeted from two hundred thousand to twenty thousand people as residents fled the occupying army.[7] Although ultimately unsuccessful, the final defense of Taiyuan by Governor Yan's forces was singled out by Japanese military officials as the most obstinate resistance faced by the invaders during the entire war in China.[8]

In 1937 the BMS had thirty-two foreign workers assigned to Shanxi (including those on furlough) with a total church membership in the province of 1,221 believers—an unimpressive number, admitted to be the lowest rate of success in all the BMS fields in China.[9] At the moment the Japanese army entered Taiyuan, fully one fourth of the BMS Shanxi staff and their families were serving in the city (including Dr. Ellen Clow's elderly mother). During the siege, the entrances to the Men's Hospital and the nurses' home had been destroyed by shelling. Ignoring the damage, the Men's and Women's Hospitals remained open despite orders from the Japanese invaders forbidding them from assisting Chinese wounded in the streets. When possible, the missionaries sought to protect the local Chinese women from the rapacious Japanese soldiery, but their requests for mercy were usually

---

6. Payne, *Harry Wyatt*, 108–9.
7. Price, "From Taiyuan to Shanghai," 46.
8. Gillin, *Warlord*, 272–73.
9. This was out of a total figure of just over 430,000 Chinese Protestant communicants nationwide. Williamson, *British Baptists in China*, 276–77, 280.

laughed at by the military officials.[10] BMS missionary Harry Wyatt supplied a firsthand account of life in Taiyuan under Japanese martial law in a letter to a friend back in England.[11]

> The hospital had many wounded, but all those who had opportunities to go south took them, even when that was not medically advisable. Consequently the number of in-patients never reached an unmanageable figure. We were able to organize the hospital so that none of the upstairs wards were in use, for they were naturally more exposed to bombs and shells. We even fitted up a cellar, but because one patient became delirious there, surrounding himself with Bibles to keep off the devils he saw, and because it was dark, we found it was not popular. Warnings of the approach of enemy aeroplanes were given by hooters several times daily, and every few days we were subjected to bombing. This was a terrific experience, being noisy even when in the distance, and when bombs fell close, as many did, the noise of the bombers overhead, the scream of the descending bombs and finally the bursting crash that rocked the walls of houses and cellars, were calculated to call up every symptom of fear. . . . Owing to the reduced population, and the shelter that most were able to take there were few casualties from these raids.
>
> . . . On November 4 General Yen left by car and it was evident that the system of defence to the north and east had been broken down, and that we might expect invasion within a few days. On Sunday, November 7, we first heard artillery fire in the distance. I moved over with Mr. Price into Dr. Bloom's house, as being farther from the street. The next day the attack on Taiyuanfu itself commenced. There was heavy bombing on the gates and on the government offices. While Dr. Clow and the Haywards were having breakfast in "The Willows" (one of the missionary houses, usually occupied by nurses) the roof was struck by a shell, and two upstairs rooms wrecked, together with many of the tiles on the roof. Later in the day the gate house of the Men's Hospital was struck, but no one on our property came to any harm.
>
> Later in the day rifle and machine gun fire could be heard to the north and east of the city. We sampled the cellars, but for the most part sat by the fireside. After we had retired for the night we received a call to the Boys' School where we had

---

10. Price, "From Taiyuan to Shanghai," 45–46.

11. The following is taken from Wyatt's personal account written to Dr. Chesterman, as recorded in Payne, *Harry Wyatt*, 108–15.

some seventy-five refugees. A group of twenty Chinese soldiers had come over the back wall to seek our protection. They had mostly been able to steal civilian clothes. They knelt and pleaded with us, saying that their lives were in our hands. We pointed out to them that we were quite unable to give protection from Japanese, and were unwilling to conceal the fact that they were soldiers. After taking two pistols from them, we escorted them through the break in the wall, advising them to get out of the city at all costs.

The next morning the Japanese entered the city and met no opposition. They shot all whom they thought might have been soldiers, including a large number of civilians. The gateman at the Salvation Army with a friend was shot. Next to the hospital some twelve men were bayoneted or shot. They were dustmen, but owing to a soldier in uniform taking a turn in there, were no doubt thought to be connected with the military. Two escaped over the Hospital wall, one with slight head wounds and the other with a bayonet wound. Another feigned death for two days, with a wound in the thigh. So that we have exact information of what happened.

During that and the subsequent ten days or so many gatemen and others were killed. Very few wounded reached the hospital, the Japanese having their own hospital arrangements. Systematic looting and destruction of property were engaged in. Before long there was not a door in the town, outside the two missions—Baptist and Catholic—that had not been broken open and not a box that had not been rifled. For these days we had to be constantly on call for soldiers who knocked at doors on our property or who scaled the walls at the back. In most instances when a foreigner appeared they were polite and easily persuaded to let us alone. In one instance I was asked in a threatening manner and on our own property to hand over my watch. They did not find it appear, however, and went away.

At an early date we were visited by an English-speaking Japanese who had official instructions to enquire after our well-being, and to make sure we had some food to eat. He obtained notices for us to place on doors forbidding the entry of soldiers, but they did not prove very effective, especially as we have so many doors. Any foreign place, not actually lived in by foreigners, was looted with the rest. The Salvation Army quarters, the Church of the Brethren and Miss Shock's house, the German residences and our Rest House outside the city were all entered and despoiled. Together with our refugees, hospital patients, staff and servants, as well as several people who at various times escaped over the walls into the comparative safety of the mission property, we must have been affording a measure of protection to about 200 persons.

On [November 17], an officer called with an interpreter and gave a long address, the gist of which was that we must put up a Japanese flag to welcome the victorious army, under threat of their displeasure. We decided later we would be willing to put up Jap flags over property where we have Chinese, if it would give them any measure of protection, but that the foreign houses would make do without. However flags of this nationality proved to give no extra protection, so they were not generally used. The same day the electric light began to function again, and with it we were able get outside news once more through the wireless.

No letters, trains or shops were functioning. The few Chinese in the city now began to loot what the Japanese did not want, and the soldiers encouraged them in this. It was a good time for the poor. One day we had to turn a soldier off our property on Ch'iao T'ou Street, who had taken refuge there unknown to us, and was using it as a center for looting. The next week it became apparent to us that no coal was likely to come into the city for some time. We therefore commenced collecting coal from various dumps in the city, as the hospitals and orphanage, as well as the rest of us, could not continue to live in this cold climate without it. It was a week before the military police stopped this as they realized that such coal as was must be conserved for the military. By this time, however, we had fitted out all our institutions with a month's supply.

On [November 26] we had quite an incident. Suddenly after breakfast we discovered about forty Japanese soldiers were seeking entry to the Girls' School. There was an officer in charge, and two of the military police. They were making a search through the town for hidden soldiers and arms, and it had come to our turn. But we soon found that the main idea of the common soldiers was to loot, and as the officer did not seem to have very effective control, this visit was anything but pleasant. They were very threatening in demanding the opening of doors and a free hand. They went through the Women's Hospital and the houses of Drs. Clow and Bloom and Mr. Price. They took a good pair of gloves, a small clock, and electric torch, a skin mat, two forks and a packet of sugar. The sugar and forks were seen at the time, and their return demanded. Upon this there was much ill-feeling, the officer, apparently saying in Japanese that these had actually been given and then demanded back in order to create an unpleasant incident. However, after much rudeness, they thought better of it and returned them and went away.

To date only two of the eight city gates are open, as it is possible for brigands or Chinese troops to descend from the mountains at any time. The town which was almost empty of people is beginning to fill up gradually. A few shops are trying to open, and it is possible to buy vegetables and a little meat. But it must obviously be some time before things become normal. Looting of empty houses by Chinese is still going on, and of course military demands must remain paramount. While it has seemed to us that the right to work here, our extensive property, and the lives of the Chinese staff and refugees here, were worth taking considerable risks to preserve, we have also been mindful all the time that we were in the hand of God. We have found that the faith of many with us has been much strengthened: and we are grateful that where so many have lost their lives or all they possessed, we have fared so well.

While the Japanese soldiers are much like those of any other country, we have found many of the officers and those who have been students not only polite, but also sympathetic. More than once I have heard an apology for the destruction caused, and the inconvenience we have suffered. It has been a terrible lesson that anti-foreign sentiments should not be given expression unless a people are prepared to defend themselves vigorously.

The ABCFM hospital in Fenzhou also struggled to stay in operation during the war years. In 1934 Walter Henry Judd had returned from a year's study at the Mayo Clinic to take up a post in Fenzhou, where he supervised the hospital with its 125 beds. Previously, Judd and his family had served in mission hospitals down south in Shaowu and Nanjing. Following the Japanese invasion of China in 1937, Judd remained at the Fenchow Christian Hospital, although his family returned to the United States. For five months he continued his work, serving under Japanese rule before returning to the United States in 1938. Judd soon resigned from the mission and then spent two years lecturing throughout the United States on the crisis in the Far East, particularly voicing his disapproval for American shipments of raw materials to Japan that could be made into war munitions.[12]

---

12. In 2005, Shanxi worker Mark A. Strand became friends with a local doctor named Li Jufen and her brother. Their father, Dr. Li Cai, had been a doctor in the Fenchow Christian Hospital in the 1930s. During those years, Dr. Li had been trained by Judd, who had also introduced him and his family to the Christian faith. Dr. Li had always considered Judd to be his personal benefactor.

As the Communist Party consolidated its control of China in the early years of the

Mission work continued in truncated form throughout the war years until the Japanese anti-British campaign commenced in the summer of 1939. On the morning of Sunday, July 16, the congregation of the Taiyuan Baptist Church (Qiaotou Jie) was summarily arrested, then held and questioned by authorities under suspicion of being in league with the Chinese Communist forces. The leader of the fellowship, an evangelist by the name of "Wang Chin Chang" was executed, supposedly for refusing to compromise his Christian faith.[13] Finally, one Sunday morning the mission premises were surrounded and many Christian workers taken as prisoners. The hospital was closed and the patients sent packing—regardless of their health or their distance from home. This led to the death of many otherwise stable patients. The missionaries were then told they had three days to leave; they had no choice, but were delayed by three weeks of heavy rains.[14]

When the missionaries made their eventual withdrawal from Shanxi they were forced to leave much property and equipment unattended. The puppet Chinese Provincial Government sent a letter to F. W. Price asking him to sign all the property over to the Chinese Church in exchange for rent. He refused on the grounds that "I had no authority to hand over property which did not belong to me." During this time, most of the BMS property in Taiyuan was occupied by Japanese authorities or business firms. One piece

---

revolution, they actively sought to root out any people who might not support them. By the late 1960s Walter Judd was known within China to be a famous politician in America who spoke out strongly against Communism. Eventually, they tracked down Dr. Li and implicated him as being a Rightist—someone who did not adequately support the Communist Party. Despite the lack of evidence of political heterodoxy, Dr. Li was falsely accused of malpractice and stripped of his job, status, salary, and home. He was homeless for several years, and had to beg for food: his children were embarrassed to be associated with him.

The family, however, still revered Walter Judd as their patron, and attributed their success in medicine and their faith in Jesus Christ to him. In the 1990s Dr. Li was rectified, his titles and salary restored, and all the false charges overturned. He was able to enjoy several happy years reestablishing the Christian church where he lived. Because of his Christian faith he had no bitterness for what had happened to him. His testimony of forgiveness helped his children to also come back to their faith in Jesus Christ, which they now cherish.

When Walter Judd departed from China, Dr. Li had traveled to Beijing to see him off, giving Judd a Chinese silk hanging as a parting gift. This scroll is now in the collection of Chinese artifacts at Carleton College in Northfield, MN.

13. Williamson, "Our Church in Post-War China," 202–3.

14. Recall that rains made the mountains impassable. Rossiter, "From the Beginning in Shansi," 41–42. It is unclear whether Rossiter's "surrounding of the mission premises" took place on July 16 or refers to a separate incident.

of property housed the Japanese consulate, while the Martyr Memorial Church was used for various business purposes, including as a cinema.[15]

During the years of Japanese occupation, none served Christ more faithfully than Hsu Ling Tsao. Shortly after the gates of the church were barred, the local fellowship began to meet at her orphanage. The furniture in the children's bedroom was all pushed aside to make room for the congregation, but even so the two hundred some people spilled out into the courtyard.[16] Soon Hsu had organized the religious life of the Taiyuan Christian community around the buildings of the orphanage, with a six o'clock prayer meeting held every Sunday morning, followed by a hymn sing and an hour-and-a-half-long service (she herself often preached).[17] The afternoon was taken up with Sunday school classes before an evening service closed the Lord's Day festivities. Meanwhile, in Xinzhou the believers met in one another's homes since all the church buildings had been requisitioned by the authorities.[18]

Throughout the occupation of Taiyuan, God miraculously intervened on a number of occasions to prevent Japanese officials from taking over the orphanage property or from taking children away from the home. Since the buildings had originally belonged to British missionaries, it seemed it was only a matter of time before they were confiscated as all the rest of the mission property in Taiyuan had been. Time and time again Japanese officials and soldiers would call on Hsu and threaten to take over the orphanage land; some came seeking money, others came seeking forgiveness. During this entire period God preserved the orphanage, and the Japanese never followed through on their threats. Perhaps most interesting of all these visitors was a "Japanese pastor" who would frequent the orphanage, praising Hsu's work, at times even bringing young soldiers to hear the gospel.[19]

During these years the Chinese Christian orphanage faced tremendous pressures, not least of which was the lack of funding due to the absence of the foreign workers. The mission's hospitals and schools were also closed, and so Hsu had to do the best she could, trusting God to provide everything—which he repeatedly did. With poor nutrition and disease so common in war-ravaged Shanxi, many of Hsu's stories revolve around God's

---

15. Price, "From Taiyuan to Shanghai," 46–47. Price admits that the BMS did eventually receive some rent for the use of their premises, though it is unclear who paid.

16. Hsu Ling Tsao, *These Little Ones*, 14.

17. Hsu's daugher later praised her courage saying, "she always confided her difficulties to God." See Rossiter's comments in Rossiter, "From the Beginning in Shansi," 42.

18. Price, "From Taiyuan to Shanghai," 50.

19. Hsu Ling Tsao, *These Little Ones*, 8–14.

miraculous care and healing for the children. On one occasion, three out of every four children in the orphanage were ill with the same infectious disease. With no functioning hospital, Hsu used what she had learned as a nurse to care for them, praying fervently. One ten-year-old girl eventually succumbed, though the rest miraculously recovered. Over the years another two children died from dysentery, while an additional two perished from tuberculosis.[20] One typical medical case demonstrates how Hsu had learned to rely on God for help when there was no help to be found.

> A friend brought a lame beggar girl to us one day. When I knew it was because of a tuberculosis bone, I thought a plaster cast would do her good, but it could not be got anywhere, so I rested her in bed. I[t] became worse and worse, and began to discharge. I use [sic] only fomentations on her. The little limited medical knowledge I had could not cure her, but I thought, why did God send her here? I said to myself one day, "It is because God loves this little child, and wants me to serve here. Then buy her a coffin to bury her in at the last." But another idea came into my heart: how can there be any difficulty if God intends to cure her? All I could do for her was to put her in bed and pray for her. So it was really God who cured her. It healed up so quickly that I could hardly believe it. She can use the leg freely now, but I have not let her do so yet. This was done when I was absolutely without hope for her. How can there be any difficulty with God?[21]

In 1942 prices in Taiyuan jumped sharply. The orphanage had its food and other needs met by miraculously-timed gifts—unexpected donations that were necessary to augment the meager government stipend that covered a mere twentieth of the orphanage's monthly expenses. In the fall of 1945 prices went up even higher, and the government subsidies disappeared altogether. Good anthracite coal from Yangquan was then quite expensive, and this period was the most difficult one for the orphanage. On more than one occasion during the early 1940s Hsu risked her life traveling to Beijing to secure funds sent from overseas supporters or from the North China Famine Relief Committee. Throughout all of these hardships, the children never went hungry.[22]

---

20. Ibid., 26.
21. Ibid., 27–28.
22. Ibid., 17–21. In 1942 flour cost over three U. S. dollars per catty, while in the difficult autumn of 1945 flour was being sold at $300 per catty.

At the close of her account of the orphanage during the years prior to the 1949 Revolution, Hsu explains the role her faith played in carrying her through these difficult times.

> Thank God, His grace is sufficient for us. This verse was given me by a very good friend of mine before she left Taiyuan in 1939. It did help strengthen me. No matter whether there was danger, suffering, [sic] poverty, riches, or disease, the children being naughty or any other thing, I was strengthened by it. Only God should be praised and given glory to. I always thanked God in those days, for I felt in my heart that there must be friends in many places praying for this work here and God heard His children's prayers, and so all things were done in us. I am nothing, but God takes charge of His own work. He uses such a mean and useless person as I am to manifest His grace, while I learnt quite a lot of lessons in this work.
>
> ... I lose hope for the children sometimes, especially a few with very strange natures. But in the Bible it says that God hath chosen the base things of the world and things which are despised and things which are not, to bring to naught the things that are. How can I despair?[23]

As things in Shanxi became more and more unstable, mission groups were forced to take action. In some cases, workers were pulled from the field over safety concerns. Other groups took measures to address Shanxi's concrete needs. In 1938 the CBM sent Howard Sollenberger to be a full-time relief worker in Shanxi. By 1939 the Brethren's work throughout all of China had already grown to include 2,670 members in five congregations with three Chinese pastors and forty-eight paid local evangelists, of whom twenty-nine were women.[24] Sollenberger, however, was only one of many missionaries who sought to bring real help and comfort to the people of Shanxi during these difficult years.

PETER TORJESEN

In 1909 in a small church in Kristiansand, Norway, seventeen-year-old Peter Torjesen responded to a call to support Christian mission by emptying his wallet into the collection plate.[25] Realizing that money was not enough,

---

23. Ibid., 28–29.
24. Tiedemann, "Church of the Brethren Mission."
25. The story of the Torjesen family is recorded in Malcolm, *We Signed Away Our Lives*.

he found a small scrap of paper and wrote three words on it before slipping it in with the offering. The words? *Og mit liv*, or "and my life."

Only two years later Peter enrolled in a preparatory course for mission at the Norwegian Evangelical Free Church Bible School in Rushford, Minnesota. He went on to study at Moody Bible Institute in Chicago before entering theological studies at the Northern Baptist Theological Seminary (a forerunner of Trinity Evangelical Divinity School). After returning to Norway to serve for two years as a military draft during World War I, Peter finally set sail for China in 1918 as an associate of the Norwegian Mission in China, a group affiliated with Hudson Taylor's CIM. Peter was making good on his offer from ten years previous, choosing for his "Motto for China" Philippians 1:20: "I eagerly expect and hope that I will in no way be ashamed, but will have sufficient courage so that now as always Christ will be exalted in my body, whether by life or by death."

After two years of formal language study, Peter found himself in Shanxi in the midst of famine. In 1921 Peter was asked to assist in the disbursement of Red Cross relief funds for the Shanxi famine victims. The immediate means of relief centered on the construction of an eighty-two-mile-long road from Fenzhou over to "Jung-tu" on the Yellow River—the first road for motor vehicles in the province. As Peter paid wages to the laborers hired by General Joseph Stillwell to build the road, those families would be saved from starvation. At this same time, his sweetheart back in Kristiansand, Valborg Tonnessen, had just completed candidate school with the CIM in England and was now in Shanxi for her two years of Mandarin study. As CIM policy forbade marriage before language school was completed, the couple had to wait before they could be together. Following the famine relief project, Peter's three years of probationary China service were complete and he was now ready to begin independent mission work. He had specifically requested to be sent to the hardest place where no church existed and where no one else wanted to go. The decision was made to send him as a pioneer into far northern Shanxi, to a small city called Hequ, located on a bend in the Yellow River. After a five-day mule trip, Peter arrived at his life's mission post on November 5, 1921.

Valborg's status as a single woman in China during her years of language study invited no end of comment from local women. As she wrote home in one letter,

> That I am thirty years old and not married the Chinese cannot imagine. Here the girls are married off as twelve- or thirteen-year-olds. So when we are visiting and a new woman comes into the room, the rest shout out, "Look at her, she is thirty and not

married." One day in a very nice home four daughters-in-law watched me with a mixture of astonishment and envy. Then the oldest said, "How wonderful that you have been kept so well till now. You are thirty and not married." She thought that was great. That I was soon to get married I didn't tell them. For then the talk would have had no end.[26]

On January 17, 1923, Peter and Valborg were married in a Norwegian ceremony in Lan County, Shanxi. The local mandarin's wife loaned her cook to the party, and this chef's "Norwegian fish balls" made from wok-fried, finely chopped chicken breast were the highlight of the meal. For their honeymoon, the couple enjoyed a mule ride to Hequ. As Valborg described it,

We had a good trip, not even cold or windy which we could expect at this time of year. God prepared everything for us in every way. The last two days were a bit rough up and down the mountains from morning till evening. After six days we were home at Saturday evening and it was good to be in our own place. Our Chinese friends have made everything so festive. The little courtyard with its flat roofs lay smiling in the sunset, and gave such a good welcome. And over the door of our new home the Christians had placed the motto: "GOD'S GRACE HAS NO LIMITS."

I felt thoroughly welcome, as we ate delicious Chinese food which they had prepared for us. Afterwards we got a few things done before the Prayer Meeting. We hung curtains up in both rooms of our apartment, and got tablecloths on the tables.

Sunday we had meetings morning and afternoon, and for the first time the women came to church in Hequ. It seemed strange, especially for the men, who are used to being there alone. We have hung a green curtain down the middle, dividing the men from the women. Behind the curtain you can hear mumblings and loud talk from the women. If it was like this during Paul's time, it is no wonder he had to tell the women to be silent in the worship services.[27]

The one hundred thousand people in the country around Hequ were a challenging group to reach. Lax regulations in Inner Mongolia—just across

---

26. Ibid., 34.

27. Ibid., 35–36. Valborg is referring to the Apostle Paul's instruction to the Corinthian Christians in 1 Corinthians 14:34–35. In later years—once the women had learned to pay attention to the sermons—Valborg would circulate among the women, encouraging them to save their questions and comments to share with their husbands after the service.

the shallow Yellow River from the city—meant that opium use was a serious problem throughout the region. Disease was another difficulty; the Torjesen children were often ill and, on one occasion, Peter nearly died from typhoid contracted while traveling in Shanxi. Finally, despite the Torjesens' efforts to adapt to local customs, superstition and fear of foreigners were endemic in Hequ. Local businessmen were unwilling to rent or sell property to the Torjesens, and Valborg found in her women's work that something as simple as sharing a cup of tea could be problematic.

> Most women are afraid to drink tea here in the women's reception room, even though it is Chinese tea, bought here in town. They think we put a kind of medicine in the tea to bewitch them to turn to our teaching about God. The men on the other hand who have had contact with us longer, have more confidence in us and are not afraid to drink our tea.[28]

In general, Valborg and Peter shared ministry and parenting duties, though Peter carried more of the itinerant load. They also respected local customs, and so in their various ministries they preserved the local sense of propriety by having women teach women and men teach men. Throughout all their work they tried to make sure there was always at least one parent at home with the children. This meant that Valborg would often hold clinic hours and some of her women's studies in the home. When she went out for home visitations or to hold studies in the homes of female inquirers, then Peter would stay with the children. This policy meant that when Peter was off on weeklong preaching tours, Valborg would necessarily limit her work.

The Torjesens' station in Hequ expanded over the years to include a school for boys and then for girls, as well as a small clinic where Valborg applied her basic nursing skills. As the only modern medical clinic in town, Valborg's station eventually invited competition. A young educated man had bought some medicines in Taiyuan, and then had someone instruct him in English writing. With a less-than-full command of English, the poor fellow hung what was to be the only English sign in Hequ for years to come: "AM I A DOCTOR."[29] Alongside their other initiatives, the gospel work progressed. In 1925 alone, Peter worked two outstations, held 367 street meetings, and visited 242 villages, enabling about 22,000 people to hear the gospel. The Torjesens had sold 2,000 Scripture portions and small books and distributed 16,000 tracts. Four men had been baptized, with now about twenty people attending Sunday morning worship services.[30]

28. Ibid., 39.
29. Ibid., 55.
30. Ibid., 44.

Peter was known for his sense of humor, a trait seen by some of his children as one of the keys to their family's happiness in their remote station. On one occasion Valborg had dared Peter to preach with only half of his face shaved. He did so, observing that foreigners appeared so strange to the local people that one more oddity would be barely noticeable.[31]

In 1927 the Torjesen family traveled to Norway for a welcome furlough. Shortly after their return, Shanxi was once again gripped by famine. Repeating patterns from the previous century, the 1929–1931 famine resulted in people selling their daughters and wives, and eating bark and leaves off of trees. As many as five million or perhaps even ten million Shanxi people perished. During these years and throughout the rest of the 1930s, bandits were a fact of life in Shanxi, and highway robberies were common. Peter and Valborg's eldest son Edvard recalled one occasion when the family's mule train was approached by bandits from the other side of a ravine. Peter crossed over to the robbers' side and after a lengthy negotiation returned—though now barefoot. The family's prayers had been answered, and all the bandit chief had wanted were Peter's shoes. On another occasion the mission community had gathered in the mountains of Shanxi for a spiritual retreat when news reached them that a bandit gang was approaching. The adults set to prayer as was their habit, but the children also gathered separately of their own accord to pray for protection. The parents did not know where their children had gone and commenced a frantic search, afraid that their little ones had been kidnapped. After the youths were discovered in prayer, the anxious missionaries returned their attention to scanning the horizon for signs of the pending bandit attack. Some time later word came from a nearby village that the brigands had fled in fear, telling others along their escape route of the men in white with shining swords lining the roofs of the building where the missionaries had gathered. The bandits wanted to know where the foreigners had kept their army.[32]

In 1934 the Torjesens' most fervent prayers were answered when revival broke out among the Hequ believers. The excitement began with a series of talks on the Holy Spirit delivered by Miss Jean Graham, a hotly sought-after New Zealand preacher with the CIM. Valborg wrote describing the initial outbreak and conviction of sin:

> It was two in the afternoon when I got home from the morning meeting. The Holy Spirit is working in the congregation and when the invitation was given for all who wanted to get rid of

---

31. Ibid., 53.

32. These stories are from the personal recollections of various Torjesen family members.

> their sin, nearly all women who had not made a stand before came forward. Others came too who had some sin hindering their walk with God—altogether fifteen to twenty women. Some were crushed under the burden of sin and wept with despair. It's a time I will never forget. Our hearts were filled with thanks that we could experience something like this . . . in Hequ. A number of women got rid of their burdens and left the church with joy on their faces. Many people have joined us these days, and among them quite a few men. The Holy Spirit is also working among the boys. . . . One boy whose parents are not believers went home last night and said he had become a Christian. He was among the first to come today. Oh, that this might be a great overturning for Hequ and many will be set free.

The event was one of the highlights of their years of service, and many encouraging stories of faith and repentance came out of it.

> Imagine experiencing the Holy Spirit reviving the whole church, like an old-fashioned Norwegian revival with aftermeetings and tears, and confession of sin. How we've been of little faith thinking this could not happen here. We have seen conviction of sin among a few before, but to see the whole congregation gripped by the Holy Spirit was something new. . . . One woman sat there so burdened when I approached her. "I am such a big sinner that there is not one of the Ten Commandments I have not broken," she confessed. After pouring out her heart in prayer she arose with a smile through her tears. Beside her sat her daughter. When she saw her mother under such conviction, she broke down too.
> . . . a man who has been a Christian several years . . . became so convicted of sin by the Holy Spirit that we had to pray for him more than once. Only when he promised God he would pay back the money he had gained in a dishonest way, did he experience peace and a special blessing. After the revival meetings were over, he took all the money he could find at home, and when it was not enough he took precious things like silver from the home and sold it so he had the sixty dollars he needed. That was a lot of money for an ordinary family. But finally when he was ready to go with the big sum, he felt happier than he had ever felt in his life. He had to walk 25 miles to the other side of the Yellow River to pay back the money. This story has spoken to many in Hequ. That a man will pay back sixty dollars in these bad times, well then—something must have happened to him.

As these stories circulated through the county, many people came to faith, often following lines of extended families.[33]

After another peaceful furlough in Norway, the Torjesens set off to return to China in August of 1937. As the ship sailed, troubling reports came from China, telling of increasingly aggressive Japanese military movements. While the Torjesens' mission society eventually gave their missionaries the mid-journey option of returning home to Norway, the passengers agreed unanimously to continue on to the field, citing Luke 9:62 as their rationale: "No one who puts a hand to the plow and looks back is fit for service in the kingdom of God." Moreover, prior to September 1939 Norway's neutral stance in the war meant that the Scandinavian missionaries had opportunities to travel and serve that were now closed to workers of other nationalities. As Peter explained, "The responsibility seems to rest more on us Norwegians and Swedes than earlier, now that the way is closed for others, and we are the only ones who can get permits to go inland."[34]

At the end of their five-week steamer passage from Genoa, Italy, to Hong Kong, the Torjesens traveled north by rail as far as Hankou. Fighting further north meant they were unable to enter Shanxi, and so the family set up residence among the refugees in the war-torn city, with Peter still trying to find secure passage to Shanxi. One fellow Norwegian missionary described Peter's role in embattled Hankou:

> We were glad to have Torejsen and his family with us. . . . But we could see the missionary in him was not totally content. . . . Then one day we woke up to the sounds of trumpets and fanfare. The troops were coming through on their way to the front with shining helmets. Another day, another group of soldiers—but no shining helmets and no fanfare. They were wounded and tattered, dirty and tired. One had a bandage on his head. Another no arm. Another was limping along on his crutches—coming from the front.
>
> The next group that came to town was the refugees—women and children, old and young. They were tired and dirty and ragged—driven from their homes and their rice fields. Their loved ones had been killed by the Japanese, or trampled under foot in the mass exodus as thousands had fled from the war zone. Now they were alone among strangers in a strange province.

---

33. The three previous quotations regarding the 1934 Hequ revival are from letters and articles written by the Torjesens as recorded in Malcolm, *We Signed Away Our Lives*, 63–65.

34. Ibid., 105.

> Most of the wounded soldiers and refugees from the north could not understand the Hunan dialect. But Torjesen they understood. Suddenly he became another person. We got a glimpse of the real missionary inside of him. Early and late he was busy. We could see him surrounded by a group of soldiers listening to his simple testimony. Next he was inside an ancestral hall where hundreds of refugees were looking for some type of shelter. Next at the temple by the river to visit Buddhist monks also in flight.
>
> His good smile brought courage to all as he spoke words of comfort to each person. There might be a tract given, or just a word about the Lord he loved. Quietly and with great inner freedom he moved among these people. This is how I remember him—always ready to comfort and help—eager to give the Good News, and filled with the missionary joy over the slightest sign of new life sprouting.[35]

By Chinese New Year of 1938 Peter was back in Hequ, albeit without his family. He had found an opportunity to carry much-needed medicines to the hospital in Linfen, an errand that warranted a letter of introduction from the Communist Eighth Route Army, the de facto rulers of Shanxi at that time. When he finally reached Hequ, Peter was welcomed in grand style by the church, with people lining the streets in joyful anticipation. As he threw himself back into the work of the Shanxi mission, Peter remarked how it was "good to find that among our missionaries as well as other missions, most have chosen to stay at their posts instead of evacuating. They have chosen to suffer with the people."[36]

The joy of returning, however, was diluted by the grim realities of life in war-torn Shanxi. The following is from Peter's report to the mission at that time:

> First came the crisis in February [1938] when 3,000 Japanese soldiers took the city. The defeated Chinese troops plundered everything they could before escaping over the river. But in the middle of this confusing time we had the most wonderful opportunity to minister to the three hundred refugees who sought shelter with us. It would not have been an easy time for the Chinese Christians to be alone. For example, one day a Japanese officer came and demanded three young Chinese girls [to use as prostitutes]. When he got a very definite refusal from me, he gave up and walked away ashamed.[37]

35. Ibid., 83.
36. Ibid., 85.
37. Ibid., 86–87.

May 1938 was similar: over one thousand refugees came to the mission compound seeking shelter as Japanese air raids shook the town for ten consecutive days. But prayers were answered, and the invading Japanese troops turned away suddenly when they were just a few short miles away from Hequ. Along with the fighting and the refugees came pestilence. A typhoid epidemic soon flared up among the wounded soldiers and civilians: that same May saw one hundred cases in Hequ. In one of the few letters that managed to get through the lines and reach his family in Hankou, Peter described some of the challenges facing the people of Shanxi during those days of war. After the epidemic passed, Peter spent an exhausting day resettling patients back in their homes. "The day after God sent a blessed rain. It poured for a day and a half and washed away all the garbage left after 1,000 refugees had stayed with us. It was also good for the farmers. This year people need a good crop to survive."[38] Summarizing the year in his annual report to the mission, Peter explained:

> It has been a year of light and shadows. I have never seen such progress in the work of the Kingdom, nor such dark clouds.... In the fall the Japanese began again to bomb Hequ and Pianguan. One reason is that the generals Fu Tso-yi and Ma Chan have their headquarters near these cities. Our station was recently hit, but no people were hurt. We had good conferences both in Hequ and Pianguan, where we have visited for the past ten years, but only now we see results.... We now have an evangelist couple living there who have the people's confidence.... In Hequ we have had meetings in the street chapel every night. The church has grown with thirty-five baptisms this year.... Both in the work in Hequ and on the long journeys to and from the field we have sensed the Unseen Power opening doors step by step.[39]

Before long Valborg and the children were forced to evacuate from Hankou to Hong Kong along with the rest of the foreign community. After a brief stay in the British colony, they headed north to Chefoo, where the children were enrolled in the CIM school for the fall of 1939. Peter quickly left Hequ to join them in Chefoo, and the family spent a pleasant summer together in a rented cabin near the ocean. When the children entered school in September, Valborg and Peter headed off once more to Shanxi.

Valborg wrote from Datong on September 20 describing her emotions upon returning to the province.

---

38. Ibid., 88.
39. Ibid., 90.

> Now we have finally reached good old Shanxi. . . . Our prayer is that if it is in agreement with God's will, that God will open doors for us all the way to Hequ, and once more allow us to work among the dear ones in that place, and seek to win new converts in the time that is left. . . . We also feel that the doors will be closed for us here in China—maybe sooner than we had thought.

When they stepped off the train at the end of the line in Ningwu, the couple still had to find transport for the last four days' journey—not an easy task at the front lines. They were only able to cross from Japanese to Chinese territory through God's miraculous provision of some very generous farmers with donkeys. Throughout the journey, Valborg marveled at how things had changed.

> The war has taken its toll on both the people and the land. . . . The first thing that struck me was the gnawing silence, as if the city had been forsaken. Many have deserted it for out of the way places in the country-side, and others have fled north of the Great Wall to Inner Mongolia. . . . Those who are left experience continued angst over the possibility of Japanese planes coming to drop bombs. . . . Tumbled down homes and ruins are seen everywhere in the city. On Main Street business has ceased and the bigger stores are closed. Only late in the afternoon there are some small shops that open. . . . And with war comes pestilence. For two years typhus and typhoid epidemics have been rampant in nearly every village around Hequ. . . . Whole families laid [sic] there sick and died due to neglect because no one dared to help the sick for fear of contagion.[40]

Shortly after they reached Hequ, the Torjesens began construction of a bomb shelter near their home. When groundwater levels made this impractical they revised their plan and built a strong shelter close to the church. Many hours were spent beneath the building "packed liked sardines in a can."

> Yesterday we were again down in the bomb shelter. We sat there for over half an hour while three planes threw twenty bombs. . . . One wonders why they continue to bomb this defenceless city. . . [with] no more soldiers in the town, just a few troops spread around the mountains. . . .

---

40. Ibid., 108. Valborg also described how famine and drought, as well as the heavy burden of feeding all the Chinese troops stationed in the area, made life in World War II Shanxi extremely difficult.

> In the ministry everything is going well. Valborg has begun daily classes for men and women. Many come to the Sunday meetings, especially in the afternoon when they are not afraid of planes. When the planes came yesterday the Sunday school had just gathered. It was good that there were only about fifty children, so there was room for all in the bomb shelter. There they stood together—some crying and some praying. The believers have many experiences of answered prayers these days. We had testimonies yesterday from three young men who were thrown in prison by the Japanese and almost shot. One had been a prisoner for seventeen months. In his need he cried to God and was set free. Through this their faith has been greatly strengthened.[41]

In the summer of 1939 Nationalist military leaders had demanded to use the mission church for a series of meetings, and the local evangelist in charge had felt powerless to refuse. When this fact—along with the news that local citizens and wounded Chinese soldiers were taking refuge in the mission compound—was reported by spies to the Japanese military officials, the neutrality the Torjesens enjoyed as Norwegian citizens was stripped away.

On the morning of December 14, 1939, the Torjesens stretched the large Norwegian flag out on the ground of their home's courtyard as always—a precaution they had taken to help the Japanese bombers avoid accidentally hitting the "neutral" Norwegian property. As was their habit, Peter and Valborg then read together the verse for the day written on the calendar tacked to their wall: "As the heavens are higher than the earth, so are my ways higher than your ways" (Isaiah 55:9). They then set about their regular daily tasks, writing reports and treating the sick until mid-afternoon when, just as they prepared to take their coffee, they heard the sound of approaching planes. Thirty or forty planes were bearing down on Hequ, and with insufficient time to seek safety in the church bomb shelter, they took refuge beneath the bed in their home. Before Peter could get completely under the bed, the first bomb burst through the air, shattering their simple mud home. In a few minutes the attack had moved past their compound and the terrifying noise and shaking stopped. Valborg was in a daze, having been thrown clear onto a pile of debris by the rush of air accompanying the explosion. Peter was nowhere to be seen. As local believers rushed from the bomb shelter to the aid of Valborg, they began to dig through what was left of the home. A half hour's exertion brought them to Peter's breathless body, his head having been struck by the central beam of the house. Valborg

---

41. Ibid., 110–11.

performed artificial respiration for two hours before she surrendered to her grief: but there was no place to lay her husband's body. As darkness fell and looters began to sweep through the devastated town, Valborg's glance turned to the calendar still miraculously hanging untouched on the one remaining wall of the home. Then, for the only time in her life, she heard the audible voice of God: "You do not realize now what I am doing, but later you will understand" (John 13:7).[42]

Peter was buried in Hequ, with some of the remaining Shanxi missionaries attending. The day's ceremonies were somber, after the Chinese fashion, with a large number of people in the procession—some carrying banners, one of which read "A good shepherd has died for me."[43] Afterward, Valborg found a new house up against the remains of the Great Wall near Hequ, complete with a dugout beneath the wall to provide shelter from Japanese bombs. By May 1940 the church in Hequ was being rebuilt, along with the school and the other buildings in the compound. Locals in Hequ had said to the believers there, "Now that your church is in ruins and your pastor dead, this must be the end of the Christian church in Hequ." "Oh, no," was the response of two of the leading local Christian businessmen, "We are all here, and we are the church." With the church recovered, Valborg set off for the coast to meet her children. The journey was hard and dangerous, and Valborg spent a time marching across the countryside as a prisoner of the Communists before finally reaching the Japanese lines, where a military officer took pity on her and gave her permission to travel to Chefoo.

By late 1940 it was already clear that no missionaries were able to return to Shanxi, and so Valborg resigned herself and turned to caring for other visitors at the mission guesthouse in Chefoo. This lasted until December 8, 1941, when all the foreigners were placed under arrest by the Japanese Navy and held at the Chefoo school. Over the next two years, the group of prisoners was moved many times, until finally they were settled at Weihsien Camp, the old Presbyterian mission compound where Henry Luce and Pearl Buck had been born. One early arrival described the place as

> Bare walls, bare floors, dim electric light, no running water, primitive latrines, open cesspools, a crude bakery, two houses with public showers, three huge public kitchens, a desecrated church and a dismantled hospital, a few sheds for shops, rows of cell-like rooms, and three-high dormitories for persons who are single.[44]

42. Ibid., 113–16.
43. Ibid., 122.
44. Ibid., 143.

The sixteen hundred foreign men, women, and children that filled the Japanese internment camp included four hundred Protestant missionaries and another four hundred Catholic priests and nuns. During their imprisonment, which lasted until the camp was liberated on September 25, 1945, the Torjesen children witnessed many examples of heroism and faith, having been particularly impressed by Eric Liddell. He was the most widely respected and loved person in the camp, as one of the Torjesen children later recalled:

> Liddell could be found putting up a wooden shelf for a former prostitute one day and carrying coal balls to an elderly person the next day.
>
> One of my great moments in camp came when I was alone in a kitchen, single handedly trying to kill hundreds of flies before 600 people would file in for their rations. Then Eric Liddell was passing by. I knew him well, both as my softball coach and as a Bible teacher. Now he stopped in and gave me his undivided attention for a few charged moments. With his steel-blue, penetrating and laughing eyes and a disarming smile, he had my complete attention. He told me that as a Christian I was bringing people nearer Christ by doing something as simple as killing flies for them. I had heard him teach that we either repel people from Christ or bring them closer. Then he heartily thanked me for what I was doing just then, with no one but God to notice what I was doing, or to give me proper credit.
>
> Next to my father, Eric Liddell was the most Christlike person I have ever met.[45]

Peter and Valborg's eldest son Edvard went on to fulfill Peter's dream of preaching north of Hequ in Mongolia, returning in 1948 to begin Mongolian language studies in Gansu province with his wife, Jenny, and their infant son, Leif.[46] Fifty years later, God revealed a key part of his plan for Peter Torjesen's sacrifice when a monument was erected on Chinese soil in his name. This unusual honor from the Chinese government—naming the Norwegian missionary Peter Torjesen as a People's Martyr—paved the way for Peter and Valborg's grandson Finn S. Torjesen to return with his family in the 1990s and continue the Torjesen family legacy in Shanxi.

---

45. Ibid., 145–46. For more on Liddell's remarkable life and ministry in China, see McCasland, *Eric Liddell: Pure Gold*.

46. Malcolm, *We Signed Away Our Lives*, 159.

GLADYS AYLWARD

The life of Gladys Aylward, "the small woman" (she stood under five feet tall), exemplified many of the changes the China field experienced during the first half of the twentieth century. Born to a postman and his wife in London in 1902, Aylward was drawn to China mission while still a child during a revival meeting at a local church. By the time she was fourteen, however, her indifferent education was over and she found herself "in service" with little money and no prospects. She eventually heard about Taylor's CIM and how they would train people with no money or education to be missionaries.[47] Aylward applied and was accepted for a probationary period of study at the China Inland Mission Centre training school in London. Unfortunately, her inability to progress in theological studies soon led to her removal from the program, as it appeared unlikely that she would be able to complete the full three-year course. Moreover, her age at the time (an "elderly" twenty-six) meant that she would be thirty by the time she completed her training and arrived in China. Experience had taught the CIM that missionaries over thirty years of age found learning Mandarin Chinese extremely difficult.[48]

Following her rejection, Aylward took a position as parlormaid for a retired CIM mission couple, finding there both encouragement and a steady income. She moved on to other positions, though still no closer to China. One night in desperation she clutched all she owned in the world—her Bible and a few coins—and cried out, "Oh God, here's my Bible! Here's my money! Here's me! Use me, God!"[49] From this point on, Aylward began saving a portion of her income in order to purchase a one-way train ticket to China, as rail was at that time the least expensive way to travel to Asia. One evening, while attending a Primitive Methodist prayer meeting, she heard of a China missionary woman named Jeannie Lawson, who, upon returning to England after her husband's death, declared that she could not settle in England and went back to China, intending to serve there until her death. This woman was now praying for a young woman to come and continue her work after she was gone. Aylward was thrilled and wrote to Lawson at once, volunteering her service. The reply came back that if Aylward could make her own way to Tianjin, a guide would meet her there and escort her over the mountains to where the now seventy-three-year-old Lawson was located.

---

47. These early details of her life are taken from Swift, *Gladys Aylward*, 8–10.

48. Burgess, *The Small Woman*, 14–15. In her later years she came to realize that the board was right for rejecting her as a student of Chinese: she was, as she described herself, "silly." Purves, *Chinese Whispers*, 115.

49. Swift, *Gladys Aylward*, 15.

On October 18, 1930, Gladys Aylward left Liverpool Station, London, by the Trans-Siberian Train bound for Tianjin, China. War and conflict made the trip almost impossible, but after being nearly kidnapped into forced labor in Vladivostok, she managed to reach her final destination—with a brief detour through Kobe, Japan.[50] Here she was told that Lawson was working in Zezhou.[51] The train ride from Tianjin carried Aylward through Beijing and west to Shanxi, eventually terminating at Yuci. From there she traveled by bus to Zezhou—where Lawson was conspicuously absent. A Mrs. Smith helped outfit Aylward with local Chinese clothes before sending her off on the two-day mule journey to Lawson's station in Yangcheng, an outpost of S. P. Smith's Tsechow Mission.[52]

The small town of Yangcheng functioned as an overnight stop for mule caravans carrying coal, raw cotton, pots, and iron goods on extended journeys.[53] Most of the residents of the town had seen no Europeans other than Lawson and now Aylward. As foreigners, they were distrusted, and few locals were willing to listen their preaching. Shortly after Aylward's arrival, the two women decided to open an inn in the hope that paying guests might be more inclined to listen to their message. They repaired their residence—a former inn—and bought food for mules and men. When the next caravan came through town, Aylward ran out and seized the reins of the first mule, turning the beast into their courtyard. The animal, eager for food and rest, followed Aylward, as did the rest of the mules. The muleteers were satisfied with their food and lodgings, and they sat happily to listen to the "entertainment"—stories about an impressive man named Jesus. The reputation of the inn soon grew, and after a few weeks, caravans would stop there of their own accord. The stories the muleteers heard at the inn were naturally repeated all along the caravan routes, and some of the men became Christians. In this environment, Aylward's Chinese language skills steadily improved, as did her confidence in ministry.[54] At just this point, Lawson fell and injured her spine, dying several months later in Yangcheng after four weeks of treatment at the mission hospital in Lu'an.[55] Gladys Aylward was now on her

50. Aylward's thrilling journey to Shanxi is recorded in Burgess, *The Small Woman*, 23–44.

51. The frontispiece of Burgess's *The Small Woman* includes a map listing "Tsehchow" as a large city located a two-days' mule ride to the east-northeast of Yangcheng.

52. At the time Aylward arrived in Shanxi it took three days to travel by train from Beijing to Yuci. Burgess, *The Small Woman*, 40–41. On the Tsechow Mission see Tiedemann, *Reference Guide to Christian Missionary Societies in China*, 224.

53. James E. Kiefer, "Gladys Aylward, Missionary to China."

54. Burgess, *The Small Woman*, 55–63.

55. Ibid., 68–73.

own, left to run the mission as best she could with the aid of their cook, a Chinese Christian named Yang.[56]

Shortly after Lawson's death, Aylward was approached by the highest-ranking official in Yangcheng. The government was looking for a "foot inspector" to carry out the decree to eliminate the oppressive practice of foot-binding, whereby the feet of young girls were wrapped so tightly that the bones were unable to grow normally producing highly-sought-after miniature "three-inch golden lotus" feet. Specifically, the official was in need of a woman (who could enter the women's quarters without scandal) with her own feet unbound (who could thus travel easily) to patrol the district, enforcing the decree.[57] It was soon clear to them both that Aylward was the only possible candidate for the job, and she accepted, realizing that it would give her undreamed-of opportunities to spread the gospel.

In her second year in Yangcheng, Aylward was summoned again by the official and sent to deal with a riot that had broken out in the men's prison. She arrived and found that several prisoners had been killed and the soldiers were afraid to intervene. The prison warden immediately turned to Aylward and commanded her to go into the prison yard and stop the rioting. When Aylward protested her own fear and inability, the warden responded with a question: "How can they kill you? You have been telling everybody that you have come here because you have the living God inside of you.... If you preach the truth—if your God protects you from harm—then you can stop this riot." Accepting the test of faith implicit in the warden's words, Aylward entered the prison courtyard unsure of what she would do. After a brief pause, she raised her voice to the wretched prisoners, ordering them to form a line and put down their weapons. She then had the men choose a spokesman to present their grievances. Aylward listened as the man explained the boredom and hunger that had led to the violence, and then relayed their concerns to the warden. At the same time, she proposed a solution: if looms were brought into the yard, the men would have an occupation as well as a source of income with which they could purchase their own food. The warden arranged for looms and a grindstone to be donated,

---

56. Aylward was supported by Mrs. Smith (until her death in 1936) and then the Davises from the Mission headquarters in Zezhou, a two-days' journey from Yangcheng. She got along well with her Zezhou colleagues, and Jean (Scottish) and David (Welsh) Davis were a particularly valuable support to her during the war years. Ibid., 118–19.

57. It would be hard to overstate the role missionaries—and particularly female missionaries—played in eliminating the Chinese practice of foot binding. See Whitefield, "The Tian Zu Hui (Natural Foot Society)," 203–12.

and from this point onward Gladys Aylward was known locally as "Ai the Virtuous" (Ai Weide).[58]

That same year she happened upon a woman begging by the side of the road. The woman was holding a filthy malnourished child, displaying her sores in order to elicit pity—and cash—from passersby. Aylward knew the woman was not the child's mother but rather a "child dealer." Aylward took pity on the child and purchased the five-year-old girl for ninepence. Young "Ninepence" soon began to bring home a steady stream of other stray children, in each case securing their place in Aylward's growing family with her promise to eat less in order that others could share in their meal.[59] Before long, Aylward had her own orphanage, feeding and caring for hundreds of children during her years in Yangcheng. Through these and other experiences Aylward, with her Chinese clothes and simple lifestyle, was becoming increasingly integrated into the local community. In 1936 she took the further step of becoming a Chinese citizen, thus removing yet one more barrier between herself and the people of Yangcheng.[60]

Everything changed in the spring of 1938 when the Japanese came to Yangcheng—first bombing the town from the air and then briefly occupying it. Many perished in the fighting, while the survivors fled into the mountains. The local official was so moved by the assistance Aylward and the local Christians provided during the invasion that he publicly announced his conversion to Christianity. Aylward then convinced him to release the convicts from the prison on bond—rather than executing them which was the traditional policy—so that they too could flee the invaders.[61]

Throughout the war years Aylward was frequently behind Japanese lines. Colonel Linnan of the Nationalist intelligence services, Aylward's love interest while in Shanxi, convinced her to pass on information regarding troop movements.[62] She also became friends with a European Catholic priest known as "General Ley," who was leading a guerilla force of Chinese fighters in the Shanxi mountains. When the Chinese forces in Zezhou were preparing for their final retreat, General Ley advised Aylward to join them. Her response of "Christians never retreat!" (*Jidutu bu tui*) was perfectly in character. However, when General Ley informed her that the Japanese were

58. Burgess, *The Small Woman*, 87–94.
59. Ibid., 97–103.
60. Ibid., 117–18.
61. Ibid., 141–45.
62. Ibid., 162–67. Whether or not Aylward shared information regarding Communist as well as Japanese troops is unclear. The chaste love affair between Linnan and Aylward ended in Xi'an when she rejected his offer of marriage convinced she had more work to do for the Lord. Ibid., 189–90, 251–52.

offering a one hundred dollar reward for information leading to the capture of "The small woman known as Ai Weide," she relented.[63]

Aylward set off across the mountains with nearly one hundred of her children in tow, hoping to bring them safely to the government orphanage at Xi'an. The journey was arduous, with some nights spent sleeping on the mountainside, others spent in the homes of kind strangers. After walking for twelve days they reached the Yellow River. All traffic had been stopped on the river in order to prevent boats from falling into Japanese hands, so there was no way across. The children, however, were confident that God could do anything, so they prayed and sang songs of praise. Their music was heard by a passing Chinese officer, who was able to secure them a boat. Eventually Aylward reached Xi'an with all her charges, where she collapsed with typhus into a delirium that lasted several days.[64]

During her slow convalescence in Xi'an Aylward started a church, spending her time living with various missionaries in the area. Eventually she moved to Chengdu, Sichuan, where she spent her last four years in China engaged in a variety of projects, including ministering to lepers in a settlement near the Tibetan border and caring for prisoners in the second largest prison in China.[65]

Since missionaries were no longer welcome in China and the Chinese Communists were seeking her as a spy (they had also put a price on her head), Aylward left China just before the Communist regime took over in 1949.[66] Back in England, she reconnected with her family and discovered that she was already famous for her mission work. One day the well-known British radio producer Alan Burgess visited Aylward, inquiring to see if she would be a suitable subject for his radio series *The Undefeated*.

> "Did anything interesting happen to you all those years you were in China?" asked Burgess.
> "No, it wasn't interesting, just hard work. No one would want to know about anything I'd done," was Gladys's humble reply.[67]

Burgess's book *The Small Woman* and later the film *The Inn of the Sixth Happiness* soon followed, as the world warmed to Aylward's remarkable story.[68]

63. Ibid., 193–97.
64. The dramatic tale of Aylward's remarkable escape from Shanxi with her one hundred orphans is told in ibid., 198–250.
65. Purves, *Chinese Whispers*, 91.
66. Ibid., 98–99.
67. Ibid., 103.
68. Responding to a review of the film in *Newsweek* magazine, one incredulous

By 1955 both of Aylward's parents were deceased, leaving her free to return to Asia. She sailed for Hong Kong in 1957, and after a brief stay there she settled in Taiwan for her remaining years of service. The unexpected surprise of a baby left in a washing basin brought Aylward back into her most beloved sphere of ministry. Before long she had a thriving orphanage, always ready to take in another of the lost.[69] The orphanage ran into financial trouble in 1963 (from which it eventually recovered) when it was discovered that the Chinese couple left in charge while Aylward toured the world raising funds for the cause had been embezzling money at the expense of the children's care. Aylward was deeply wounded and spent her remaining years wary of trusting others with the care of her orphans.[70] Gladys Aylward, the Small Woman of China known as Ai Weide, passed away on January 3, 1970.[71]

PAUL E. ADOLPH

Paul Adolph was first compelled to take up mission in China by the accounts of heroism and suffering under the Boxers recorded in Archibald Glover's *A Thousand Miles of Miracle in China*.[72] Once Adolph completed his Bible school diploma plus two years of medical study at Wheaton College in Illinois, he set sail for China. When he arrived in 1929, the twenty-eight-year-old visited his brother, who was teaching biochemistry at a university in Beijing, before heading to the CIM training school in Anqing to commence his language studies. Following just six months of formal Mandarin instruction, Adolph moved on to the Shanxi city of Linfen, where he completed his residency at the local mission hospital.[73]

---

reader expressed criticism: "In order for a movie to be good, the story should be believable!" Kiefer, "Gladys Aylward, Missionary to China."

69. Given her welcoming heart and love for children, Aylward was a fairly lax disciplinarian with the children she herself adopted. This was particularly true with regard to her youngest adopted son, Gordon. For one example, see the incident recorded in Purves, *Chinese Whispers*, 119.

70. The details of the criminal case can be found in ibid., 118–19.

71. Long-serving missionary to Asia Richard Olson recalls visiting Aylward's Taiwan home when he first arrived on the field in 1973. He and some of the other workers on the field were charged with disposing of the refuse and cleaning the home so it could be used again. Olson recalls that Aylward was still greatly revered—as a legend—by most workers on the field at that time. Her orphanage was still in operation.

72. Adolph, *Surgery Speaks to China*, 34. This book is Adolph's own account of his time as a surgeon in China—both with the CIM and the U.S. Army. It is a fascinating record with fantastic details regarding all aspects of medical work in 1930s Shanxi.

73. Ibid., 29–33.

Shortly after, Adolph began his years of service in the CIM hospital in Lu'an, where he discovered that Wheaton College classmates Claude H. Thomas and his wife were serving as "evangelistic missionaries."[74] The one-hundred-bed mission hospital in Lu'an had been built in 1916 and then left empty for many years due to the lack of suitable medical personnel to operate the facility. Before he could begin work, Adolph made trips to Beijing and Tianjin to purchase necessary medical equipment.[75] Adolph was so successful in this respect that, as he said, "Our operating instruments were equal in quality and variety to those which are available in any good hospital of similar size in America today."[76] Unfortunately, Lu'an itself had much less to offer in the way of supplies. Though the Japanese invaders eventually extended railroads to Lu'an after it was occupied in 1939, prior to that the city was isolated, lacking the cosmopolitanism of the bigger coastal cities.[77]

Practicing Western medicine in 1930s Shanxi was challenging, and Adolph's creativity and flexibility were often put to the test. On one occasion Adolph was extracting decayed teeth from an elderly believer to relieve him of back pain—but the terrified patient resisted Adolph's ministrations. Once he realized that the patient feared that the foreign doctor's poor grasp of Chinese had led him to confuse the Chinese words for backache (*yao teng*) and toothache (*ya teng*), Adolph was able to calm the man and perform the extractions. On another occasion Adolph amazed a group of local doctors by conducting a surgery using chopsticks when clean forceps were unavailable.[78] Similarly, when Adolph first arrived in Lu'an, the hospital used kerosene lamps and a flashlight for performing operations. Though electrification did not come until years later, Adolph improved conditions dramatically by rigging an electrical lamp in the operating theater using a spare battery from an old Ford V8.[79]

Many of the difficulties Adolph faced in his medical practice were related to Shanxi's conservative birth customs.[80] The traditional Chinese one-month period of post-birth confinement (*zuo yuezi*) was typically extended in Shanxi to a full three months or "one hundred days." Post-birth restrictions on bathing, going outdoors, and eating food other than millet and

74. Ibid., 34.
75. Ibid., 31–32.
76. Ibid., 38.
77. Ibid., 33.
78. Ibid., 104.

79. Ibid., 87–88. At that time the two cars operated by the missionary doctors had the highest license plate numbers in all of Shanxi: eighty-nine and ninety. Ibid., 97.

80. The details in this paragraph are taken from the chapter "Combatting Hospital Problems" in ibid., 80–93.

other coarse grains resulted in many health complications for both mothers and infants.[81] Shortly after arriving in Lu'an, Adolph attempted to overcome the malnutrition endemic in the Shanxi countryside by supplying infants and mothers with meat concentrate in capsule form; once local people found out, they were horrified by his blatant disregard for local confinement customs. When Adolph heard that the Republican government had begun a massive obstetrics propaganda campaign, he bought posters from Beijing and hung them in the Lu'an Hospital. In a few cases the official nature of the campaign helped convince families to change.

Sanitation was another frequent source of frustration throughout Adolph's time in China. Much attention was given to improving the sanitary practices of local midwives—though, admittedly, Shanxi midwives habitually severed umbilical cords with hot pokers, unlike even less sanitary practices in other parts of China. Bathing before surgery was considered dangerous by most Shanxi people, but once hot and warm baths were installed in the hospital, patients gradually acquiesced to the idea. On one occasion Adolph was mistaken for being in his twenties, but the patient instantly realized his error: Adolph's skin lacked the typical thirty-years' worth of dirt. "It's the way of these foreigners," the man remarked. "They are always taking baths."[82]

In 1936 Adolph and his family traveled back to the United States for a welcome furlough, leaving Drs. D. Gordon Anderson and Helen Neve (both Scottish) in charge of the hospital.[83] When they returned to China in 1937, they were warned that access to Shanxi was limited. With the Communists actively resisting Japanese advances in Shanxi, travel by train was increasingly dangerous and unreliable. As telegraph lines were sabotaged by the Communists, Japanese forces were forced to use carrier pigeons to secure right of passage for trains. In the resulting confusion, Japanese soldiers often attacked or blockaded their own trains.[84] Eager to return despite the difficulties, Adolph decided to leave his family on the coast, traveling inland by train from Beijing to Shunde, Shanxi. On this journey he had the good

---

81. In modern Shanxi it is still common in the countryside and not unusual in the city to find these folk customs practiced and even enforced by local women. As a result of extended confinement indoors, Shanxi has historically had some of the highest rates of incidence in the world of the Vitamin D deficiency known as rickets.

82. Adolph, *Surgery Speaks to China*, 87.

83. Ibid., 113–14. For some reason, Adolph's account contains almost no details about his family and their life in China.

84. Ibid., 119.

fortune to be accompanied by Dr. Harry Wyatt (see below), one of the chief medical workers at the BMS mission hospitals in Taiyuan.[85]

Although back in Shanxi, Adolph was initially unable to return to Lu'an due to fierce fighting in the south of the province. He made the best of his situation, working in Shunde with Dr. H. E. Henke until 1938, by which time Communist victories throughout Shanxi made it possible for him to complete his journey. People in Lu'an were amazed that Adolph returned to the mission hospital when conditions in Shanxi were so dangerous and chaotic. This opened a new season of ministry for Adolph. As he explained, "We found ourselves looked upon as their friends more than ever, since they realized that we were willing to endure inconvenience and even suffering for the Chinese people, and this increased our opportunities many fold."[86] Similarly, many Communist soldiers were quite willing to hear the nurses and doctors at the hospital tell them about the gospel while they treated their wounds. Adolph recalled that there had been one fellow, in particular, who was violently opposed to any talk of divine things. Having rested in the hospital for some time, this man was prepared for amputation after his leg wound suddenly began hemorrhaging uncontrollably. His military unit was asked to provide blood donors; they refused, and since no plasma was available, a local Christian male nurse offered his blood free of charge for the poor soldier. This powerful example of Christ's love broke the man's heart and made him receptive to the gospel.[87]

After less than a year at his station, Adolph headed to the coast to join his family for a well-earned few months of respite. In 1939, leaving his family alone once more, Adolph attempted to return to Lu'an. He spent the better part of that year wandering from village to village in embattled Shanxi. Lice, a broken leg, official interference, Japanese marauders, and threats of bandit attacks ultimately prevented him from reaching his mission hospital. At one point an injury required him to reside for a few weeks in a small village where he entered into the local life in a remarkable way: he was eventually requested by the village to explain to them the religion that had brought him as an American to help China.[88] As it was no longer practicable to return to Lu'an, Adolph agreed to serve briefly as director of the CIM hospital in Kaifeng (renamed the "American Hospital" by Adolph in the wake of the Japanese-sponsored anti-British campaign), before fi-

85. Ibid., 116.
86. Ibid., 134.
87. Ibid., 136–38.
88. For his convalescence, Adolph was practically adopted by a local mountaineer outside of Handan, Hebei: it was this time of immobility and dependence that created his unique witnessing opportunity. Ibid., 159.

nally returning with his family to the United States in 1942—just after the Japanese attack on Pearl Harbor.[89] Adolph's determination to serve with his medical skills during a time of danger and conflict provided many Shanxi people with a practical demonstration of the radical love of others that is central to the gospel.

HARRY WYATT

Born in 1895 into the family of a Baptist Nonconformist minister, Harry Wyatt lived in many different English towns during his childhood. Following his baptism at the age of eighteen, he threw himself into a range of service projects in the church and community, often finding opportunities to speak to groups on topics dear to his heart. A keen interest in scouting and years of varied schooling prepared him well for his service as an army dentist during the First World War. An address he delivered to the Bridgewater Scouts from around that time shows already the bent his life would eventually follow.

> For instance you know that many thousands of people have given their lives as martyrs in the cause of Christ. Why? Well the truth is they could not help it. Yet it is just as true that as boys they were ordinary normal fellows just like you are, with exactly the same thoughts, feelings and wishes as you. Yet do you think they would be likely to die for Christ, whom you have never seen, whom maybe you have never heard, and have not yet felt as being *present* with you? You may take it as a fact that something changed them, or took hold of them. And that something may change you from an ordinary healthy honest chap to—a Christian. And that something is the "Love of Christ."[90]

By 1918 Wyatt was back from the war, his foreign service having confirmed him in his career: medical missions. Sponsored by the Medical Missionary Society of London, he began his medical studies under the guidance of the BMS. He immediately impressed his fellow students, with one classmate describing him as "a fine fellow—the real thing. He was no pietist, though he had plenty of piety of the right sort, but he lived his Christianity."[91] In 1924 Wyatt finally made his formal application to

---

89. The story of Adolph's last few years in China gives a valuable portrait of what life in war-torn Shanxi must have been like during the years of Japanese aggression. See especially the last five chapters in ibid.

90. Payne, *Harry Wyatt*, 32–33.

91. Ibid., 42.

the BMS. Though he had struggled much to make his faith his own—he often lamented the lack of spiritual guidance during his early years—he was quickly accepted by the BMS Candidate Board. When asked where he would like to serve, he replied, "I have been too pre-occupied with things in this country to consider the various fields." He was appointed to sail for China in only a few weeks' time. As he prepared to leave for the other side of the world, one friend asked Wyatt when he would come back. His answer: "I am not going—to come back."[92]

Beginning studies at the Peking Language School in March 1925, Wyatt saw clearly the tensions of living in an increasingly nationalistic China.

> I like the look of the Chinese. . . . There is a delightful element of uncertainty in the air—revolutions, students organized and largely Bolshevistic, nurses on strike at Taiyuanfu, BMS hospitals probably turn on almost impossible lines, and so on. It makes me stretch myself in anticipation. . . .
>
> One hears bugles blowing in the barracks or sees a troop train on the railway line, some big general is escorted by horsemen down the street, or a band of students bearing banners go by. . . . It is strange to feel one is in a hostile country.[93]

Wyatt was initially wary of the missionary community: "When I came out first there was one thing, which I own I did dread a little, and that was the missionaries. But I know now at first hand what homely, kind-hearted people they are, and I am not afraid of them any more."[94] Quickly acclimating to his new peers, Wyatt spent his first summer at Beidaihe where he mingled with Eric Liddell and many other expatriate missionaries. Eager to sample the many ministry possibilities provided by his new environment, Wyatt traveled throughout China visiting various mission hospitals, spoke to expatriate groups in and around Beijing, and taught English to classes of local students. In late 1925 Wyatt was especially moved during a Christmastime stint volunteering at the Peking Union Medical College. Fighting in and around Tianjin had produced an appalling influx of wounded and, despite planned anti-Christian demonstrations on Christmas Day, the college put out a call for volunteers—a request which many foreigners answered. Though conditions were primitive, and the suffering quite acute, Wyatt was impressed to see Chinese and foreigners working so closely together. This was not the only incidence of violence that Wyatt, now known as Huai Anli,

---

92. Ibid., 47–48.
93. Ibid., 51–52 and 52–53.
94. Ibid., 57.

would see as he persevered in his language studies amid bombings, political coups, demonstrations, and war.[95]

Wyatt's own letters give an indication of his impressions and thoughts during these early days in China:

> I am speeding across Shantung in a comfortable train. The sun in setting picks out the distant ranges of mountains with deep shadows. The countryside is dotted with blue-coated, sun-bronzed field-labourers. The autumn crops have been gathered in; and now they are ploughing the wide stretches of the plains to put in their winter wheat. There are no walls or hedges, only border–stones; and where there is rising ground it is cut into terraced plots. Here and there, as far as the eye can reach, are small groves of cypress sheltering a few graves. Each grave is a conical mound of earth. There are also memorial tablets, and small altars for the offerings to the dead. Many of the graves are in the open plain, and the plough must wend its way about these sacred monuments of the dead past. They dot the plain in far greater number than the healthy bronzed toilers. For thousands of years the autumn sun has set on just such a scene, and life has been lived peacefully, frugally and simply. . . .
>
> And what do I represent in this scene, comfortably seated, rushing along the railroad? A representative of a young virile, restless people who are antagonizing these quiet country folk: a bearer of the strong wine of a new commercial and scientific civilization, the unprecedented product of yesterday. Are these factors which have come to end the serenity of the past centuries? What will the next hundred years mean for the ancient customs and modes of life of this agricultural people?
>
> Yet I am more than that—I am a representative of a society of Christian people who have been teaching and preaching over these rural plains for fifty years now. This Society has built up a native church of seven thousand adherents scattered through these villages. They are self-governing and self-supporting, and they should stand, however great the anti-foreign feeling may become. . . .
>
> But there is something deeper here than commercial change or church organization. Has not God spoken again, and the time now come when these people are being called from the circling sequences of their past ages to a new and progressive

---

95. Wyatt's Chinese name was taken from a Christmas card the family had printed (presumably) in Taiyuan and sent back to friends in England. Wyatt's son Dr. Arthur Wyatt kept a copy of the card in his private collection, the text of which reads: "*gonghe jiuzhu shengdan, bing zhu xinnian hong xi*. Huai Anli, Hou Meide, Tong Jugong."

spiritual life? Has not the time come when in Christ's name not only are social customs going to change, tumults and wars arise, and many strange things come to pass, but also the humble people are going to put their trust in a Heavenly Father and set their faces toward a better land?

There is something enjoyable in the rush of the train over these brown plains, as the sun sinks lower and lower in the hills. How much more fascinating the rushing of the purposes of God, the coming of a new age.[96]

In January of 1926, R. H. P. Dart arrived on the field, accompanied by two young female recruits for the BMS. Dart was headed to Taiyuan to serve as business manager of the BMS hospital, while the women were committed to language studies. One of the women—Edith Holden—quickly became the focus of Wyatt's particular attention. Like Dart, Wyatt was also bound for Taiyuan where the two bachelors were to become roommates. Fighting in north China prevented Wyatt from moving to Shanxi until the end of April, after which he dove immediately into part-time work at the Taiyuan mission hospital. Wyatt's life during these years was disciplined and busy, with his time divided between medical work and continuing language studies.

> I am back at routine work again. This morning we were operating. . . . I had my Chinese teacher at 8.30 a.m. and again at four this afternoon. Then an hour on the tennis courts and then trying to memorise some wiggly characters in a cold room, because R. H. P. Dart, my companion in this bachelor's den, had two student visitors by our only fire. Then a carpenter called and I put him up to making a trouser press. Then one of our Chinese doctors came to dinner. Then more Chinese [study] and the newspaper. I broke fresh ground.[97]

Fighting in northern Shanxi in 1926 and 1927 threw missionary work on the field into disarray at the same time that heavy deficits on the home front were driving retrenchment within the BMS. Times were tight and stress levels were high for the Baptist missionaries in Shanxi. In the midst of all this, Wyatt took time to reflect on his first taste of real mission life.

> This end of mission service is great fun, with all the novelty and romance. It is the older people who feel the strain—strain of jogging along without much progress, and out of contact with home life and all that means both intellectually and spiritually.

---

96. From a letter written to a Mr. Paterson in the fall of 1925 titled "Across Shantung in a Train," as recorded in Payne, *Harry Wyatt*, 54–55.

97. Ibid., 74–75.

> Then there is the strain of living apart from the children, and the difficulty of making ends meet, and the bereavements that come to most in a land where mortality is high. A glance at the cemetery here would enlighten you on this point. So I am very happy indeed at present, but I must be prepared to pay the price of the road I have chosen.[98]

It was not long before Wyatt was tested: during his first year in Taiyuan, Wyatt was dispatched to Xi'an to negotiate the evacuation of fifteen adults and nine children representing four different mission societies besieged by the new governor of neighboring Shaanxi province.[99] The experience was sobering, but Wyatt returned impressed by God's faithful provision in the midst of difficulties.

Late in 1926 Wyatt's particular friend Edith Holden took up residence at the BMS Xinzhou station, a short trip north from Taiyuan. Wyatt managed the journey a number of times before the couple were married in Beijing on Easter Sunday, 1927. By this time fighting in the north had led to the evacuation of most expatriates from the interior, and by June even Beijing was considered unsafe for female residence. The newlyweds retreated to the peaceful seaside resort of Beidaihe where they waited anxiously to return to their work in Shanxi—now completely stopped due to lack of workers. The members of the Shanxi BMS station felt uncomfortable sitting idly by while conditions in Shanxi worsened, and toward the end of summer they decided to return to Taiyuan in blatant disregard of the British Consul's advice.[100]

Until their home leave in 1932, the Wyatts worked hard in Taiyuan, supporting both the Men's and Women's Hospitals while growing their own family as well (they eventually had four children). Bible studies for students and impromptu hymn-sings in the hospital courtyard on his harmonium rounded out Wyatt's already hectic medical schedule. And throughout all these years, fighting, famine, staffing shortages, air raids, and a too-frequent lack of supplies brought strain and tension into an already challenging

---

98. From a letter written during his first few weeks in Shanxi, as recorded in ibid., 61. The cemetery which Wyatt mentions—the cemetery especially established for foreigners—no longer exists, although the location is attested to by older members within the Taiyuan Christian community as resting in or around Sanercun on the Eastern Hills just north of the Donghuayuan housing district. Villagers from Sanercun affirmed in 2000 that much of the surrounding area had been marked with graves for as long as they could remember.

99. The details are recorded in Wyatt's own words in ibid., 67–72.

100. Shortly after, in November 1928, Grace Mann—Edith's companion prior to her marriage to Harry—was killed by brigands on the road between Taiyuan and Xinzhou. Ibid., 88.

situation. Note the determination evident in Wyatt's own account of work conditions in 1930s Shanxi:

> In the mornings I work in the Men's Hospital where we keep between thirty and forty beds open. On outpatient mornings I see about fifty patients, and this comes twice a week. The whole gamut of human illness seems to come trooping into our chapel to wait under the evangelists' words to see the doctor. Here I have to see to all the details of the professional side of the work, touring the dispensary, the laboratory, the sterilizing room, the wards and the out-patient department in turn. . . . In the afternoon I go to the Women's Hospital, where we have thirty more beds. Here I am merely a doctor and Nurse Jaques makes things go. Then the foreign community use me as being the only available foreign doctor. There must be about thirty Germans alone living in the town. There are French on the railway, and a few English people, and also several continental nationalities in the Roman Catholic mission. Of operations I have done quite a wide and varied selection during my six months here. At one time we were very busy with wounded soldiers, and at another the wounded from a bomb dropped by an aeroplane kept us busy. Latterly a diphtheria epidemic caused some anxiety, particularly as two nurses caught the infection. Now I am faced with the problem of keeping dust out of the theatre during the spring dust storms. We are also beginning to run out of some kinds of medicine and antiseptics. . . . The railway has not run through to the coast since last summer, and we see no prospect of it doing so yet.[101]

Wyatt and his family returned from their home leave in the fall of 1933, after which his work expanded rapidly. He began having more interactions with Chinese medical doctors in and around Taiyuan, sharing interesting cases with them. He opened clinics staffed by local nurses in Shouyang, Taizhou, and Xinzhou, and also started a dental department at the Men's Hospital in Taiyuan. This was a time of tremendous advance for the BMS Taiyuan team, an impression confirmed by a very encouraging visit from Generalissimo Chiang and his wife in early 1935. In a letter to a friend at his home church in England, Wyatt effused over his growing scope for ministry: "I do not know when it has been so easy to speak to people of Christianity and to follow up interested patients in their homes. . . . I

---

101. Ibid., 86–88.

have two Bible classes, two prayer meetings and sundry odds and ends every week so that clear evenings are few."[102]

By 1937 Wyatt was one of the senior BMS workers in China, owing largely to the retirement of many post-1900 missionaries. This brought him into leadership even as things in China grew progressively worse. Japan commenced formal hostilities, and earthquakes, typhoons, and air raids seemed almost commonplace. Before long the BMS decided to evacuate the women and children to the safer coastal regions, as it was clear that Shanxi and Shaanxi would face the brunt of the Japanese invasion. After escorting his family and the rest of the team to Hankou, Wyatt returned to Taiyuan, determined to stay at his post no matter what happened. Along with a handful of others, Wyatt served in Taiyuan throughout the Japanese siege and occupation of the city.[103]

Fighting spread throughout much of Shanxi, with the Japanese occupation focused primarily on the larger cities, the rail lines, and major roads. Though travel was difficult and officially restricted, Wyatt secured a permit in December of 1937 and left Shanxi for a brief visit to his family along the coast. After the joyous reunion, he established them in the relative safety of Beijing before returning to Taiyuan in February of 1938. By this time he was already writing home to the mission, calling for the return of the missionaries and the rapid bolstering of the field: "We have found that the open door does not always mean the open mind or the open heart; but a time like this provides an unexampled opportunity for getting the message home. This is the time to take the opportunities that present and not to hang fire."[104]

On May 4, 1938, Harry Wyatt hopped into a Ford truck and headed north toward Xinzhou to assist in the redistribution of mission workers throughout the province. The driver for this trip, Hu Shifu, was a volunteer. Hu's father had driven for the mission until the previous summer when he had become involved in a charge of espionage; he was first tortured and then put to death by the government. On the return trip from Xinzhou, Wyatt was joined by Beulah Glasby, a veteran from Xinzhou who had stayed in Taiyuan to manage the orphanage during the Japanese siege, and the Jaspers, newlyweds accompanying Glasby to staff the mission station in Taizhou.

About seven miles south of Guo County, a shot rang out from the hilly wilderness, and Hu Shifu—the artery in his arm bleeding profusely—brought

102. Ibid., 100–101.

103. Ibid., 107–8. Payne gives the names of those workers who remained in Taiyuan at the time of the siege: F. W. Price, V. E. W. Hayward and his wife, S. R. Dawson, Beulah Glasby, Ellen Clow and her mother, Bloom, and Wyatt. They were later joined by Salvation Army missionaries Major Marcel Beney and his wife.

104. Ibid., 117.

the truck to a stop. Bullets rained down on the vehicle from all around. Glasby was soon hit, and Wyatt proceeded to gather the group under the relative protection of the truck's engine block. While attending to the party's wounds, Wyatt seized the Union Jack from the back of the truck and raced into the open, waving the flag and calling out that they were a party of Britons, all to no avail. Hand grenades and bullets continued to fly in their direction. When Glasby expired from her wounds, the party decided to attempt to run to safety. They split up, with the Jaspers running for a nearby rail embankment while Wyatt ran for a nearby ditch carrying the seriously injured driver as best he could. Wyatt was hit by a bullet just before he reached the ditch. The Jaspers were surrounded and taken prisoner as the gunmen advanced on Wyatt and Hu Shifu, pouring bullet after bullet into their motionless bodies.

Once captured, the Jaspers realized their attackers were Chinese. Only after the truck had been looted and the Jaspers had been handled roughly did they manage to convince the Chinese bandits that they had ambushed British missionaries, and not a group of Japanese spies. The attackers were horrified by their mistake, and out of fear they refused to return to the site of their error, leading the Jaspers on a lengthy journey by foot back to Taiyuan.

It took some time to recover the bodies of the fallen, but on May 19 Glasby and Wyatt were laid to rest in the Martyrs Memorial Cemetery next to the other expatriate saints who had earlier given their lives in Shanxi. Various ceremonies and services were held for them in Taiyuan—and eventually England—with guests from the foreign community, various mission societies, the local Christian community and hospitals, and even a few Japanese officers attending. The concluding section of Romans 8 was read, and the hymn "O Sacred Head Now Wounded" —one of Wyatt's favorites—was sung. In the local tradition, silk banners were hung in the chapel with various inscriptions: "His spirit will never die." "His benevolent influence has penetrated through the whole province of Shansi." "A true hero."[105]

Only two days before his death, Dr. Harry Wyatt had written a note to his wife in Beijing: "You do not want a husband who would fail others any more than one who would fail you."[106] Wyatt had given everything in order to bring spiritual and physical aid to the people of Shanxi during a time of great difficulty and suffering.

---

105. Details on the funeral are taken from ibid., 123–26. Old photographs of the memorial service preserved by the Wyatt children show the interior of the Taiyuan chapel decorated for a Chinese funeral, complete with the white silk banners with black writing so characteristic of Chinese funerary practices.

106. Ibid., 125–26.

With Harry gone, Edith Wyatt decided to leave embattled Shanxi and return to England with her children. Shortly after, in December 1940, all Brethren missionaries were evacuated from Shanxi.[107] As fighting continued in Shanxi, expatriate life and ministry in the province became increasingly untenable, and many other missionaries left to seek the relative security of coastal China. This safety, however, proved fleeting as Japanese forces began to round up expatriates in the larger cities and place them in internment camps.

MISSIONARY LIFE IN THE INTERNMENT CAMPS

By the autumn of 1942, Shanxi missionary F. W. Price was being held and interrogated by the Japanese along with three hundred or so other expatriates in the Columbia Country Club near Shanghai. On March 17, 1943, he and the other prisoners were transferred to the Lunghua Camp—a former Chinese high school outside of Shanghai. At the new location Price and some of the other foreigner leaders quickly set up committees to provide all eighteen hundred internees with various tasks and responsibilities in order to keep the camp organized and to keep people occupied. Over the two and a half years of his confinement, Price served successively as watchman, road maker, laundry worker, dispensary assistant, librarian, and—throughout his entire stay—hospital chaplain. Not surprisingly, given the high concentration of missionaries in the camp, religious services at this particular site were planned by a multi-denominational committee and included Church of England and Free Church services, as well as Sunday schools, lectures, and even a ministers' fraternal society.

BMS Taiyuan missionary Annie Rossiter remembered life in the camps as consisting of stiflingly hot summers and freezing cold winters. While food tapered off to "a suspicion of meat and vegetable soup" as the years progressed, the monotony was relieved by curious events such as a feast of "three tasty herrings" on the occasion of the Japanese Emperor's birthday. For Rossiter, the greatest thrill of the camp years was the monthly arrival of the International Red Cross parcels. News from the outside came

---

107. The Brethren returned again briefly in 1941 when Ernest Wampler and O. C. Sollenberger were sent to serve the American Advisory Committee for Relief—thought to be suitable wartime service for the pacifists. The men intended to do ambulance and emergency relief work: however, they were forced to close the work a year later when the United States State Department refused to issue passports to conscientious objectors. Tiedemann, "Church of the Brethren Mission."

in the form of daily deliveries of pro-Japanese newspapers; this increased the sense of isolation felt by the prisoners.[108]

Japanese authorities were generally decent toward their foreign prisoners, although they often slapped the faces of male and female prisoners for trivial offenses. At first, relations between prisoners were also tense, with the non-Christian internees wary and even derisive of their fellow prisoners from the missions:

> . . . but this changed to admiration and respect as they saw how missionaries undertook and tackled the hardest and most undesirable forms of work. Long before our release some expressed their agreeable surprise at the way missionaries had worked and said that they wished the camp might have been in the hands of a missionary council.[109]

Langdon Gilkey in his account of prison camp life, *Shantung Compound*, analyzed this difference in character as he witnessed it.

> There was a quality seemingly unique to the missionary group, namely, naturally and without pretense to respond to a need which everyone else recognized only to turn aside. Much of this went unnoticed, but our camp could scarcely have survived as well as we did without it. If there were any evidences of the grace of God observable on the surface of our camp existence, they were to be found here.[110]

For the missionaries and their families who had elected to stay behind, the years of internment were bittersweet. Living conditions were very poor, and many found the psychological privations of imprisonment unbearable; at the same time, the camps provided families with a degree of protection from the possibility of greater violence outside the prison walls. The intimacy of overcrowding also presented the mission community with new

---

108. "Suspicion of meat" is Price's own phrase, while the other comments are from Rossiter. Price, "From Taiyuan to Shanghai," 49; Rossiter, "From the Beginning in Shansi," 43. Malcolm claims there were sixteen hundred prisoners in the Weihsien Internment Camp, including four hundred Protestants, but not including another four hundred or so Catholics who were transferred to Beijing just before the Protestant group arrived. Malcolm, *We Signed Away Our Lives*, 151.

109. Price, "From Taiyuan to Shanghai," 50. Many unbelieving internees became Christians during internment.

110. As quoted in Malcolm, *We Signed Away Our Lives*, 150. Situated on the premises of a former Presbyterian mission compound known as the Courtyard of the Happy Way (Ledaoyuan), the Weihsien Internment Camp (Weixian Jizhongying) near modern-day Weifang, Shandong, is described in detail in Cliff, *Courtyard of the Happy Way*; and Gilkey, *Shantung Compound*.

opportunities to serve their neighbors. Valborg Torjesen and several other women formed a Service Committee to provide childcare and other forms of assistance for the weak and ill within their camp.[111] As one missionary recalled, life in the camps

> ... was missionary work—with a difference! Instead of putting a dollar in the collection, you shared a newly-opened tin of tomato juice with a friend. Instead of sending your cook's son to kindergarten, you gave a loaf of bread and half a jar of peanut butter to a hungry boy. Instead of taking Scripture classes with Chinese women, you explained the Bible to Russian women.[112]

Children's memories of internment camp are particularly vivid, often tinged with joy. Snatches of camp ditties sung to fend off boredom or discouragement surface in their memoirs, alongside anecdotes about collecting bedbugs and swatting flies. In many cases their recollections offer revealing portraits of the older missionaries. One young internee recalled that famed Olympian and second-generation China missionary Eric Liddell was a particular favorite with the children. On Sunday afternoons children would join in soccer matches with Eric—the very man who eschewed competing on the Sabbath—happily serving as referee.[113]

With the Japanese surrender in 1945, the internment camps were liberated, and many mission workers looked eagerly to return to their fields of service. With World War II only recently concluded, funding and personnel were tight in the home offices of the mission societies. At the same time, civil war in China was now being waged in earnest, and travel in many parts of the country was dangerous if not impossible. As Nationalist forces retreated and pulled back, the advancing Communists gained ground almost daily, leaving missionaries with few options. Some were able to return to their passport countries; others were forced to either seek asylum outside of Europe, or remain in China and await the decision of the civil war. Each society made its own decision. The CBM, as one example, attempted to reopen China work several times during the 1940s—most notably through their 1946 to 1948 agricultural tractor training and livestock donation program—but by 1953 the Brethren had ceased all missionary work in China.[114]

111. Malcolm, *We Signed Away Our Lives*, 149.

112. Pearson, "Loyalty," 120.

113. Malcolm, *We Signed Away Our Lives*, 144–47. Liddell was happy to arrange exercise on the Sabbath for the children in prison, reasoning that the Sabbath should be a taste of heaven, a flavor far too rare in the internment camps.

114. All told, approximately one hundred Brethren missionaries served in China from 1908 to 1953—many in Shanxi. Tiedemann, "Church of the Brethren Mission."

Years of observing the fighting between the various forces in China had led most missionaries early on to question the capacity of the Nationalist regime to rule China. On the other hand, events in Russia caused most missionaries to be wary of Communism. Not surprisingly, the late 1940s were a confusing time for many expatriate workers in China. Allegiances were difficult to gauge, and always the question remained—what would things be like *after* the fighting ended? Most missionaries just wanted a peaceful place to continue ministering faithfully to their flocks. Many also hoped that things would be better once the question was settled—that there would be an end and a purpose to all the suffering the last century had brought upon the Chinese people.

There are not many pretty walks around Taiyuan. The weird loess cliffs are quaint but hardly beautiful because so bare. But there is one walk we often take when we want to escape from the dusty city into the fresh air, and that is to a bush garden about a mile outside the city on the slope to the eastern hills. Here one can find quiet repose amongst the trees and shrubbery. It is the foreign cemetery. Here lie the remains of those thirty-five martyrs who were killed in Boxer days, and several who died before 1900, while other mounds and stones have been added since.

About this time of year the flowering bushes burst forth into glory and hide the barren shame of winter. The green of new buds overhead stands out against the deep blue sky, and in the distance the brown mountain sides are taking on their first tinge of green. In the plain between stand up the far-flung walls of the martyr city. Away to the north the smoking arsenal chimneys make one sure that this is no visionary city. Yet here all is restful and quiet, and that not the peace of death, but the peace of life and faith. The flowers tell of everlasting purity, while the leaves whisper that life is born again. Where there was death, life has sprung up again. Where there was defeat and horror in an ancient city, now there are Christian hymns and Christian homes.

It is an inspiration to work in a martyr city. It makes plain to us that we do not depend on human protection for security, but depend on God for victory over malice. Not in pomp and power, but in lowly service and simple kindness, lies the security of everlasting life. Who knows what the future holds? I know it holds joy and peace and victory through Jesus Christ, and I believe it holds a time when the martyr city shall be a Christian city, and over those grey walls will tower spires that point to God.

And why not now? That is because most of the people do not know their need of God. They know the need of bread and money and new friends, but to have a place in life for God seems strange and unnecessary to them. Likeable in many ways, quiet and peace-loving, fond of little children, and a simple life, yet the greater number remain strangers to the love of God. It is still the day of sowing, of teaching day by day, of patiently witnessing to the riches in Christ Jesus. One day if we have faith, they will become aware of something missing in life, and wonder why they were content without it for so long. And they will only find rest in God.

—From "A Garden Reverie" by Dr. Harry Wyatt (BMS Taiyuan)

Written in Taiyuan ca. 1929
as recorded in Payne, *Harry Wyatt*, 91–93.

5

Legacy (1949–2015)

WHEN THE COMMUNISTS FORMALLY "liberated" China in 1949, the Chinese Christian community was composed of approximately one million Chinese Protestants and three million Chinese Catholics.[1] For the Protestants, this was the result of nearly a century and a half of massive nationwide missionary effort. From 1807 to 1949, one hundred sixty sending organizations had employed around ten thousand missionaries who collectively built 6,812 elementary schools, 4,726 churches, 332 hospitals, 240 middle schools, 174 orphanages, 69 public service organizations, 58 nurse training schools, 39 publishing houses, 28 teachers' schools, 13 colleges, and 10 medical schools in the hopes that the Kingdom of God would be firmly established within the Middle Kingdom.[2] Yet despite auspicious beginnings, the extensive mission effort in Shanxi had produced only a comparatively small Christian community.[3]

---

1. These are my interpretations of the somewhat anti-Catholic figures in Williamson, *British Baptists in China*, 273–74. One Chinese source lists a total of seven to eight hundred thousand Protestant Christians in 1949, of whom 70 percent were from rural areas and 40 percent were illiterate. Yu Ke, *Dangdai jidujiao*, 293.

2. Yu Ke, *Dangdai jidujiao*, 293. While they provide some sense of the scale of the China mission project, these numbers are likely inaccurate, given Yu Ke's limited use of archival materials. The original Chinese text gives a total figure of one thousand missionaries: this is clearly inaccurate, either a typographical error (for ten thousand) or simply a fabrication.

3. As early as 1920 the Shanxi Christian community—despite the extensive and early establishment of mission stations throughout the province—remained one of the smallest in China. Stauffer, *The Christian Occupation of China*, 286, 293. The growth of the church in China in the second half of the twentieth century is an enormous topic. This chapter will give limited attention to the national trends, focusing instead on presenting the limited Shanxi-specific information that is available. For a helpful

By 1949 the combined Catholic and Protestant missionary population was reduced to some four thousand expatriates still residing in China. With the Communist Party firmly in control of China, Protestant sending agencies and home churches expected the extensive property, foreign identities, and religious convictions of the missionaries to lead to their rapid expulsion from the country. Those on the ground, however, were much more hopeful. Since 1948 the Communists had adopted a more tolerant approach to foreign missionaries, with most missionaries reporting a very peaceful handover in 1949. And while by 1950 the Chinese state was refusing new missionaries and missionaries returning from furlough permission to enter the country, resident missionaries who avoided politics and possessed technical skills were supposedly still welcome to remain and continue serving in the new China. The remaining expatriate workers in China interpreted this as an invitation to further service—a promising sign for the future. One group of American Protestants associated with China mission even went so far as to formally petition the United States government to recognize China's Communist rulers, convinced that doing so would help ensure the continued advance of God's Kingdom in China.[4]

Taiyuan came under Communist control in October of 1948. At that time there were few foreign mission workers left in the city, and most mission property was either already transferred or ready to be transferred into local hands. Once divested from mission control, however, church schools, hospitals, and orphanages throughout the province were gradually handed over to the government, as Chinese Christians struggled and then failed to meet the exorbitant taxes and fines levied by local officials. At the same time, the humanitarian institutions of the church were further threatened by populist accusations of imperialism and criminal activity, as Christianity became increasingly suspect. On July 19, 1949, the last BMS expatriates left the province with their hearts warmed by the promises of their local colleagues that "with God's help they would continue to witness faithfully to Him."[5] Over the next few years nearly all the rest of the foreign missionaries in Shanxi departed, leaving the future of the church in the hands of the local Christians.

At the time, many Protestant missionaries looked back on the previous one hundred fifty years of missionary effort with regret, interpreting the forced missionary exodus as God's judgment for their cultural pride and

---

summary of post-1949 Chinese Protestantism, see Dunch, "Protestant Christianity in China Today," 195–216. For an overview of the rapid growth of Protestantism in China toward the end of the twentieth century, see Lambert, *China's Christian Millions*.

4. Tucker, "An Unlikely Peace," 97–116.
5. Williamson, *British Baptists in China*, 190–91.

their failure to address China's real needs.⁶ This pessimistic view, however, failed to recognize two important facts. First, while no mass conversion of the Chinese nation had occurred, Christianity had nevertheless been planted in a very challenging and often frustrating mission field. The sixty-five hundred or so mission centers and churches that existed across the country in 1949 were evidence of this success.⁷ Second, the departure of the foreign missionaries provided ideal conditions for Chinese Christians to finally take full ownership over the Chinese church. In this sense, the "reluctant exodus" of the expatriate missionaries was necessary in order to allow the Chinese church to escape the label of "foreign religion" that was such a liability under Communist rule. In the case of Shanxi, the final departure of the last expatriate workers was not a particularly traumatic event. Years of fighting had accustomed Shanxi Christians to ministry with very limited numbers of foreign missionaries. With the final departure of their Western brothers and sisters, Chinese Christians were now positioned to grow the Shanxi church beyond what the earliest missionaries could have imagined.

The initial challenge for Chinese Christians during the early years of Communist rule was to find room within Chinese Communism for public Christian faith. Within a few years an accommodation was reached that resulted in the formation of the Three-Self Patriotic Movement (Sanzi Aiguo Yundonghui) or TSPM, a political organization focused on directing Christianity to contribute positively to the goals and ideals of the Communist Party. Much has been written elsewhere about the positive and negative implications of the TSPM adaptation, but at the very least it offered some hope that the church might continue to exist legally under atheist Communist rule. The divisions in the Chinese Protestant community that arose out of the varied responses to this party-sanctioned Christian association still shape the religious landscape in China today.⁸

The provincial arm of the TSPM was established in Shanxi in 1950.⁹ Local reactions to the TSPM varied, with some fellowships joining quickly in an effort to preserve their freedom to worship. Others refused, convinced that the broadly ecumenical organization represented at best the establishment of a state church and at worst a compromise of the gospel. For example, former ABCFM Christians in Taigu joined the TSPM in April 1951, while

---

6. See the discussion in Tiedemann, *Handbook of Christianity in China. Volume 2, 1800–present*, 766–80.

7. Ibid., 793.

8. On Chinese Communist religious policy, see MacInnis, *Religion in China Today*. On the emergence of the TSPM, see Merwin and Jones, *Documents of the Three-Self Movement*; and Wickeri, *Seeking the Common Ground*.

9. *Shanxi tongzhi*, vol. 42: 455.

their denominational brothers and sisters in Fenyang resisted association until August 1956.[10] Churches previously associated with the Shanxi CBM lost many of their believers after the departure of the foreign missionaries; of the Chinese congregants who continued to identify as Christians, some joined the TSPM while others started their own home fellowships.[11]

Independent Christian groups at first were at an advantage but over time faced the same pressures to conform. The True Jesus Church had fared comparatively well in Shanxi during the civil war years, and their anti-foreign stance initially won them the support of party officials. They formally established their own Shanxi branch in 1953, but factionalism brought on by a "small number" (*ji gebie*) of their leaders led to the suppression of their sect by the state.[12] The Jesus Family (Yesu Jiating), a similarly independent Chinese church that had been active in Houma, enjoyed independence from the TSPM until the official labeling of several Shandong Jesus Family leaders as reactionaries led to the group's suppression in 1952.[13] Watchman Nee's local church movement (Jidutu Juhuichu), sometimes known as the "Little Flock" (Xiaoqun) because of their use of the Plymouth Brethren's *Hymns for the Little Flock*, was active in Shanxi throughout the 1940s and 1950s. Their members were often disaffected believers from other Christian groups, and their church's aggressively inclusive nature—Nee insisted that there should be only one church in any given city—placed them in direct competition with the TSPM. While some Shanxi Little Flock followers joined the TSPM in 1951, many continued to worship on their own. In Taigu and Yuci over eighty Little Flock followers went further, signing a public statement of intent to oppose the state and the TSPM. Resistance continued until January 1956, when members of the main Shanghai branch of the Little Flock were accused of espionage, resulting in the arrest of the primary Shanxi leaders and a complete ban on the organization.[14]

Catholic leaders in China were typically less likely to embrace socialist ideals than Protestants, and their comparatively independent alternative society attracted relatively more hostility from political activists. Moreover, even though local Catholic priests in Shanxi unanimously supported the formation of the Catholic TSPM, they maintained their membership in the

---

10. Ibid, vol. 42: 468.

11. Ibid, vol. 42: 465. There appears to have been a strong presence of local Brethren Christians in Taiyuan right up until the Cultural Revolution. In the early 2000s an older local believer gave me a hand-copied Brethren church manual he claimed was from the 1950s.

12. Ibid, vol. 42: 455.

13. Ibid, vol. 42: 486.

14. Ibid, vol. 42: 487–88.

global Catholic Church by continuing to send statistics on the provincial church to Rome. In the increasingly radical political environment of the early 1950s, these international connections left the Church vulnerable to political attack. Not surprisingly, by the summer of 1954 all Catholic missionaries had been deported from the province.[15]

By 1955 or 1956, the legally sanctioned church in Taiyuan was largely under the control of former YMCA leaders. Having indigenized early and rapidly, the Chinese YMCA was home to many local political activists, most of whom embraced modernist or liberal theologies. One Shanxi pastor remembers attending Christmas services at the main church with her father during this period and finding the atmosphere "cold, chilly."[16]

By the mid-1950s nearly all of the expatriate missionaries had been forced out of the province. Nevertheless, the increasingly radical nature of the Chinese Communist Revolution made even the faintest foreign associations politically suspect—including membership in a "foreign" religion. In Taiyuan, party officials sought to discredit and ultimately dismantle the church by taking advantage of the factionalism that existed between the various Protestant groups. According to one pastor in the Taiyuan registered church, in 1958 all Protestants in the city were forced to worship together in the same location (at the present Qiaotou Jie site) and all denominations were eliminated under the guise of eliminating factionalism. An official document from that time regarding the unification of the Protestant churches in the city of Taiyuan instructed that:

(1) The Little Flock shall abolish all its women's meetings, its weekly breaking of bread, its personal interview with members before the breaking of bread, and its rule against women speaking in the church.

(2) The Salvation Army shall give up its military regulations.

(3) The Seventh-day Adventists (Jidu Fulin Anxirihui) shall abolish their daily morning prayers, and they shall work on

---

15. Reporting did not cease until 1955. Harrison, *The Missionary's Curse*, 147–48.

16. Much of the information in this chapter comes from oral interviews with current Shanxi church leaders. Two of the older sisters from one of Taiyuan's most influential Christian families have been particularly helpful. One of the sisters is a leading pastor in the local church, and another works at the church bookstore. Their father, after spending years as an itinerant evangelist throughout northern Shanxi and Inner Mongolia, eventually settled in Taiyuan, though it is not clear with which sect—if any—he was primarily associated.

> the Sabbath. Their tithe system for the support of the clergy shall be abolished.[17]

For Chinese revolutionaries, the elimination of foreign denominational affiliations was hailed as a critical blow to the foreignness of Christianity—and to Christianity itself. Forcing all Protestants to worship together also made it possible to revise all aspects of church life and faith in accordance with the dictates of socialism. A 1958 article published in the official church publication *Tian Feng* or "Heavenly Wind" describes the way in which the TSPM leaders in Taiyuan sought to carry out their program of reform.

> [A]ll books and journals used in the interpretation of the Bible shall be examined and judged and those containing poisonous thoughts shall be rejected. Teaching conducive to cooperation [with the government] and in tune with socialism shall be promoted. At the same time, all books and journals coming from outside [China] must be critically examined before being accepted. There shall be no more preaching about the "Last Day" or about "vanity" of this world which is other-worldly, negative, and pessimistic.[18]

Not surprisingly, in this politically charged environment the more radical, separatist Christian sects suffered the most. In addition to attacks from the party targeting their "superstitious" practices and beliefs, these groups also had to face attacks from their brothers and sisters within the more "orthodox" (politically and/or theologically) Christian sects. As one modern scholar analyzed the situation,

> [T]he persecution of sectarian heterodoxy by the state is not new in China. To the extent that religious sects rejected integration and challenged social harmony, they were viewed as threatening to the traditional order and were suppressed by the authorities. . . . The issue was not Christianity *per se*, but the threat which separatist religious sects, some with foreign connections, might pose to social unity.[19]

For political activists looking to prove their hatred for imperialism or Chinese Christians eager to demonstrate their "normalness" to the new state, Christian sects that refused to accept TSPM integration were convenient targets.

---

17. Gao Wangzhi, "Y. T. Wu," 347.

18. As translated from the original article in *Tian Feng* 561, no. 18 (1958), in Deng Zhaoming, "The Church in China," 112.

19. Wickeri, *Seeking the Common Ground*, 155.

In 1957 and 1958 China's supreme leader Mao Zedong advocated his own radical agricultural and economic policies in order to help China "catch up" with England and America in the space of just a few years. Known as the Great Leap Forward (Dayuejin), this campaign was quickly adopted by the entire nation. Mao's idealistic plans combined with the growth of the personality cult that surrounded him to create a crisis of over-reporting and squandered resources. Mao's Great Leap Forward generated so much enthusiasm that it was impossible to say anything negative about its effects, with many officials outdoing each other in exaggerated reports of the campaign's success. One Shanxi man recalled that at first in the early stages of the Great Leap Forward "we ate a lot of meat. It was considered revolutionary to eat meat. If you didn't eat meat, it wouldn't do. . . . People even vied with each other to see who could eat the most."[20] This confidence in the abundance that Mao's policies would produce did not match reality, as the massive scale of participation in the movement literally ate away at China's wealth. In just a short period of time surpluses and reserves of food and other raw materials were exhausted, and it was clear that Mao's "scientific" theories on agriculture and manufacturing were not yielding results. Instead of leaping forward, China was falling back.

In the space of a few short years, the loss of crops and production capacity due to Mao's Great Leap Forward created a desperate famine that devastated the nation. While it is nearly impossible to say precisely how many died during the famine years, recent scholarly estimates place the total number of premature deaths near forty-five million.[21] The famine reached Shanxi in 1961, rapidly making its effects known. Fortunately, strong memories of the previous century's North China Famine and a relative lack of revolutionary enthusiasm led many Shanxi residents to hide food and take steps to avoid complying with official demands for increased contributions. While Shanxi may have suffered less than places in southern China, to this day Shanxi recollections of the "three years of suffering" (*san nian kunnan*) are strong, eliciting long sighs and furrowed brows from all those old enough to remember.[22]

---

20. From William S. Hinton's Shanxi research as recorded in Becker, *Hungry Ghosts*, 81. Meat was a rare and expensive commodity in revolutionary China. Many Shanxi seniors recall eating meat only once a year, at the Spring Festival holiday.

21. Dikötter, *Mao's Great Famine*, 324–34. Several scholars have challenged Dikötter's handling of Chinese archival materials. See the discussion at H-PRC, "Looking for Great Leap 'Smoking Gun' Document."

22. On Shanxi's limited suffering during the famine, see Yang Jisheng, *Tombstone*, 394–406.

In the wake of his disastrous Great Leap Forward, Mao found himself sidelined and discredited by the more conservative economists. Mao fought back by launching his Great Proletariat Cultural Revolution (Wuchan Jieji Wenhua Da Geming), a bid to wrest power from the hands of the conservative reformers and restore the true revolution. As the new movement rose to dominate nearly all social interactions, Taiyuan Christians initially faced the same fears and troubles as others in society. Government officials and their usurpers fought for authority, using persecution and fear of persecution to gain support from the populace.[23] In this environment, association with a bourgeois foreign religion was quickly identified as an incontrovertible indicator of bad class background. In Taiyuan, Christians were forced to abandon church property, and many were sent to prison or labor camp alongside many other non-religious "anti-revolutionaries." In some cases, Taiyuan Christians were sent back to their home villages. One influential local Christian family was sent to their hometown, where they were kept under house arrest until near the end of the Cultural Revolution. The main Taiyuan church on Qiaotou Jie was occupied by Buddhists in 1961 and 1962, though only a year or two later the local police station evicted the Buddhists and seized the property to use as offices.

Older Taiyuan Christians recount the story of one German missionary who had worked in Taiyuan for many years and continued to preach right up until the Cultural Revolution. Known by the local believers as Teacher Qi (Qi *jiaoshi*), the missionary was soon placed under house arrest in Nanyang (this location is unclear, but most likely somewhere in Jinzhong). Despite the tremendous pressure at the time to avoid association with anything foreign, some local Christians persisted in visiting the missionary, keeping the expatriate fed and warm through those years of struggle. Teacher Qi eventually died in Nanyang of natural causes in the 1970s, sometime prior to the end of the Cultural Revolution.[24]

---

23. Though primarily viewed as an urban phenomenon, the Cultural Revolution has been shown to have had a great impact on rural communities as well—predominantly through the organized political programs of the latter years of the movement. Walder and Su, "The Cultural Revolution in the Countryside," 74–99.

24. This general narrative of Teacher Qi is attested to by many local believers in Taiyuan and Yuci. One gentleman recalls that his father was brave, visiting Teacher Qi three times during the turmoil. Many believers claim that Teacher Qi was to some degree protected by local authorities, perhaps even receiving food and aid from the government. Gary Tiedemann's research into the German missionary Anna Ziese raises the possibility that she was Teacher Qi. Ziese served with the American AG in Shanxi from 1920 until her death in 1969, having refused the US Consulate order to leave China in 1948.

The 1960s were especially tumultuous for Shanxi's Catholics. While the economic and political sufferings of these years struck all Shanxi residents with little discrimination, Catholic believers were especially open to political attack because of their identification with a foreign religion and the unique cultural and religious practices that marked them as outside of mainstream Chinese culture.[25] In the midst of these trials, Shanxi Catholics reported experiencing a striking number of miracles. In the early spring of 1965, a cross reportedly appeared on the face of a cliff in the hills just to the north of Taiyuan, attracting many pilgrims looking for solace or supernatural assistance. Catholics who preached boldly in the face of political oppression were frequently credited with miraculous powers as they challenged fellow believers to resist the official pressure to recant. According to one frequently-repeated story, a revered preacher, one of "the Four Fragrances" (*si xiang*), escaped from pursuing soldiers when the bicycle she was riding miraculously took flight. The prevalence of miracles, alongside Cold War fears and local turmoil, led many Shanxi Catholics to believe that they were living in the last days. Accordingly, in Shanxi local Catholics began to avoid wearing rubber-soled shoes: many believed that cotton or leather soles would better resist the consuming fire that was about to rise up from the earth in judgment. All this religiously-motivated activity attracted the violent attention of Red Guard factions and government officials, with many Catholics imprisoned or publicly beaten before yet another political shift in the spring of 1970 resulted in the execution of many Catholic leaders.[26]

Protestant Christians also suffered during the Cultural Revolution, with many believers experiencing deprivation or imprisonment. While many individual Protestants recount instances of God's miraculous provision and comfort during these times of suffering, the most common theme in Shanxi Christian Cultural Revolution narratives was betrayal. Older Christians today are often quick to recall the names and stories of believers who not only recanted their faith but also informed on their fellow Christians during those difficult years. In most cases, these stories concluded with the disloyal Christian receiving divine justice—typically involving either persecution at the hands of revolutionaries or physical disease and pain. As recently as the mid-2000s, elderly Taiyuan believers interpreted the painful death from breast cancer of one prominent female pastor as judgment

---

25. Many scholars see these differences—the outgrowth of centuries of conversion patterns rooted in families, villages, and lineage lines—as sufficient to grant Chinese Catholics their own distinct "ethnicity." This idea is discussed in Madsen, *China's Catholics*, 50–75.

26. Harrison, *The Missionary's Curse*, 145–71. The story of the melting shoes is from an informal presentation Harrison gave in Taiyuan in 2007.

from God for her betrayals during the 1960s. When the churches began to resurface in the 1980s, the persistence of these narratives of betrayal formed a substantial impediment to trust and cooperation among Christian leaders.

THE REEMERGENCE OF THE TAIYUAN CHURCH IN THE ERA OF OPENING AND REFORM

By the early 1970s it was clear that Mao's Cultural Revolution had gotten out of control, and efforts were made to slowly rein in the more violent and disruptive aspects of the movement. Mao's death in 1976 signaled the final end to the tumult, as the nation cried tears of sorrow mixed with joy. By 1978 China was embarking on a new path toward reform and opening, with restored leader Deng Xiaoping heralding a more pragmatic form of governance. With most of the nation weary and cynical from years of revolution, religious activity began to reappear in public. Now, however, years of political scrutiny and the absence of foreign missionaries meant that this reemerging church was finally able to present itself as a *Chinese* church—even if the faith it carried was still broadly perceived as a foreign one.

In the mid-1970s older believers in Taiyuan began surreptitiously approaching the daughters of a man named Wang, a popular pastor and evangelist known for his ministry throughout Shanxi and Inner Mongolia in the years before the Chinese Communist Revolution. Christians were waiting expectantly for larger worship services to recommence after the death of Mao, and Pastor Wang seemed the most likely person to organize a meeting. Pastor Wang eventually agreed, and slowly believers began to gather secretly in his home, grateful for the chance to fellowship with other Christians.

In October of 1979, the Taiyuan Protestant Church met openly for the first time since the Cultural Revolution began. Only seven or eight believers attended the service officiated by Pastor Wang at the Qiaotou Jie property. The front portion of the old church had been returned in the mid-1970s, though the police continued to occupy the back sections of the property until the comings and goings of criminals posed a safety issue for the believers. A photograph exists from these early years of a young American university student who was teaching at Shanxi Agricultural University (Shanxi Nongye Daxue) in Taigu posing with one of Pastor Wang's daughters following what may have been the church's first post-Cultural Revolution public Christmas celebration. Pastor Wang officiated the holiday service at the main sanctuary on Qiaotou Jie.[27]

---

27. Pastor Wang's oldest daughter, who has seen the photo and recalls the foreign woman's presence at the service, reported these events. The foreigner was quite likely

In 1980 the China Christian Council (Zhongguo Jidujiao Xiehui) or CCC was created to provide publishing, theological education, and other services to the registered Protestant churches in China. From this point onward, decisions affecting the day-to-day operations of local registered churches were often made at each administrative level by selected representatives of both the TSPM and CCC gathered together into what became known as the Protestant Twin Committees (Lianghui).[28]

In addition to participating in the worship services at the officially registered Qiaotou Jie church on Sunday mornings, Pastor Wang also began gathering with a few believers in his Taiyuan home near Dayingpan on Sunday afternoons for further fellowship and teaching. This fellowship group, one of the earliest post-Cultural Revolution home fellowships in Taiyuan, met independently for a year, quickly growing to include people who would walk to Dayingpan all the way from the Children's Hospital (Shanxi Sheng Ertong Yiyuan) on the north end of town. Pastors Tong Yiqiang (a physicist educated at Qinghua University (Qinghua Daxue)) and Qi Hong'en (a physical education teacher trained at the Christian Yenching University (Yanjing Daxue) in Beijing prior to 1949) soon become involved. At first the three pastors were carefully observed by local officials, although the person sent to spy on them quickly became a supporter and so stopped reporting on their activities. Eventually the pastors were invited to move their fellowship onto the registered church premises. Since they had never opposed the newly-opened, officially-recognized church at Qiaotou Jie, the three men were happy to move—although they felt that the atmosphere of open sharing and fellowship they had enjoyed in their home was never quite recaptured. After the move, this home fellowship slowly evolved into an informal support group—eventually one of many—for the larger officially recognized congregation.

By the late 1980s the main Taiyuan church had grown to three hundred people—almost all of them believers from before the Cultural Revolution

---

an Oberlin student or graduate who was teaching at the Provincial Agricultural University as part of the two schools' special relationship. She is remembered for having purchased a small hearing aid for Pastor Wang; devices that small (this one hung on his ear) were not available in China. At that time, around 1982, things had just begun to relax, so the Wangs hid this American connection, claiming that the piece had been purchased in Taiwan and sent over by the brother of one of Pastor Wang's daughters' husband's brothers. Unfortunately, the family eventually lost the hearing aid during a bouncy bicycle ride across town.

28. The Protestant Twin Committees (Lianghui) should not be confused with the national twin committees (*quanguo lianghui*), the annual plenary session composed of representatives of both the National People's Congress and the National Committee of the Chinese People's Political Consultative Conference.

who had simply come back into the open. In Taiyuan the leaders appointed to govern the newly opened churches were primarily the same ones who had led the "cold" church of pre-Cultural Revolution days. Typically politically motivated and with little or no faith, these leaders were initially happy for their jobs, viewing their positions as "official" careers with great political potential. However, as the church grew and the number of true believers increased, these leaders found themselves more and more at odds with the people in the pews—most of whom were economically disadvantaged and poorly educated. With little opportunity for profit or gain, and chafing under the critical eye of the faithful believers, these leaders also became increasingly hostile toward the more influential evangelicals.

At about this time, after over a quarter-century's absence, foreigners began to reappear in Taiyuan—some serving as independent teachers or business people, others as part of a larger sending agency. Starting in 1982, Educational Services Exchange with China (ESEC) was placing expatriate English teachers at Shanxi University and Taiyuan University of Technology (Taiyuan Ligong Daxue). Typically serving for just one or two years, this consistent presence created a notable and early witness on the campuses of two of Shanxi's premier universities. Under the auspices of the still-functioning Oberlin Shansi Memorial Association, Oberlin College students were also sent to teach English at Shanxi Agricultural University beginning in 1980. The total number of expatriates in Shanxi during these years was quite small, and the feeling of isolation was often acute. In most cases their religious activity was confined to individual discipleship and evangelism, with small numbers of expatriates often meeting together for worship and spiritual encouragement.

Pentecostal evangelist Dennis Balcombe is known today for his early and dynamic ministry in post-Cultural Revolution China: on one famous occasion he was smuggled between Chinese villages in a coffin to elude authorities.[29] Although there is no evidence that he ever visited Shanxi, his anything-goes attitude toward expatriate ministry in China typified the sensationalist methods justified by many expatriate Christian workers seeking to minister behind China's "closed doors." One American man spent five to ten years in Taiyuan beginning in the 1980s planting churches and running underground Bible training seminars. On an early 1990s trip smuggling Christian literature into Shanxi, he was caught by police at the Taiyuan airport, his materials were confiscated, and he was evicted from China.[30] Shanxi, however, was never a priority for "cowboy" missionaries

---

29. Balcombe, *China's Opening Door*, 126–27.

30. According to longtime Shanxi worker Mark A. Strand, this man reentered China a few years later but never returned to Shanxi.

such as this, as its remote location and lack of minority people groups made the province less "attractive" to expatriate evangelists. In a stark departure from these more aggressive methods, teachers working for Educational Services Exchange with China in Shanxi and elsewhere were forbidden by their founding director Danny Yu to start churches on their own and were encouraged instead to attend services at the local registered church.[31] This was a very progressive and yet humble approach to expatriate service in China at a time when most mission organizations felt that the "desperate" state of the Chinese church justified almost any action on the part of missionaries.

Shortly after the birth of one of his daughters, Pastor Wang decided to dedicate the child to a life of gospel ministry (and singleness). In the 1980s this daughter expressed interest in studying at the officially-registered Yanjing Seminary (Yanjing Shenxueyuan) in Beijing. Her father was initially against her decision, fearing that the environment might cause her to lose her faith and her love for the Lord. She went anyway, convinced that the official credential would enable her, an evangelical, to hold positions of authority within the officially registered churches in Taiyuan. Returning to Taiyuan in 1990 after two years of seminary studies, Pastor Wang's daughter, now known as Sister Wang, was surprised to discover that the Christian community was growing rapidly—and this time from new converts.[32] In the wake of the violent Beijing Spring of 1989, a broad sense of disillusionment was leading many Chinese people to abandon their faith in Communism, resulting in a wave of newcomers—especially young people—flocking to the churches in search of a new faith.[33] At the same time, years of faithless religious "leaders" had made it difficult for people to trust the official church. So-called underground churches were proliferating throughout the city against the wishes of official church leaders, the State Administration for Religious Affairs (Guojia Zongjiao Shiwu Ju) or SARA, and the Public Security Bureau (Gong'an Ju) or PSB.[34] Sister Wang and other influential evangelicals (most of them evangelists or teachers) within the officially registered churches visited these home fellowships in secret to provide training—all without the knowledge or approval of the official leaders of the registered church.

31. Yu's positive yet nuanced attitude toward China's registered church can be seen in his article "Into the Future."

32. This is the same daughter who posed for the photo with the American woman following that first Christmas service.

33. For a sociological study of the keen interest in religion demonstrated by Beijing youth during these years, see Li Suju and Liu Qifei, *Qingnian yu "zongjiao re."*

34. Provincial level and lower offices of the SARA are still commonly referred to by the older name of Religious Affairs Bureau.

The old church building on Qiaotou Jie, the primary sanctuary for the registered church in Taiyuan, had a capacity of three hundred people—far too small to accommodate the rapid growth from the "Christianity fever" (*Jidujiao re*) that seized China in the late 1980s and early 1990s in particular.[35] The church was granted permission to tear down the historic building and rebuild a much larger sanctuary on the same site. During the construction phase from 1991 to 1994, the main Taiyuan registered fellowship moved from location to location, spending the first two years meeting at a dance hall on Fuxi Jie located where the current World Trade Center stands. Though the church held the deed to this piece of land, their claims were rejected in favor of demands from the local community to continue the site's role as a social hub. Similar difficulties arose at other temporary worship sites, forcing the congregation to relocate many times. One spot—located on Qiaodong Jie—was known as the "Red Door Church" by the fledgling foreign community. Though it was an actual church building, its small size meant a courtyard overflowing every Sunday with worshipers, all of them waiting eagerly for the new Qiaotou Jie sanctuary to reach completion.

The wisdom of Sister Wang's decision to pursue formal training in Beijing was soon evident. The evangelical classmates and teachers she met while at Yanjing Seminary provided her with an excellent channel for recruiting ministers to fill newly opened positions in the growing Taiyuan official church. Many of the ideas she acquired while at seminary were also new to Shanxi. She recalled learning in Beijing that under Chinese law, unregistered home fellowship groups were not necessarily illegal—as long as they were not too big. Sister Wang and her new coworkers quickly began sharing this information with the various Taiyuan fellowship groups, as well as the local PSB and SARA officials. The official church leaders were still unfriendly toward the home fellowship groups, perceiving them to be a source of trouble and a potential threat to their positions of authority. Whenever opportunities arose, these leaders used the bureaucracy and the state security apparatus to block the returning seminary students' efforts to help the local fellowships.

The Seventh-day Adventists were also growing in influence in Taiyuan during the early 1990s.[36] Influential evangelicals in Taiyuan took advantage of the Adventists' expansion to approach the leaders of the official church, explaining that they were concerned that the Adventists might sway the unregistered home fellowship groups into heresy. The official church leaders

---

35. Fiedler, "China's 'Christianity Fever' Revisited," 71–109; Hunter and Chan, *Protestantism in Contemporary China*, 1–8.

36. For an introduction to Adventism in contemporary China, see Lee and Chow, "Christian Revival from within," 45–58.

were concerned about losing members and being accused of associating with a heretical cult, so they authorized the evangelicals to "check up" on the home fellowships. This provided yet another opportunity to provide care and support for the many new meeting points in and around Taiyuan.

As work progressed on the new official church building at Qiaotou Jie, the home fellowship groups continued to grow in number and size. Before long there were not enough leaders to keep track of all the home groups, and so the church began a Lay Training Program (*yigong peixunban*) targeted at providing training to leaders within the local fellowships. The courses were held twice a year, in August and over the Chinese New Year holiday, with most of the instruction focused on teaching through the different books of the Bible. It was difficult to get the official church leaders and the SARA to agree to the new proposal, but eventually the training program was approved with the requirement that the church bring in fully qualified teachers from the official registered church seminaries. In practice this proved difficult to arrange, and so over time the church relied more and more on their own local staff to provide the actual training.

As China's economy developed it soon became clear to church authorities that the best paths to power, fame, and fortune lay outside the church, and so those not committed to serving Christ gradually shifted their attentions elsewhere. Accordingly, the day-to-day operations of the church were increasingly taken over by the evangelical leaders who had returned from seminary to Taiyuan in the early 1990s. Unfortunately, lack of consensus between the official church leadership and the SARA made it impossible to hold meaningful elections to replace the church leaders. While the old guard continued to hold their seats on the Provincial Protestant Twin Committees, the evangelical leaders proceeded to expand training and pastoral care in the church and the many fellowships. By now there were in Taiyuan nearly one hundred separate gatherings associated with the official church through various teaching and relational networks.

In 1993 Finn S. Torjesen and his wife, Sandy, moved to Taiyuan with two other families to found a new Christian development organization called Evergreen Family Friendship Service (Shanxi Yongqing Jiating Fuwushe). Back in 1990, following the dedication of the Torjesen memorial tablet in Hequ, Vice Governor Guo Yuhuai had invited Torjesen to move to Shanxi and continue the work of his grandfather Peter Torjesen (see above).[37] Recalling Peter Torjesen's earlier ministry, Evergreen sought to provide public benefit services for the common people of Shanxi, while be-

---

37. Peter Torjesen's Chinese name was "Leaf Evergreen" (Ye Yongqing). For more on the organization's development and operations in Shanxi, see Andrew T. Kaiser, "Peter Torjesen's Legacy" in Malcolm, *We Signed Away Our Lives*, 179–97.

ing open about the organization's faith commitment. The new agency began to attract bi-vocational cross-cultural workers—men and women trained in ministry who were ready to use their professional skills and experience to be a blessing and a witness within Shanxi communities. These early Evergreeners formed the nucleus of Taiyuan's first officially-registered foreign fellowship, joined by a handful of other expatriate Christians from around the world, meeting weekly for prayer and fellowship in one of Evergreen's residential apartments.[38] By this time in the mid-1990s there was a consistent presence of twenty to thirty foreign Christians working in the Taiyuan region for a period of one or more years, with university campuses hosting many of these expatriates as either English teachers or students of Mandarin Chinese.

While Evergreen's arrival in 1993 marked the return of long-term expatriate Christian service in Shanxi, this was a different kind of mission. Evergreen members were public about their identity as Christians; however, as employees of a legally-registered, wholly foreign-owned enterprise, they chose to constrain their regular religious life to legally acceptable channels and venues—to the registered church—in order to ensure their ability to secure annual visa renewals. Founder Finn S. Torjesen drew on the lessons of mission history and his own experience growing up on the mission field, placing long-term service and linguistic ability at the core of Evergreen's identity. Rejecting older models of expatriate leadership in local ministry, and recognizing the tendency of on-the-ground foreign-local ministry partnerships to draw resources away from the developing local churches, Evergreen leaders pushed the ministry toward a new model of service. By grounding their expatriate as well as local personnel within the local church community and allowing local Christian leaders to guide Evergreen's service, the new mission considered itself as located within the Shanxi church. Ultimately, it was hoped that this approach to ministry in China would make possible the gradual transfer of formal ministry authority into local hands.

In that same year (1993), Arthur Wyatt—son of BMS Missionary Harry Wyatt—returned to Taiyuan with his wife Margaret to lecture at the Shanxi Tumor Hospital (Shanxi Sheng Zhongliu Yiyuan). During their time in Taiyuan, the Wyatts were taken to the official Taiyuan church bookstore by Evergreen member Mark A. Strand. In the 1990s the bookstore was located

---

38. When the Taiyuan Foreign Fellowship registered in the mid-1990s, it was officially listed as meeting in Evergreen's first legally owned apartment (67 Fuxi Jie) with one of Evergreen's expatriate workers serving as the fellowship's legal representative. During these early years there were other regular gatherings of expatriate Christians, at least one of which served those who preferred a more charismatic worship environment.

in an old two-story European-style home on Xinghualing Xiang, complete with bay windows and large fireplaces. After examining the books and Bibles on the ground floor, Dr. Wyatt expressed a desire to see the upstairs of the building. Upon reaching the top of the stairs, he paused and uttered a gasp: the simple swinging gate at the top of the staircase had been installed in the 1930s by Harry Wyatt to keep Arthur and his siblings safe upstairs while their parents were studying Chinese with their tutors downstairs.[39]

The new Taiyuan church building on Qiaotou Jie was finally completed in late 1994, located on the site of the first Protestant sanctuary in Shanxi, built by Timothy Richard back in 1879. With seating for nearly thirteen hundred people, the sanctuary was soon filled to capacity each Sunday morning. In addition to the regular weekly attendees, many outlying fellowships sent representatives to attend the monthly communion services and bring elements back to share with their associates. Taking advantage of the building's size and prime location in the heart of the city's shopping district, the pastors were soon holding seven or eight Christmas services each year, presenting the gospel in dramatic and musical form to ten to twenty thousand people every holiday season.

A year or two after the new building opened, the young pastors were eager to begin providing religious instruction to the growing number of children (many brought by their grandparents) who were attending Sunday morning services. As Chinese citizens under the age of eighteen do not have freedom of religious belief, and proselytizing children is forbidden in China, this ambition was far from straightforward. They eventually decided to present the Taiyuan SARA officials with a problem, explaining that the large number of children in the sanctuary during worship services was causing great disruption and disorder. The pastors proposed that the children be removed from the sanctuary and placed in some of the nearby church meeting rooms. While the adults were worshiping, the children could then be entertained with songs, stories, and games—anything that might keep them settled so that the services could go on without interruption. The officials agreed to the church's proposed "child care" plan, and so began Taiyuan's first modern Sunday school program.

In 1995 the Yuci Christian community opened their newly built four hundred-seat sanctuary. The original church building had been reopened in 1981, although church life and ministry remained restricted for several

---

39. This property—identified by the Wyatts in 1993 as the former missionary residence of their parents—was demolished in 2008, but has yet to be developed by the church due to lack of planning permission. A few Christian slogans on the walls and a forest of rebar from an aborted attempt at construction mark the location of the site, currently being used as a parking lot and recycling center.

years with close surveillance from government officials. It wasn't until 1989 that Bibles were regularly available for purchase within the Yuci church.

Situated just north of Taiyuan, Yangqu County had been the center of Timothy Richard's earliest Shanxi relief work during the 1877–1879 North China Famine. By 1996 expatriates were residing in Yangqu, once again providing humanitarian service—this time offering medical training in partnership with the local Public Health Bureau. At that time the few Protestants in the county were disconnected and no legally registered fellowship existed, though Catholics were numerous with an active religious life centered on the Holy Mother shrine (Shengmu Tang) located on top of a local mountain fifteen kilometers southeast of the Yangqu county seat.

Within a few years, the expatriate Christians living and working in Yangqu helped a small number of local Christians form a fellowship. While Yangqu officials refused to register the group, the registered church in Taiyuan agreed to support them, sending pastors or elders to provide solid teaching and experienced management during its early phases of development. One elder by the name of Hao, in particular, became very involved in supporting the Yangqu fellowship. He naturally came to know some of the expatriates living and working in Yangqu, and in 1998 when they began a one-room schoolhouse to educate their children, Elder Hao recommended his wife, Zhang Xinrong, one of the key organizers of the Taiyuan registered church Sunday school program, for the position of Chinese language instructor. Zhang Xinrong and the new school's founding teacher, Edie Eager, soon became close friends, and before long Eager was also providing training and assistance to the Taiyuan church Sunday school teachers.

Finally, in 1998, the Taiyuan City and Shanxi Provincial Protestant Twin Committees held elections for the first time since the churches were reopened in 1979. The evangelical leaders fared well in the elections, having in practice already taken over most of the leadership positions in the official church. Tensions with the Seventh-day Adventist leadership, however, resulted in less-than-complete evangelical control of the Provincial Twin Committees. That same year the Qiaotou Jie church formed its first musical ensemble and drama troupe. While a few expatriate Christians provided encouragement and technical training (voice, piano, and instrument instruction), the impetus for these new areas of ministry came from younger believers within the Christian community. These ministries expanded rapidly, engaging more and more youth in witnessing to their communities through weddings, funerals and holiday celebrations.

In 1999, the church called an additional three new Bible teachers to join the work in Taiyuan. These men were evangelical graduates of Yanjing Seminary, former classmates of the newly-elected church leaders. Eager to exercise their newfound authority, the Taiyuan pastors invited their classmates to leave their work in different parts of northern China, in the hope that they would become the teaching core of the nascent Taiyuan Bible School. Located just south of Taiyuan, the school had already been built, but had yet to receive formal permission from the Taiyuan SARA. Official approval was repeatedly postponed due to a supposed need to investigate and see if the small number of believers and staff in that area could support the school. The school was eventually allowed to open a few years later, but its physical location within the boundaries of Jinzhong Municipality rather than Taiyuan enabled officials to restrict its enrollment and management to citizens of Jinzhong.[40] While approval was welcome, this limitation meant that there was still no training center for future church leaders in Taiyuan. Further efforts to expand Bible training were hampered by the anti-religion/anti-superstition wave that swept the country during the aggressive 1999 repression of the Buddhist-Daoist hybrid cult known as Falun Gong.

With a cohort of evangelical leaders in positions of authority, the official church was growing and expanding its ministry to the people of Taiyuan. In the spring of 2000, four pastors were ordained—all from among the evangelical spiritual leaders. For the first time since 1949 the church also was able to commission thirty-one deacons and four elders. That summer, the church held its seventh lay leaders training session, with over one hundred people attending the twenty days of Bible teaching led by the pastors and some of their former classmates from Beijing. That same year, with the encouragement of some of the local religious affairs officials, the official church took the first steps toward beginning a sanctuary-building program in the south part of the city. Taking advantage of land they already owned as compensation for property lost in the 1960s and 1970s, they hoped to build a thousand-seat sanctuary to meet the demands of some of the large home fellowships in that area. The newly-arrived teachers and pastors would staff and manage the new site. Unfortunately, high real estate costs and internal fighting between different Christian factions slowed progress on this urgently needed project.

By the early 2000s the Taiyuan Christian community was expanding rapidly with perhaps twenty or thirty thousand worshipers attached to the various registered fellowships and an additional forty to eighty thousand Christians worshiping in unregistered house churches.[41] While some un-

40. Jinzhong is the modern name for the old county seat of Yuci. In 2010 the elder in charge of the Jinzhong Bible School drove away all the students and locked the doors, effectively closing the school.

41. These are extremely loose estimates based on personal conversations with local church leaders and expatriate missionaries.

registered fellowships elected to associate with the evangelical pastoral leadership team of the official registered church in Taiyuan, a growing number of groups were choosing specifically not to associate with the registered church leadership. In many cases the reasons were personal, reflecting old and new networks of friendship and loyalty, with stories of betrayal from the Cultural Revolution looming large in the hearts of many older Christians. In some cases, divisions emerged over differing views of the degree of theological accommodation involved in joining the TSPM/CCC associated church. In rare cases, divisions among Christians were rooted in theological differences. One older woman had a falling out with Sister Wang and left the registered church to start her own fellowship where she could propagate her belief in faith healing. Her son, who was well known to the foreign Christian community because of his habit of sitting in the balcony at Qiaotou Jie church and offering to translate sermons for English speakers, followed. Years later, the young man returned with the remnants of his mother's fellowship and reconciled with Sister Wang. His mother's confidence in faith healing had led her to reject the medical care that might have saved her from death, and the experience had greatly humbled her son.

Unfortunately, the increasing presence of foreign Christians often exacerbated already existing divisions within the local Christian community. The resources that the expatriates promised—though always less than what they actually provided—made them attractive commodities. Often unaware of their outsized influence, foreign Christians carried great authority with some local Christians, at times unwittingly allowing their personal preferences for either more or less charismatic expressions of Christianity to perpetuate previous local divisions. Unregistered fellowships, in particular, were far more likely to espouse faith healing, gifts of prophecy, and other more radical charismatic practices and beliefs, and were often eager to latch on to visiting expatriates who shared their experience. While believers on both sides of the debate were often quick to ostracize their opponents, expatriates with limited connections to other foreign or local Christians were especially likely to be drawn into relationships that strengthened fractures within the Christian community. One American woman made frequent trips to Taiyuan during this period in an effort to develop Christian orphan care programs in the city. With her strong personality, charismatic worship style, and purported access to vast financial resources, local and expatriate Christians in the city were compelled to either agree with her methods of ministry and assumptions about the local church or get out of her way.

There were other fault lines within the Christian community as well. Adventism's traditional emphases on family and adherence to Mosaic Law coincided nicely with Chinese cultural tendencies, making the Adventist church attractive to many Shanxi people. Taiyuan Seventh-day Adventists worked hard for several years to convince local SARA and PSB officials that they should be considered Protestants, and as such should be eligible for registration within the official church. Evangelical leaders within the registered church resisted Adventists appeals, arguing that the group was legalistic and heretical; however, SARA officials consistently replied by criticizing all Christians for being divisive and unable to get along.

The Qiaotou Jie church leadership won a major victory over the Seventh-day Adventists in the first few years of the new century. Because of the SARA's persistence in recognizing the Adventists as an official part of the registered Protestant community, the evangelical pastors were forced to share their property with the sect. On Saturday mornings it was common to see Adventist deaconesses handing out tracts on the busy shopping street in front of the Qiaotou Jie church, urging passersby to join their worship service inside. If any vaguely Christian person walked by, the Adventists would drag the wanderer in, convincing them to share in their Christian worship. Eventually the pastors hit upon a solution: they told the SARA that some recent property damage had almost certainly occurred on Saturday. Since this was the pastoral staff's day off, there was really no one on the church property to maintain security. They suggested that the best way to keep things safe—including the Adventist worshipers inside—was to lock the front gate of the church on Saturdays. The appeal to safety and order won the day, and the Seventh-day Adventists were restricted to using the difficult-to-find back gate of the church during their services. Their attendance dropped off, and their influence began to wane.[42]

In November 2000 Arthur Wyatt returned with his brother to visit once more the Xinghualing neighborhood. Wyatt had received an invitation to deliver medical lectures at the Taiyuan City Number One Hospital (Taiyuan Shi Diyi Renmin Yiyuan) located on the site of the old BMS Taiyuan Women's Hospital. A number of older buildings still remained within the hospital complex, and the Wyatts were able to tour these after they had amazed the hospital staff with their family's stories from old Shanxi.[43]

---

42. In the 1990s the evangelical leadership had been asked by local SARA officials to perform an ordination ceremony for a Seventh-day Adventist pastor in southern Shanxi. The evangelicals resisted as long as they could, though their own need for SARA support as well as the accusations of not "loving one another" eventually left them with no choice but to comply.

43. During their visit I took the Wyatt children on a tour of the old neighborhood. As we stood in front of what had likely been their parents' residence, an elderly woman approached and asked if I spoke Chinese. I explained my guests' interest in the old house and the woman became excited, begging us to follow her back into the neighboring courtyard. An elderly gentleman was seated inside one of the buildings.

In 2002–2003 the Taiyuan Foreign Fellowship began meeting on Sunday afternoons in one of the classrooms of the Qiaotou Jie church. The Fellowship established a governing committee external to Evergreen in order to recognize and take full advantage of the contributions of non-Evergreen expatriate workers in the small congregation. The committee then invited one of the local pastors to officiate communion for the expatriate community on a monthly basis. While growth in numbers—on a crowded Sunday the Fellowship might have as many as fifty attendees—was one of the main reasons for the move, it was also hoped that meeting in the local church would help shorter-term expatriate workers to recognize the authority of local Chinese pastors. It was also believed that meeting at the church would provide an avenue for other foreign Christians to become legally involved with the local church.

By this time the number of foreign Christians living and serving in Shanxi had also expanded dramatically, with expatriates—mostly Protestants, though there were a few Catholics as well—witnessing on many university and school campuses as teachers or students. Transportation options and the standard of living had improved, making things more welcoming to foreigners—though Shanxi was still far behind the more prosperous coastal provinces. Taiyuan's total expatriate population was still under six hundred people, including businessmen and students on shorter-term visas, many of whom were from Taiwan or Hong Kong; of those, approximately fifty (including children) were Christian professionals committed to more than three years of service in Shanxi. Taiyuan was also receiving infrequent visits from Baha'i, Mormon, and Jehovah's Witness missionaries; however, none of these groups managed to establish a large following in the city.[44]

Perhaps more importantly, the kind of work that expatriate Christians were engaged in was broadening considerably. In addition to teaching English and studying Mandarin Chinese, foreign Christians were now involved

---

After introductions he explained that he had lived there all his life and—pointing at the Wyatts—remembered very clearly his boyhood playmates from next door. Once during his youth he had injured his leg; Harry Wyatt came directly over and set his leg in a plaster cast. On another occasion Wyatt had treated him for a fever. He went on to describe the courtyard and street in front of the Wyatt house, the names of their household staff, even the pet goat they had kept in the yard. The man's father had been a practitioner of Chinese medicine and had been good friends with Harry Wyatt.

44. As of 2014 all expatriate Mormons have left Taiyuan having failed to establish a business foothold, while the Baha'i adherents have all married locals and returned to their passport countries. The Jehovah's Witnesses complained so much about their living conditions while teaching at local schools that after a year no school was willing to employ them. These three cults still have influence in Taiyuan, though their presence is largely restricted to literature sent into Shanxi by overseas relatives of local people.

in business ventures, agricultural development, professional training, and medical work, as well as more traditional poverty relief and community development efforts. While many different models for mission work are employed in China today, a sizable portion of Shanxi's expatriate Christians chose deliberately to work alongside the existing local Christian communities. Rather than leading and directing local churches, these new foreign workers were advising and supporting, enabling Shanxi Christians to build their own church. Discipleship and fellowship, along with participation in local church activities were some of the main venues for service available to this new generation of Shanxi missionaries.[45]

While in many ways this attitude toward China missions was dictated by the unique political climate in which the Christian community was forced to operate, it was a change that was welcomed by local church leaders. One Chinese pastor had watched over the years since opening and reform, as foreigners in his local area planted churches and evangelized on the university campuses. He had also witnessed the fruits of a foreign non-profit organization's long-term presence throughout the province. When asked what purpose he felt foreigners could best serve, he responded simply: "Foreigners are able to go to places where we Chinese Christians rarely go. They can talk to people we rarely meet. Foreign Christians are like the spade that breaks up the soil." Though not spoken, the implication of his comment was that the rest of the work—planting seeds, watering the seedlings and eventually harvesting the crop—was best carried out by the local church.[46]

Still, there were clashes with local officials. Campus Crusade's earliest activities in Taiyuan attracted more than their share of police attention. One spring in the early 2000s, a group of thirty or so American college students arrived at Shanxi University for a month-long "Chinese culture and language" course. Teachers at the university quickly approached other long-term expatriates in the hope that they would encourage these young students to actually attend their classes and respect their teachers. In fact, the group comprised short-term missionaries tasked with showing *The Jesus Film* to as many university students as possible. This evangelistic "blitz" was supposed to generate a list of names for follow-up by longer-term Crusade

---

45. A partial list of some of the Christian organizations that had worked in Shanxi since the beginning of the period of opening and reform would include: the Association for Christian Conferences Teaching and Services or ACCTS, Campus Crusade for Christ, Educational Services Exchange with China or ESEC, English Language Institute China or ELIC, the Evangelical Alliance for Mission or TEAM, Jian Hua Foundation or JHF, Mennonite Central Committee Canada, Overseas Missionary Fellowship or OMF, Team Expansion, and a handful of other denominational organizations as well.

46. Personal interview with local Taiyuan pastor, summer 2002.

workers in Taiyuan, but instead contributed to an amendment to foreign teacher contracts at Taiyuan universities specifically prohibiting religious activities on campuses.

On another occasion, police were called to investigate complaints of a late-night prowler in an old Taiyuan neighborhood. They arrived and captured a young American student who was going through apartment hallways at night surreptitiously inserting literature under residents' doors. One long-term Christian expatriate heard all of this the next day from a friend in the police who asked him if he recognized the literature carried by the young man who had just been escorted to the airport and sent home: it was a gospel tract printed in the United States. The small number of expatriates in Shanxi and the early influence of more progressive groups like Evergreen and ESEC means that there are fewer incidents like this—and thus more trust from local officials—than what would be typical of many of the more-developed coastal cities. This has resulted in a more harmonious official environment for expatriate Christians—despite Shanxi's comparatively conservative political and legal climate.

In late 2004 the Taiyuan Twin Committees were granted permission to open a Bible training school for the purposes of training new pastors from the Taiyuan region. The first class of twenty-eight students enrolled for a yearlong course of study in the fall of 2005 in a facility on the edge of Jinyuan, still within reach of Taiyuan City public transportation. The pastoral staff from Taiyuan handled all the teaching themselves, with the various pastors teaching one subject for an entire day once a week. The content of the training focused primarily on mastering the books of the Bible, though other topics such as music, administration, finances, and homiletics were covered as well. On a few occasions Bible school teachers consulted with resident expatriate Christians regarding curriculum questions, but course selection, design, and instruction were all carried out by local church workers.

Along with the biannual lay training programs, the new Bible school was seen as a valuable tool in resisting the growing influence of cults and heresies in and around the Taiyuan Christian community. Faith healers and radical millenarian sects have come and gone throughout Taiyuan's modern history: the 1990s saw a faith-healing sect active to the west of Taiyuan and an end-times sect growing in Yushe just outside Jinzhong. One particularly unusual recent heresy involved a pseudo-Christian sect of Japanese origin that advocated drinking one's first morning urine in order to guarantee health and vitality. This group's literature circulated among some of the fellowships near the train station, and eventually reached some of the workers at the Qiaotou Jie church bookstore. Trusted long-term resident expatriate Christians were often called upon by local Christian leaders to assess other newly arrived expatriate Christians for their orthodoxy: over the years, this has helped local Christians avoid predation from several different foreign "prophets." In one memorable instance, expatriate Christian workers were asked to evaluate an Australian national who had set herself up as a prophet in a Taiyuan home fellowship and was collecting tithes from and giving "words of power" to local Christians. On another occasion, long-term resident expatriates were asked to assess the orthodoxy of an older English-speaking tourist who approached the pastors, offering to give them a suitcase full of English-language paper gospel tracts.

No cult was more active in Shanxi than the Eastern Lightning (Dongfang Shandian) or Church of the Almighty God (Quannengshen Jiaohui). Relying on their own set of sacred writings to help them properly interpret the Bible, Eastern Lightning asserts that Jesus's promise in Matthew 24:27 has been literally fulfilled with the Christ's return to Zhengzhou—this time in female form.[47] Beginning in the 2000s, the cult made a determined effort to expand into Taiyuan, having already made tremendous inroads in the rural parts of the province. The group aggressively targeted Christians—foreign and local—for conversion and absorption into their group. In other parts of China they had resorted to kidnappings and violent attacks on local Christian leaders; in Shanxi they used promises of marriage and various brainwashing techniques to draw unsuspecting believers into their network. In Taiyuan, Eastern Lightning followers would sit in the back of regular services at the Qiaotou Jie church and then chat with the stragglers after the service. Once the deacons and deaconesses discovered their strategy, the cultists moved to the street in front of the church, where they approached a number of expatriate Christians using passable English to explain that they were Christians, just like the foreigners! The church's response to Eastern Lightning's efforts was twofold: they expanded lay training programs emphasizing methods for identifying and refuting the lies of the cult while also encouraging believers to report all Eastern Lightning followers to the local police.

In 2004 the leader of the main registered Protestant church in Yuci was ordained as an elder. A year later, twenty deacons, deaconesses, and evangelists were commissioned to minister throughout the area. Three thousand or so believers had either been baptized in the Yuci church or considered it their home church, though only around 275 worshipers attended their weekly Sunday afternoon services. The congregation was composed of

---

47. Dunn, "'Cult,' Church, and the CCP," 96–119. For a detailed examination of Eastern Lightning's publications, see Dunn, *Lightning from the East*.

around 70 percent women and most of the believers were between forty and sixty years of age, although the number of younger believers was slowly increasing year by year.

That same year the tiny Yangqu fellowship was formally registered as a meeting point (*juhuidian*) in the home of one of the local Christian leaders. Four years later they purchased property for dedicated use as church building, a move that enabled expatriates in Yangqu to attend their weekly services. In 2011 they began construction on the site of a new church building, changing their official registration status formally to "church." The believers completed and began using the new facility in 2012 and, with some encouragement and training from the Yangqu expatriate Christians, they now have a growing Sunday school program run by a team of younger local believers determined to raise their children in the faith.

With the support of the city SARA, in 2005 the Taiyuan City Twin Committees began pursuing registration and ultimately property purchases or leases for over thirty new locations around the edges of Taiyuan City. All the proposed locations reflected existing fellowships with connections to the main registered church—some of them quite large with memberships of well over one hundred believers. Within a year, over half of the locations had been approved, bringing the total number of registered meeting points and sanctuaries (*tangdian*) in Taiyuan to nearly thirty locations. As the new fellowships grew and moved into more fixed sites, the pastors assigned new ministers to serve in the specific locations.

By 2007 the biannual lay training sessions at the main registered church in Taiyuan were still well attended. The effectiveness of these programs was visible in the rising number of commissioned deacons and deaconesses—by this time approaching three hundred workers spread throughout the Christian community associated with the Taiyuan registered churches. Church attendance was also up, with the earliest of the two weekly Sunday morning services at the Qiaotou Jie church routinely spilling out into two or three nearby overflow rooms. There were now officially fifteen ministers and seven elders serving the many registered believers in the greater Taiyuan area, and there were plans to ordain two new workers.

CHRISTIANITY IN POST-OLYMPIC SHANXI

As the 2008 Beijing Olympics turned the world's eyes toward China, the vision for Taiyuan shared by the pastors in the registered churches was simple—a dream inspired by a trip to Baotou they made in 2003. They wanted Taiyuan citizens to see the cross of Christ wherever they turned their eyes: a skyline riddled with steeples so that no one would miss the gospel for lack of a place to hear about it. This confidence continued following the success of the Beijing Olympics, as the church began to act in accordance with its own expanding human and financial resources.[48] No longer concerned with matters of survival, Shanxi Christians turned their focus outward. Younger Christians, many of whom had grown up in the church and had little or no experience of government interference, were now expecting to carry their faith out into society. The Taiyuan registered church became increasingly involved in raising funds to assist building projects throughout the province, as well as participating financially in various national relief efforts. In one especially prominent example, Taiyuan Christians collected funds and materials to assist with the May 2008 Wenchuan Earthquake relief work. Several teams of Christians—both local and expatriate—traveled from Shanxi to the disaster area to participate in the aid effort.

More remote areas of Shanxi also shared in the growing mood of confidence. In 2011 local believers in Xinzhou, Shanxi, were assisted by a cohort of national and international Chinese Christian intellectuals to publish an open appeal for the return of the Baptist mission property purchased in the city in 1899 by Timothy Richard. Despite the international attention and strong historical documentation, the Buddhist community occupying the land and the relevant local officials resisted local church pleas, leaving the dispute unresolved.[49]

In the post-Olympic years, however, state resistance to the increasingly vocal and confident Christian community became more and more common. The September 2009 detention and imprisonment of several pastors at the Fushan and Golden Lampstand (Jin Dengtai) churches from the unregistered Linfen Church garnered international attention. The violence of the confrontations, with supposedly hundreds of thugs representing the security forces beating worshipers and destroying property at both sites, was particularly egregious. Nevertheless, the buildings had not received construction approval and the fifty-thousand-member church was not legally registered, and so with little or no due process the church leaders received long sentences.[50] Several years later a group of expatriate Christians work-

---

48. Fulton, *China's Urban Christians*, 22–46.

49. The May 2011 open letter, along with a list of supporting archival documents, is available in many places online, including He Guanghu et al., "*Zunjing lishi wenhua yiji.*" As recently as October 2015 foreigners were blocked from visiting the disputed property.

50. For a recent update, see the 2013 open letter from the Linfen believers to Xi Jinping posted on China Aid's Linfen webpage: "*Gei Xi Jinping zhuxi de yifeng gongkai xin.*"

ing in Shanxi made a business trip to Linfen. Local and provincial officials politely yet firmly escorted them out of Linfen and onto the freeway in order to prevent them from meeting with Linfen Christians.

Around the time of the Olympics a group of Christians from Taiyuan house churches registered and opened a store in the city specifically aimed at providing Christian media to local believers. The first and only private Christian bookstore in Taiyuan, the Enyu or "Rain of Grace" bookstore was soon popular for the many Christian gift items it sold in addition to the more traditional print and video offerings.[51] Within a year or two the bookshop moved to a slightly larger location, using the extra space for Christian salons, English corners, and training events. A 2012 visit from Li Wenxi, a worker from a Beijing Christian bookstore, to provide advice for the Enyu staff attracted the attention of local government officials, and resulted in the arrest of both Li and Ren Lacheng, a Taiyuan house church leader and Enyu sponsor. The two men were given multiple-year imprisonments for receiving illegal profits of 5460 RMB from the sale of 780 hymnals.[52] Books seized by officials from the bookstore as evidence of illegal business dealings were subsequently seen for sale in Taiyuan book markets.[53] Perhaps most troubling was the wording of the official press release from the Taiyuan City government offices: "Yingze District successfully clamped down on a case of Christianity."[54]

By the second decade of the twenty-first century, the Christian population in Shanxi had expanded to perhaps as many as 2.9 million believers, of whom roughly one quarter were Catholic. Taiyuan was home to many of those Catholics, with an estimated two hundred fifty thousand followers—many located in the suburbs. The Protestant population was smaller, with approximately one hundred fifty thousand believers living in the Taiyuan municipality. Statistically, the unregistered church population was growing most rapidly with one hundred twenty thousand believers in their fellowships.[55] While in the 1990s this imbalance in growth was envied

---

51. Since the late 1990s the Qiaotou Jie church bookshop has bosted a surprisingly large selection of Christian literature. Shortly after the Enyu bookstore opened, the Qiaotou Jie church bookshop further expanded its offerings in order to compete with Enyu and the many online alternatives operating in China today.

52. China Aid, "*Huyu shifang*;" and Voice of the Martyrs, "Prisoner Alert: Lacheng Ren."

53. China Aid, "Original Verdict Upheld."

54. Amy Li, "'Don't you dare bring Christianity to Shanxi.'" There is currently no private Christian bookstore in Taiyuan.

55. These numbers are taken from Hattaway's 2010 research. Paul Hattaway, "How Many Christians Are in China?" The total number of Christians (Catholic, Orthodox, and Protestant) in China is still disputed, with informed scholars placing the figure

or even resented by the pastors in the official churches, by this time they were much more at peace with this pattern. As they explained, the visibility and accessibility of the registered churches—particularly their large public Christmas outreaches—provided an easy access point for Chinese people curious about Christianity. After coming to faith, many of these new believers then chose to move from the larger registered churches to the more intimate pastoral environment of unregistered communities.

In the mid-2000s churches had begun to emerge in China's more affluent cities which, while not being formally registered with the TSMP or CCC, nevertheless sought to be public in their worship and Christian identity. Often rooted in urban professional communities, these churches proactively announced their identities and their main worship services to the local public security bureau, in many cases renting local restaurants or conference halls for their gatherings. The most prominent of these fellowships was Shouwang Church in Beijing, a large house church begun in the early 1990s.[56] Since 2005 the church, led by pastor Jin Tianming, has rented a series of office spaces and hotel ballrooms to house their worship gatherings. Buoyed by the heady confidence surrounding the Beijing Olympics, the large fellowship attempted to chart a new course between the two options of registered or unregistered meeting points. However, the state responded quickly, using its influence on several occasions beginning in 2008 to prevent Shouwang from renting or purchasing premises for their worship services. For years, the fellowship has been holding services out of doors, braving further official interference as they struggle to find a space to worship.[57] With little indication of resolution any time soon, early hopes for creating a new path to legal recognition for religious activities outside of the TSPM/CCC have since faded, though conditions vary from city to city.[58]

Unregistered groups like Beijing's Shouwang Church that are eager to be public in their Christian identity have been slow to form in Taiyuan. By

---

somewhere between the 2010 Hattaway study's 105 million and the Pew Research Center's 2011 estimate of 67 million. Pew Forum on Religion and Public Life, "Appendix C: Methodology for China," 97–110.

56. Promise Hsu, "Why Beijing's Largest House Church Refuses to Stop Meeting Outdoors."

57. Shouwang Church has been covered extensively in Western media. See, for example, China Aid's useful online summary "About Shouwang."

58. Insiders report that Shouwang Church is divided over the question of how hard to press for reform, with some prioritizing Shouwang's desire to worship without interference while others feel obligated to use their church's notoriety and influence to actively pressure the government to revise Chinese regulations regarding religious faith and practice.

2013 at least one of these so-called "third church" fellowships was meeting in Taiyuan, comprising around one hundred people meeting weekly in smaller groups and joining together for corporate fellowship on a monthly basis. Known as the Cultural Springs Fellowship, the group's membership comes primarily from Taiyuan's educated professionals and young middle-class families, including a few government officials and a growing number of young graduates. There are a few "sea turtles" or returnees from overseas in the fellowship as well, although Taiyuan's economic situation has resulted in a smaller population of returnees than its status as provincial capital might suggest.[59] Several of the leaders from this group were discipled within the Medical Fellowship attached to the Qiaotou Jie church. Perhaps best labeled as an "urban professional church," the vision for this currently unregistered fellowship is to eventually seek some kind of official recognition. As one of the leaders said, "How can we be faithful, healthy Christians if we have to hide our faith?" Cultural Springs Fellowship often partners with the registered church at Qiaotou Jie for training opportunities, maintaining a close relationship that belies their status as an unregistered house church.

Indeed, for many younger believers in Taiyuan today, the boundaries between registered and unregistered are porous. For Chinese Christians born after 1990, there is an expectation that religious faith can be an acceptable and public part of one's life. These same younger believers are increasingly comfortable moving back and forth among the various Christians groups in the city, showing less allegiance to the old personal divisions and more of a desire to be a part of any Christian activities that feed their souls. These dynamic Christians will participate in Bible studies, volunteer work, social events, and worship services wherever they experience Christian community—regardless of legal status or affiliation.[60]

Out of this population, a host of new explicitly Christian associations are emerging, largely organized through social media, and often with little awareness of the possibility of government interference. Christian retreats and tourism are expanding, and there are the beginnings of the kinds of short-term mission trips that are already common in many southern China and coastal city churches. There are currently several experiments in Taiyuan developing small Christian schools and, while none have achieved any measure of success, interest is very high, with many young professional

---

59. The Mandarin Chinese term for a Chinese citizen who has returned to China after a time of work or study overseas (*hai gui*) is a homophone for the word for sea turtle.

60. This phenomenon is illustrated in Liao Yiwu, *God Is Red*. See, especially, chapter 18, "The New Convert."

families eager to find a Christian alternative to China's constricting educational system.

Despite years of encouragement from expatriate Christians, older generations of Shanxi church leaders still find it difficult to trust up-and-coming Christians with leadership authority and responsibility. At the same time, the extreme level of personal loyalty demanded by many of these older Christian leaders is unattractive to younger Christians. Undaunted, this next generation of Chinese believers continues to engage dynamically with society, attracting more and more believers to their fellowships and ultimately leaving older Christian leaders little choice: they must either join or be relegated to the past. At the same time, today's expatriate Christians are increasingly placing themselves under the authority of these young local Christians—an encouraging sign that the "three-self" goals of many of the earliest Shanxi missionaries are now being realized. Armed with the growing financial and human resources God has given them, Shanxi Christians are actively pursuing new and winsome ways to witness to the gospel in their own communities.

In the fall of 2015 a conference was held for representatives of unregistered house churches from a handful of cities across southern Shanxi.[61] The purpose of these meetings was to establish a local sending agency (*chaihui*) to mobilize, train, equip, and send out Shanxi Christians as missionaries. With roots in the 1920s "Back to Jerusalem" movement, the current indigenous mission movement is gaining momentum across China—even if it has only recently touched Shanxi.[62] Initial efforts during the early 2000s to send Chinese missionaries overseas to engage in cross-cultural evangelism were most often unsuccessful, with would-be missionaries returning after only a few years, complaining of insufficient financial backing, struggles with language and cultural issues, and a lack of pastoral support. This new wave of missionaries is smaller in scale, but much more determined to learn from the past and invest the time and resources necessary to become faithful effective cross-cultural workers. Only time will tell what fruits will come from this new initiative, but it surely marks a new and exciting stage in the development of the Shanxi church. The rushing on of God's purposes has

---

61. The timing of this meeting suggests it may be related to Mission China 2030, a group of Chinese Christian leaders that have committed to repaying China's "gospel debt" by sending out 20,000 missionaries from China by the year 2030. Arising after Chinese delegates were blocked from travelling to the Third Lausanne Congress in 2010, the group met in Hong Kong for its first conference in September 2015. Lausanne Movement, "Nine Hundred from Mainland China Participate in Inaugural Mission China 2030 Conference"; and Ro, "The Rising Missions Movement in China."

62. For a helpful summary of this exciting new trend, see Fulton, *China's Urban Christians*, 94–108.

come full circle as Shanxi Protestants step out into the world, this time as ambassadors of the same gospel that was preached to them at such great price over the last one hundred fifty years.

Pray that God would bless Shanxi . . .
And through Shanxi, bless the world.

—Finn S. Torjesen
Founding Director, Shanxi Evergreen Service.

Selected List of Chinese Terms

Ai Weide	艾伟德
a mi tuo fa	阿密托法
Anqing	安庆
Anze	安泽
Baguolianjun	八国联军
Baibancun	栢板村
Baidengzhao	白灯照
Bailianjiao	白莲教
Baoding	保定
Beidaihe	北戴河
Beimei Rui-Nuohui	北美瑞娜会
bing zhu xinnian hong xi	并祝新年鸿禧
Bo'ai Yiyuan	博爱医院
bu wei qiangpao	不畏枪炮
Cai Hesen	蔡和森
Cai Yuanpei	蔡元培
Cen Chunxuan	岑春煊
chaihui	差会
Changzhi	长治
Chen Duxiu	陈独秀
Cheng Jingyi	诚静怡
Chiang Kai-shek (Jiang Jieshi)	蒋介石
Cixi	慈禧
cunmiao	村庙

Dadaohui	大刀会
Daizhou	戴州
dalu	大路
da maozi	大毛子
Dananmen	大南门
Daning	大宁
Datong	大同
Daying Anliganhui	大英安立甘会
Daying Xundaohui	大英循道会
Dayingpan	大营盘
Dayuejin	大跃进
Dingwu Qihuang	丁戊奇荒
Dingxiang	定襄
dishang kan Shanxi	地上看山西
dixia kan Shaanxi	地下看陕西
Dongfang Shandian	东方闪电
Donghuayuan	东华苑
Dongjia Xiang	东夹巷
Dongjihuying	东辑虎营
Duan Qinwang	端亲王
Enyu	恩雨
er maozi	二毛子
Falun Gong	法轮功
fan Qing mie yang	反清灭洋
feng	风
feng zhi mie jiao	奉旨灭教
fengshui	风水
Fenyang	汾阳
fu/xing Qing mie yang	扶/兴清灭洋
Fushan	浮山
Fuxi Jie	府西街
Fuzhou	福州
Gao Daling	高大龄
Gengzi	庚子
gong xi	公戏
Gong'an Ju	公安局
gonghe jiuzhu shengdan	恭贺救主圣诞
Guan	冠

Selected List of Chinese Terms

Guan Di	关帝
Guangxu sannian	光绪三年
Guangxuehui	光学会
Guan Yu	关羽
Guguan	固关
Guojia Zongjiao Shiwu Ju	国家宗教事务局
guo li di san daxue	国立第三大学
Guoyangzhen	崞阳镇
Guo Yuhuai	郭裕怀
hai gui (returnee)	海归
hai gui (sea turtle)	海龟
Hai Ying	海英
Hankou	汉口
hanyu pinyin	汉语拼音
Hanzhong	汉中
henggu weiyou	亘古未有
Hequ	河曲
Hongdengzhao	红灯照
Hongdong	洪洞
Hongshizi Kouqiang Yiyuan	红十字口腔医院
Houma	侯马
Hou Meide	候美德
Huai Anli	怀安理
hui	会
Huolu	获鹿
Huozhou	霍州
Hu Shi	胡适
Jia	价
jiangshen futi	降神附体
Jiangzhou	绛州
jiao'an	教案
Jiaocheng	交城
jiaohui	教会
Jiaozhou	胶州
Jidu Fulin Anxirihui	基督复临安息日会
Jidujiao Nüqinghui	基督教女青年会
Jidujiao Qingnianhui	基督教青年会
Jidujiao re	基督教
Jidutu bu tui	基督徒不退

Jidutu Juhuichu	基督徒聚会处
Jiexiu	介休
ji gebie	极个别
jin	斤
Jincheng	晋城
Jinci	晋祠
Jindanjiao	金丹教
Jin Dengtai	金灯台
jinshi	进士
Jinyuan	晋源
Jinzhong	晋中
Jiushijun	救世军
jiushi tang	救世堂
juhuidian	聚会点
junfa	军阀
juren	举人
Juye	巨野
Kaifeng	开封
kang	炕
Kangxi	康熙
ketou	磕头
Kongming	孔明
Kong Xiangxi	孔祥熙
Lan	岚
Ledaoyuan	乐道院
li	里
liang	两
Lianghui	两会
liangting	凉亭
Liaozhou	辽州
libai	礼拜
Li Dazhao	李大钊
Li Hongzhang	李鸿章
Li Jufen	李菊芬
Linfen	临汾
Lingde Tang	令德堂
Lingqiu	灵丘
Liu Bei	刘备
Liu Dapeng	刘大鹏

Selected List of Chinese Terms

Li Wenxi	李文习
Liu Xiang	柳巷
liyi lianchi	礼仪廉耻
liyi zhizheng	礼仪之争
Liyuantun	梨园屯
Li Yuehan	李约翰
Lu'an	潞安
Lucheng	潞城
lujun xuetang	陆军学堂
Lundun Chuandaohui	伦敦传道会
Lüshouzhao	绿手照
Meiguo Gonglihui	美国公理会
Meiguo Zhanglaohui	美国长老会
Meihuaquan	梅花拳
min bu liao sheng	民不聊生
mu	亩
Nanguan	南关
Nian	捻
nianshu de haizi	念书的孩子
Ni Tuosheng	倪柝声
Nuoweihui	挪威会
Pianguan	偏关
Pingding	平定
Pingyang	平阳
Pingyao	平遥
Puyi	溥仪
Qiaodong Jie	桥东街
Qiaotou Jie	桥头街
Qiao Yisheng	乔义生
qigong	气功
Qi Hong'en	祁宏恩
Qi *jiaoshi*	祁教师
Qingdao	青岛
Qinghua Daxue	清华大学
Qinglong Guzhen	青龙古镇
Qingzhou	青州
quanfei	拳匪

quanguo lianghui	全国两会
Quannengshen Jiaohui	全能神教会
Quwo	曲沃
renao	热闹
Ren Lacheng	任拉成
renmin bi	人民币
Ruidian Shengjiehui	瑞典圣洁会
Rui-Huahui	瑞华会
Rui-Meng Xuandaohui	瑞蒙宣道会
san bu	三不
Sanercun	伞儿村
san nian kunnan	三年困难
Sanqiao Jie	三桥街
Sanzi Aiguo Yundonghui	三自爱国运动会
Senluo	森罗
Shaanxi	陕西
Shangdi Jiaohui	上帝教会
shangfa	上法
Shangma Jie	上马街
Shanxi	山西
Shanxi Daxue	山西大学
Shanxi Nongye Daxue	山西农业大学
Shanxi Sheng Ertong Yiyuan	山西省儿童医院
Shanxi Sheng Zhongliu Yiyuan	山西省肿瘤医院
Shanxi Yiyong Dianzi Yiqichang	山西医用电子仪器厂
Shanxi Yongqing Jiating Fuwushe	山西永青家庭服务社
Shanxi, bu dong bu xi, bu shi dongxi	山西，不东不西，不是东西
Shen Dunhe	沈敦和
Shengmu Tang	圣母堂
Shenquan	神拳
Shentie	什贴
Shenzhaohui	神召会
Shijiazhuang	石家庄
Shipin Jie	食品街
Shitu Xinxinhui	使徒信心会
Shouyanghui	寿阳会
Shuoping	朔平
si xiang	四香
Song Ailing	宋蔼龄

Selected List of Chinese Terms 265

Song Meiling	宋美龄
Song Qingling	宋庆龄
Song Shangjie	宋尚节
Sugelan Shengjinghui	苏格兰圣经会
Sun Wukong	孙悟空
Sun Yatsen	孙中山
Taigu	太谷
Taihang	太行
Taiyuan Ligong Daxue	太原理工大学
Taiyuan Shi Diyi Renmin Yiyuan	太原市第一人民医院
Taiyuan Shi Minzheng Ju	太原市民政局
Taiyuan Shifan Xueyuan Fushu Zhongxuexiao	太原师范学院附属中学校
tangdian	堂点
Tangseng	唐僧
Tianan Jie	天安街
Tiananmen	天安门
Tian Feng	天凤
Tianlong Shan	天龙山
timing bei	提名碑
ting hao	挺好
Tong Jugong	仝鞠躬
Tong Yiqiang	童义强
tongzijun	童子军
tu huangdi	土皇帝
wawa xiefashi	娃娃邪法司
wawadui	娃娃队
Wei	魏
Wei Enbo	魏恩波
Weifang	潍坊
Weixian Jizhongying	潍县集中营
wen	文
wenmiao	文庙
Wenshui	文水
Wuchang	武昌
Wuchan Jieji Wenhua Da Geming	无产阶级文化大革命
Wuhu	芜湖
Wutai Shan	五台山
wuxing	五行

Wuyi Guangchang	五一广场	
Wuyi Lu	五一路	
Xi'an	西安	
Xiangdao Zhoubao	向导周报	
Xiaodian	小店	
Xiaoqun	小群	
xiaoti zhongxin	孝悌忠信	
Xiaoyi	孝义	
Xi Jinping	习近平	
Xinghualing Xiang	杏花岭巷	
Xinhai	辛亥	
Xin Wenhua Yundong	新文化运动	
Xin Yesu Jiaohui	新耶稣教会	
Xinzhou	忻州	
Xi Shengmo	席胜魔	
Xixiao Qiang	西肖墙	
Xixinshe	洗心社	
xixue zhuanzhai	西学专斋	
Xi Zizhi	席子直	
Xizhou	隰州	
Xu Baoqian	徐宝谦	
Xu Shihu	徐士珩	
yamen	衙门	
yang guizi	洋鬼子	
Yangqu	阳曲	
Yanjing Daxue	燕京大学	
Yanjing Shenxueyuan	燕京神学院	
Yantai	烟台	
Yan Xishan	阎锡山	
yaodong	窑洞	
yao teng	腰疼	
ya teng	牙疼	
Yesujiao Yiyuan	耶稣教医院	
Yesu Jiating	耶稣家庭	
Ye Yongqing	叶永青	
yigong peixunban	义工培训班	
Yihequan	义和拳	
Yihetuan	义和团	
yin	阴	

Yingguo Jinlihui	英国浸礼会
Yingze	迎泽
Yongning	永宁
You'aihui	友爱会
yuan	元
Yuanlin Ju	园林局
Yuan Shikai	袁世凯
Yuci	榆次
Yudaohe	峪道河
Yuncheng	运城
Yuxian	毓贤
Zeng Guofan	曾国藩
Zeng Guoquan	曾国荃
Zezhou	泽州
Zhang Er	张二
Zhang Fei	张飞
Zhang Hanzhong	张汉中
Zhangjiakou	张家口
Zhang Lingzao	张灵造
Zhang Xinrong	张新荣
Zhang Xueliang	张学良
zhaobi	照壁
Zhaocheng	赵城
Zhao Sanduo	赵三多
Zhao Yun	赵云
Zhao Zicheng	赵紫宸
Zhengzhou	郑州
Zhen Yesu Jiaohui	真耶稣教会
Zhifu	芝罘
Zhili	直隶
zhi Qing mie yang	支清灭洋
Zhongguo Gongchangdang	中国共产党
Zhongguo Guomindang	中国国民党
Zhongguo Jidujiao Xiehui	中国基督教协会
Zhongguo Neidihui	中国内地会
Zhonghua Jidujiao Zilihui	中华基督教自立会
zhongxue zhuanzhai	中学专斋
Zhongyang	中阳
Zhu Bajie	猪八戒
Zhuge Liang	诸葛亮

Zhutou Xiang	猪头巷
Zongli Yamen	总理衙门
Zouping	邹平
zouzhe	奏折
zuo yuezi	坐月子

Bibliography

Adolph, Paul Ernest. *Surgery Speaks to China: The Experiences of a Medical Missionary to China in Peace and in War.* Philadelphia: China Inland Mission, 1945.
Anderson, Gerald H., ed. *Biographical Dictionary of Christian Missions.* New York: Macmillan Reference, 1998.
"Assemblies of God Mission." Ricci Roundtable Database. http://ricci.rt.usfca.edu/institution/view.aspx?institutionID=175.
Austin, Alvyn. *China's Millions: The China Inland Mission and Late Qing Society, 1832–1905.* Grand Rapids: Eerdmans, 2007.
Balcombe, Dennis. *China's Opening Door: Incredible Stories of the Holy Spirit at Work in One of the Greatest Revivals in Christianity.* Lake Mary, FL: Charisma House, 2014.
Baller, F. W. *Letters from an Old Missionary to his Nephew.* Shanghai: American Presbyterian Mission Press, 1907.
Barber, W. T. A. *David Hill: Missionary and Saint.* London: C. H. Kelly, 1899.
Bays, Daniel H. "Christian Revival in China, 1900–1937." In *Modern Christian Revivals*, edited by Edith L. Blumhofer and Randall Balmer, 161–79. Urbana: University of Illinois Press, 1993.
———. "Christianity and the Chinese Sectarian Tradition." *Ch'ing-shih wen-t'i* 4, no. 7 (1982) 33–55.
———, ed. *Christianity in China: From the Eighteenth Century to the Present.* Stanford: Stanford University Press, 1996.
———. "The Growth of Independent Christianity in China, 1900–1937." In *Christianity in China: From the Eighteenth Century to the Present*, edited by Daniel H. Bays, 307–16. Stanford: Stanford University Press, 1996.
Beach, Harlan P. *Dawn on the Hills of T'ang, or Missions in China.* Revised ed. New York: Student Volunteer Movement for Foreign Missions, 1905.
Beauchamp, Montagu Harry Proctor. *Days of Blessing in Inland China: Being an Account of Meetings Held in the Province of Shan-si, etc.* London: Morgan & Scott, 1887.
Bebbington, David W. "Evangelicalism." In *The Blackwell Companion to Nineteenth-Century Theology*, 235–50. Malden, MA: Wiley-Blackwell, 2010.
Becker, Jasper. *Hungry Ghosts: Mao's Secret Famine.* New York: Free Press, 1996.

Bell, Prudence, and Ronald Clements. *Lives From A Black Tin Box*. Milton Keynes, UK: Authentic Media, 2014.

Benson, Lisa K. *Across China's Gobi: The Lives of Evangeline French, Mildred Cable, and Francesca French of the China Inland Mission*. Norwalk, CT: EastBridge, 2008.

Bohr, P. Richard. *Famine in China and the Missionary: Timothy Richard as Relief Administrator and Advocate of National Reform, 1876-1884*. Cambridge, MA: Harvard University Asia Center, 1972.

Brandt, Nat. *Massacre in Shansi*. New York: toExcel, 1999.

Broomhall, A. J. *Hudson Taylor & China's Open Century*. Vol. 6, *Assault on the Nine*. Sevenoaks, UK: Hodder and Stoughton with Overseas Missionary Fellowship, 1988.

———. *Hudson Taylor & China's Open Century*. Vol. 7, *It is Not Death to Die!* Sevenoaks, UK: Hodder and Stoughton with Overseas Missionary Fellowship, 1989.

Broomhall, Marshall. *The Jubilee Story of the China Inland Mission*. London: Morgan & Scott, 1915.

———, ed. *Last Letters and Further Records of Martyred Missionaries of the China Inland Mission*. London: Morgan & Scott, 1901.

———, ed. *Martyred Missionaries of the China Inland Mission, with a Record of the Perils & Sufferings of Some who Escaped*. London: Morgan & Scott, 1901.

Burgess, Alan. *The Small Woman*. London: Evans Brothers Limited, 1957.

Cabot, Mabel H. *Vanished Kingdoms: A Woman Explorer in Tibet, China & Mongolia 1921-1925*. New York: Aperture Foundation, 2003.

Chang, Irene, et al., eds. *Christ Alone: A Pictorial Presentation of Hudson Taylor's Life and Legacy*. Hong Kong: OMF Hong Kong, 2005.

Chang, Jung. *Empress Dowager Cixi: The Concubine Who Launched Modern China*. New York: Knopf, 2013.

Chao, Samuel Hsiang-En. "John Livingston Nevius (1829-1893): A Historical Study of his Life and Mission Methods." PhD diss., Fuller Theological Seminary, 1991.

China Aid. "About Shouwang." Help China. http://www.helpsw.org/p/about-shouwang.html.

———. "*Huyu shifang Li Wenxi he Ren Lacheng dixiong!* Free Li Wenxi and Ren Lacheng! " YouTube. https://www.youtube.com/watch?v=SGsX5VHjxKw.

———. "*Gei Xi Jinping zhuxi de yifeng gongkai xin* [An Open Letter to Chairman Xi Jinping]." Help Linfen. http://www.helplinfen.com/2013/06/blog-post.html.

———. "Original verdict upheld after second-instance trial in March 28 Enyu Bookstore case." China Aid Association. http://www.chinaaid.org/2013/12/original-verdict-upheld-after-second.html.

China Mission Yearbook. CLS periodical, 1910-1925.

China's Millions. OMF periodical, 1876-1952.

The Chinese Recorder and Misionary Journal. American Presbyterian Mission periodical, 1867-1941.

Clark, Anthony E. *Heaven in Conflict: Franciscans and the Boxer Uprising in Shanxi*. Seattle: University of Washington Press, 2014.

———. "Mandarins and Martyrs of Taiyuan, Shanxi, in Late Imperial China." In *A Voluntary Exile: Chinese Christianity and Cultural Confluence since 1552*, edited by Anthony E. Clark, 93-116. Lanham, MD: Rowman & Littlefield, 2013.

Cliff, Norman Howard. *Courtyard of the Happy Way*. Evesham, UK: Arthur James, 1977.

———. *A Flame of Sacred Love: The Life of Benjamin Broomhall, 1829–1911*. Carlisle, UK: OM, 1998.
———. *How the Gospel Came to South East Shanxi*. Rumford, UK: Kall Kwik, 2000.
Cohen, Paul A. *History in Three Keys: The Boxers as Event, Experience, and Myth*. New York: Columbia University Press, 1997.
Crumpacker, Frank H. *Brethren in China*. Elgin, IL: Brethren Publishing House, 1937.
Daily, Christopher. *Robert Morrison and the Protestant Plan for China*. Hong Kong: Hong Kong University Press, 2013.
Deng Zhaoming. "The Church in China." In *The Church in Asia Today: Opportunities and Challenges*, edited by Saphir Athyal, 103–26. Singapore: Asia Lausanne Committee for World Evangelization, 1996.
Dikötter, Frank. *Mao's Great Famine: The History of China's Most Devastating Catastrophe, 1958–1962*. New York: Walker, 2010.
Dong Conglin. *Long yu shangdi: Jidujiao yu zhongguo chuantong wenhua* [The Dragon and God: Christianity and Chinese Traditional Culture]. Beijing: Sanlian shudian, 1992.
Dunch, Ryan. "Protestant Christianity in China Today: Fragile, Fragmented, Flourishing." In *China and Christianity: Burdened Past, Hopeful Future*, edited by Stephen Uhalley Jr. and Xiaoxin Wu, 195–216. Armonk, NY: M. E. Sharpe, 2001.
Dunn, Emily C. "'Cult,' Church, and the CCP: Introducing Eastern Lightning." *Modern China* 35, no. 1 (2009) 96–119.
———. *Lightning from the East: Heterodoxy and Christianity in Contemporary China*. Leiden: Brill, 2015.
Edgerton-Tarpley, Kathryn. *Tears From Iron: Cultural Responses to Famine in Nineteenth-Century China*. Berkeley, CA: University of California Press, 2008.
Edwards, E. H. *Fire and Sword in Shansi: The Story of the Martyrdom of Foreigners and Chinese Christians*. London: Fleming H. Revell, 1903.
Elvin, Mark. "Who Was Responsible for the Weather? Moral Meteorology in Late Imperial China." *Osiris* 13, 2nd Series (1998) 213–37.
Esherick, Joseph W. *The Origins of the Boxer Uprising*. Berkeley, CA: University of California Press, 1987.
Evans, Edward William Price. *Timothy Richard, a Narrative of Christian Enterprise and Statesmanship in China*. London: Carey Press, 1945.
Fairbank, John King, and Merle Goldman. *China: A New History*. 2nd ed. Cambridge, MA: Belknap, 2006.
Fiedler, Katrin. "China's 'Christianity Fever' Revisited: Towards a Community-Oriented Reading of Christian Conversions in China." *Journal of Current Chinese Affairs* 39, no. 4 (2010) 71–109.
Fishburn, Janet F. *The Fatherhood of God and the Victorian Family: The Social Gospel in America*. Philadelphia: Fortress, 1981.
Forsyth, Robert C. *The China Martyrs of 1900: A Complete Roll of the Christian Heroes Martyred in China in 1900 with Narratives of the Survivors*. London: Religious Tract Society, 1904.
———. *Shantung: The Sacred Province of China in Some of its Aspects*. Shanghai: Christian Literature Society, 1912.
Fortosis, Stephen, and Mary Graham Reid. *Boxers to Bandits: The Extraordinary Story of Jimmy and Sophie Graham, Pioneer Missionaries in China, 1889–1940*. Charlotte, NC: Billy Graham Evangelistic Association, 2006.

Fulton, Brent. *China's Urban Christians: A Light That Cannot Be Hidden.* Eugene, OR: Pickwick Publications, 2015.

Gao Pengcheng, and Chi Zihua. "Li Timotai zai 'dingwu qihuang' shiqi de zhenzai huodong [On the Influence of Timothy Richard's Relief in 'Ding-wu Disaster']." *Shehuikexue*, no. 11 (2006) 132–38.

Gao Wangzhi. "Y. T. Wu: A Christian Leader Under Communism." In *Christianity in China: From the Eighteenth Century to the Present*, edited by Daniel H. Bays, 338–52. Stanford: Stanford University Press, 1996.

Gilkey, Langdon. *Shantung Compound: The Story of Men and Women Under Pressure.* New York: Harper & Row, 1966.

Gillin, Donald G. *Warlord: Yen Hsi-shan in Shansi Province 1911–1949.* Princeton, NJ: Princeton University Press, 1967.

Glover, Archibald E., and Leslie T. Lyall. *A Thousand Miles of Miracle in China.* Expanded centenary ed. Sevenoaks, UK: Christian Focus; Overseas Missionary Fellowship, 2000.

Goforth, Jonathan. *By My Spirit.* Elkhart, IN: Bethel, 1983.

Groot, J. J. M. de. *Sectarianism and Religious Persecution in China.* Taipei: Ch'eng Wen, 1970.

Grossi, Ken, and Carl Jacobson. "Oberlin in Asia: A Digital Collection Documenting the Sharing of the Ideals of Learning and Labor." Oberlin College Archives. http://oberlin.edu/library/digital/shansi/intro.html.

Guo Jinfeng. "Shanxi jindai jidujiao jiaohui yiyuan jianzhu yanjiu [Architecture of Pre-Modern Christian Hospital in Shanxi]." MA thesis, Taiyuan Technical University, 2007.

H-PRC. "Looking for Great Leap 'Smoking Gun' Document." H-NET Discussion, December 1, 2015. https://networks.h-net.org/node/3544/discussions/99266/looking-great-leap-smoking-gun-document#reply-100102

Haar, Barend J. ter. *Telling Stories: Witchcraft and Scapegoating in Chinese History.* Leiden: Brill, 2006.

Hao Ping. "Guangxu chu nian Shanxi zaihuang yu jiuji yanjiu [Research on Emergency Relief and the Famine in Shanxi During the First Year of the Guangxu Reign Period]." PhD diss., Shanxi University, 2007.

———. "Shanxi 'dingwu qihuang' bingfa zaihai shu lue [A Brief Record of the Complications Related to the Dingwu Famine in Shanxi]." *Jinyang xue kan*, no. 1 (2003) 86–89.

Hao Ping, and Zhou Ya. "'Dingwu qihuang' shiqi de Shanxi liangjia [The Food Price of Shanxi in the Great Famine in 1877 and 1878]." *Shi lin*, no. 5 (2008) 81–89.

Harlan, Rolvix. "John Alexander Dowie and the Christian Catholic Apostolic Church in Zion." PhD diss., University of Chicago, 1906.

Harrison, Henrietta. *China.* Edited by Robbins, Keith. New York: Arnold, 2001.

———. *The Man Awakened from Dreams: One Man's Life in a North China Village, 1857–1942.* Stanford: Stanford University Press, 2005.

———. *The Missionary's Curse and Other Tales from a Chinese Catholic Village.* Berkeley, CA: University of California Press, 2013.

———. "Narcotics, Nationalism and Class in China: The Transition from Opium to Morphine and Heroin in Early Twentieth-Century Shanxi." *East Asian History* 32/33 (2007) 151–76.

———. "Village Industries and the Making of Rural-Urban Difference in Early Twentieth-Century Shanxi." In *How China Works: Perspectives on the Twentieth-Century Industrial Workplace*, edited by Jacob Eyferth, 25–40: New York: Routledge, 2006.

———. "Village Politics and National Politics: The Boxer Movement in Central Shanxi." In *The Boxers, China, and the World*, edited by Bickers, Robert A. and R. G. Tiedemann, 1–15. Lanham, MD: Rowman & Littlefield, 2007.

Hattaway, Paul. "How Many Christians Are in China? Statistical Tables." *Asia Harvest* (2010). http://asiaharvest.org/how-many-christians-are-in-china-tables/.

He Guanghu, et al. "*Zunjing lishi wenhua yiji, jiujiu bainian fuyin jiaotang* [Respect cultural and historic remains, save the hundred year-old Gospel Church]." *Shi Hengtang de boke* [Shi Hengtang's Blog]. http://blog.sina.com.cn/s/blog_4a90a2340100u6w9.html.

Hill, David. "The Triennial Examinations for the Ku Jen Degree." *CR* 10, no. 6 (1879) 463–64.

Horning, Emma, Anna Seese, Grace Clapper, and F. H. Crumpacker. *Junior Folks at Mission Study—China: A Symposium Written by Missionaries in China*. Elgin, IL: Church of the Brethren General Mission Board, 1921.

Hsu Ling Tsao. *These Little Ones*. 1946.

Hsu, Promise. "Why Beijing's Largest House Church Refuses to Stop Meeting Outdoors." *Christianity Today* (April 26, 2011). http://www.christianitytoday.com/ct/2011/aprilweb-only/beijinghousechurch.html?start=2.

Hu Shixiang. *Hondong jidujiao shi* [History of the Hongdong Christian Church]. Hongdong: Hongdong xian renmin zhengfu minzu zongjiao ke, 1990.

Hunter, Alan, and Kim-Kwong Chan. *Protestantism in Contemporary China*. New York: Cambridge University Press, 1993.

Hunter, Jane. *The Gospel of Gentility: American Women Missionaries in Turn-of-the-Century China*. New Haven: Yale University Press, 1984.

Hyatt, Irwin T. "Protestant Missions in China, 1877–1890: The Institutionalization of Good Works." In *American Missionaries in China: Papers from Harvard Seminars*, edited by Kwang-Ching Liu, vol. 21, 93–126. Cambridge, MA: Harvard East Asian Research Center, 1966.

Janku, Andrea. "The North-China Famine of 1876–1879: Performance and Impact of a Non-Event." In *Measuring Historical Heat: Event, Performance, and Impact in China and the West*, 127–34. Heidelberg: n.a., 2001.

Jacobson, Carl. "H. H. Kung: Strengthening China through Education and the 'Oberlin Spirit.'" Oberlin College Archives. http://www.oberlin.edu/library/digital/shansi/bios.html.

Jen Yu Wen, and Adrienne Suddard. *The Taiping Revolutionary Movement*. New Haven: Yale University Press, 1973.

Johnson, David G. *Spectacle and Sacrifice: The Ritual Foundations of Village Life in North China*. Cambridge, MA: Harvard University Asia Center, 2009.

Johnson, Eunice V. *Timothy Richard's Vision: Education and Reform in China: 1880–1910*. Eugene, OR: Pickwick Publications, 2014.

Kaiser, Andrew T. "Encountering China: The Evolution of Timothy Richard's Missionary Thought (1870–1891)." PhD thesis, University of Edinburgh, 2014.

———. "S. Wells Williams: Early Protestant Missions in China." MA thesis, Gordon-Conwell Theological Seminary, 1995.

Kane, Herbert J. "J. Hudson Taylor, 1832–1905, Founder of the China Inland Mission." In *Mission Legacies: Biographical Studies of Leaders of the Modern Missionary Movement*, edited by Gerald H. Anderson, 197–204. Maryknoll, NY: Orbis, 1994.

Kiefer, James E. "Gladys Aylward, Missionary to China." *Biographical Sketches of Memorable Christians of the Past*. http://justus.anglican.org/resources/bio/73.html.

Kilcourse, Carl S. "Son of God, Brother of Jesus: Interpreting the Theological Claims of the Chinese Revolutionary Hong Xiuquan." *Studies in World Christianity* 20, no. 2 (2014) 124–44.

Lambert, Tony. *China's Christian Millions*. Oxford: Monarch, 2006.

Landor, Henry Savage. *China and the Allies*. 2 vols. New York: Charles Scribner's Sons, 1901.

Latourette, Kenneth Scott. *A History of Christian Missions in China*. New York: Macmillan, 1929.

The Lausanne Movement. "Nine Hundred from Mainland China Participate in Inaugural Mission China 2030 Conference." *Lausanne Movement* (October 26, 2015). https://www.lausanne.org/news-releases/inaugural-mission-china-2030-conference.

Lee, Joseph Tse-Hei, and Christie Chui-Shan Chow. "Christian Revival from within: Seventh-day Adventism in China." In *Christianity in Contemporary China: Socio-cultural Perspectives*, edited by Francis Khek Gee Lim, 45–58. New York: Routledge, 2013.

Lewis, W. J., W. T. A. Barber, and J. R. Hykes, eds. *Records of the General Conference of the Protestant Missionaries of China: Held at Shanghai, May 7–20, 1890*. Shanghai: American Presbyterian Mission Press, 1890.

Li Aisi. "Competition and Compromise between British Missionaries and Chinese Officials: The Founding of Shanxi University in 1902." DPhil thesis, University of Oxford, 2012.

———. "Towards Building Direct Educational Partnership: The Foundation of Shanxi University in 1902." *Frontiers of Education in China* 9, no. 2 (2014) 188–210.

Li, Amy. "'Don't you dare bring Christianity to Shanxi,' says official before detaining Beijing believer." *South China Morning Post* (April 4, 2013). http://www.scmp.com/news/china/article/1206848/dont-you-dare-bring-christianity-shanxi-says-official-who-jails-beijing?page=all.

Li Suju, and Liu Qifei. *Qingnian yu "zongjiao re"* [Youth and "Religion Fever"]. Beijing: Zhongguo qingnian chubanshe, 2000.

Li Weihui. "'Shanxi daxue tang sheli xixue zhuan zhai shimo ji' zhushi [Annotations for the 'Record of the Establishment of the Western Studies Department of Shanxi University']." *Taiyuan shizhuan xuebao*, no. 3 (1998) 75–78.

Li Wenhai. *Zhongguo jindai shi da zaihuang* [The Ten Great Disasters of Modern China]. Shanghai: Shanghai renmin chubanshe, 1994.

Lian Xi. *The Conversion of Missionaries: Liberalism in American Protestant Missions in China, 1907–1932*. University Park, PA: Pennsylvania State University, 1997.

———. "A Messianic Deliverance for Post-Dynastic China: The Launch of the True Jesus Church in the Early Twentieth Century." *Modern China* 34, no. 4 (2008) 407–41.

———. *Redeemed by Fire: Popular Chinese Christianity in the Twentieth Century*. New Haven: Yale University Press, 2010.

Liao Yiwu. *God Is Red: The Secret Story of How Christianity Survived and Flourished in Communist China*. New York: HarperCollins, 2011.
Litzinger, Charles A. "Temple Community and Village Cultural Integration in North China." PhD diss., University of California, Davis, 1983.
Liu Dapeng. *Tuixiangzhai riji* [Diary from the chamber to which one retires to ponder]. Taiyuan: Shanxi renmin chubanshe, 1990.
Longenecker, Carol. "Progressivism and the Mission Field: Church of the Brethren Women Missionaries in Shanxi, China, 1908–1951." MA thesis, Clemson University, 2007.
Lu Yao. "Yihetuan yundong fazhan jieduan zhong de minjian mimi jiaomen [Non-Governmental Secret Religious Societies in the Course of the Evolution of the Yihetuan Movement]." *Lishi yanjiu*, no. 5 (2002) 53–65.
Lutz, Jessie G. *Chinese Politics and Christian Missions: The Anti-Christian Movements of 1920–28*. Notre Dame: Cross Cultural Publications, 1988.
MacGillivray, Donald. *A Century of Protestant Missions in China (1807–1907), Being the Centenary Conference Historical Volume*. Shanghai: American Presbyterian Mission Press, 1907.
MacInnis, Donald E. *Religion in China Today: Policy and Practice*. Maryknoll, NY: Orbis Books, 1989.
Madsen, Richard. *China's Catholics: Tragedy and Hope in an Emerging Civil Society*. Berkeley, CA: University of California Press, 1998.
Malcolm, Kari Torjesen. *We Signed Away Our Lives: How One Family Gave Everything for the Gospel*. Tenth Anniversary ed. Pasadena, CA: William Carey Library, 2004.
McCasland, David. *Eric Liddell: Pure Gold*. Grand Rapids: Discovery House, 2001.
McIntosh, Gilbert, ed. *China Centenary Missionary Conference Records: Report of the Great Conference Held at Shanghai, April 5th [25th] to May 8th, 1907*. New York: American Tract Society, 1907.
Merwin, Wallace C., and Francis P. Jones, eds. *Documents of the Three-Self Movement*. New York: National Council of the Churches of Christ in the USA, 1963.
Michie, Alexander. *Missionaries in China*. London: E. Stanford, 1891.
Middlebrook, J. B. *Memoir of H. R. Williamson: In Journeyings Oft*. London: Baptist Missionary Society, 1969.
Minamiki, George. *The Chinese Rites Controversy: From its Beginning to Modern Times*. Chicago: Loyola University Press, 1985.
Miner, Luella. *China's Book of Martyrs: A Record of Heroic Martyrdoms and Marvelous Deliverances of Chinese Christians during the Summer of 1900*. New York: Pilgrim, 1903.
The Missionary Herald. BMS periodical, 1819–2000.
Morrison, Robert, and Eliza A. Morrison. *Memoirs of the Life and Labours of Robert Morrison*. London: Longman, Orme, Brown, and Longmans, 1839.
Nathan, May R. "From Miss May Nathan's Last Letter." In *Last Letters & Further Records of Martyred Missionaries of the China Inland Mission*, edited by Marshall Broomhall, 38–46. London: Morgan & Scott, 1901
Nevius, Helen Sanford. *The Life of John Livingston Nevius, for Forty Years a Missionary in China*. New York: Fleming H. Revell, 1895.
Nevius, John Livingston. *Methods of Mission Work*. Shanghai: American Presbyterian Mission Press, 1886.

Newman, R. K. "Opium Smoking in Late Imperial China: A Reconsideration." *Modern Asian Studies* 29, no. 4 (1995) 765–94.

Ng, Peter Tze Ming. "Cheng Jingyi: Prophet of His Time." *International Bulletin of Missionary Research* 36, no. 1 (2012) 14–16.

Nichols, Francis H. *Through Hidden Shensi*. New York: Charles Scribner's and Sons, 1902.

Nyström, Erik. *Det nya Kina* [The New China]. P. A. Norstedt, 1913.

Ogren, Olivia C. "A Great Conflict of Sufferings." In *Last Letters & Further Records of Martyred Missionaries of the China Inland Mission*, edited by Marshall Broomhall, 65–83. London: Morgan & Scott, 1901.

———. *The Last Refugees from Shansi in the Hands of the Chinese Boxers (An Eyewitness Account)*. Victoria, BC: Trafford, 2004.

Patterson, James Alan. "The Loss of a Protestant Missionary Consensus: Foreign Missions and the Fundamentalist-Modernist Conflict." In *Earthen Vessels: American Evangelicals and Foreign Missions, 1880–1980*, edited by Joel A. Carpenter and Wilbert R. Shenk, 73–91. Grand Rapids: Eerdmans, 1990.

Payne, Ernest A. *Harry Wyatt of Shansi, 1895–1938*. London: Carey Press, 1939.

Pearson, Mary. "Loyalty." In *Through Toil and Tribulation*, 111–20. London: Carey Press, 1947.

Pew Forum on Religion and Public Life. "Appendix C: Methodology for China." In *Global Christianity: A Report on the Size and Distribution of the World's Christian Population*, 97–110. Washington, DC: Pew Research Center, 2011.

Pfister, Lauren F. "Rethinking Mission in China: James Hudson Taylor and Timothy Richard." In *The Imperial Horizons of British Protestant Missions, 1880–1914*, edited by A. N. Porter, 183–212. Grand Rapids: Eerdmans, 2003.

Pollock, John C. *The Cambridge Seven*. London: Inter-Varsity Fellowship, 1955.

Preston, Diana. *The Boxer Rebellion: The Dramatic Story of China's War on Foreigners That Shook the World in the Summer of 1900*. New York: Walker, 1999.

Price, Eva Jane. *China Journal 1889–1900: An American Missionary Family During the Boxer Rebellion*. New York: Scribner, 1989.

Price, F. W. "From Taiyuan to Shanghai." In *Through Toil and Tribulation*, 45–50. London: Carey Press, 1947.

Purves, Carol. *Chinese Whispers: The Gladys Aylward Story*. Leominster, UK: Day One Publications, 2004.

Qiao Zhiqiang, ed. *Yihetuan zai Shanxi diqu shiliao* [Local Historical Materials on the Boxers in Shanxi]. Taiyuan: Shanxi renmin chubanshe, 1980.

Ren, Fuxing. "'Xinzhou Yesu jiao jinlihui shengtu xunnan bei ji' yu Shanxi Xinzhou jiao'an [The 'Xinzhou Christian Baptist Saints Martyrdom Tablet Inscription' and the Religious Cases of Xinzhou, Shanxi]." *Xinzhou wen shi*, no. 3 (2003?) 103–16.

Richard, Mary Martin. *Jiaoshi liezhuan* [Christian Biographies]. 10 vols. Shanghai: SDCK, 1898.

———. *Paper on Chinese Music*. Shanghai: American Presbyterian Mission Press, 1899.

Richard, Timothy. "China." *MH* 72, no. 12 (1876) 246.

———. *Fifteen Years' Missionary Work in China: An Address by Rev. Timothy Richard*. London: Baptist Missionary Society, 1885.

———. *Forty-Five Years in China: Reminiscences*. London: T. Fisher Unwin, 1916.

Ro, David. "The Rising Missions Movement in China (the World's New Number 1 Economy) and How to Support It." *Lausanne Global Analysis* 4, no. 3 (May 2015).

Rossiter, E. Annie. "From the Beginning in Shansi." In *Through Toil and Tribulation*, 41–44. London: Carey Press, 1947.

Schofield, A. T. *Memorials of R. Harold A. Schofield: First Medical Missionary to Shan-Si, China*. London: Hodder and Stoughton, 1885.

Schofield, R. H. "Medical Mission, Tai-yuen fu, 1882." *CM* 135–36.

Seagrave, Sterling. *The Soong Dynasty*. New York: Harper & Row, 1985.

Semple, Rhonda Anne. *Missionary Women: Gender, Professionalism, and the Victorian Idea of Christian Mission*. Rochester, NY: Boydell, 2003.

Spence, Jonathan D. *The Search for Modern China*. New York: W. W. Norton, 1990.

Spurgeon, Charles H. "The Wordless Book." January 11, 1866. The Spurgeon Archive. http://www.spurgeon.org/sermons/3278.php.

Stanley, Brian. *The History of the Baptist Missionary Society, 1792–1992*. Edinburgh: T. and T. Clark, 1992.

Stark, Joel. "Reexamining Chinese Student Nationalism: The Anti-Christian Protest of 1925 at Mingyi School." Comprehensive Excersise Thesis Paper, Carleton College, 2003.

Stauffer, Milton T., ed. *The Christian Occupation of China*. Shanghai: China Continuation Committee, 1922.

Steer, Roger. *J. Hudson Taylor: A Man in Christ*. Singapore: OMF Books, 1991.

Swift, Catherine. *Gladys Aylward*. Minneapolis: Bethany House Publishers, 1984.

Taylor, Howard. *One of China's Scholars: The Culture and Conversion of a Confucianist*. Fifth ed. London: Morgan & Scott, 1905.

Thompson, Roger R. "'If Shanxi's Coal is Lost, Then Shanxi is Lost!': Shanxi's Coal and an Emerging National Movement in Provincial China, 1898–1908." *Modern Asian Studies* 45, no. 5 (2011) 1261–88.

———. "Reporting the Taiyuan Massacre: Culture and Politics in the China War of 1900." In *The Boxers, China, and the World*, edited by Robert A. Bickers and R. G. Tiedemann, 65–92. Lanham, MD: Rowman & Littlefield, 2007.

———. "Twilight of the Gods in the Chinese Countryside: Christians, Confucians, and the Modernizing State, 1861–1911." In *Christianity in China: From the Eighteenth Century to the Present*, edited by Daniel H. Bays, 53–72. Stanford: Stanford University Press, 1996.

Tiedemann, R. G. "Christianity and Chinese 'Heterodox Sects': Mass Conversion and Syncretism in Shandong Province in the Early Eighteenth Century." *Monumenta Serica* 44 (1996) 339–82.

———. "Church of the Brethren Mission." Ricci Roundtable Database. http://ricci.rt.usfca.edu/institution/view.aspx?institutionID=242.

———, ed. *Handbook of Christianity in China. Volume 2, 1800–present*. Leiden: Brill, 2010.

———. "Not Every Martyr Is a Saint! The Juye Missionary Case of 1897 Reconsidered." In *A Lifelong Dedication to the China Mission*, edited by Noël Golvers and Sara Lievens, 589–617. Leuven: Ferdinand Verbiest Institute K.U. Leuven, 2007.

———. *Reference Guide to Christian Missionary Societies in China: From the Sixteenth to the Twentieth Century*. Armonk, NY: M. E. Sharpe, 2009.

Tucker, Nancy Bernkopf. "An Unlikely Peace: American Missionaries and the Chinese Communists, 1948–1950." *Pacific Historical Review* 45, no. 1 (1976) 97–116.

The Voice of the Martyrs. "Prisoner Alert: Lacheng Ren." Accessed January 20, 2016. http://www.prisoneralert.com/pprofiles/vp_prisoner_228_profile.html.

Walder, Andrew G., and Yang Su. "The Cultural Revolution in the Countryside: Scope, Timing and Human Impact." *The China Quarterly*, no. 173 (2003) 74–99.

Walls, Andrew F. "The Multiple Conversions of Timothy Richard: A Paradigm of Missionary Experience." In *The Cross-Cultural Process in Christian History: Studies in the Transmission and Appropriation of Faith*, 236–58. Maryknoll, NY: Orbis Books, 2002.

Wang, Xiaojing. "The Church Unity Movement in Early Twentieth-Century China: Cheng Jingyi and the Church of Christ in China." PhD diss., University of Edinburgh, 2012.

Wei Yisa, ed. *Zhen Yesu jiaohui chuangli sanshi zhounian jinian zhuankan* [Special Volume Commemorating the Thirtieth Anniversary of the Founding of the True Jesus Church]. Nanjing: Zhen Yesu jiaohui, 1948.

Whitefield, Douglas Brent. "The Christian Literature Society for China: the Role of its Publications, Personalities and Theology in Late-Qing Reform Movements." PhD thesis, Cambridge University 2001.

———. "The Tian Zu Hui (Natural Foot Society): Christian Women in China and the Fight against Footbinding." *Asian Studies* (2008) 203–12.

Wickeri, Philip L. *Seeking the Common Ground: Protestant Christianity, the Three-Self Movement, and China's United Front*. Eugene, OR: Wipf and Stock Publishers, 2011.

Wigram, Christopher E. M. *The Bible and Mission in Faith Perspective: J. Hudson Taylor and the Early China Inland Mission*. Zoetermeer: Boekencentrum, 2007.

Williamson, Alexander. *Journeys in North China, Manchuria, and Eastern Mongolia; With Some Account of Corea*. 2 vols. London: Smith, Elder, 1870.

Williamson, H. R. *British Baptists in China, 1845–1952*. London: Carey Kingsgate, 1957.

———. "Our Church in Post-War China." In *Through Toil and Tribulation*, 197–208. London: Carey Press, 1947.

Williamson, Isabelle. *Old Highways in China*. London: Religious Tract Society, 1884.

Wood, E. M. "A Mandarin Primer." *CM* (March 1895) 36.

Xing Long. *Shanda wangshi* [Shanxi University's Past]. Taiyuan: Shanxi renmin chubanshe, 2002.

———. "Wusi qianhou [Before and After May Fourth]." *Maotouying* 12 (2004).

Xu Shihu. *Li Timotai zhuanlue* [A Brief Biography of Timothy Richard]. Taiyuan, Shanxi: A Publication of the Shanxi University Ninetieth Anniversary School Historical Archives, 1992.

Yang Jisheng. *Tombstone: The Great Chinese Famine, 1958–1962*. New York: Farrar, Straus and Giroux, 2012.

Yu, Danny. "Into the Future: Ding's Theology and China's Church," *ChinaSource Quarterly* 3, no. 1 (March 2001). http://www.chinasource.org/resource-library/articles/into-the-future.

Yu Ke, ed. *Dangdai jidujiao* [Contemporary Christianity]. Beijing: Dongfang chubanshe, 1993.

Yuan Yingying. "'Dingwu qihuang' zhong chuanjiaoshi zai Shandong de zhenzai huodong kaocha [An Investigation of Missionary Disaster Relief Activities During the 'Dingwu Famine']." *Liaocheng daxue xuebao (Shehuikexue ban)*, no. 6 (2007) 98–102.

Zhang Lingzao. "Shen de weida zuowei—zai Taiyuan gu'eryuan (1924–1945) [God's Great Accomplishments—at the Taiyuan Orphanage (1924–25)]." http://www.tyjdj.org/_d276673639.htm.

Zhang Wenjian. *Tianguo zhi dao: Jidujiao* [The Way of the Heavenly Kingdom: The Christian Church]. Beijing: Shijie zhishi chubanshe, 1998.

Zheng Yangwen. "The Social Life of Opium in China, 1483–1999." *Modern Asian Studies* 37, no. 1 (2003) 1–39.

Index

1910 World Missionary Conference, 140

Adolph, Paul E., 208–12
Allen, Roland, 141
American Board of Commissioners for Foreign Missions (ABCFM), 7n4, 26n102, 28, 40, 41, 43–44, 47, 52–56, 58–60, 75, 79–80, 84, 88n89, 89n93, 93n106, 96–97, 101, 107, 110–11, 124, 136, 145, 165, 186, 227
American Presbyterian Mission, 6, 15, 21n84, 118, 129n38, 165
Anderson, D. Gordon, 210
Anqing, 48n177, 49–50, 143, 208
Anti-Christian Students Federation, 156
Anze, 72
Apostolic Faith Missionaries, 165
Atwater, Ernest and Lizzie (Graham), 55, 59, 61, 93n106, 96
Atwood, Iranaeus, 106–7
Aylward, Gladys, xii, 46, 203–8

Backhouse, Edmund, 89n90
Baibancun, 20
Balcombe, Dennis, 236
Baller, Frederick W., 18, 49–51
Baoding, 48, 52, 65, 80, 106–7
Baotou, 250

Baptist Missionary Society (BMS), 5–6, 22–24, 27–30, 37, 41, 44, 45n166, 53n193, 56, 57n208, 58, 81, 91–92, 94n111, 95, 100–101, 103, 107, 111, 113, 117, 122–23, 125–26, 128, 131, 134, 136–37, 144–46, 159, 166, 178, 181–83, 187, 188n15, 211–20, 224, 226, 245
Beauchamp, Montagu, 44
Beidaihe, 213, 216
Beijing University, 154
Beijing, 3–4, 5n16, 44, 48, 52n190, 65–67, 74, 77–78, 81, 89n90, 100, 103–4, 107, 112, 116, 121, 128, 132, 134, 138, 140, 142–43, 144n89, 147–48, 150, 154, 156, 163, 179, 187n12, 189, 204, 208–10, 213, 216, 218–19, 221n108, 235, 237–38, 243, 250–53
Bell, Prudence, 108n160
Beney, Marcel, 182, 218n103
Bethany Biblical Seminary, 148
Beynon, W. F., 92
Bible House of Los Angeles (BIOLA), 125n24
Big Sword Society, 61–63, 73
Bird, Rowena, 75, 83, 96n118
Bloom, C. V., 183, 185, 218n103
British and Foreign Bible Society, 28, 56, 91n97, 92
Brook, S. P., 65

281

Index

Brooks, Rachel, 171–72
Broomhall, Amelia, 18
Broomhall, Benjamin, 27
Broomhall, Hudson, 27, 57n207
Buck, Pearl S., 173, 201

Cable, Mildred, 121n11
Cai Yuanpei, 154
Cambridge Seven, xii, 27, 30, 44–45, 49, 57
Cameron, James, 18n72
Campus Crusade, 247
Cassels, William, 44, 49
Cen Chunxuan, 110n166, 111–14
Changzhi, 30, 41n143, 98
Chao, T. C., 169
Chefoo, 5, 27, 35, 198, 201
Chen Duxiu, 180
Cheng Jingyi, 140, 158
Cheng Xiuqi, 58
Chengdu, 207
Chiang Kai-shek, viii, 124n21, 160n133, 179, 181, 217
China Centenary Missionary Conference, 139–40
China Christian Council (CCC), 136n65, 235, 244, 253
China Inland Mission (CIM), 5, 8, 9, 14n56, 18–19, 21n86, 22–28, 30–31, 32n124, 33–37, 43–46, 48–51, 53, 55–59, 70, 79, 83, 88–92, 98–99, 100, 101n132, 102n140, 106, 110–11, 113n178, 121n7, 125, 126n28, 136–37, 142, 145, 149, 163, 166–67, 181, 191, 194, 198, 203, 208–9, 211
Chinese Communist Party, 95, 150, 159–61, 179–82, 186n12, 187, 197, 201, 206–7, 210–11, 222, 225–30, 234
Chinese Nationalist Party, 124, 127n32, 130n39, 159, 160–61, 179–82, 200, 206, 222–23
Christian and Missionary Alliance, 90
Christian Literature Society for China (CLS), 21n84, 30, 140
Church of Christ in China, 140, 158, 161
Cixi, Empress Dowager, 64n9, 66–67, 73, 88, 96n118, 104, 107n158, 110, 116

Clapp, D. Howard and Jenny, 58, 96n117–18
Clarke, George, 18n72
Clow, Ellen, 182–83, 185, 218n103
Coombs, Edith, 55n199, 90–92, 93n107, 95n113, 107n159
Cooper, E. J. and Margaret, 97–99
Cultural Revolution, 144n90, 145n91, 228n11, 232–36, 244

Daizhou, 108, 123
Daning, 44, 57, 70
Dart, R. H. P., 145, 215
Datong, 57, 88, 198
Davis, David and Jean, 205n56
Davis, Francis, 96n118
Dawson, S. R., 218n103
Dayingpan, 235
Deng Xiaoping, 234
Dewey, John, 154, 158
Dingxiang, 56
Dixon, Herbert and Elizabeth, 29, 95n114, 108nn160–61, 117
Dongjia Xiang, 91n96, 107n159, 144–45
Dongjihuying, 141
Dowie Sect, 30
Dreyer, F. C., 92, 125, 137
Duan Qinwang, Prince, 65
Duncan, Moir, 107, 115
Duval, Mary, 55n199, 93n106

Eager, Edie, 242
Eastern Lightning, 249
Educational Services Exchange with China (ESEC), 236–37, 247n45, 248
Edwards, Eben Henry, 37, 53–55, 58, 81, 92n100, 93n106, 94, 95n115, 100, 106–7, 109–11, 113, 121–22, 123n18, 128, 130, 134, 145
Edwards, George, 122, 131–32, 144
Edwards, Marjory, 122
Eight-Nation Army, 65, 103
Eldred, Annie, 89
England, 2, 18–19, 29, 32–37, 44, 48, 55, 121, 127, 129–30, 133, 136, 145, 149, 155, 165–67, 178, 182–83, 191,

Index   283

203, 207, 212, 214n95, 217, 219–20, 231
Ennals, Sidney, 95n114
Enyu bookstore, 252
Evergreen Family Friendship Service, 145n93, 239–40, 246, 248
Ewing, Archibald Orr, 106

Famine Relief Committee, Shanghai, 15n60, 16n62, 16n65
Farthing Memorial School. *See* Taiyuan Boys' School
Farthing, George, 41, 81, 113
Federal Council of the Chinese Christian Churches of North China, 138–39
Fenchow Christian Hospital, 186
Fenyang, 41, 89n93, 93n106, 145, 149, 228
Fenzhou, 7n24, 41, 44, 53n192, 55, 60, 79, 84, 88n89, 89n91, 96–97, 186, 191
Flory, B. M., 170n165
Ford, K., 131
Forth, M. L., 46
Foster, Arnold, 8
Franson, Frederick, 27
French, Evangeline, 89, 121
Fuxi Jie, 92n102, 238, 240n38

Gao Daling, xii, 20, 21, 58, 115, 141–42
Garnier, A. J., 123, 133n50
Gauntlett, E., 89
General Council of the Assemblies of God (AG), 135, 151, 165, 166n148, 166n149, 232
General Mission Board of the Church of the Brethren (CBM), 146, 147–48, 165n147, 166, 170n165, 184, 190, 220, 222, 228
Glasby, Beulah, 136, 218–19
Glover, Archibald, 41n143, 48–49, 208
Goforth, Jonathan, 119–20
Graham, Jean, 194
Graham, Jimmy and Sophie, 118–19
Great Leap Forward, 231–32
Guan Di, 71–72, 74
Guangdong, 2, 139n72
Guangxu Emperor, 67, 104, 116

Guguan Pass, 106
Guizhou, 49
Guo County, 108, 181, 218
Guo Yuhuai, 239

Hankou, 5, 8, 97, 102, 163, 196, 198, 218
Hanzhong, 49
Harlow, J. C., 146n95
Hayward, V. E. W., 218n103
Heart-Washing Society, 133n49
Hebei, 27, 45, 62–63, 66n13, 100, 101n131, 106, 151, 211n88
Henan, 36, 88, 97, 119
Henke, H. E., 211
Henle, Richard, 62
Hequ, 191–202, 239
Hiel Hamilton Memorial Hospital, 146
Higgs, Edith, 89
Hill, David, 8n29, 10, 14–15, 16n63, 18, 20, 34–35
Hodgkin, H. T., 173
Hong Kong, 196, 198, 208, 246, 255n61
Hongdong, 4, 27, 45, 57–58, 79, 88, 125, 142
Horne, Celia, 18
Hoste, Dixon, 27, 44–45, 49, 58, 79, 106, 109, 163
Hoste, Gertrude (Broomhall), 27, 57n207
Houma, 121, 228
Hsi, Pastor. *See* Xi Shengmo
Hsu Ling Tsao, 144, 188–90
Hu Shi, 154
Hubei, 97, 139n72
Hunan, 58, 155, 197
Huolu, 27
Huozhou, 57–58, 121n11
Huston, Mary, 98–99

Independent Mission. *See* Shouyang Mission
Inner Mongolia, 58n215, 192, 199, 229n16, 234

Jakobsen, Anna, 58
James, Francis H., 5, 8, 9, 18, 53n193, 57n208

Japan, xii, 62, 66, 103, 133, 150, 152, 154–55, 179–88, 196–202, 204, 206–7, 209–12, 218–22, 248
Jaques, V. G., 122, 217
Jasper, Vincent, 218–19
Jesus Family, 228
Jiangzhou, 10
Jiaocheng, 145
Jiaozhou, 62
Jiexiu, 89
Jin Dengtai, 251–52
Jin Tianming, 253
Jincheng. *See* Zezhou
Jinci, 7, 19, 38, 81, 104, 112, 151
Jinzhong Bible School, 243
Jinzhong. *See* Yuci
John Sung, 158
Judd, Walter Henry, 186
Juye Incident, 62–63

K'ung, H. H., viii, 124
Kemp, Emily, 134n52
Kingsbury, Emily, 18n72

Lan County, 192
Lancaster, Agnes, 18n72
Landale, Robert, 18n72, 44n159
Lane, Katherine, 122
Lanterns (Green, Red, and White), 70–71
Lawson, Jeannie, 203–5
Lees, Jonathan, 5
Lewis, John, 122, 131
Li Cai, 186n12
Li Dazhao, 180
Li Hongzhang, 12, 17, 106–7
Li Wenxi, 252
Li Yuehan, 142
Liaozhou, 146
Liddell, Eric, 202, 213, 222
Linfen, 10, 13–14, 16, 18, 89n93, 110, 197, 208, 251–52
Lingqiu, 16n65
Little Flock, 228–29
Liu Dapeng, 38, 81, 104, 105n153, 152
Liu Xiang, 71
Liyuantun, 62

London Missionary Society (LMS), xvii, 4–6, 8, 110
London, 8, 18, 30, 32, 98, 131n41, 203–4, 212
Lovitt, Arnold E., 55n199, 91
Lu'an Hospital, 181, 204, 209
Lu'an, 30, 44, 48–49, 57, 88, 98n121, 166, 204, 209–11
Luce, Henry, 201
Lucheng, 41n143, 56n204, 57, 98–99, 166n149
Lundgren, Anton and Elsa, 89

Maier, Paula, 122
Mann, Grace, 216n100
Mao Zedong, 155, 181, 231–32, 234
Martyr Memorial Cemetery, 107n159, 109, 135, 216, 219, 224
Martyr Memorial Church, 145, 188
Mateer, Calvin, 21n84
May Fourth Movement, 154–55
May, Matilda, 95n112, 102
McCurrach, Adam and Clara, 95n114
McKee, Stewart and Kate, 88n89
McKie, Graham, 102
Michie, Alexander, 38–39, 54–55
Miles, Alice, 57n207
Ming Hsien School, 124–25
Mongolia, 1–2, 99, 100, 166n151, 202
Mongolia, Inner, 58, 192, 199, 229n16, 234
Moody Bible Institute, 191
Moody, Dwight L., 32–33, 44
Morrison, Robert, 3n6, 4, 57
Müller, George, 51
Murray, Marianne, 50

Nagnone, Alfonso, 3
Nanetti, Barnaba, 112
Nanjing, 4, 126, 143, 159–60, 186
Nanking Incident, 159–61
Nathan, May, 70
National Association of Chinese Independent Churches, 138–39
National Bible Society of Scotland, 5, 46
National Christian Conference, 137n66, 156, 173

Index 285

National Christian Council of China, 140, 156
Neve, Helen, 210
Nevius, John Livingstone, 6, 141
New Culture Movement, 169
New Jesus Church, 141–42
Nian Rebellion, 61
Nichols, Francis, 86, 104n148, 109n164
Nies, Francis Xavier, 62
Ningwu, 107n158, 199
North China Famine, 6n22, 8–17, 20, 24, 49, 109n162, 153, 231, 242
Northern Baptist Theological Seminary, 191
Norway, 151, 190–92, 194–96, 200, 202
Norwegian Evangelical Free Church Bible School, 191
Norwegian Mission in China, 166

Oberlin Band, 28, 43, 44n159
Oberlin College, 43, 124, 125, 235n27, 236
Oberlin Shansi Memorial Association (OSMA), 124, 125n22, 136, 236
Ogren, Olivia, 70, 81, 102
Olson, Richard, 208n71

Partridge, Mary, 96n118
Peking Language School, 147n101, 213
Peking Union Medical College, 213
Pianguan, 198
Pigott, T. W., 18n72, 27, 53, 54, 55, 81, 93n106, 130–31
Pingding Brethren Hospital, 146
Pingding, 146
Pingyang, 4, 13–15, 21, 28, 37, 44, 49, 57, 63, 101
Pingyao, 51n187, 57, 83, 89, 106n156, 121
Pitkin, Horace, 80
Plum Flower Boxers, 62
Plymouth Brethren, 43, 228
Polhill-Turner, Arthur, 45, 49
Polhill-Turner, Cecil, 45, 49
Presbyterian Church USA, 160
Price, Charles, 29n114, 41, 52n188, 79, 84, 88n89, 93

Price, Eva Jane, 7n24, 53n192, 54, 109n162
Price, Frank M., 28–29
Price, Frank W., 183, 185, 187, 188n15, 218n103, 220–21
Public Security Bureau (PSB), 237–38, 245

Qi County, 152
Qi Hong'en, 235
Qiao Yisheng, 141
Qiaodong Jie, 238
Qiaotou Jie, 21n85, 91n96, 91n97, 113n177, 122, 123, 185
Qiaotuo Jie church, 17, 95n113, 113n177, 123, 141, 187, 229, 232, 234–35, 238–39, 241–42, 244–46, 248–50, 252n51, 254
Qinghua University, 156, 235
Qinglong Guzhen, 104n147
Quwo, 57, 82n68

Red Cross Dental Hospital, 91n96, 107n159, 145n93
Ren Lacheng, 252
Renaut, Bessie, 95n114
Ricci, Matteo, 3, 100n128
Rice, Hattie, 98–99
Richard, Mary (Martin), 18–19, 44
Richard, Timothy, xii, 3n8, 5–21, 22–30, 35, 40, 44, 53n195, 56n202, 57n208, 58, 79n54, 106, 111, 113–15, 122n12, 123–24, 131, 241–42, 251
Ritter, Richard, H., 174–76
Robinson, John, 55n199, 93n106
Rossiter, E. Annie, 122, 144n88–89, 187n14, 220
Russell, Bertrand, 158
Russia, 1–2, 70, 103, 121, 222–23

Salvation Army, 30, 151n108, 166, 182, 184, 218n103, 229
Sanercun, 216n98
Sankey, Ira, 33, 44
Saunders, Alexander R., 51n187, 53, 83, 85, 98n121
Scandinavian Alliance Mongolian Mission, 100

Schofield Memorial Hospital, 37, 41, 45, 56, 90, 113n174, 122
Schofield, R. Harold, 18n72, 25, 35–40, 44–45, 78
Schroeder, Oscar and Esther, 150–52
Searell, Edith, 89–90
Senluo Temple, 63–64
Seventh-day Adventists, 229, 238–39, 242, 244–45
Shaanxi, viii, xi, 1n1, 27n111, 44, 97, 104n148, 126n29, 132, 182, 216, 218
Shandong, 5–6, 12–14, 17, 21n84, 25, 44, 46, 49, 52, 61–65, 72, 73, 87–88, 89, 122n12, 131, 143, 214, 221n110, 228
Shanghai, 6, 44, 48, 98, 106, 115, 130, 139, 143, 158, 161, 173, 180, 220, 228
Shangma Jie, 144
Shanxi Agricultural University, 125n22, 234, 236
Shanxi Bible Institute, 125
Shanxi Tumor Hospital, 240
Shanxi University, 113n178, 114–15, 123, 127–28, 154, 236, 247
Shekleton, M. E., 113
Shentie, 71n32, 112
Shijiazhuang, 151
Shouwang Church, 253
Shouyang Mission (SYM), 37, 55–56, 88, 90, 91, 95, 100, 107, 107n159, 110–11, 113, 122
Shouyang Women's Hospital, 146
Shouyang, 27, 55–56, 81, 93, 101, 113, 122, 130–31, 146, 148, 150–51, 162, 170n165, 217
Shunde, 129, 210–11
Shuoping, 90
Sichuan, 45, 207
Smith, Creasy, 107
Smith, Harlan and Frances, 147–50, 162–63
Smith, Stanley Percival, 30–31, 41n143, 44–45, 48, 49, 53, 120–21, 166n149, 204
Social Gospel, 140n77, 168–69, 174

Society for the Diffusion of Christian and General Knowledge Among the Chinese (SDCK), 29–30
Society for the Propagation of the Gospel (SPG), 15, 65
Society of the Divine Word, 62
Sollenberger, Howard, 190
Sowerby, Arthur, 29, 40, 113, 125, 128
Spirit Boxers, 61–63, 72
Spurgeon, Charles, 32
State Administration for Religious Affairs (SARA), 237–39, 241, 243, 245, 250
Stenz, Georg, 62
Stimson, Martin and Emily, 43, 44n159
Stockley, C. I., 131
Stokes, George and Margaret, 55n199
Strand, Mark A., 147n100, 151n107, 186n12, 236n30, 240
Stuart, J. Leighton, 168
Studd, C. T., 44, 49
Sun Yatsen, 124n21, 126–27, 179
Swedish Holiness Mission, 90, 100, 166
Swedish Mission in China, 166
Swedish Mongol Mission, 100

Taigu, 40, 41, 44, 75, 79, 83, 96, 101–2, 106n156, 124, 146, 160, 180, 227–28, 234
Taihang Mountains, 48
Taiping Rebellion, 3–4, 70
Taiwan, 124n21, 208, 235n27, 246
Taiyuan Bible School, 243, 248
Taiyuan Boys' School, 18, 21, 22n90, 91n97, 113, 123, 183
Taiyuan Chinese Independent Church, 141
Taiyuan City Number One People's Hospital, 122n14, 245
Taiyuan Girls' School, 19, 45n168, 56, 90–91, 113, 185
Taiyuan Men's Hospital, 45n167, 107n159, 113n174, 122, 128, 145, 182–84, 216–17
Taiyuan Teachers Technical College Middle School, 115n186
Taiyuan University of Technology, 236

Taiyuan Women's Hospital, 45n167, 122, 128n36, 144, 146, 182, 185, 216–17, 245
Taylor, Ernest, 106
Taylor, J. Hudson, xii, 18–19, 22–31, 32–33, 43–44, 50–51, 52n191, 55–56, 58, 126n28, 191, 203
Taylor, James Hudson, IV, 125n24
Taylor, Jennie (Faulding), 9n33, 18–19, 33, 45n168, 49
Teacher Qi, 232
The Evangelical Alliance Mission (TEAM), 27n111, 247n45
The Scandinavian Alliance Mission, 27
Thomas, Claude H., 209
Three-Self Patriotic Movement (TSPM), 227–28, 230, 235, 244, 253
Tiananmen Square, 154
Tianjin, 1, 11–12, 52, 54, 65–67, 72–73, 75, 82, 100, 103, 116, 138, 203–4, 209, 213
Tianlong Shan, 151
Tjader, C. H., 106
Tong Yiqiang, 235
Torjesen, Edvard, xv, 194, 202
Torjesen, Finn S. and Sandy, 202, 239–40, 257
Torjesen, Peter, xii, 148n103, 190–202, 239
Torjesen, Valborg (Tonnessen), 191–202, 222
Trinity Evangelical Divinity School, 191
True Jesus Church (TJC), 142, 172, 228
Tsechow Mission, 166, 204
Tsechow. *See* Zezhou
Turner, Anna (Crickmay), 18, 35
Turner, Joshua J., 5, 8, 9n32, 14–15, 16n63, 18, 21, 29, 44, 53n193, 57n208, 128
Twin Committees, 235, 239, 242, 248, 250

Underwood, Thomas and Fanny, 95n114
United Presbyterian Mission, Scotland, 17
United States of America, 30, 48n176, 52n190, 54, 59, 103, 110–11, 116n188, 132n45, 135, 142, 147–51, 154–55, 158, 160–63, 166–67, 169, 174, 186, 209–12, 220n107, 226, 231, 232n24, 234–36, 237n32, 244, 247–48

Wales, 5, 120, 205n56
Wang, Pastor, 234–35, 237
Wang, Sister, 237–38, 244
Watchman Nee, 158, 228
Wei Enbo, 142
Weihsien Internment Camp, 201, 221n108, 221n110
Wenshui, 14, 123, 145
Wheaton College, 208–9
Whitchurch, Emily, 89–90
White Lotus Rebellion, 61, 69
Whitehouse, S. Frank, 92
Whitewright Institute, 122n12, 123, 131, 135
Whiting, Albert, 15, 109n162
Williams, George, 79–80, 96n118
Williams, Samuel Wells, 26n102
Williamson, Alexander, 2, 5, 46
Williamson, Emily (Stevens), 131–33
Williamson, H. R., 121, 127n30, 130–36
Wilson, Millar, 37, 88, 92
Wordless Book, 32–35
World Student Christian Federation, 156
Wuchang, 126, 143, 159
Wuhu, 48
Wulsin, Frederick and Janet, 129–30, 163–65
Wutai Shan, 2, 32
Wuyi Lu, 91n96, 145n91
Wyatt, Arthur and Margaret, 214n95, 240–41, 245
Wyatt, Edith (Holden), 215–16, 220
Wyatt, Harry, xii, xv, 109n162, 136, 145n92, 149n105, 178, 183, 211, 212–20, 224, 240–41, 245n43

Xi Shengmo (Zizhi), 20–21, 28, 42, 45, 51, 56, 58, 79, 88n87, 120, 125, 142
Xi'an, 4n9, 97, 109n164, 126n29, 206n62, 207, 216
Xiaodian, 74
Xiaoyi, 57, 89–90

Xinghualing Xiang, 91n96, 107n159, 122, 145, 241, 245
Xinzhou, 44, 45n166, 56, 58n212, 74, 76n46, 78–79, 82–83, 95, 101, 106n156, 107n158, 108, 117, 123, 181, 188, 216–18, 251
Xixiao Qiang, 71
Xizhou, 57
Xu Baoqian, 169–70

Yan Xishan, 124, 127–30, 132–34, 141, 152, 179–82
Yangcheng, 204–6
Yangqu, 13, 20, 56, 74, 77, 102n141, 242, 250
Yangzhou, 49
Yanjing Seminary, 237–38, 242
Yanjing University, 158n127, 174n173, 235
Yantai. *See* Chefoo
Yellow River, 61, 179, 191, 193, 195, 207
Yongning, 70, 81
Young Men's Christian Association (YMCA), 123, 124, 134n55, 135, 143, 145, 153n114, 158, 166, 169, 170, 229
Yu, Danny, 237
Yuan Shikai, 65, 127
Yuci, 56, 71, 82n68, 105, 112, 135, 150–52, 204, 228, 232, 241–43, 249
Yudaohe, 149
Yuncheng, 57
Yuxian, 64–65, 67n17, 87–89, 92–97, 107, 109n161, 118

Zeng Guoquan, 13, 109n162
Zezhou, 15, 30, 58n216, 76–77, 85, 166n149, 204–6
Zhang Hanzhong, 142
Zhang Lingzao. *See* Hsu Ling Tsao
Zhang Xinrong, 242
Zhang Xueliang, 179
Zhangjiakou, 90
Zhao Sanduo, 62–63
Zhaocheng, 142
Zhili, 101n131, 129n38
Zhutou Xiang, 92n102, 107n159
Ziese, Anna, 232n24
Zongli Yamen, 42, 65, 77